UPPER INTERMEDIATE

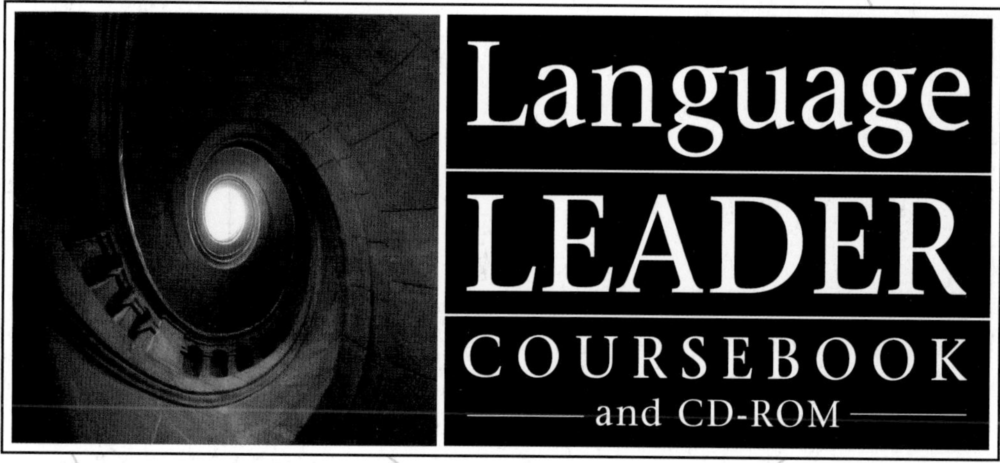

Language LEADER

COURSEBOOK and CD-ROM

David Cotton David Falvey Simon Kent

Language Reference and Extra Practice by Mark Foley

CONTENTS

Listening	Speaking/ Pronunciation	Scenario	Study and Writing Skills
Opinions on what makes a good communicator Introducing the achievements of a well-known person Part of a radio series	Discussing communication Discussing trends (in communication and research)	**Flat sharing** **Key language:** outlining problems, offering solutions **Task:** solving communication problems	Note-taking Structure of talks Note-taking Writing and checking emails Register Peer checking
Vox pops about where people live Questions and answers about volcanoes Advice on designing questionnaires	Information gap: comparing the results of two surveys Discussing changes in one's environment Preparing a fact sheet about volcanoes **Pronunciation:** stress in word combinations, contractions	**Sparrow Hill wind farm** **Key language:** agreeing and disagreeing politely, polite questions **Task:** attending a public meeting	Designing a questionnaire Question types Writing a questionnaire
Interview with a karate teacher A lecturer giving advice on essay writing	Sports quiz Discussing sport and games Discussing men and women in sport **Pronunciation:** the definite article	**Who was the greatest?** **Key language:** emphasis and comparison **Task:** choosing the greatest modern sportsperson	Understanding essay questions Understanding key words Essay writing For-and-against essays Introductions Formal expressions
Talk by a professor about issues with medical treatments A lecture on using the Internet for research	Assessing what makes a good doctor Discussing medical and ethical issues Planning an awareness-raising day **Pronunciation:** stressed syllables	**The Dowling Hospital** **Key language:** predicting **Task:** making a difficult decision	Evaluating resources on the Internet Writing short reports Making recommendations
BBC news report about a new type of transport	Discussing methods of transport Role play: road safety Discussing a difficult journey	**Transport: a new plan** **Key language:** persuading, recommending action **Task:** making an action plan	Describing graphs, charts and tables Describing information in a table Comparison and contrast
Book group discussion Monologues about characters in literature Book extracts	Talking about books you like/dislike Discussion about childhood beliefs and practices **Pronunciation**: *used to*	**A book deal** **Key language:** proposing, bargaining, talking about needs/expectations **Task:** negotiating a contract	Improving listening skills Predicting from clues Guessing meaning of words A travel blog Adverbs of degree

CONTENTS

Listening	Speaking/ Pronunciation	Scenario	Study and Writing Skills
Interview with an architect	Discussing and describing buildings Discussion about space hotels Comparing two bridges **Pronunciation:** word stress, stress and intonation	**On the horizon** **Key language:** talking about requirements **Task:** deciding on facilities in a hotel	Identifying fact and opinion A description of a building Avoiding repetition: nouns, verbs, clauses
Podcasts about globalisation	Discussing positive and negative aspects of globalisation Comparing good and bad experiences	**Supermarket superpower** **Key language:** clarifying **Task:** a TV debate	Summarising Topic sentences Paraphrasing A summary Editing to shorten
Conversation about exhibitions and opinions of them	Discussion: what is art? Discussing works of art and art exhibitions Describing photos and a work of art **Pronunciation:** stress and intonation	**The new exhibition** **Key language:** sequencing information, moving to a new point **Task:** giving an informal presentation	Expanding your vocabulary Collocations An online review Adverbs
Part of a lecture on group dynamics	Discussing team roles Organising a group activity Discussing crime books **Pronunciation:** stress patterns in adjective-noun pairs	**Ask Vanessa** **Key language:** giving advice **Task:** an advice phone-in	Writing a bibliography, referencing A discursive essay Linking words Conclusions
Vox pops about one's own culture Monologue about experiencing culture shock Description of cultural mistakes A radio discussion	Time capsule Comparing two descriptions of changing cultures Debate on cultural differences	**Kaleidoscope World** **Key language:** creating impact in a presentation **Task:** giving a formal presentation	Improving reading skills Chunking Prefixes and suffixes Linkers A formal letter Letter layout Formulaic language
Descriptions of gadgets and opinions of them	Discussing technology and its benefits Debate on the rate of technological progress	**Computer crash** **Key language:** reassuring and encouraging **Task:** problem-solving meeting	Plagiarism: what it is and how to avoid it An article Identifying the writer's position
Audioscripts (p175–190)			

1 Communication

In this unit

Grammar
- the continuous aspect
- the perfect aspect

Vocabulary
- communication
- idioms

Scenario
- Flat sharing

Study skills
- note-taking

Writing skills
- writing and checking emails

1.1 GREAT COMMUNICATORS

The most important thing in communication is to hear what isn't being said.
Peter Drucker, 1909–2005, Austrian–US management guru

SPEAKING AND VOCABULARY

1 In small groups, discuss these questions.

1 Who do you communicate with every day? Do you communicate well with them? Why / Why not?

2 Who is the best communicator you know? Why?

3 When did you last have a communication problem? Who was it with? What happened?

2a Complete the sentences on the right with the words in the box.

appearance charisma cultures digressions eye humour language listener nerves pace rambler vocabulary

2b Which of the points do you agree/disagree with? Is there anything else you would add?

What makes a good communicator?

A good communicator is someone who:

1 is a good _____ and shows interest in other people.
2 has an awareness of body _____.
3 is not a _____ and doesn't get easily sidetracked.
4 doesn't suffer from _____ and is relaxed when meeting new people.
5 is sensitive to people from other _____.
6 has an extensive _____.
7 has a good sense of _____.
8 has an attractive _____ and is well dressed.
9 maintains _____ contact with the listener(s).
10 speaks at a reasonable _____ – not too fast and not too slow.
11 has _____ and can hold the attention of the listener(s).
12 keeps to the point and doesn't have a lot of long _____.

LISTENING

3 1.2 Listen to seven people talking about what makes a good communicator. Match the person with the main point they make.

They ...

a) listen carefully.
b) don't ramble. *1*
c) clarify difficult expressions.
d) don't digress too often.
e) don't confuse listeners.
f) explain clearly.
g) don't interrupt.

4 Ask and answer the following questions.

1 How do you feel when someone interrupts you?

2 What do you do when someone isn't paying attention to you?

3 How do you deal with someone who is rambling?

4 What techniques do you use to explain complicated things?

5 Is it always bad to digress when talking?

A

B

C

READING

5a Do you know of any great public speakers? What do you know about any of the people in the photos?

5b Read the speeches below and try to match them with the people.

1

'In the long history of the world, only a few generations have been granted the role of defending freedom in its hour of maximum danger. I do not shrink from this responsibility – I welcome it. I do not believe that any of us would exchange places with any other people or any other generation. The energy, the faith, the devotion which we bring to this endeavor will light our country and all who serve it. And the glow from that fire can truly light the world.

And so, my fellow Americans, ask not what your country can do for you; ask what you can do for your country.

My fellow citizens of the world, ask not what America will do for you, but what together we can do for the freedom of man.' (1961)

2

'I have a dream that one day this nation will rise up and live out the true meaning of its creed: "We hold these truths to be self-evident, that all men are created equal."

I have a dream that one day on the red hills of Georgia the sons of former slaves and the sons of former slave owners will be able to sit down together at the table of brotherhood.

I have a dream that one day even the state of Mississippi, a state sweltering with the heat of injustice, sweltering with the heat of oppression, will be transformed into an oasis of freedom and justice.

I have a dream that my four little children will one day live in a nation where they will not be judged by the color of their skin but by the content of their character.

I have a dream today.' (1963)

3

'I know full well the responsibilities that await me as I enter the door of No. 10 and I'll strive unceasingly to try to fulfil the trust and confidence that the British people have placed in me and the things in which I believe. And I would just like to remember some words of St Francis of Assisi which I think are really just particularly apt at the moment. "Where there is discord, may we bring harmony. Where there is error, may we bring truth. Where there is doubt, may we bring faith. And where there is despair, may we bring hope."' (1979)

6 What is the main topic of each speech? Choose from the following.

a) clean forms of energy
b) the defence of liberty
c) racial equality
d) moving into a new home
e) going to the moon
f) signing a treaty
g) becoming prime minister

7a Which speech does the following? There is one extra option.

a) gives a warning
b) outlines a hope
c) asks people to make a choice
d) makes a promise

7b Find examples in the speeches of the following:

a) repetition
b) tripling (saying things in threes), e.g. past, present and future; the sun, moon and stars
c) contrast, e.g. love → hate
d) a quote (repeating another person's words exactly)

8 'Good communicators are born, not made.' Do you agree with this statement?

9a 1.3 Now listen to the speeches. Which impresses you most? Why?

9b Listen again and follow the text. Mark where the speaker pauses and which words they emphasise. Practise saying one of the speeches.

WRITING

10 Write the beginning of your own speech. Choose from the following situations.

1 the opening of a new building
2 accepting an award for an achievement
3 your hope for the future of your town

READING

1a In groups, tell each other how you feel when you have to:

- give a presentation.
- participate in a seminar or meeting.
- meet new people.

1b What advice would you give to people who were nervous about all the situations above?

2 Read the leaflet on the right quickly. Are any of the points similar to your answer to Exercise 1b?

3 Read the leaflet again. Match the following extracts from Andrea Barnard's course handouts with the weeks in the leaflet.

A Decide what you want to say before the seminar. Review it in your mind. Keep rehearsing it until you can say it confidently. There's truth in the old saying, 'Think before you speak'.

B People from Britain and the US often leave more space around them than other nationalities. They are more likely to move away when they feel that others are invading their space.

C People judge you very quickly so it is very important to make a good first impression. You look much more confident and capable when you have made an effort to smarten your appearance.

D Your voice gives people a clear indication of how you are feeling. If we are stressed, our voices can crack under pressure and get louder – giving away our emotions.

E Even when you are sitting still, your body is communicating with everyone in the audience. Aim to look confident. Remember, 'Actions speak louder than words'.

4a Read the statements below. With your partner, decide whether they are true or false.

This course ...

1 will help you if you have a speech impediment such as a stammer.
2 will teach you how to walk properly.
3 will teach you how to be assertive and aggressive.
4 will teach you to understand and be aware of your listeners.
5 will teach you how to interact successfully with other participants in a seminar.
6 will not help you to prepare for a presentation.
7 will help you to show your true nature.

Do you want to communicate confidently?

If you find it difficult to speak up during seminars or if you feel you can't get a word in edgeways when others are talking, then this small, friendly group will help you to manage these situations with more ease and confidence.

More and more people are taking communication courses these days to help them in both work and home life.

The course lasts for 12 weeks and aims to help you communicate more effectively.

You will learn how to:

Week

1 Remain in control of your emotions and your voice
2 Maintain good posture
3 Prepare what you want to say before the event
4 Use tone to engage people with interest and excitement
5 Dress smartly to make a good impression
6 Communicate in an assertive and not a passive or aggressive style
7 Stay calm and polite at all times
8 Participate actively in seminars
9 Consider your potential listeners
10 Be a good listener
11 Understand cultural differences
12 Be yourself

Dates: 10 Sept to 30 Nov

Location: Frobisher Library meeting room

How to join: Please ring Student Services on 020 5312 3310

Facilitator: Andrea Barnard

Andrea is currently carrying out research for her doctorate on communication barriers. She was voted best communicator of the year while she was studying for her Masters at Edinburgh University.

4b Which communication skills mentioned in the leaflet are you good at? Which areas do you need to develop?

VOCABULARY: idioms

5a Match the idioms with their definitions.

1 actions speak louder than words
2 think before you speak
3 (can't) get a word in edgeways
4 hear it on the grapevine
5 be on the same wavelength
6 get straight to the point
7 have a quick word with someone

a) talk about the most important thing immediately
b) share similar ideas
c) hear about a rumour passed from one person to another
d) (not) get a chance to say something
e) talk briefly to someone
f) what you do is more important than what you say
g) don't start talking until you have thought about what you want to say

5b In pairs, answer the following questions.

1 Does it irritate you when people do not get straight to the point?
2 When was the last time you felt you were really on the same wavelength as someone else?
3 Who was the last person to ask to have a quick word with you?
4 What have you heard on the grapevine recently?

GRAMMAR: the continuous aspect

6a Look at these examples of the continuous aspect from the leaflet and course handouts.

1 Andrea *is currently carrying out* research ...
2 She was voted best communicator of the year while she *was studying* ...
3 More and more people *are taking* communication courses these days ...
4 ... your body *is communicating* with everyone in the audience.

6b Tick the four words/phrases below that can describe the continuous aspect.

temporary habitual complete permanent
unfinished in progress changing

The three words you did not tick can describe the simple aspect.

7 In pairs, look at the verb forms in the sentences below. Name the verb form and say why it is used.

1 a) I'm writing an email to my parents.
b) I write a letter to my parents every week.
2 a) I work in London.
b) I'm working in London, but I'm looking for a job in Paris.
3 a) She wrote the report on the flight home.
b) She was writing the report on the flight home.

GRAMMAR TIP

The following verbs are rarely used with the continuous aspect: *agree, believe, know, like, want, hear, see*.

~~*I'm liking this course very much.*~~ ✗

➡ Language reference and extra practice, pages 134–135

8 Five of the following sentences are wrong. In pairs, identify which they are and discuss why they are wrong.

1 You're absolutely right! I am agreeing with you.
2 I was writing a letter to my mum on the train, but I didn't have time to finish it.
3 She's working as an au pair until she goes to university.
4 We stay with my parents until the work on our house is finished.
5 My grandfather is knowing how to text.
6 Look. He talks to the Linguistics professor.
7 Peter is studying telecommunications at the moment.
8 These days mobile phones get smaller.

SPEAKING

9 The present continuous is often used to talk about trends. In groups, talk about current trends in communication. Think about:

reading texting the Internet audiobooks
telephoning writing letters writing emails
using libraries for research

People are reading less these days because they're using computers more.

LISTENING

1 Look at the front cover of a well-known academic book on the right. What is it about?

2a 1.4 Listen to an introduction to a radio programme about Deborah Tannen. Check your answer to Exercise 1 and say what she is famous for.

2b Listen again. Say when Deborah Tannen did these things, or if the information is not given.

1 publish *You Just Don't Understand*
2 write *Talking from 9 to 5*
3 appear on the Larry King and Oprah shows
4 join the Linguistics Faculty at Georgetown University

GRAMMAR: the perfect aspect

3 Look at Track 1.4 on page 175 and underline examples of the present perfect, past perfect and past simple.

4 Complete the following explanations with *past simple, past perfect* and *present perfect*.

We use the perfect aspect to look back from one time to another:

- the _____ looks back from now to a time before now.
- the _____ looks back from a time in the past to another time before that.
- the _____ refers to a completed event at a definite time in the past.

➡ Language reference and extra practice, pages 134–135

5 Complete this report about a communications company with the verbs in the box in the past simple or a perfect tense.

build	contribute	employ	go up	grow
have	move	reach	rise	start	take on

Technicom [1]_____ 15 years ago as a small training company dedicated to improving communication in the workplace. We [2]_____ a reputation over the last 15 years for the delivery of quality information management solutions, and we [3]_____ just _____ another successful year. When we started the company, we [4]_____ only 12 people. By 2006, that figure [5]_____ to over 100. In 2007 we [6]_____ to larger premises near Dublin. Since then we [7]_____ a lot more staff and that number [8]_____ to the present 500. Although salary costs [9]_____ sharply over the last few years, profits have risen steadily as well. By early 2008, our turnover [10]_____ 27 million euros. Thank you to everyone who [11]_____ to Technicom's success.

Deborah Tannen

AN INTERNATIONAL BESTSELLER
DEBORAH TANNEN
Women and Men in Conversation
You Just Don't Understand
The classic book that shows us why we find it difficult to talk to the opposite sex

READING

6 Do you agree with these statements?

1 Women talk far more than men.
2 Men talk about sport. Women talk about their feelings.
3 Women and men communicate differently.

7 The two extracts opposite are from *You Just Don't Understand*. Read them quickly. What does the author say about the statements above?

8a Read the extracts again and complete these statements with M (men) or W (women).

1 _____ like to stand out.
2 _____ prefer private speaking.
3 _____ often speak for longer.
4 _____ are concerned about their rank and position in society.
5 _____ like to find things that are almost the same between people.
6 _____ don't like speaking in front of large audiences.

8b Underline the sections that gave you this information and compare with your partner.

VOCABULARY: idioms

9a Match the expressions a–d with the ideas in 1–4.

a) burst into (laughter)
b) run out of (things to say)
c) the life of the party
d) hold centre stage

1 get a lot of attention
2 fun and exciting to be with
3 suddenly start to do something (e.g. cry)
4 use all of (something)

Extract 1

YOU JUST DON'T UNDERSTAND

"PUT DOWN THAT PAPER AND TALK TO ME!"

I was sitting in a suburban living room, speaking to a women's group that had invited men to join them for the occasion of my talk about communication between women and men. During the discussion, one man was particularly talkative, full of lengthy comments and explanations. When I made the observation that women often complain that their husbands don't talk to them enough, this man volunteered that he heartily agreed. He gestured toward his wife, who had sat silently beside him on the couch throughout the evening, and said, 'She's the talker in our family.'

Everyone in the room burst into laughter. The man looked puzzled and hurt. 'It's true,' he explained. 'When I come home from work, I usually have nothing to say, but she never runs out. If it weren't for her, we'd spend the whole evening in silence.' Another woman expressed a similar paradox about her husband: 'When we go out, he's the life of the party. If I happen to be in another room, I can always hear his voice above the others. But when we're home, he doesn't have that much to say. I do most of the talking.'

Who talks more, women or men? ...Women are believed to talk too much. Yet study after study finds that it is men who talk more – at meetings, in mixed-group discussions, and in classrooms where girls and young women sit next to boys or young men. For example, communications researchers Barbara and Gene Eakins tape-recorded and studied seven university faculty meetings. They found that, with one exception, men spoke more often and, without exception, spoke for a longer period.

Extract 2

YOU JUST DON'T UNDERSTAND

"PUT DOWN THAT PAPER AND TALK TO ME!"

For most women, the language of conversation is primarily a language of rapport: a way of establishing connections and negotiating relationships. Emphasis is placed on displaying similarities and matching experiences. From childhood, girls criticise peers who try to stand out or appear better than others. People feel their closest connections at home, or in settings where they *feel* at home – with one or a few people they feel close to and comfortable with – in other words, during private speaking. But even the most public situations can be approached like private speaking.

For most men, talk is primarily a means to preserve independence and negotiate and maintain status in a hierarchical social order. This is done by exhibiting knowledge and skill, and by holding centre stage through verbal performance such as story telling, joking, or imparting information. From childhood, men learn to use talking as a way to get and keep attention. So they are more comfortable speaking in larger groups made up of people they know less well – in the broadest sense, 'public speaking'. But even the most private situations can be approached like public speaking, more like giving a report than establishing rapport.

9b Complete the text with the four expressions.

Eduardo is a really good communicator. He puts people at ease and listens carefully to you. He never [1]_____ topics of conversation. He doesn't try to [2]_____ all the time and dominate a group, but he is always [3]_____. He doesn't really tell jokes but he's very funny and people often [4]_____ around him.

SPEAKING

10 In groups, talk about the following.

- problems you have experienced recently communicating with men and women
- problems you have experienced communicating in your life

1.4 SCENARIO

SITUATION

1 Look at the poster and discuss the questions.

1 What services does the Advice Centre offer?
2 Have you ever used a service like this? Would you use it?
3 What kind of problems do you think the Advice Centre has to deal with?

Bradfield University

Student Advice Centre

Got a problem? We're here to help.

- Come and see us with any problem, big or small.
- We deal with emotional matters, financial difficulties, problems with studies, problems between flatmates ... anything you want.

Just make an appointment

2a 1.5 **Listen to two counsellors from the Advice Centre discussing the problems of Marco, a student. What kind of problem does he have?**

2b Listen again and answer the questions.

1 Why can't Marco pay his rent?
2 Why is it a 'difficult situation'?
3 What solution does Jean propose?

KEY LANGUAGE: outlining problems, offering solutions

3a Listen to the counsellors again and complete these sentences. Then check your answers in Track 1.5 on page 175.

1 ... you know. The __________ that he's been spending too much recently.
2 Well, __________, can't we?
3 The best way __________ is to tell him to get a loan.
4 It's the obvious solution, but __________ is that it's the third time he's run out of money.
5 It's __________ – he can't escape from it.
6 It's a __________ because it's not just about the rent.
7 Mmm, he's really got problems, hasn't he? It's __________, isn't it?
8 Give him some advice ... that might __________, – at least in the future.
9 Yes, that seems __________, but will he listen to us?

3b Match each expression you have written in Exercise 3a with the correct function.

a) Outlining problems
b) Offering solutions
c) Reacting to suggestions

TASK: solving communication problems

4 Martin, Carlos, Paul and Stewart are students sharing a flat for a year. Read about them and discuss what problems could arise because of their different personalities.

Martin (English), aged 21, is studying Engineering. A strong personality, he is extrovert and sociable. He can often upset people because he usually speaks his mind. He likes to organise things, and plans his life carefully. A tidy person, he has already put up several notices reminding his flatmates to keep the flat clean.

5a 1.6 **The four flatmates talk about how to organise their life in the flat. Listen and note down which rules Martin wants to introduce.**

5b Listen again. What does Martin say about each rule? Do the others agree with him?

Flat sharing

Paul (American), aged 22, comes from a very wealthy family – both his parents are top lawyers in the United States. Encouraged by his parents, he is also studying Law. Ambitious and very hard-working, he spends most of the day and night reading law books and writing assignments. He likes to communicate by email and often sends messages to his flatmates.

Stewart (English), aged 20, is the youngest flatmate. He is studying Modern Languages. Shy and lacking confidence, he is a typical introvert. He loves travelling, and spends his vacations going all over Asia, alone. He is continually saving money for these trips and eats little food. He does not like face-to-face communication or telephoning.

Carlos (Brazilian), aged 21, is studying Media. Easy-going, confident, he is always happy and relaxed. He spends a lot of time late at night telephoning his family in Rio de Janeiro, Brazil. He loves talking and chatting to friends. An untidy person, his favourite pastime is playing Brazilian music as loudly as possible.

6a **Work in groups of four. You are counsellors at the Advice Centre. Each of you has had a conversation with one of the flatmates. Read the extra information about your student and note down the key points.**

Counsellor A: turn to page 158.
Counsellor B: turn to page 161.
Counsellor C: turn to page 167.
Counsellor D: turn to page 169.

6b **In your group, share information about the four students. Explain the point of view of the student you met.**

6c **Discuss the flatmates' problems and suggest solutions. These questions might be helpful to you:**

- Why are the students having so many problems?
- Do they need more rules to improve relations in the flat?
- Should they continue to live together?
- Should they try to cancel their contract with the landlord?
- What is the best solution to their problems?

7 **As a class, discuss the solutions you have thought of. What's the best solution?**

OTHER USEFUL PHRASES

Outlining problems

The trouble is ... (he can't pay the rent).

It's a delicate situation.

Offering solutions

We can remedy the situation by ... (giving him some financial advice).

The way to sort it out is to ... (find someone to lend him the money).

Reacting to suggestions

That might be the answer.

That could be the best thing to do.

I'm not sure it's the right thing to do.

1.5 STUDY AND

STUDY SKILLS: note-taking

1a Read the extract from a radio guide on the right. What other topics do you think will be covered in the series?

1b What do you think will be covered in this week's episode of the radio series? What would you like to know about?

2a Structure of talks Formal talks, such as lectures, are usually structured in a very clear way, with 'signposts' to help listeners. Match these headings with the examples.

1 Introducing what is to come
2 Sequencing
3 Signalling the main point
4 Rephrasing
5 Exemplifying

a) For instance, …
b) I intend to discuss …
c) In other words …
d) The most important thing …
e) Firstly, I want to …

2b What other phrases do you know for each heading?

3a 1.7 Note-taking Listen to Part 1 of the talk by James Hammond in the *Communication World* series, and take notes of the main points.

3b Compare your notes with another student and discuss these questions.

1 Did you note the same information?
2 Did you make notes in the same way?
3 Which of the phrases from Exercise 2a did you hear? Which did you find most useful for your notes?

3c Which of the following techniques did you use?

- arrows
- using headings/colours
- using a lot of space
- underlining key words
- using capital letters for very important ideas and points
- your own system of abbreviations and short forms
- using one letter to mean a word or topic, e.g. S = speech, C = communication

4a 1.8 Listen to Part 2 of the talk and take notes of the main points. Try to use some of the techniques above which you think will be useful for you.

4b Compare your notes with your first set of notes. Is the second set of notes better/clearer?

5 In small groups, reconstruct what you heard from your notes. Check your ideas with Track 1.8 on page 176.

Communication World (Episode 3)

20:00–20:30

The new series produced by the ever-popular Louise Duncan looking at all aspects of human communication, from the earliest cave paintings to today's high-tech world. The 12 guest presenters all focus on their area of expertise in what has so far proved to be an entertaining and informative series. After last week's fascinating look at the history of codes and codebreaking, this week James Hammond (speechwriter to royalty, politicians, celebrities and the odd dictator or two) looks at public speaking.

WRITING SKILLS: writing and checking emails

6 What information do you find at the top of an email? In what ways is an email different from a letter?

7a Register Read the two emails sent to James Hammond, the speaker from the radio programme. In each case, what is the relationship between the writer and James? How do you know this?

1

Dear Mr Hammond,
I attended your lecture on public speaking at the Communication Skills conference in London last week and I was very impressed. I am involved in organising something similar and I would like to invite you to speak at our conference in Milan, Italy, on 15 May. The talk would need to last for 60 minutes (45 minutes for the talk and 15 minutes for questions).
Please find attached a document giving full details of the programme.
Should you have any further questions, please do not hesitate to contact me.
I look forward to hearing from you.
Yours sincerely
Elena Conti
Conference Organiser

2

Hi James,
Great talk last week on public speaking. Really enjoyed it.
Fancy giving a talk at an industry thing I'm getting together in Italy in May?
Session needs to be an hour (45 mins for the talk and 15 mins questions).
See attached for the full prog.
Any problems or queries, just let me know.
Hope to hear from you soon.
Best,
Lisa

7b Complete the chart below with expressions from the emails.

	Formal/neutral	Informal
Greeting		
Request		
Mention of attachment		
Additional information		
Future contact		
Ending		

8a The replies to the two emails are below, but they are jumbled. Decide which sentences go with which email and number them in the correct order.

	1	2	3	4	5	6	7
Email 1 (formal)	*a*						*g*
Email 2 (informal)	*h*						*n*

a) Dear Ms Conti

b) Sorry, but I won't be able to make it this year as I've already got something on.

c) Once again I would like to apologise for not attending this year and for any inconvenience caused.

d) I am afraid that I will be unable to attend the conference this year due to a prior engagement.

e) If you want, I can see if I can find someone to step in.

f) Anyway, sorry again for not coming and I hope it doesn't put you out too much.

g) Yours sincerely, James Hammond

h) Hi Lisa,

i) Thank you for your email of 5 February inviting me to speak at the conference in Milan, Italy.

j) Please let me know about any other stuff you are doing in the future.

k) If you wish, I could recommend one of my colleagues to speak in my place.

l) Thanks for the invite to talk at the conference in Italy.

m) Please do not hesitate to contact me should you organise another conference in the future.

n) Best, James

8b Now complete the table with expressions from the two replies.

	Formal/neutral	Informal
Thanking		
Giving bad news		
Offering help		
Apologising		
Future contact		

9 From your analysis of the four emails, list the general features of formal and informal language.

In informal language: missing out words, …

10a Peer checking Work in pairs. Look at the following situations and choose one each. Write your chosen email.

1 Your college or workplace is opening a new building. Last week, you saw a television news item about the project. There was an interview with a former employee who worked in the old building for 50 years. Write an email inviting him/her to make a speech as part of the opening ceremony.

2 You are getting married next summer. You are starting to plan and organise the wedding. Write an email to a friend who lives abroad, inviting him/her to make a speech at the wedding reception. Explain your reasons for choosing him/her.

10b Exchange your email with your partner. Check your partner's email for mistakes, using the system described below.

Unlike notes which are only for you to understand, writing needs to be accurate to communicate effectively. People will also judge you on the accuracy of your writing whereas they may judge speaking on communicative ability alone. Readers need to GRASP your message:

G – Grammar: check it!

R – Register: is the level of formality correct and consistent?

A – Appropriacy of vocabulary: is it the right meaning and register?

S – Spelling

P – Punctuation (commas, full stops, capital letters, etc.)

11 Write a suitable reply to your partner's email.

2 Environment

In this unit

Grammar
- present perfect simple and continuous
- indirect questions

Vocabulary
- local environmental issues
- word combinations
- adverbs

Scenario
- Sparrow Hill wind farm

Study skills
- designing a questionnaire

Writing skills
- writing a questionnaire

2.1 LOCAL ENVIRONMENT

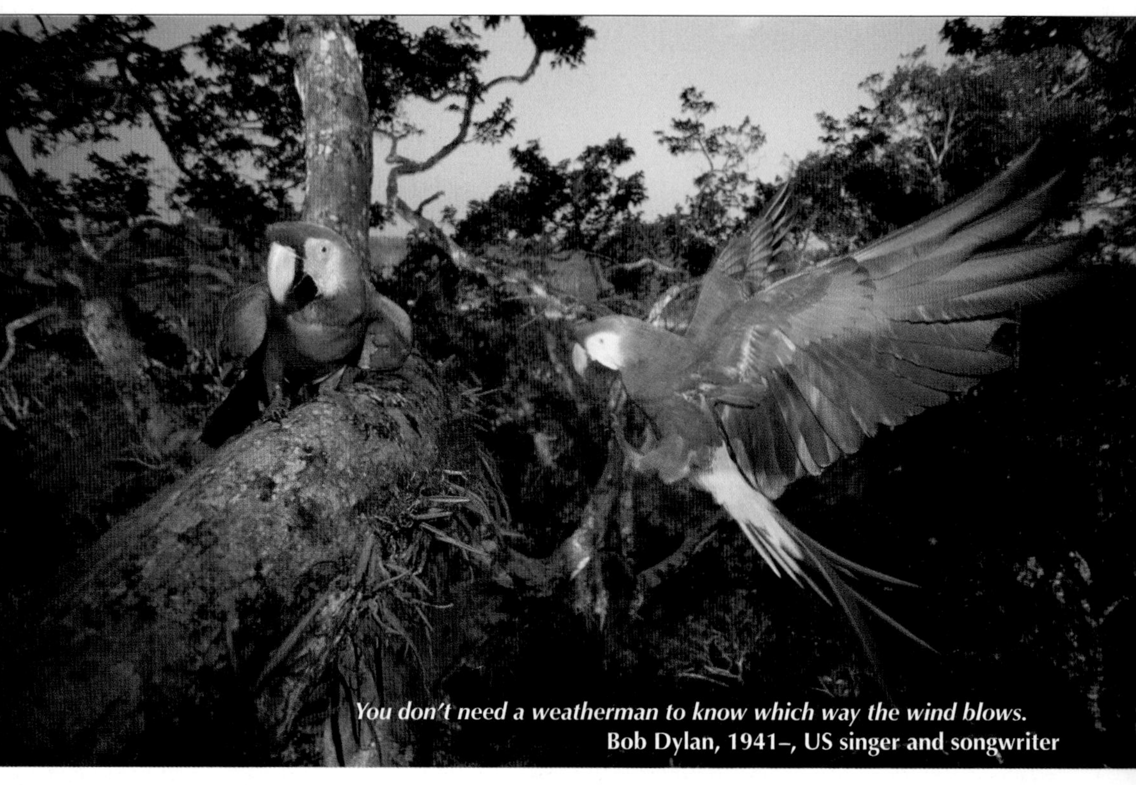

You don't need a weatherman to know which way the wind blows.
Bob Dylan, 1941–, US singer and songwriter

LISTENING AND VOCABULARY

1a Discuss your environment.

1 Where do you live, e.g. urban/rural area?

2 What do you like or dislike about where you live?

1b 1.9 Listen to three people taking part in a survey about their local area. Complete the chart.

	Person 1	Person 2	Person 3
Type of building			
Where they live			
What they like			
Problems			

2a Complete the following word combinations. Listen again to check your answers.

atmosphere hour house pollution rate ~~spaces~~

1 open *spaces* 2 noise _____ 3 cosmopolitan _____
4 crime _____ 5 detached _____ 6 rush _____

abandoned apartment mindless stunning traffic transport

7 _____ views 8 _____ block 9 _____ cars
10 _____ connections 11 _____ vandalism 12 _____ congestion

pronunciation

2b 1.10 Word combinations Mark the stress on the word combinations. Then listen and check.

READING

3a What don't you like about your local environment? Discuss the following list of problems people experience. Which are the worst for you? Can you add any others to the list?

- noise from traffic
- graffiti
- people drinking in the street
- abandoned vehicles
- young people / children misbehaving
- dog mess
- litter/rubbish
- vandalism
- noise from neighbours

3b Put the problems above in order of importance for your area. Compare your ideas with a partner.

Noisy neighbours and all the things that drive us mad

By Ross Lydall

1 Noisy neighbours, uncollected litter and graffiti are among the things that really annoy us, according to a new survey.

2 The findings come from a Mori poll of more than 2,000 residents in three UK cities – London, Dundee and Newcastle.

3 The government-commissioned survey revealed that other issues, such as dog mess and abandoned vehicles, also cause so much anxiety that they can affect our quality of life.

4 Designed to measure how people respond to noise, the survey also established the extent to which we are troubled by other anti-social problems.

5 While almost one in three people said noisy neighbours were a problem, they placed it eighth on a list of what troubled them most.

6 They were more than twice as concerned about litter and rubbish – the main problem to affect their quality of life. They said noise was a problem of similar scale to abandoned cars and drinking in the street.

7 However, the effect of noisy neighbours ranked much more highly among residents already dissatisfied with their home – jumping to second place.

8 It is also the second biggest quality-of-life issue among residents in medium- or high-rise flats.

9 The study – carried out for the Department for Environment, Food and Rural Affairs – found that loud music, shouting and banging attracted far more complaints than noisy parties. As many as two in five people annoyed by noise have complained to their council or the police, while one in four have complained directly to neighbours.

10 The survey finds that people are able to develop 'immunity' to traffic and trains while neighbourhood noise is synonymous with a 'lack of consideration'.

11 The Environment Minister said tackling noise pollution was a government priority.

The Evening Standard

4 Read the article and answer the questions.

1 How many people took part in the survey?
2 Which groups of people have a particular problem with noisy neighbours?
3 According to the survey, how many people have protested:
   a) to their local government or the police?
   b) to their neighbours?
4 According to the article, why is transport noise not a bigger problem?

5a Find words or phrases in the article which mean:

1 results (paragraph 2)
2 survey (para. 2)
3 subjects often discussed / argued about (para. 3)
4 size/level (para. 6)
5 become unaffected by (para. 10)
6 closely connected with (para. 10)
7 not thinking about other people's feelings (para. 10)
8 something very important (para. 11)

5b Which of the highlighted phrases in the article do the following?

1 introduce who asked for the survey (2 phrases)
2 gives the purpose of the survey (1 phrase)
3 compare two results of the survey (2 phrases)
4 introduce facts from the survey (3 phrases)

SPEAKING AND WRITING

6 Discuss these questions about local environmental issues.

1 What are the issues in your local area?
2 What questions would you like to ask in an opinion poll about the environment?
3 What should the government priorities for the environment be?

7a Now discuss the results of two other surveys.

Half the class (A): turn to page 158.

The other half (B): turn to page 161.

7b Now form pairs – one Student A and one Student B – and discuss your information.

8 Write a report for a university lecturer of 150–180 words describing the information in the two tables. Use some of the phrases from Exercise 5b in your writing.

READING

1 In groups, look at the headline and answer the questions.

1 Why do you think polar bears are in danger of becoming extinct?

2 What other animals are in danger of dying out?

Polar bears are facing extinction in the wake of retreating sea ice

2a Look at the headline again and predict which ten of the following words will appear in the article.

banks cubs deserts fast (n) fat (n) icebergs mammals marine penguins prey seals species thrive waves

2b Match six of the words in Exercise 2a with these definitions.

1 eating no food at all for a period of time

2 a group of animals or plants of the same kind

3 an animal that is hunted and eaten by another animal

4 young bears, lions, tigers, etc.

5 animals that feed their young with milk from their body

6 relating to the sea and creatures that live there

3 Scan the introduction and the article and check your answers to Exercise 2a.

4 Read the introduction to the article and answer the following questions.

1 How long have sea levels been rising? Are they still rising?

2 How long has polar ice been shrinking? Is it still shrinking?

3 What success have environmentalists had in their fight against global warming?

We all know that sea levels have been rising for the last 20 years, but the rate of rise has increased rapidly in recent years. Polar ice has been shrinking at a rate of nearly 75,000 square kilometres a year over the last 30 years. Unfortunately, environmentalists have not achieved any significant results in their fight against global warming. So what effect has all this had on Arctic wildlife?

1 The retreat of sea ice in the Arctic is forcing the world's wild polar bear population into an unnatural fast, which threatens the species with extinction.

2 Scientists said yesterday that the earlier annual break-up of sea ice caused by climate change is cutting short the spring hunting season for the bears, which rely on floating banks of ice to reach their prey.

3 The disappearance of the sea ice in summer months is forcing hungry polar bear populations to spend longer on land, giving a false impression that numbers are increasing as they encroach on human settlements in search of food.

4 Travel agencies in Canada and the US offering Arctic tours have begun boasting of the increased likelihood of spotting the bears.

5 But a joint study by the Canadian Wildlife Service (CWS) and Nasa published in the scientific journal *Arctic* this week has found that, far from thriving, the polar bear is at potentially irreversible risk from global warming.

6 The research into bears in five Arctic regions found that sea ice has begun retreating progressively earlier each year when satellite images from 1979 to 2004 are compared.

7 Female bears rely on the spring hunting season to build the fat reserves needed to see them through the summer months. The retreating ice means they have not had time to build up normal levels of fat – which can reach a thickness of 12cm.

8 The study found the spring hunting season was being reduced by nearly three weeks in some places – reducing the fat levels by up to 80kg in each animal.

9 As females become thinner, they are more susceptible to disease. Their ability to reproduce and the survival chances of their cubs decline significantly.

10 Claire Parkinson, a Nasa scientist and co-author of the report, said: 'Our research strongly suggests that climate warming is having a significant and negative effect on a primary species reliant on the sea ice for survival.'

11 The sea ice provides a waterborne hunting ground for polar bears from which they can find their prey – seals and other marine mammals. The polar bear can detect a seal from 20 miles.

12 Ms Parkinson said: 'Our concern is that if the length of the sea ice season continues to decrease, polar bears will have shorter periods on the ice to feed.'

5 Read all the article carefully and complete the following sentences in your own words, with between two and five words.

1 Polar ice is shrinking because of climate change.
2 Polar bears are getting closer to where people live in order to _____.
3 Travel companies are saying that there is a better chance of _____ on an Arctic tour.
4 Polar bears are at risk from global warming, according to the _____.
5 When female bears cannot build up fat reserves, they are _____.
6 Polar bears need _____ to catch the animals they hunt for food.

VOCABULARY: word combinations

6a Match the words on the left with the nouns on the right.

1 climate	a) images
2 false	b) change
3 scientific	c) journal
4 global	d) effect
5 satellite	e) impression
6 significant	f) warming

6b Complete the text with word combinations from Exercise 6a.

I read in a respectable [1]_____ recently that [2]_____ is already happening. [3]_____ have shown that [4]_____ is even reducing the legendary African snow on the top of Mount Kilimanjaro. Since 2000, observations of the [5]_____ of rising temperatures have started to mount up. Even the American business community has stopped trying to give a [6]_____ that everything is all right.

GRAMMAR: present perfect simple and continuous

7 Look at these sentences from the article and answer the questions.

1 ... sea levels *have been rising* for the last 20 years, ...
2 What effect *has all this had* on Arctic wildlife?

a) Which sentence focuses on an activity that is still continuing? Which tense is used?
b) Which sentence focuses on the result (or lack of result) of an activity? What tense is used?
c) Which tense is used for an activity that is completed?

GRAMMAR TIP

With *since* and *for* you can use some verbs in the present perfect simple and continuous with no difference in meaning, e.g. *live, stay, work, study, teach, wait, drive.*

She's lived / She's been living in that house for 20 years.

➡ Language reference and extra practice, pages 136–137

8 Underline the most appropriate form. Sometimes both forms are correct.

1 In Iceland, the ice *has disappeared* / has been disappearing at an alarming rate.
2 Since 1990, the Quelccaya ice cap in South America *has shrunk / has been shrinking* at the rate of about 30 metres a year.
3 Rising sea levels mean that some reclaimed land in low-lying areas *has already vanished / has already been vanishing.*
4 *We've waited / We've been waiting* for weeks to see Al Gore's film *An Inconvenient Truth.*
5 To stop the rise of sea levels, the president of the Maldives *has sent / has been sending* 200 copies of the book *Global Warning: The Last Chance for Change* to heads of state.
6 The environmental lobby *has tried / has been trying* to get the government to reduce CO_2 emissions for ages.

SPEAKING

9 Discuss changes in your environment. Use the present perfect simple and continuous.

LISTENING

1 In pairs, guess the answers to this quiz.

What do you know about volcanoes?

Decide if these statements are true or false.

1 Volcanoes are a natural way that the Earth and other planets have of cooling off.
2 The biggest volcano on Earth is Mauna Loa in Hawaii.
3 Most volcanoes are found around the rim of the Atlantic Ocean.
4 There are volcanoes around the coastline of Antarctica.
5 There are no underwater volcanoes.
6 Between 1975 and 1985 more than 35 volcanoes erupted each year.
7 The temperature of lava flows can reach 1,250°C.
8 People can never go inside volcanoes.
9 There is a large volcano under Yellowstone Park in the USA.
10 Vesuvius is a famous active volcano in Italy.

2a 1.11 **Listen to someone talking about volcanoes and check your answers to the quiz questions above.**

2b **Listen again. What is the situation? What is the relationship between the speaker and the listeners?**

GRAMMAR: indirect questions

3 **Look at the questions in the table. Then look at Track 1.11 on pages 176–177, find exactly how they were asked and note them down.**

Direct questions	Indirect questions
1 What is the biggest volcano in the world?	*Can I ask what the biggest volcano in the world is?*
2 Can people go inside volcanoes?	
3 Is Vesuvius an active volcano?	
4 Why do volcanoes stop erupting?	

4 **Why does the professor use a direct question (*What is a volcano?*) and the students use indirect questions?**

5 **Look at the indirect questions in Exercise 3. Are these statements true or false?**

1 We use the word order of affirmative statements in indirect questions.
2 We use *if* or *whether* to introduce indirect *yes/no* questions.
3 We use a question word, e.g. *what*, to introduce indirect *Wh-* questions.
4 We use the auxiliary *do / does / did* in present simple indirect questions.
5 Indirect questions always end with a question mark.

➡ Language reference and extra practice, pages 136–137

6a **Change the direct questions into indirect questions. Use introductory phrases from Exercise 3.**

1 How high is Mauna Loa?
I'd like to know how high Mauna Loa is.
2 How many volcanoes erupt each year?
3 How many eruptions were reported between 1975 and 1985?
4 Can you go inside an erupting volcano?
5 What causes a volcano to erupt?
6 What is the biggest volcano in the USA?
7 Which volcano has been showing a lot of activity recently?
8 When did Vesuvius destroy Pompeii?
9 When did Vesuvius last erupt?
10 Do a lot of people live near Vesuvius?

6b **In pairs, ask and answer the indirect questions, using information from Track 1.11 on pages 176–177.**

READING

7 **Read the extracts from Bill Bryson's *A Short History of Nearly Everything* and answer the questions in your own words.**

1 What does the title *'dangerous beauty'* mean?
2 What are the approximate dimensions of Yellowstone Park?
3 Why, if Yellowstone blew, is 'the cataclysm pretty well beyond imagining'?
4 Does Doss know how much warning would be given if Yellowstone was 'going to go'?
5 Why does Doss say that warning signs of an eruption would not be easy to predict at Yellowstone?
6 Why would evacuating Yellowstone 'never be easy'?

VOCABULARY: adverbs

8 **Look at the highlighted adverbs in the extracts and match them with the adverbs in the box.**

deliberately relatively normally perhaps mainly slowly and pensively

SPEAKING AND WRITING

9a **In pairs, discuss the five or six most important facts about volcanoes that would be interesting for schoolchildren.**

9b **In pairs, write a short fact sheet on volcanoes for a local school magazine.**

Yellowstone – dangerous beauty

Yellowstone, it turns out, is a supervolcano. It sits on top of an enormous hot spot, a reservoir of molten rock that begins at least 2,000 kilometres down in the Earth and rises to near the surface, forming what is known as a superplume. The heat from the hot spot is what powers all of Yellowstone's vents, geysers, hot springs and popping mud pots. Beneath the surface is a magma chamber that is about 72 kilometres across – roughly the same dimensions as the park – and about 13 kilometres thick at its thickest point. The pressure that such a pool of magma exerts on the crust above has lifted Yellowstone and its surrounding territory about half a kilometre higher than they would otherwise be. If it blew, the cataclysm is pretty well beyond imagining.

...

'It may not feel like it, but you're standing on the largest active volcano in the world,' Paul Doss, Yellowstone National Park geologist, told me soon after climbing off an enormous Harley-Davidson motorcycle and shaking hands when we met at the park headquarters at Mammoth Hot Springs early on a lovely morning in June.

...

I asked him what caused Yellowstone to blow when it did.

'Don't know. Nobody knows. Volcanoes are strange things. We really don't understand them at all. Vesuvius, in Italy, was active for three hundred years until an eruption in 1944 and then it just stopped. It's been silent ever since. Some volcanologists think that it is recharging in a big way, which is a little worrying because two million people live on or around it. But nobody knows.'

'And how much warning would you get if Yellowstone was going to go?'

He shrugged. 'Nobody was around last time it blew, so nobody knows what the warning signs are. Probably you would have swarms of earthquakes and some surface uplift and possibly some changes in the patterns of behaviour of the geysers and steam vents, but nobody really knows.'

'So it could just blow without warning?'

He nodded thoughtfully. The trouble, he explained, is that nearly all the things that would constitute warning signs already exist in some measure at Yellowstone. 'Earthquakes are generally a precursor of volcanic eruptions, but the park already has lots of earthquakes – twelve hundred and sixty of them last year. Most of them are too small to be felt, but they are earthquakes nonetheless.'

...

Evacuating Yellowstone would never be easy. The park gets some three million visitors a year, mostly in the three peak summer months. The park's roads are comparatively few and they are kept intentionally narrow, partly to slow traffic, partly to preserve an air of picturesqueness, and partly because of topographical constraints. At the height of summer, it can easily take half a day to cross the park and hours to get anywhere within it.

SCENARIO

SITUATION

A British power company has identified a commercially viable site for a wind farm in the north of England. The proposal is for a wind farm of 80 turbines over a large area. Each tower will be 60 metres tall and have a turbine of 35 metres diameter. The wind farm will cover an area of several kilometres and take five years to complete.

As fossil fuels such as coal, gas and oil are being used up, governments are keen to find alternative sources of energy, especially those that do not emit carbon dioxide. Nuclear power is one possible source, but many people have doubts about its safety. Renewable energy sources include solar, wave and wind power. The UK Government is keen to use these sources of power, and hopes to generate 10% of its energy needs from renewable sources by 2010 and 20% by 2020. However, many people feel that onshore wind farms spoil the landscape, particularly in countryside areas where they are usually sited. It is argued that they are eyesores which damage people's enjoyment of areas of outstanding natural beauty. Other people argue that wind power is simply not reliable as an energy source as wind power output is variable and unpredictable.

1 Read the situation and the leaflet and answer the questions.

1 Which facts and figures indicate that the wind farm will be large?
2 Which phrase indicates that the wind farm will be profitable?
3 What sources of energy are mentioned? What advantages and disadvantages are given for the energy sources?

2 1.12 Listen to a government official talking to a power company representative. They are discussing the proposed wind farm.

1 What is the attitude of each speaker to a public meeting?
2 What is John Reynolds worried about?
3 What do they decide in the end?

Sparrow Hill wind farm

KEY LANGUAGE: agreeing and disagreeing politely, polite questions

3a **Write these expressions from the conversation in the correct order. Use contractions where necessary.**

1 looking one it way is but at that of
2 are because right you absolutely
3 like I know to would
4 point you have but a think do not you
5 interested I knowing am in
6 very is true that because
7 go there I because you along would with

3b **Now listen again and check your answers.**

4 **Practise saying the expressions. Pay careful attention to pronunciation and use contractions.**

TASK: attending a public meeting

PUBLIC MEETING

To discuss the
Sparrow Hill wind farm
proposals

Date: 15th July • Time: 7.00p.m.
Venue: Merlin Sports Centre

All Welcome

5 **Work in groups of five. You are going to attend the Public Meeting. Read your role cards and prepare for the meeting. You can add any other ideas of your own.**

Student A: turn to page 158. **Student B:** turn to page 161.
Student C: turn to page 167. **Student D:** turn to page 169.
Student E: turn to page 170.

6 **Now hold the meeting. Ask your questions and give your opinions. Try to persuade the other people at the meeting to accept your ideas.**

7 **Meet as a class. Report back on the result of your meeting.**

8 **What do you think would happen in your country with a similar proposal?**

OTHER USEFUL PHRASES

Asking polite questions
Could you tell me (if/what) …
I was wondering (if/what) …

Putting your point of view forcefully
I'm absolutely certain that …
I really believe that …
There's no doubt in my mind that ...
I'm totally convinced that …

Being diplomatic
I see where you're coming from, but …
Yes, I see what you mean, but ...

STUDY SKILLS: designing a questionnaire

1 Questionnaires are used to gather data for surveys and reports. They usually provide up-to-date information or find out people's attitudes and behaviour.

1 If you have answered a questionnaire recently, what was it about?
2 Which organisations frequently use questionnaires to gather information?

2a 1.13 Listen to a lecturer giving advice to a student about questionnaires. Answer the questions.

1 What two key points does she mention about designing questionnaires?
2 What two types of question are mentioned?
3 What is the lecturer's final piece of advice?

2b Listen again and answer the questions.

1 Why should questions be fairly short, if possible?
2 What is the difference between open and closed questions?
3 What warning does the lecturer give about open questions?
4 According to the lecturer, questions should be 'clear and well structured'. What does she mean?
5 What kind of questions are good at the beginning of a questionnaire?

2c What are the advantages and disadvantages of asking open questions and closed questions?

3a Question types Look at the following extracts from a questionnaire and match A–G with the descriptions of the types of question below.

Descriptions of question types

1 Closed questions requiring the answer 'yes' or 'no'.
2 Questions which require a respondent to indicate how frequently they do something.
3 Questions requiring respondents to tick items in lists or boxes.
4 Questions requiring a choice between alternatives.
5 Straightforward questions which require a figure or limited number of words.
6 Open questions beginning with *what, who, why,* etc.
7 Questions which require the respondent to choose a number on a scale.

A What department are you in? ....
How many students are in your class? ....

B Tick the box in each group which applies to you.
1 undergraduate ☐
post-graduate ☐
other ☐
2 course ☐
research ☐

C Do you feel stressed during your studies?
Tick the appropriate box.
Yes ☐ No ☐

D Put a cross (✗) on the scale to indicate your level of stress.
(1 = no stress, 5 = average stress, 10 = very stressed)
1 ——— 5 ——— 10

E What do you think are the main causes of stress for students?

F Which would you prefer? Circle the letter to show your preference.
a) fewer course assignments and more tests and examinations?
b) fewer tests and examinations, and more course assignments?

G How often do you feel stressed? Circle the appropriate letter.
a) never b) rarely c) sometimes d) often
e) always

3b **Look at the following questions from a questionnaire. Tick the good questions. Put a cross against the poor questions.**

3c **Discuss how to improve the 'poor' questions. Suggest alternatives.**

1 How old are you? Tick the appropriate box.
15–20 ☐ 20–30 ☐ 30+ ☐

2 Do you believe it is necessary to save energy in the home? Tick the appropriate box.
Yes ☐ No ☐

3 Do you have a gas boiler and is it new and fuel-efficient?

4 Do you replace light bulbs in your house/flat?

5 Which of the following energy-saving activities are you doing? Tick the appropriate boxes.
Wearing jumpers and cardigans in the house to keep heating at a low temperature. ☐
Having fewer baths and more showers. ☐
Driving an energy-saving car, e.g. a hybrid car. ☐
Using as few lights as possible and turning them off as soon as you don't need them. ☐
Installing solar panels to light and heat your house. ☐

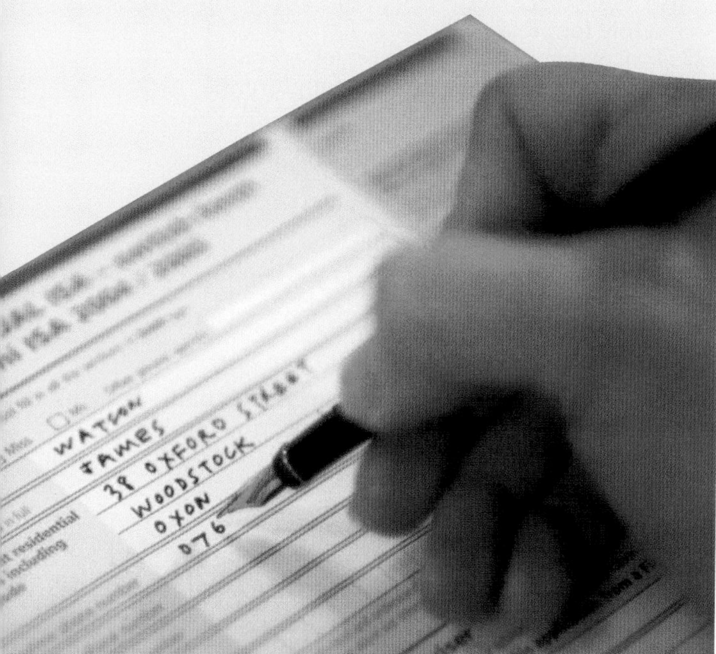

WRITING SKILLS: writing a questionnaire

4 **Read about the organisation Save Our Earth. What issues do you think SOE will list in the questionnaire they are going to prepare? Note down a few key environmental issues.**

Save Our Earth (SOE) is an environmental organisation founded two years ago. It aims to raise awareness among young people of environmental issues and to encourage them to take action to protect the environment.

Members of SOE are meeting to prepare a questionnaire which will be sent to young people aged 15–30. The questionnaire will gather information about young people's attitudes to a number of environmental matters.

5a 1.14 **Listen to the first part of an SOE meeting. Fill in the missing words in the following:**

Basic information about respondents will include their:

Age	Marital ____
Sex	____ qualifications
Nationality	Work or ____ status

5b **Listen again. Note down the issues they plan to include in their questionnaire. Are they the same as the ones you chose in Exercise 4?**

6 1.15 **Listen to the next part of the meeting and tick the questions which will be included in the questionnaire.**

1 How important each issue is for them.
2 Why they chose the most important issue.
3 What they do to protect the environment.
4 How aware and worried respondents are about each issue.
5 If respondents are able to give money to SOE.
6 If respondents are willing to join SOE's campaigns.

7a **You work for SOE. In groups of four, each student chooses one issue from Exercise 5b. Write six questions to find out respondents' attitude to your issue.**

7b **Show your questions to the other members of your group and correct them if there are language errors.**

8a **Make suggestions for adding two more questions to each issue.**

8b **Prepare the questionnaire, adding in the basic questions about the respondents from Exercise 5a.**

3 Sport

In this unit

Grammar
- quantifiers
- definite and zero articles

Vocabulary
- idioms
- prefix *self-*
- abstract nouns
- adjectives

Scenario
- Who was the greatest?

Study skills
- understanding essay questions

Writing skills
- for and against essays

3.1 FAIR PLAY

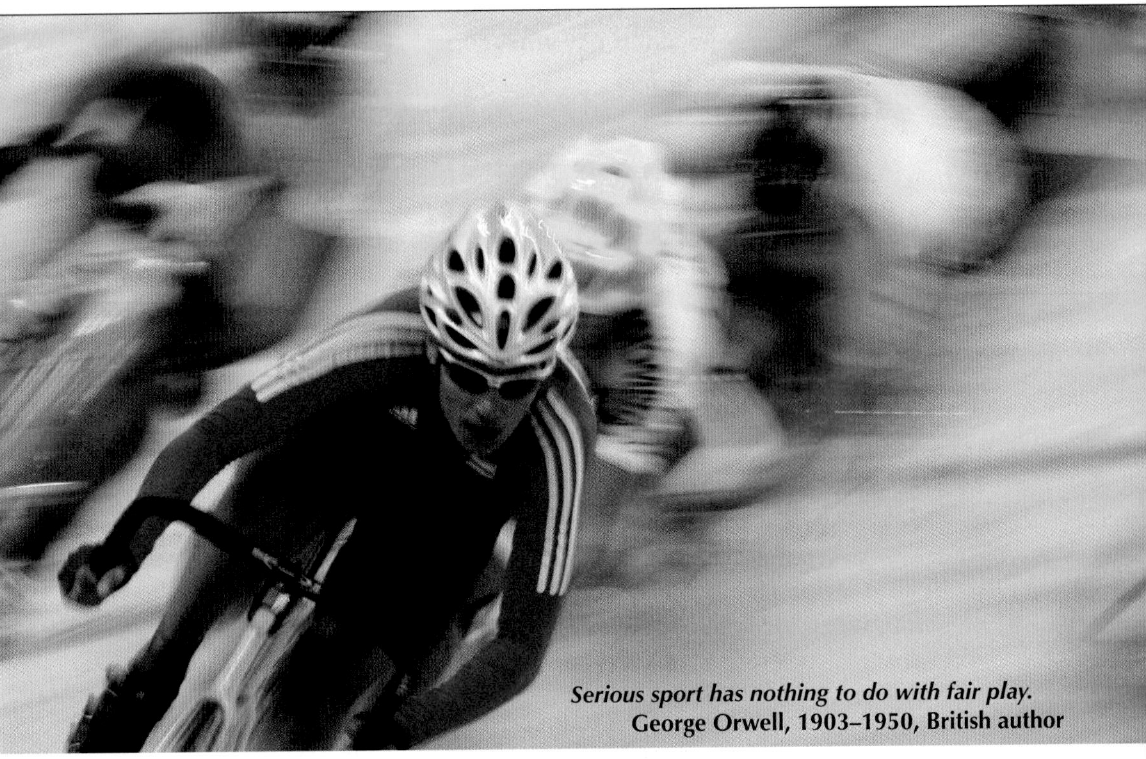

Serious sport has nothing to do with fair play.
George Orwell, 1903–1950, British author

SPEAKING

1a Sports quiz **Work in pairs. You have three minutes to think of a different sport for each of the categories below.**

Name a sport where:

1 people often get injured
2 people wear special clothes
3 people have physical contact
4 you can only do it indoors
5 you can only do it outdoors
6 you usually compete as an individual
7 you are part of a team
8 you compete against the clock
9 animals are involved
10 men and women compete together

1b Compare your ideas with another pair.

2 Which of the sports you discussed do you think:

1 is the most competitive?
2 is the most dangerous?
3 has the most complicated rules?
4 is the most difficult to be good at?
5 is the most exciting to watch?
6 you would like to take up?

READING

3 You are going to read an article about football. Read it quickly and match the titles to the correct paragraph. There are two extra titles.

a) More than a player
b) Breaking the rules
c) Taking football further
d) A football education
e) A final honour
f) The world's favourite sport
g) The best player in the world
h) Only for pleasure

4 Read the article again carefully. Are the statements true, false, or not given?

1 Miller played football professionally.
2 Miller was educated in England.
3 Miller scored a lot of goals.
4 Brazil first played against England in 1914.
5 Miller played for several teams in England.
6 Brazil has won the World Cup four times.
7 Miller has a football move named after him.
8 Miller started a football club in Brazil.

Charles Miller Father of the beautiful game

1 ______

Football is the most popular spectator sport in the world – possibly the only global sport – and Brazil is arguably the greatest footballing nation in the world, having won the World Cup more times than any other country. Even people who are not keen on football have heard of Pelé, often considered the world's greatest player. However, how many football fans are familiar with the name of Charles Miller and his contribution to what Pelé called 'the beautiful game'?

2 ______

Known as the father of Brazilian football, Charles William Miller was born on 24 November 1874 in São Paulo to a Scottish father and Brazilian mother. In 1884, young Charles was sent to school in England, where he learned to play both football and cricket. Miller became skilled in running with the ball, heading and taking free kicks.

3 ______

In 1894 Miller returned to Brazil with two footballs and a copy of the rules of football. The São Paulo Athletic Club (SPAC) had been formed in 1888 by a group of British men who played mainly cricket. Miller persuaded them to take up football. He was also instrumental in setting up the Liga Paulista, the first football league in Brazil. Over the first 20 years of the next century, state championships were formed throughout Brazil and in 1914 the first national side played against Argentina.

4 ______

Miller was not only a great player, but also an excellent coach and administrator. In Brazil he spent a lot of time and effort teaching and coaching Brazilians. After retiring as a player, he continued to be a referee until the age of 50.

5 ______

When football became professional in Brazil in 1933, Miller was disappointed and decided to have no more contact with the game. He felt that sportspeople should be amateurs – he didn't like the introduction of money and business into sport. For Miller, football was a game, and about participation and doing your best, not money.

6 ______

Charles Miller's memory lives on in the skilful individual game which is Brazilian football. It is also kept alive in another way. When the São Paulo sports writers association brought out a dictionary of football terms in Portuguese, only one word survived from the vocabulary of the past: the *charles* or *chaleira*. Named after Charles Miller, it is a clever pass with the heel of the foot. The exciting ball skills of all the great Brazilian players, including Pelé, owe something to the pioneering spirit of Charles Miller and his passion for the game of football.

5 Underline all the words in the article which refer to people in sport. Which one refers to a person who:

1 watches sport 2 loves sport 3 teaches sport
4 makes sure rules are followed
5 plays a sport without being paid

VOCABULARY: idioms

6a A lot of idioms are based on sport, and on football in particular. Complete the idioms with the words in the box.

~~ball~~ ball eye field game goal goalposts

1 be on the *ball*
2 move the ______
3 take your ______ off the ball
4 a level playing ______
5 a whole new ball ______
6 score an own ______
7 start the ______ rolling

6b Now match the idioms with their meanings.

a) a completely new/different situation
b) able to think or react very quickly
c) start something happening
d) change the rules/limits, making something more difficult
e) lose concentration
f) do/say something which has the opposite effect to your intention
g) a fair situation

SPEAKING

7 In groups, discuss these questions about sport.

1 Do you think football is 'the beautiful game'? Which other sports do you think are beautiful? Why?
2 What's the difference between a sport and a game?
3 Does sport bring people together or divide them?

3.2 MARTIAL ARTS

LISTENING

1 In pairs, tell each other about any martial arts you know. Think of five reasons for doing martial arts.

2a 1.16 Kevin Coles is a karate teacher. Listen to him talking about his experiences and answer the questions.

1 How long has he been doing karate, and how often does he train?
2 What gives him the most satisfaction?
3 What is the advantage of having belts?
4 How does he feel when students get their belts?

2b 1.17 Now listen to Mr Coles talking about karate. Answer the questions.

1 Is karate a hobby or a way of life for most people?
2 Give at least two reasons why people start karate.

READING

3a You are going to read a leaflet to attract students to a university karate club. Which five of the following do you think will be mentioned in it?

1 the founder of karate – Gichin Funakoshi
2 the benefits of doing karate
3 the location of the karate club
4 days and times
5 the increase in violence recently
6 karate competitions and championships
7 a free introductory lesson

3b Read the leaflet quickly and check your answers.

University Shotokan Karate Club

Learn karate – the ultimate in self-defence and fitness

The university karate club was founded in 1962. All grades from beginners to advanced are welcome. The classes are suitable for both men and women and several women have obtained their black belt.

TUESDAYS AND THURSDAYS
6.00–8.00 p.m.
WEAVER HOUSE GYM
FIRST LESSON FREE

Hardly any of us have experienced real violence, but, over the last few years, assaults on innocent people have increased. Each of us has some ability to defend ourselves, and by learning a form of self-defence, we are not only increasing that ability, but also doing something to build our own sense of self-respect. Karate will show you a lot of simple and effective techniques to protect yourself, giving you increased self-confidence.

Far too many people think martial arts are about violence. Martial arts training is based on a lot of respect, self-discipline, self-control and non-violence. We learn basic etiquette, courtesy and tolerance. Good manners and consideration for others are expected at all times.

Karate is the practice of blocking and striking techniques for the purpose of self-defence, health and self-development. Karate exercises the entire body. Techniques are practised on both sides of the body, therefore muscle imbalances do not occur and the strength, coordination, flexibility and agility of both sides of the body are improved. Regular training in karate improves the body's physical stamina and suppleness. It also helps concentration and produces the mental calm and assurance that come from knowing we can defend ourselves.

Karate has many benefits but they do not come easily or overnight. Training requires ongoing commitment and hard work. Some of you will give up, but a few of you will get your black belt.

For further information visit:

4 Read the leaflet again and cross out the options below that are *not* correct. (You can cross out one, two or three options.)

1 Classes are suitable for
a) beginners b) intermediate students c) women d) children.

2 Martial arts are based on
a) violence b) self-defence c) respect d) self-discipline.

3 Which of the following does karate improve?
a) stamina b) concentration c) politeness d) aggression

4 Which of the following relate to the physical aspects of karate?
a) flexibility b) agility c) courtesy d) suppleness

VOCABULARY: *self-*, abstract nouns

5a Find all the words beginning with *self-* in the leaflet and match them with these meanings.

1 being happy about your character and abilities
2 the certainty that you can do something successfully
3 behaving calmly and sensibly even when you are angry, excited or upset
4 the use of force to protect yourself when you are attacked
5 making yourself do the things you should do
6 becoming better at something

5b Underline the most appropriate combination with *self-* in each sentence below.

1 He shot her in *self-defence / self-respect*.
2 He lost his *self-control / self-development* and screamed.
3 It is difficult to keep your *self-respect / self-control* when you have been unemployed for a long time.
4 He can only develop *self-defence / self-confidence* if he is told he is good and clever.
5 The children are so badly behaved. They have no *self-confidence / self-discipline*.

6a Find the abstract nouns in the leaflet related to the following adjectives.

courteous tolerant coordinated flexible agile calm

6b Which three of the words in Exercise 6a are related to the body? Which two of the words are related to polite behaviour?

GRAMMAR: quantifiers

7a Complete the following scale with the quantifiers highlighted in the leaflet.

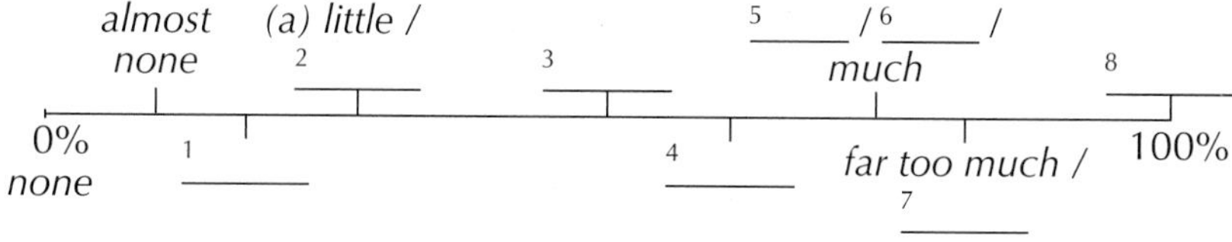

7b Divide the quantifiers into three groups: those used with plural countable nouns, those with uncountable nouns, and those used with both.

GRAMMAR TIP

All of the quantifiers in the scale can be used with *of + the / my / these*, etc. + noun/pronoun:
Hardly any of my friends are taking exams this year.

Language reference and extra practice, pages 138–139

8 Look at the following sentences. In which ones can you replace *few/little* with *not many/much*? In which ones do *few/little* mean *some*?

1 I'm pleased to say that *a few* of you will get your black belt next year.
2 Unfortunately, *few* of you are likely to pass the exam.
3 There's *little* time to practise for the grading next week.
4 We've got *a little* time left. What shall we practise?

9 Correct the mistakes in these sentences.

1 Several my friends have taken up volleyball recently.
2 Far too much children lack discipline these days.
3 Could you give me little help?
4 A little of the parents take up martial arts with their children.
5 Hardly any the spectators left before the end of the game.
6 It's great that we managed to get few tickets.
7 This sport is so new that we have a little information about it.

10 Make the sentences true for you by adding a quantifier (with *of*). Then compare your answers with a partner.

1 My friends play football.
2 My family watches sport on television at the weekend.
3 My friends have full-time jobs.
4 The people I work/study with exercise a lot.
5 Houses in our street have a garden.

3.3 What a babe!

READING

1a Which sportswoman/women do you most admire? Why?

1b Read the text quickly. How did your choice compare with Babe Didrikson?

2 Read the article again and number the following information in chronological order.

a) died of cancer ☐
b) married George Zaharias ☐
c) won first prize at a fair for sewing ☐
d) was born in Texas ☐
e) set five world records ☐
f) became an Olympic Games track and field star ☐

VOCABULARY: adjectives

3 Find adjectives in the article with these meanings.

1 having special skills or knowledge of a subject (line 11)
2 annoyed or upset about something that is not acceptable (line 30)
3 very great or impressive (line 33)
4 not allowed by the law (line 42)
5 very determined to succeed or get what you want (line 45)
6 sudden, surprising, exciting and impressive (line 46)
7 doing a sport or activity as your job (line 48)

FIFTY YEARS AGO last week an American woman died of cancer in Texas. She was arguably the best sportswoman ever, anywhere in the world, and she lived at a time when sporting ability was considered to be the province of the male. Jon Henderson recalls the amazing life of Babe Didrikson, who could run, jump, throw, hit, swim – and sew – better than anyone.

You cannot help but feel just a little sorry for George Zaharias, even if he was a 20-stone wrestler with cauliflower ears. This is how *Time* magazine reported his wedding in 1939: 'Married. Mildred ("Babe") Didrikson, famed woman athlete, 1932 Olympic Games track and field star, expert basketball player, golfer, javelin thrower, hurdler, high jumper, swimmer, baseball pitcher, ... and George Zaharias, heavyweight wrestler; in St Louis.'

The marriage notice might have added that Didrikson was also expert at cooking, sewing – she won first prize at the 1931 Texas State Fair for her box-pleated dress – and harmonica playing ... Asked if there was anything she did not play, Didrikson shot back: 'Yeah, dolls.'

Didrikson, who was christened Mildred and became Babe because of Babe Ruth-like feats at baseball, was the sixth child of seven born to Ole, a Norwegian ship's carpenter, and his wife, Hannah. The first three children were born in Norway; Babe and the other three arrived when the family settled in Port Arthur, Texas.

Didrikson began her sporting career before graduating from high school. Then, at the 1932 Amateur Athletic Union track-and-field championships, Didrikson won the team award by finishing first in six events and setting five world records. She was disgusted that she was allowed to compete in only three events at the Olympics that followed. It was at these games that the 21-year-old announced to a world audience her phenomenal ability: 'I am out to beat everybody in sight and that's just what I'm going to do,' she said when she stepped off the train in California.

GRAMMAR: definite and zero articles

4a Find these phrases in the article and match them with the uses of the definite article below.

1 *the* family settled in Port Arthur ... (line 24)
2 *the* Olympics that followed. (line 31) / *the* sporting scene in the US. (line 50)
3 Didrikson won the team award ... It was at these games that *the* 21-year-old ... (line 32)
4 *the* best sportswoman ever (line 2)

We use the definite article when ...

a) a noun is defined by a phrase that follows it.
b) it is obvious from the context what is referred to.
c) we mention the noun a second time or use a substitute noun.
d) we refer to something unique (including superlatives).

4b Look at the highlighted phrases in the text and match them with uses a–d above.

In fact, she nearly succeeded. She won the javelin comfortably, throwing just over 44 metres despite, she said, the spear slipping out of her hand; took the 80 metres hurdles in a world record 11.7 seconds; and finished equal first in the high jump, but lost the title on a technicality. Her highly individual style, the judges said, was illegal.

Golf was what eventually claimed her attention. She was soon winning titles. One golf writer described her as having an aggressive and dramatic style and being able to hit balls as powerfully as a man.

When she turned professional, she was chiefly responsible for establishing the women's pro game as part of the sporting scene in the US. The other pros understood her importance to the tour and admired rather than resented her success. One of them, Patty Berg, said: 'When I come in second to her I feel as though I have won.'

5 Now look at the sentences below and match them with the uses of the zero article.

1 She lived at a time when sporting ability was …

2 Didrikson began her sporting career before graduating from high school.

3 She was soon winning titles.

We use the zero article …

a) when we focus on the type of institution rather than a particular or specific building.

b) before plural nouns that are general, not specific.

c) before abstract nouns.

GRAMMAR TIP

When we refer to a particular building, we use the definite article before the noun:

Could you tell me where the university is?

➡ Language reference and extra practice, pages 138–139

6 Edit the text about Mia Hamm, finding and correcting 12 mistakes in the use of articles. The first one has been done for you.

At the age of 15, Mia Hamm became the youngest player ever to play for national soccer team of the United States. She was the first international star of women's game and eventually became one of most famous women athletes in the world, giving the hope to the young sportswomen.

She was born in 1972 and went to the high school in Northern Virginia. In 1989, she entered North Carolina University, where Michael Jordan had also studied.

She became youngest American woman to win a World Cup championship at the age of 19. As part of the US women's soccer team, she won World Cup in 1991 and 1999, and also Olympic gold medals in 1996 and 2004. In addition to winning four major championships, the US women finished third in the 1995 and 2003 World Cup tournaments.

Mia devotes much of her free time to the charities, and in 1999, she began the Mia Foundation to help with bone marrow research and to develop sports programmes for women with the sporting ability. Her book, *Go for the Goal*, was published in 1999. Book, aimed at young female athletes, has proved inspirational for a generation of young women.

pronunciation

7 1.18 **Definite article Listen carefully to the five sentences. Is there a definite article before these nouns in the sentences? Use the context to help you.**

1 university 2 university 3 game, captain

4 tennis players, wrist injuries 5 tennis players, courts

SPEAKING AND WRITING

8a In small groups, decide whether you think men and women in sport should compete equally, and in which sports.

8b Now write a paragraph about your discussion from Exercise 8a.

3.4 SCENARIO

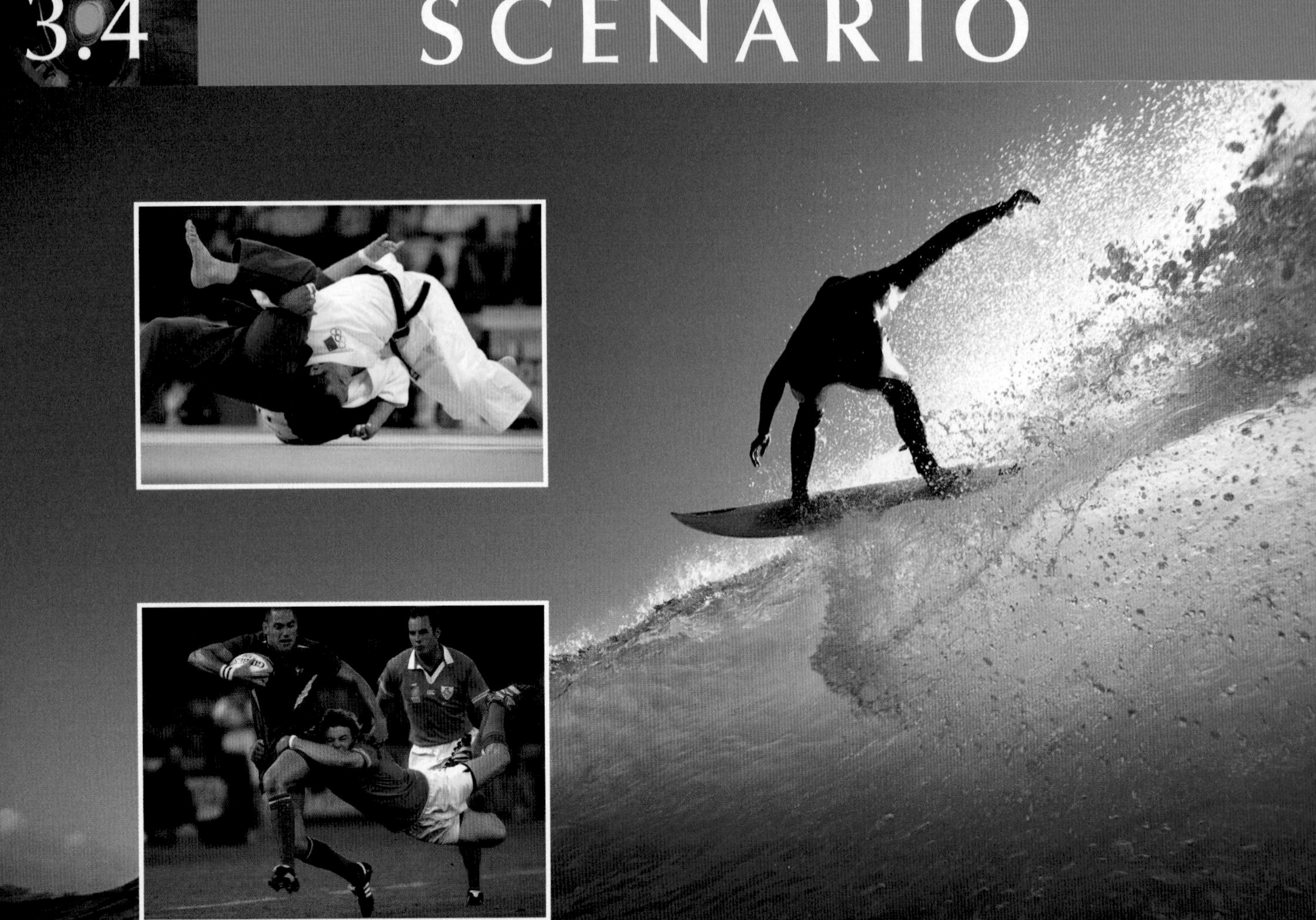

SITUATION

1a In pairs, write the names of two famous sportspeople in as many of the sports as possible.

boxing swimming athletics football tennis baseball basketball motor racing golf ice hockey

1b Now compare your choices with another pair.

2 Read the situation on the right and answer the questions.

1 Why has the sports channel decided to have a competition?
2 What does the channel mean when it says 'modern sportsperson'?
3 How will the winner be chosen?

A new television channel, Global Sports, has just started broadcasting. To attract viewers' interest, it has announced a competition to decide the greatest modern sportsperson, male or female. The channel has invited viewers to write or email the sportsperson they consider to be the greatest in the last 20 years. They have to make a case for their chosen sportsperson. The writers of the most interesting emails/letters will be invited to the studio to take part in a debate. They will present their case and attempt to persuade the audience that their sportsperson should win the competition. Finally, a vote will be taken and the winner announced.

3a What should be used as the criteria for choosing the greatest modern sportsperson? In small groups, choose the five things below which you consider to be most appropriate for the competition.

The sportsperson's:

- achievements
- competitors' level
- fair play
- status as a role model
- fame
- exceptional personal qualities
- contribution to their sport
- time at the top of their sport
- ability to overcome difficulties

3b Now, as a class, agree on five of the above criteria to be used in the competition.

Who was the greatest? 3.4

4 1.19 **Maria is practising a short talk about Ellen MacArthur. Listen and answer the questions.**

1 What is the Vendée Globe?
2 How did Ellen MacArthur perform in the event?
3 What is Ellen MacArthur's greatest achievement, according to Maria?

KEY LANGUAGE: emphasis and comparison

5a **Listen again. Note down words and phrases that Maria uses to emphasise her points. Think about:**

Adjectives – an *amazing* achievement

Adverbs – a *truly* remarkable person; *particularly* impressed

Expressions – *most of all; What's extraordinary is …*

5b **Check your answers to Exercise 5a in Track 1.19 on page 178. The emphatic words/phrases are in italics.**

6 **The following emphatic statements are jumbled. Put them in their correct order.**

1 Pelé Brazilian was footballer a fantastic truly
2 Tiger Woods the golfer in the best world is definitely
3 Andre Agassi charismatic a was tennis player particularly
4 what's Serena Williams about is determination her extraordinary
5 I'd stress to Ellen MacArthur incredibly is courageous that like
6 Mohammed Ali most of all will for his be against George Foreman remembered match

7 **Look at Track 1.19 on page 178 and underline all the words and phrases which are used to make comparisons.**

TASK: choosing the greatest modern sportsperson

8a **You are going to give a short talk (2–3 minutes) on your outstanding modern sportsperson. Choose from the following.**

Either choose one of the personalities on page 171 or choose a sportsperson you know well (someone active in the sport within the last 20 years).

8b **Prepare your talk by making suitable notes. You can use the headings in the information given or you can use your own headings.**

9a **In small groups, make your case for your sportsperson. When you listen to the other presentations, ask questions at the end of each one.**

9b **After all the presentations, take a vote. (You may not vote for your own candidate.) Then discuss your choice with other groups.**

OTHER USEFUL PHRASES

Emphasising

Adjectives

exceptional fantastic great impressive incredible outstanding tremendous wonderful

Adverbs

clearly incredibly indisputably remarkably totally unbelievably undeniably

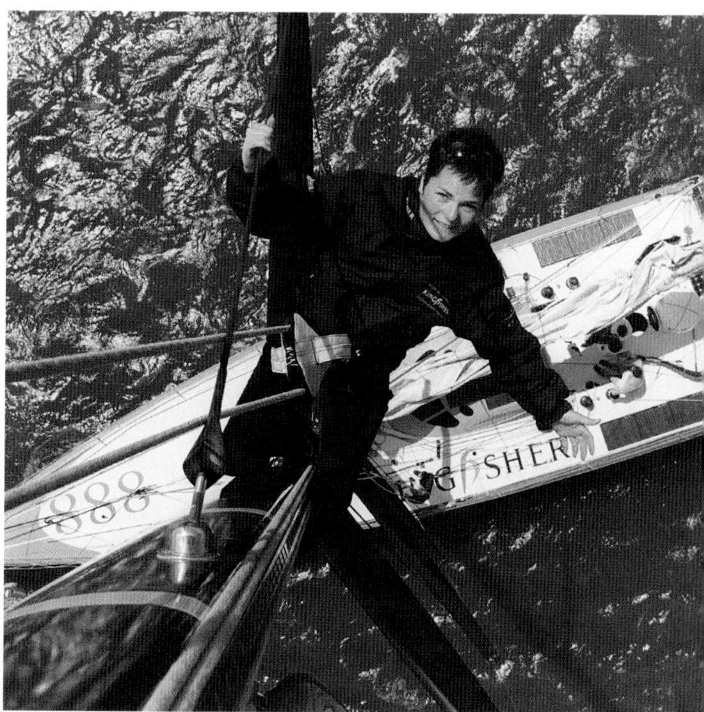

3.5 STUDY AND

STUDY SKILLS: understanding essay questions

1 What makes a good essay? Make a list.

It should have a clear structure ...

It should answer the question ...

2a Understanding key words Look at the essay questions and discuss what you think each question is asking. Underline the key words in each.

1 Analyse the reasons why the bad behaviour of spectators at sports events has increased in recent years.
2 Compare and contrast the achievements of two sports stars.
3 To what extent is winning the most important aspect of sport?
4 Account for the success of the sport of Association Football around the world.
5 Outline the benefits of children doing sport at school.
6 In most sports fitness is more important than skill. Discuss.
7 Describe the role of a captain in team sports.

2b Match words and expressions from the essay questions in Exercise 2a with the meanings below.

a) give reasons for, explain
b) give a description of the main features or characteristics of something
c) look at in detail
d) talk about how far something is true or not
e) give both sides of an argument, e.g. for and against
f) briefly give (the positive aspects)
g) show how two or more things are similar or different

3a 1.20 Essay writing A lecturer has just finished a study skills workshop and is answering questions. Listen and identify the main point he makes at the beginning.

3b Listen again and complete the following notes about essay writing.

Preparing to write

1_____ *the title –* 2_____ *the key words.*
3_____ *if the title indicates a clear structure.*
4_____ *some notes.*
5_____ *your ideas.*
6_____ *yourself questions.*
7_____ *your notes.*

Writing

Use the beginning, 8_____ *and* 9_____ *approach.*
In the first paragraph you should 10_____.
In the final paragraph you should 11_____.

Language

Academic writing tends to be 12_____ *in tone.*
Try to leave 13_____ *out of your writing.*
14_____ *structures are common.*
Avoid 15_____ *and contractions.*

4 In pairs, choose one of the essay titles from Exercise 2a, analyse it and discuss what you would include in it.

WRITING SKILLS: for-and-against essays

5 Work in pairs. How do you feel about the amount of money top sportspeople earn?

6 Read the essay opposite and answer the questions.

1 Which sports are mentioned?
2 What sources of income are mentioned?
3 What is the writer's opinion?

7 Read the essay again and match the ideas with the correct paragraph.

a) arguments against the proposition
b) conclusion and opinion
c) introduction and restatement of question
d) arguments for the proposition
e) background information

8a Introductions Which of the following might you find in the opening paragraph of an essay?

1 your opinion
2 a context for the question / background information
3 your aim/target, i.e. what you are going to argue in the essay
4 a restatement of the question
5 arguments and examples
6 a recommendation

8b Look at the introduction in the essay and check your answer.

Top sportsmen and women are paid too much. Discuss.

In recent years the amount of money earned by top sportsmen and women has risen and attracted a lot of media attention. Stars of high-profile sports such as football, golf, tennis, boxing and motor racing often feature in lists of the world's richest people. The objective of this essay is to decide if these sportspeople should receive such large amounts of money.

It is true that not all sports stars are very well paid, but certain individuals do earn an enormous amount. The earnings of these sports stars come from a number of sources. Firstly, there are the huge salaries for some stars, for instance footballers. Secondly, there is the prize money available for winning major sporting competitions and trophies. Finally, and perhaps most lucrative for many top sports stars, are sponsorship deals and advertising contracts.

Many people argue that these stars deserve their earnings for a number of important reasons. Sports players provide entertainment, like any well-known actor or pop star. They are professional people at the top of their chosen career. In simple terms, they are the best at what they do and so should be paid accordingly. They have put in years of training to be as good as they can be at their sport. It can also be argued that most sports stars have a relatively short career, and so need to earn a lot of money in a short time to support them when they retire. In some sports there is a risk of serious injury and death. Sportsmen and women should be compensated for this risk.

In contrast, some people argue that it is wrong to pay sports stars these huge amounts of money when there is so much poverty in the world. Sports stars do not save lives or really contribute much to society, apart from providing entertainment, which can be seen as unnecessary. It is also clear that these sports stars often have extravagant lifestyles, appearing in celebrity magazines and generally not using their wealth in a positive way. Some, even though they are role models for young people, actually behave very badly.

In conclusion, it is obvious that there are differences not only between sports, but also between individuals in the same sports. On balance it can be said that sports stars are worth the money they earn as they have the ability to enhance people's lives by their achievements. They manage to unite whole countries during significant competitions, which is something even politicians are rarely able to do.

Anna Kournikova, Lewis Hamilton

9a The introduction also engages the reader with the topic. Two common ways of doing this are to talk about changes over time or to generalise about the current situation. Which does each opening expression below do? Which tenses are used with each?

1 Over the last 20 years …
2 Many people nowadays …
3 In the past decade …
4 Since the late 1990s …
5 These days …
6 For centuries …
7 At the present time …

9b Look back at the essay questions in Exercise 2a and write some opening sentences using the phrases above.

10 Formal expressions Find some formal expressions in the essay which mean the following.

1 My aim here is to look at ... (paragraph 1)
2 like (para. 2)
3 A lot of people feel ... (para. 3)
4 In other words, ... (para. 3)
5 On the other hand, ... (para. 4)
6 It also seems to me that ... (para. 4)
7 To sum up, ... (para. 5)
8 Overall, ... (para. 5)

11a Work with a partner to discuss the following essay questions.

There is too much emphasis on winning in sports today. Discuss.

Sports involving animals should be banned. Discuss.

Men are more interested in sport than women. Discuss.

11b Choose one essay to plan together. Then write your essays individually, using the notes you made in Exercise 3b, the structure in Exercise 7, and some of the expressions in Exercise 10.

REVIEW

GRAMMAR

1a Work with a partner to discuss the following.

1 What can you see in the photo in the text opposite?
2 Who was the first person to climb this mountain?
3 How many people do you think climb it each day?
4 What sort of things do you think people leave there?

1b Read the article and find the answers.

2 Read the article again and complete the gaps with the words below.

1 a) a mountain b) the mountain c) mountain
2 a) have reached b) had reached c) were reaching
3 a) a lot of b) many c) a few
4 a) were reaching b) had reached c) have reached
5 a) a little b) few c) little
6 a) were b) was being c) was
7 a) top b) the top c) a top
8 a) discovered b) were discovering c) have discovered
9 a) was leaving b) had left c) was left
10 a) had generated b) was generating c) has generated
11 a) had complained b) was complaining c) have been complaining
12 a) was calling for b) called for c) has called for
13 a) a tourism b) the tourism c) tourism
14 a) the government b) government c) a government
15 a) had decided b) decided c) has decided
16 a) A deposit b) The deposit c) Deposit

3a Work with a partner. Imagine you are interviewing Sir Edmund Hillary, the first person to climb Mount Everest. Make a list of questions to ask him.

How long did it take you to get to the top?

3b Choose five questions from your list and rewrite them using indirect language.

Could you tell me how long it took you to get to the top?

Rubbish on the roof of the world

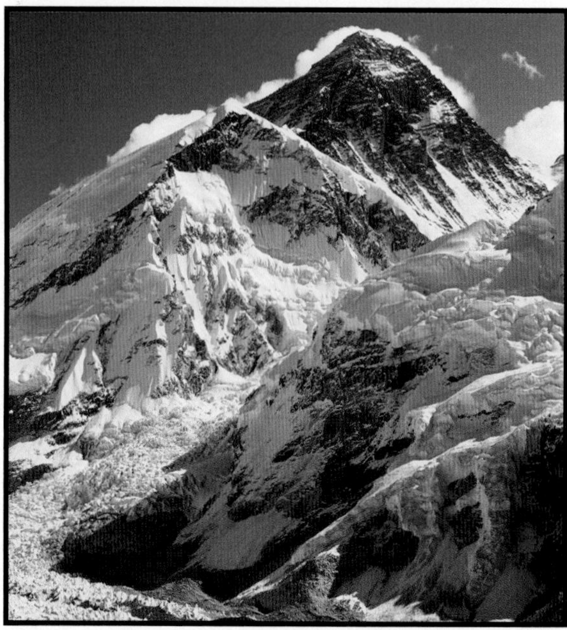

You might think that the top of Mount Everest, the highest point in the world, would be one of the few places left on our planet that is free from human rubbish. You'd be wrong. In fact, 1_____ is covered with the debris and litter left behind by the thousands of climbers who 2_____ the summit over the last 50 years.

Climbing Mount Everest is an arduous task that requires 3_____ equipment. Oxygen tanks, tents, sleeping bags and food and water supplies are all necessary for a successful ascent. Once climbers 4_____ the top, they no longer need as much equipment and there is 5_____ reason to carry heavy loads back down the mountain, so the temptation is to leave everything behind. In the days when climbing the mountain 6_____ a rare occurrence this wasn't a problem. But now, with more than 40 people getting to 7_____ on some days, the amount of litter has become unacceptable.

In 1988 climbers 8_____ a huge quantity of rubbish at base camp. The piles of trash included Frisbees, baseball bats and cans. A US expedition from the previous year 9_____ it behind. Incredibly, a group of only 16 people 10_____ over a ton of rubbish!

Recently, many well-known mountaineers 11_____ about the problem and Sir Edmund Hillary (1919–2008), the first man to climb Mount Everest (with Tenzing Norgay in 1953), 12_____ a five-year ban on climbing the summit. But thousands of local people rely on 13_____ and the government of Nepal is keen to encourage visitors rather than put them off.

But now 14_____ of Nepal, in the face of international criticism, 15_____ to take action. Each expedition that wants to climb the mountain has to pay a $4,000 deposit to the Nepalese authorities. 16_____ is only refunded if the climbers bring their rubbish back down the mountain. Climbers are also encouraged to use metal containers rather than plastic or glass. These can be crushed once they are empty and then recycled by local businesses which turn them into knives and forks.

UNITS 1–3

VOCABULARY

4 Complete the sentences with words from the box.

aggressive block congestion culture global intentionally rush self-discipline sense transport

1 I didn't do it _____; it was an accident.
2 You should learn about the _____ of countries you're going to visit so you know how to behave.
3 I like people with a good _____ of humour.
4 This part of the city has excellent _____ connections – you can get a bus anywhere.
5 _____ warming is one of the most serious problems facing the modern world.
6 Michael Schumacher was possibly the most _____ racing driver. He was so determined to win.
7 We live on the third floor of the apartment _____.
8 I avoid the traffic _____ by cycling everywhere.
9 Trains are very crowded during the _____ hour.
10 Martial arts need a lot of _____.

5 There is one incorrect word in each sentence. Find the mistakes and correct them.

1 She talks too much. I can't get a word in sideways.
2 He did an own goal when he was late for the test.
3 You should always think before you say.
4 Jane, would you like to start the topic rolling?
5 Are you sure or did you see it on the grapevine?
6 This project is a whole modern ball game for me.
7 I'm afraid we're not in the same wavelength.
8 Police officers can never put their eye off the ball.

KEY LANGUAGE

6 1.21 Listen to three people talking about a football team. Match the names with a–f.

1 Marek
2 Steve
3 Patrice
4 Sinan
5 Giancarlo
6 Kenny

a) has never played for the first team.
b) is the team manager.
c) has got a knee injury.
d) certainly won't be able to play on Saturday.
e) could be a very good footballer in the future.
f) is a good striker.

7 Complete the extracts. Then look at Track 1.21 on page 179 and check your answers.

1 Marek _____ isn't going to be fit by Saturday.
2 It's a very tricky _____.
3 The _____ with that is we'll be very weak in defence.
4 OK. You _____ a point.
5 That could _____ the problem.
6 _____ to Sinan, I think he's got a lot more potential.

LANGUAGE CHECK

8 Write in the missing words in sentences 1–10. Look at the pages to check your answers.

1 Fewer and fewer people studying chemistry courses these days. (page 9)
2 Actions speak louder words, so do something instead of just talking! (page 9)
3 By 1998 she written ten plays. (page 10)
4 Everybody is aware that average temperatures have going up for the last 20 years. (page 19)
5 How long the sea level been rising? (page 19)
6 Even the government has stopped trying to give a false that taxes are going down. (page 19)
7 We like to know why rivers start freezing. (page 20)
8 Miklos lost his control and started shouting at everyone. (page 29)
9 I'm happy to say that few of you will get a place on the course next month. (page 29)
10 In 2004 she entered Royal College of Art, where David Hockney had also studied. (page 30)

LOOK BACK

9 Find the exercises in Units 1–3 where you ...

- read a speech by Martin Luther King. (Unit 1)
- learn about verbs we rarely use with the continuous aspect. (Unit 1)
- check your partner's email for mistakes. (Unit 1)
- discuss the results of two surveys. (Unit 2)
- learn about using *since* and *for* with the present perfect simple and continuous. (Unit 2)
- design a questionnaire. (Unit 2)
- read about the father of Brazilian football. (Unit 3)
- learn seven idioms connected with sport. (Unit 3)
- prepare a talk about the greatest sportsperson. (Unit 3)

4 Medicine

In this unit

Grammar
- future continuous, *going to*, present continuous
- future perfect, *will*

Vocabulary
- medical terms
- illness and medicine
- dependent prepositions

Scenario
- the Dowling Hospital

Study skills
- evaluating resources on the Internet

Writing skills
- writing short reports

4.1 MEDICAL BREAKTHROUGHS

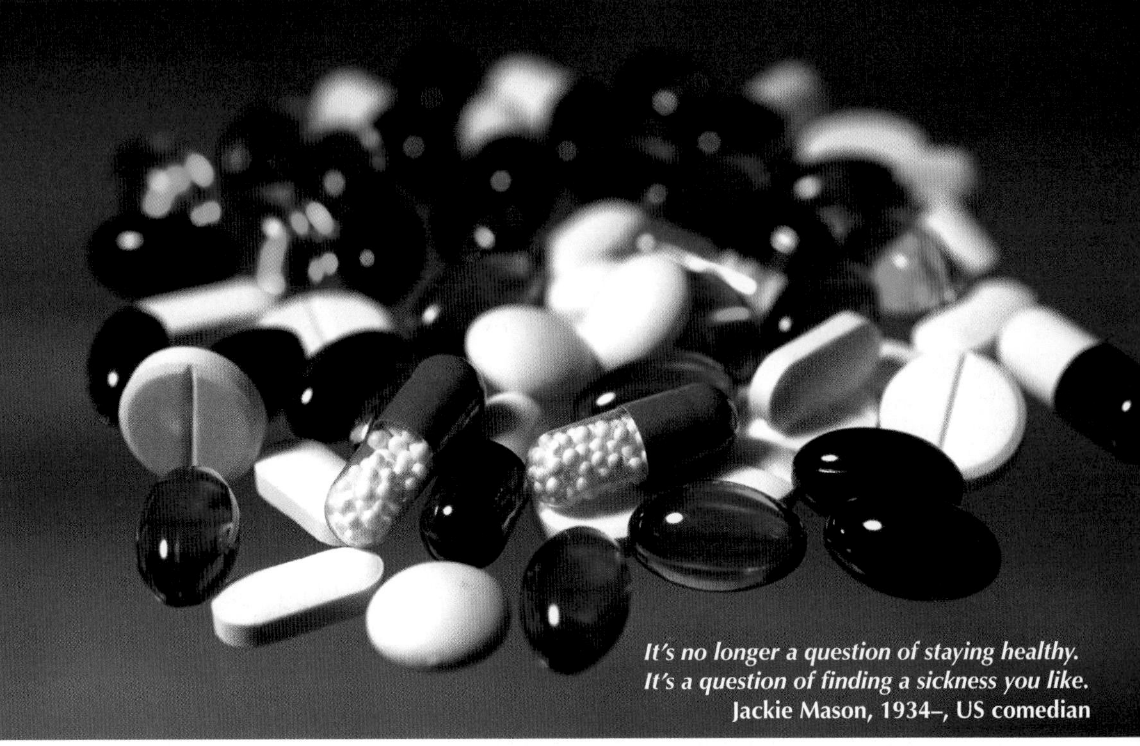

It's no longer a question of staying healthy. It's a question of finding a sickness you like.
Jackie Mason, 1934–, US comedian

SPEAKING

1 Work in pairs. Look at the statements. Which do you agree with? Which are the most important? Give your reasons.

A good doctor …

1 knows the names of all his/her patients.
2 listens sympathetically to people who are not really ill.
3 accepts alternative treatments such as hypnosis, acupuncture and aromatherapy.
4 tells people how to live a healthy life.
5 uses everyday language rather than medical terms in discussions with patients.
6 acts on instinct rather than using logical reasoning.
7 makes home visits in the evenings and/or at weekends.
8 recognises emergency cases immediately.
9 usually prescribes medication, for example, anti-depressant tablets.
10 treats the person rather than the disease.

VOCABULARY: medical terms

2a Look at the words in the box and find the following.

1 six people who work in medicine
2 six treatments / types of drug
3 six medical conditions

Alzheimer's anaesthetist antibiotic arthritis cancer chest infection diabetes heart disease injection midwife morphine painkiller pharmacist physiotherapy psychiatrist radiologist surgeon transplant

2b Complete the sentences with some of the words in the box.

1 A doctor writes a prescription, but you need to take it to a _____ to get the medicine.
2 After my operation, I had _____ twice a week for three months until I could walk again.
3 They found an organ donor in time, so it looks like the _____ will go ahead as planned.
4 People who suffer from _____ need to take insulin or regulate their diets.
5 People with eating disorders, like anorexia and bulimia, are usually treated by a _____.
6 Some drugs are best given to patients by _____.
7 Often caused by poor diet, _____ is the biggest killer in the western world.

pronunciation

3 2.2 **Stressed syllables Mark the stressed syllable on the words in Exercise 2a and say what the stressed vowel sound is. Listen and check your answers.**

READING

4 **You are going to read about some important medical advances. What medical breakthroughs can you think of?**

5a **Work in pairs. Each student reads two texts. Make notes about the medical advances, using the questions below. You may not find answers to all the questions.**

- What?
- Where?
- How?
- Results/benefits?
- Who?
- When?
- Problems?

Student A: look at the texts below.

Student B: turn to page 162.

5b **Using your notes, tell your partner about the two breakthroughs.**

The first text is about …

X-RAYS

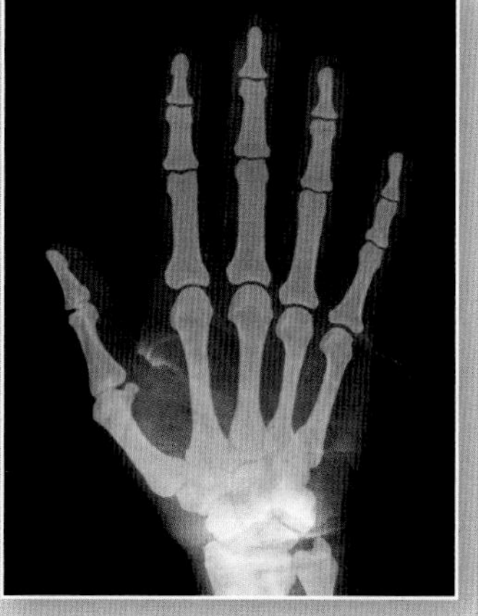

X-rays are images which are used to diagnose disease. They were discovered by Wilhelm Röntgen, a German scientist working in Munich, in 1895. He was working on a cathode ray tube* developed by one of his colleagues, when he noticed that it was projecting a green light on the wall. Strangely, the light was passing through some materials, including paper, wood and books. As he experimented by placing other materials in the way, he noticed that the outline of the bones in his hand was projected onto the wall. In the following weeks he continued to investigate the new rays, which he temporarily called X-rays. Two months later, he published his paper 'On a new kind of X-rays', and in 1901 he was awarded the first Nobel Prize in Physics. Although the new rays would eventually be known as Röntgen rays, he always preferred the term *X-rays*. Today, Röntgen is considered the father of Diagnostic Radiology, a medical speciality using images to diagnose disease. Nowadays, radiologists can examine all areas of the body for different types of disease.

*A cathode ray tube is a piece of equipment which can produce an image on a screen, as in a television.

6 **In pairs, discuss these questions about the medical advances.**

1 Which do you think is the greatest of the advances?
2 What other medical inventions do you think are very important, e.g. the thermometer, the scalpel, the stethoscope?

SPEAKING

7 **Look at these general issues about medicine and the medical profession. Talk about them in small groups.**

1 Should people have to pay for health care?
2 Do you think nurses and midwives are paid enough in your country? Why / Why not?
3 Soon medical advances will allow people to live to a very old age. Is this desirable? Why / Why not?
4 Should new drugs be tested on both animals and humans before being prescribed by doctors?

PENICILLIN

This was the first effective antibiotic. It was discovered by Alexander Fleming, who was a brilliant medical researcher at St Mary's Hospital, London. He was also careless, and his laboratory was often untidy. In 1928, after returning from holiday, he noticed a glass dish that had some mould growing on it. His analysis of this and its effect on the bacteria in the dish led to the discovery of penicillin. This paved the way for the treatment of infectious disease. Fleming published his findings in 1929, but little attention was paid to them. He continued his research, but found it was difficult to grow penicillin mould and even more difficult to refine it.

Fleming shared the 1945 Nobel Prize in Physiology or Medicine with Ernst Chain, who worked out how to isolate and concentrate penicillin. Howard Florey also shared the prize for his work on mass producing penicillin. Fleming's accidental discovery marks the start of modern antibiotics. It is estimated that penicillin has saved nearly 200 million lives.

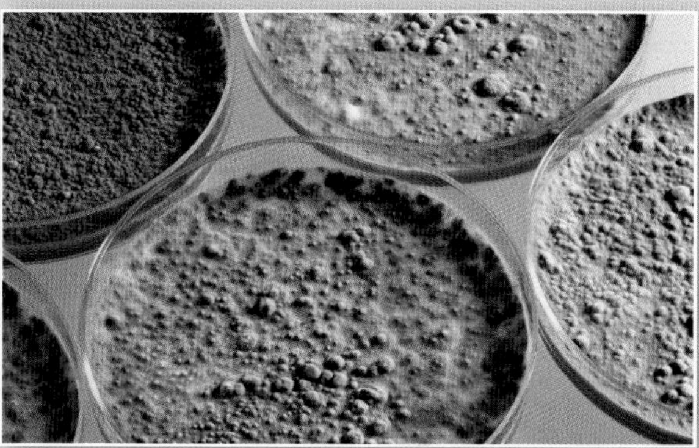

LISTENING

1 Which illnesses are the biggest killers in your country? In the world? Do you know what scientists are doing to try to prevent these illnesses?

2a 2.3 Listen to a talk by Professor John Dodge, honorary Professor of Child Health at the University of Wales, Swansea. What reason does he give for some people not getting effective drugs?

2b Listen again and answer the questions.

1 Why do we need new anti-malarial drugs?
2 Why are pharmaceutical companies unlikely to develop them?
3 What can international agencies do?

READING

3 Is malaria a problem in your country? What do you know about malaria and ways of fighting it?

4a Scan these four texts about malaria and check your answers to the second question in Exercise 3.

Facts about malaria

- Malaria kills more people than any infection apart from HIV/Aids.
- Malaria is spread by the single-celled parasite *plasmodium* and it is endemic in parts of Asia, Africa and Central and South America.
- 90% of malaria deaths occur among young children in sub-Saharan Africa.
- Malaria kills up to 2.7 million people a year.
- Symptoms of malaria include neck stiffness, fits, abnormal breathing and fever.
- Alexander the Great and Genghis Khan died of malaria. John F. Kennedy and Mahatma Gandhi contracted malaria but recovered.
- There is currently no effective vaccine against malaria.

World Swim against Malaria

**The Carleton Place Water Dragons (Ontario, Canada) will be doing their swim between December 5 and 9.
On Friday December 9, from 6 to 7 p.m., the club will be asking parents, friends and siblings to swim and help the global initiative reach their target of one million swimmers and increase funds for the fight against malaria.**

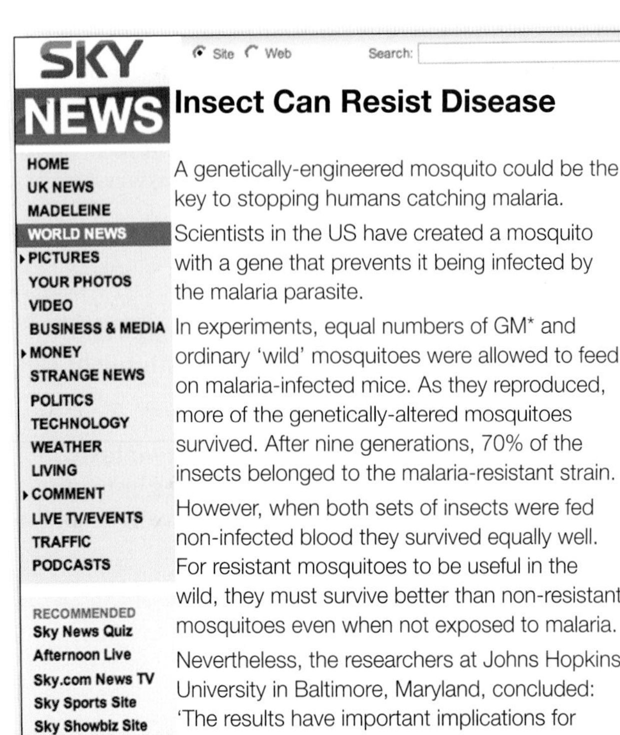

SKY NEWS

Site Web Search:

HOME
UK NEWS
MADELEINE
WORLD NEWS
PICTURES
YOUR PHOTOS
VIDEO
BUSINESS & MEDIA
MONEY
STRANGE NEWS
POLITICS
TECHNOLOGY
WEATHER
LIVING
COMMENT
LIVE TV/EVENTS
TRAFFIC
PODCASTS

RECOMMENDED
Sky News Quiz
Afternoon Live
Sky.com News TV
Sky Sports Site
Sky Showbiz Site
Planet News

EXTRA
Radio
About Sky News

Insect Can Resist Disease

A genetically-engineered mosquito could be the key to stopping humans catching malaria.

Scientists in the US have created a mosquito with a gene that prevents it being infected by the malaria parasite.

In experiments, equal numbers of GM* and ordinary 'wild' mosquitoes were allowed to feed on malaria-infected mice. As they reproduced, more of the genetically-altered mosquitoes survived. After nine generations, 70% of the insects belonged to the malaria-resistant strain.

However, when both sets of insects were fed non-infected blood they survived equally well. For resistant mosquitoes to be useful in the wild, they must survive better than non-resistant mosquitoes even when not exposed to malaria.

Nevertheless, the researchers at Johns Hopkins University in Baltimore, Maryland, concluded: 'The results have important implications for implementation of malaria control by means of genetic modification of mosquitoes.'

*GM=genetically modified

Africa Malaria Day

The Roll Back Malaria partnership has decided that Africa Malaria Day will be commemorated on 25 April every year. In Africa many countries will be organising events and activities in the run-up to 25 April and on Africa Malaria Day itself. In Europe, coalitions and alliances against malaria will be lobbying in parliaments. And the malaria community of the United States will be highlighting this day with its Malaria Awareness Day. Many governments are planning to increase their funding in the fight against malaria.

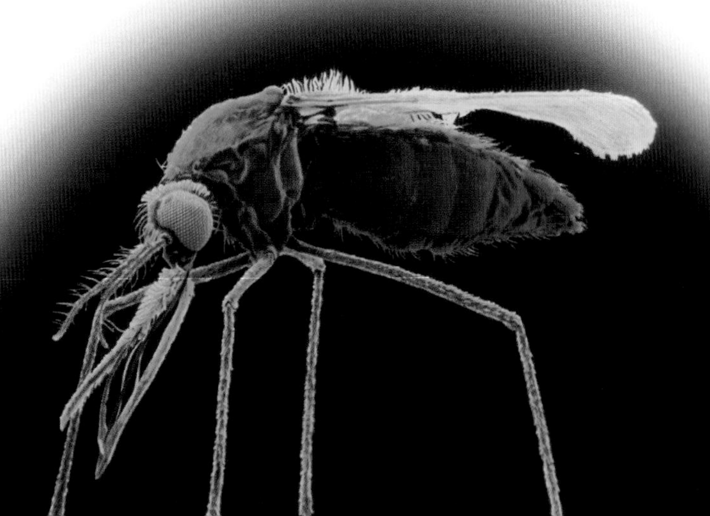

4b Scan the texts again and find the following.

- two famous people who were killed by malaria
- three continents where malaria is common
- a university
- a North American swimming club
- the name of the parasite that spreads malaria
- the animal that was infected by malaria in tests
- the date of Africa Malaria Day

5 Are the statements about the information in the texts true or false?

1 It is not possible to recover from malaria.
2 The 'Swim against Malaria' campaign wants one million swimmers to raise money.
3 Malaria Day takes place only in Africa.
4 The genetically-modified mosquitoes can't be infected by malaria.

VOCABULARY: illness and medicine

6 Find words in 'Facts about malaria' which mean the following.

1 a disease in part of your body caused by bacteria or a virus
2 a plant or animal that lives on or in another plant or animal and gets food from it
3 something that shows you have an illness
4 a symptom of illness in which you have a very high body temperature
5 to get a serious illness
6 a substance used to protect people against a disease, which contains a weak form of the virus that causes the disease

GRAMMAR: future continuous, *going to*, present continuous

7a Look at these sentences from the texts and complete the rules below with the words in the box.

1 In Africa many countries *will be organising* events ... in the run-up to 25 April ...
2 On Friday December 9 ... the club *will be asking* parents, friends and siblings to swim ...

be time future progress *will*

We use the future continuous to talk about an action in _____ at a particular _____ in the _____. It is formed with _____ + _____ + the *-ing* form of the verb.

7b Look at these three ways of talking about an action in the future. Match them with the meanings below.

1 I'm doing a charity swim next Thursday afternoon.
2 I'm going to do a charity swim next Thursday afternoon if I have time.
3 I won't be here. I'll be doing a charity swim next Thursday afternoon.

The speaker:

a) is stating his/her intention – it may not happen.
b) is simply stating a fact about an action happening next week.
c) is talking about a fixed arrangement.

➡ Language reference and extra practice, pages 140–141

8 Which form is correct? Cross out the incorrect form. (In some cases, both are possible.)

1 *I'm going to study / I'm studying* medicine, but I don't know where yet.
2 *Will you be passing / Are you passing* the doctor's when you're out? I need my prescription.
3 I can't see you next Monday as *I'm going to start / I'll be starting* my new job that day.
4 *I'm seeing / I'm going to see* the doctor next week.
5 Don't contact me between 2.00 and 3.00 as *I'll be operating / I'm going to operate* on a patient then.
6 *I'm starting / I'm going to start* a new job at the hospital next week.
7 In a few minutes, *we are landing / we will be landing* in Lusaka.
8 I'm having an operation on Monday. *I'll be recovering / I'm recovering* next week and will miss the monthly meeting.

9 In pairs, ask and answer the questions.

What will you be doing ...

- at 6.00 p.m. this Sunday?
- this summer?
- this time next year?
- when you are 60?

SPEAKING AND WRITING

10a In pairs, plan a day to raise awareness for an illness (similar to the Africa Malaria Day).

10b In pairs, write the text for a poster or leaflet for the awareness-raising day.

The world's first partial face transplant

2004

2007

Most people agree that November 24 and 25, 2005 are important dates in the history of modern medicine. At that time, a team of surgeons in France achieved a remarkable medical breakthrough when they succeeded in performing the first partial face transplant.

A 38-year-old Frenchwoman, Isabelle Dinoire, had been badly disfigured when her dog tried to wake her after she had taken some sleeping pills. After the dog's 'attack', she had terrible injuries. She had lost most of her nose, lips and chin. As a result, she had difficulty eating and drinking. The doctors at the hospital decided to improve the quality of her life by giving her a partial face transplant.

Ms Dinoire is making a good recovery after her operation. However, she will have to take drugs for many years to come so that her body does not reject the new face tissue. No one really knows what the effects of these drugs will be on her health in the long term. She will probably also need psychological counselling as she adjusts to her 'new face'.

Dr Jean-Michel Dubernard, a leading transplant expert who participated in the surgery, explained that the woman's face 'will not exactly resemble her face before, but neither will it completely resemble that of the donor.' He said, 'It will be a new face.'

While some people approve of the operation, others have been more critical. They question whether Ms Dinoire was able to consent fully to the operation when she was in such an emotional state at the time. Other medical experts say that the team should have tried more conventional reconstruction surgery before risking a face transplant.

READING

1 In pairs, answer the following questions.

1 Which organs are most commonly transplanted?
2 What problems can arise after someone receives an organ transplant?

2 Read the article quickly and answer the following questions.

1 Why did Isabelle Dinoire need a transplant?
2 Was it successful? How do you know?
3 Is the operation likely to be repeated?

3 According to the article, which of the following will probably happen? Find the actual predictions in the text to support your answers.

1 Isabelle Dinoire will need to be on medication for many years.
2 She will need to see a psychologist.
3 There may be many transplants in the US, UK and China.
4 There is unlikely to be further discussion of the pros and cons of face transplants.
5 It will be illegal to buy and sell organs on the Internet.

VOCABULARY: dependent prepositions

4 Write the prepositions that follow these verbs. Then check your answers in the article.

1 succeed	2 adjust	3 participate
4 approve	5 consent	6 relate

GRAMMAR: future perfect, *will*

5a Look at these examples of the future perfect from the article and choose the correct alternative in the explanation.

1 In a few years' time, surgeons … will probably *have carried out* many such transplants …
2 … by the end of the next decade, it *will have become* legal for people to buy and sell organs … on the Internet.

We use the future perfect for an action *completed before a point in time in the future / in progress at a time in the future.*

5b Now complete this rule for the formation of the future perfect.

The future perfect = _____ */won't* + _____ + past participle (e.g. *carried*).

➡ Language reference and extra practice, pages 140–141

The operation was the first partial face transplant using skin from another person. Apparently, skin from another person's face is usually a better match than skin from another part of the patient's body.

Since the French operation, surgeons in other countries have received permission to perform face transplants. In a few years' time, surgeons in such countries as the United States, Britain and China will probably have carried out many such transplants, and the debate about the ethical and moral issues relating to face transplants will undoubtedly continue.

Indeed, the whole issue of the modern medical practice of organ transplants will be a subject for ethical debate for some time: the need for organ transplants definitely won't decrease in the future, and, even more controversial, some scientists predict that by the end of the next decade, it will have become legal for people to buy and sell organs for transplant on the Internet.

6 Put the following words in the correct order to make future perfect sentences.

1 I'm afraid have won't I by then finished
2 in the field of transplants have we'll by the year 2050 made progress
3 had the operation have I'll by the time you get here
4 come out the hospital won't have of they yet
5 in weeks three term have will finished the

7a Find examples of the following from the article.

1 the modal verb *will* to make a prediction
2 examples of adverbs of certainty, e.g. *certainly, possibly*

Do the adverbs come before or after *will* and *won't*?

7b Complete the following sentences so they are true for you. Use *will* + infinitive or the future perfect, and an adverb of certainty where you can.

1 I _____ (pass) my next English exams.
2 I _____ (finish) all this week's work by Friday.
3 I _____ (learn) something new by the end of this class.
4 I believe there _____ (be) a cure for cancer in the next 20 years …
5 … and that we _____ (replace) surgery for some types of cancer by less invasive treatments.
6 Scientists _____ (develop) a vaccine against malaria by the end of the decade.

8 Complete this company announcement with the verbs in brackets, using *will* or the future perfect.

Anderson Bio-Sciences announces its takeover next week of the Essex-based company HGP. Together, ABS and HGP [1]_____ (form) the largest genetic engineering company in the UK, and by 2020, we [2]_____ (expand) to employ over 1,000 people. In addition, by 2020 the company [3]_____ (become) the largest employer of medical researchers in the country. HGP is close to determining the entire sequence of the human chromosome set and we [4]_____ (publish) that knowledge base over the Internet. This [5]_____ (revolutionise) biology and medicine and [6]_____ (give) researchers huge potential to develop new drugs.

In 2020 medical records [7]_____ (include) people's complete genomes and this [8]_____ (permit) doctors to treat people as biochemical and genetic individuals. By 2020, the company [9]_____ (make) substantial progress towards true 'cloning' of certain organs.

Investors interested in purchasing shares in this company should request further information at http

9 Predict where you will be, what you will be doing and what you will have achieved at these future points. Discuss the predictions in pairs.

- this time tomorrow
- this time next year
- in ten years' time
- when you retire

This time tomorrow I'll be at my physics lecture, so I'll be taking notes. I hope by this time tomorrow I'll have learned a bit more physics.

SPEAKING

10 In groups, discuss the following ethical questions.

- Should people who have a better chance of survival be given priority over other people urgently needing organ transplants?
- Should young children be given priority for transplants?
- Should those whose lifestyle choices (smoking, obesity, etc.) have damaged an organ be given the chance of an organ transplant?
- Should financial incentives be offered to encourage people to donate organs?

SITUATION

1 Read the extract from the information leaflet. If you lived in St Lucia and had a low income, what facts might encourage you to have medical treatment at the Dowling Hospital?

The Dowling Hospital is situated on the English-speaking island of St Lucia in the Caribbean. In cooperation with the Boston Medical Foundation (BMF), it offers a comprehensive range of health care. The hospital was founded in 1956 by a talented doctor, Edgar Dowling, who had high ideals about a fair society for all. The money to build the hospital came from a wealthy benefactor. Dowling wanted the hospital to provide low-cost treatments and medical care for the poorer sections of the community. Over the years, he built up a team who shared his principles.

Nowadays, the Dowling Hospital has an international reputation. However, at present the hospital is having financial problems, as costs have risen but the fees for treatments have remained low. Funds from charities have also decreased in recent years.

2 Read the article from a local English-language newspaper. Answer the questions.

1 Who is giving money to the hospital?

2 What two reasons are given for the grant coming at the 'right time'?

3 How have grants from foundations helped the Dowling Hospital?

Million-Dollar Grant for Dowling Hospital

THE DOWLING HOSPITAL has announced that it will receive a grant of $1 million from the US-based Goldwater Foundation. This is welcome news for the hospital as it is known to be experiencing financial difficulties.'We are very pleased to receive the grant,' said Director, William Garvey. 'We have a number of projects which need to be funded, so the grant has come at the right time. We are grateful to the Goldwater Foundation for their generosity. The Dowling Hospital has always depended on funds from organisations such as Goldwater to provide high-quality treatments for our patients and to maintain our fees at an affordable level.'

We will inform our readers how the money will be spent as soon as the hospital management makes its decision.

The Dowling Hospital 4.4

KEY LANGUAGE: predicting

3a 2.4 Listen to the Dowling's Medical Director talking to the Nursing Director about the grant. Tick the reasons they mention for NOT spending the money on the gardens and full-time gardeners.

1 One million dollars would not be enough to landscape the gardens.
2 The Boston Medical Foundation might not approve their decision.
3 They need new equipment to improve their medical care.
4 Medical research needs to be financed.
5 The local newspaper would want the money to be spent on poor people.
6 Diana Marsden would not approve of this kind of expenditure.

3b Listen again and complete each prediction with words or phrases from the dialogue.

1 ... the gardens are in a dreadful state. But it __________ quite a lot to have them landscaped.
2 I don't have precise figures, but I'd say it __________ over half of the grant.
3 If we __________ the gardens, I don't think the Boston Medical Foundation will be very pleased.
4 They __________ to spend the grant on up-to-date equipment.
5 They're very keen for us to get a new scanner. They think it __________ our treatments.
6 Another thing to think about, ... is __________ an effect on other projects.
7 Exactly. It __________ a big impact on research.
8 I __________ to Diana Marsden some time this weekend ...

OTHER USEFUL PHRASES

Considering implications

We need to look at the implications ... (of that option).

If we do X, it could ... (upset the Boston Medical Foundation).

Well, one consequence could be ... (we'll harm our image).

It'll have a (big) impact on ... (research).

It's bound to have an influence on ... (hiring new staff).

It could be good/bad for ... (our image).

It will lead to ...

It could result in ...

It will/may contribute to ...

It could influence ...

TASK: making a difficult decision

4 You are members of the hospital management. Work in small groups to discuss each option below for using the grant. Use the following criteria to guide your discussion.

1 cost
2 time to implement the option
3 impact on the hospital's image
4 benefits to the patients and to the hospital
5 drawbacks of the option
6 the implications of each option

Options

1 Send some patients to Boston for urgently needed operations and post-operative care.
Cost: approximately \$200,000–\$250,000 per patient
2 Hire a research assistant to investigate the causes of cot deaths (unexpected deaths of young children in their sleep). The death rate of children from this cause is high in the local community.
Cost: approximately \$300,000 for five years
3 Build new facilities for physiotherapy. Hire new staff to work in the rooms.
Cost: approximately \$1million (at least)
4 Buy new equipment: an up-to-date MRI (magnetic resonance imaging) scanner.
Cost: at least \$600,000
5 Upgrade the facilities and accommodation at the hospital: the hospital needs to be redecorated and the fittings and furniture renovated.
Cost: \$800,000
6 Invest in a new facility: set up a cosmetic surgery clinic run by the hospital's gifted surgeon, Mr Mack. This will bring in a lot of money from wealthy American and European clients.
Cost: approximately \$700,000
7 Erect a bronze statue of Edgar Dowling (who died two years ago) in the hospital grounds.
Cost: \$150,000, but \$50,000 already raised from public donations

5a Choose the best three options and rank them. (1 = your first choice)

5b Meet as a class. Try to persuade the other groups that your solution for spending the money is the best one. Decide which option(s) you will spend the money on. If you cannot agree, take a vote.

STUDY SKILLS: evaluating resources on the Internet

1 In pairs, look at the suggestions for evaluating websites used for research. Discuss which you agree/disagree with and give reasons for each answer.

1 You should always find out who runs the website.
2 You need to find out the purpose of the website. The best way to do this is to click on 'About us'.
3 Websites run by governments are usually fairly reliable.
4 Commercial websites, which try to sell products or raise money, give a lot of reliable and accurate information.
5 Professional associations, such as scientific and medical research societies, tend to be reliable.
6 A reputable website will not give you links to other websites.
7 A website will be a useful source of information only if it is updated regularly.
8 A website is usually reliable if it contains facts and opinions, and the names of experts.
9 An article on a website will probably be worth reading if it has been reviewed by someone well known in the field.

2 2.5 Listen to Part 1 of a lecture on evaluating websites that you use for research. Answer the questions.

1 What are the speaker's two main points?
2 What warning does she give her audience?

3 2.6 Listen to Part 2 of the lecture. Tick the points that the lecturer makes in this section of her talk.

1 Government and educational websites are generally reliable.
2 Commercial organisations are often non-profit making.
3 If there is no review by a specialist in the field, the information needs to be checked carefully.
4 Websites must be kept up-to-date regularly.
5 Websites should contain only facts or results.
6 Links can help to support the results of research.
7 The lecturer thinks that libraries are still the most reliable source of information.

4 Imagine you are going to write an article on hypnotherapy. Look it up on the Internet and choose the three best websites to get information. Compare your choice with other students.

WRITING SKILLS: writing short reports

5 A consumer research agency, Up-Date.co.uk, is currently doing an online series on alternative therapies: acupuncture, osteopathy, aromatherapy, massage, homeopathy and herbal medicine. Discuss these questions.

1 What do you know about each therapy?
2 Have you ever used any of the therapies?
3 If so, did you get any benefit from it?

6 Read Up-Date's report on homeopathy. In which section of the report can you find the following?

1 a summary of the writer's main points
2 the key facts discovered in the research
3 advice to consumers who read the report
4 where the information comes from

7a Making recommendations Study the Recommendations section and answer the questions.

1 What words does the writer use to introduce each recommendation?
2 Which recommendations are strongest? Which are weakest? How do you know?
3 Which recommendations use the passive form of the verb?
4 Why is the passive form sometimes used in recommendations?

7b Rewrite each recommendation using one of the alternative grammatical structures. Make any necessary changes.

must + verb / passive verb
It is advisable to … It is vital that …

might/could + verb / passive verb
It is a good idea to …

Members must understand that symptoms can get worse before they get better.

8a You work for Up-Date.co.uk. You have to write a report on herbal remedies, i.e. plant-based treatments to improve health. Use the notes on page 170 to write the report.

8b In pairs, look at each other's reports and try to improve them.

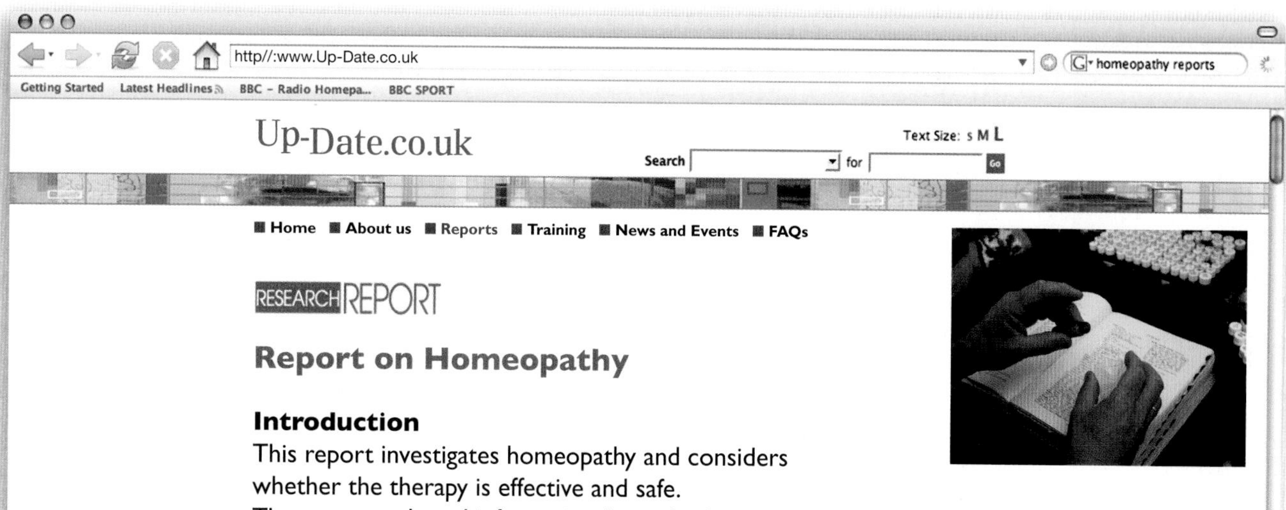

RESEARCH REPORT

Report on Homeopathy

Introduction

This report investigates homeopathy and considers whether the therapy is effective and safe.
The report gathered information from the following sources:

- 3,500 of our members were sent questionnaires asking them about their experience of using the therapy. We received 2,560 completed surveys.
- Leading medical journals and experts in the field were consulted.

Facts and findings

1. Homeopathy was developed in Germany in the late 1700s. Illnesses are treated with very small samples of natural materials such as plants, minerals and some animal products.
2. Homeopathic prescriptions are tailored to each patient. Two patients may have the same symptoms but be given different remedies.
3. Homeopathy is considered safe by most users and experts because the ingredients are used in small quantities and are diluted.
4. Opinion is divided about the effectiveness of homeopathic remedies. Some leading medical journals say that the therapy does not have any real benefits. However, some studies have found that homeopathic remedies are 'equivalent to conventional medicines' in treating certain illnesses.
5. Our members used homeopathy to treat a wide range of medical problems. Just over 52% said that they would recommend the treatment to friends.

Conclusion

Scientific experts and users of the therapy are divided about its benefits. However, homeopathy is considered to be safe.

Recommendations

1. You should consult your doctor before using homeopathic remedies.
2. It is vital to consult a registered homeopath before taking a remedy.
3. The instructions on homeopathic products must be read carefully before use.
4. It is essential to understand that symptoms can get worse before they get better.
5. Homeopathic products should be bought from an established outlet, for example a reputable health care store.
6. Homeopathic remedies may alleviate hay fever, coughs and colds, stress and depression.

■ Aileen McGuire

Done

Transport

In this unit

Grammar
- modal verbs (future)
- modal verbs (past)

Vocabulary
- transport
- safety features

Scenario
- Transport: a new plan

Study skills
- describing graphs, charts and tables

Writing skills
- describing information in a table

5.1 GETTING FROM A TO B

Everywhere is walking distance if you have the time.
Steven Wright, 1955–, US comedian
KLM

VOCABULARY: transport

1 **What methods of transport do you use most often? Which do you prefer? Why?**

2a **Add some of your own ideas to the word map.**

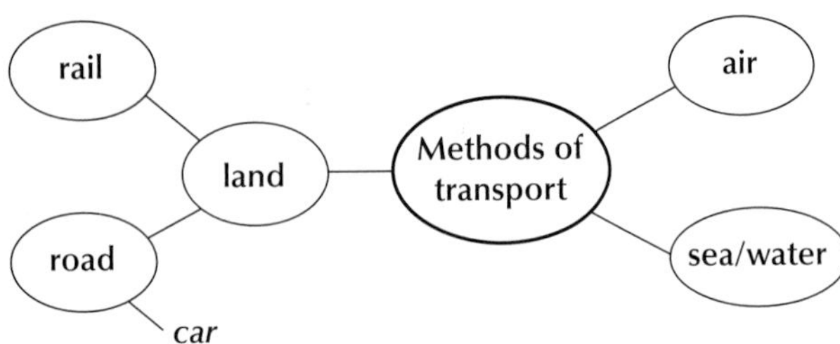

2b **Add the methods of transport in the box to the word map.**

balloon barge cable car coach ferry glider helicopter hovercraft hydrofoil lorry/truck Maglev train motorbike quad bike scooter submarine tram van

2c **What type of transport do you associate these problems with?**

fogbound runway lane closure low tide platform alteration puncture rough weather signalling problems tailback turbulence

fogbound runway = air transport

3 **Discuss the questions.**

1 What is your preferred method of transport?
2 Which methods of transport in the word map haven't you used?
3 Which would you like to try? Which wouldn't you like to try? Why?
4 What are the advantages and disadvantages of the methods of transport you have discussed?

READING

4 **What adjectives would you use to describe the cars in the pictures? Which do you think looks the safest? Why?**

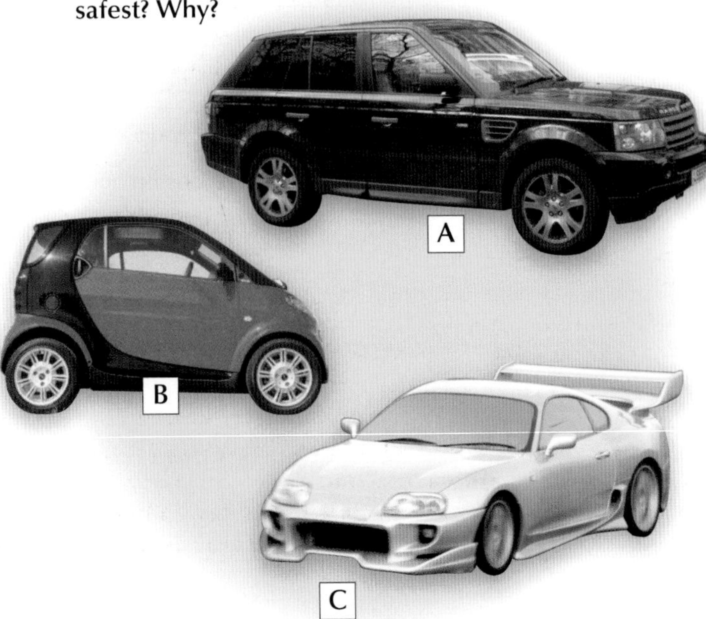

5a How important do you think the following are as causes of crashes on the road today?

- the age of drivers
- speed
- the number of cars on the road
- the weather
- mechanical problems
- the sex of drivers
- the psychology of drivers
- the quality of roads

5b Read the article quickly and decide which the writer feels is the biggest cause.

6 Read the article again and decide which of the methods of making roads safer listed below are mentioned. Support your choices with examples.

- restricting the speed at which people can drive
- introducing technological innovations to make people slow down
- educating drivers
- improving safety features in cars
- having tough penalties for drivers who break the law
- introducing an upper age limit for drivers
- assessing drivers' abilities and issuing of documents
- introducing street lighting to improve visibility

VOCABULARY: safety features

7 Without looking back at the article, complete these safety features.

1 speed _____
2 anti-lock _____
3 traffic _____
4 air_____
5 _____ cameras
6 seat _____
7 one-way _____

SPEAKING AND WRITING

8a Work in groups of three. You are going to have a debate about the best ways of making the roads safer.

Student A: turn to page 158.
Student B: turn to page 162.
Student C: turn to page 167.

8b Discuss the ways of improving road safety. Decide together which method you think would be the most effective.

8c Report your decisions to the class.

9 As a class, give your own opinions and try to reach a decision together as to the best course of action on this issue.

10 Write your recommendations for a report on road safety.

The dangers of safety

Travelling by road is widely accepted as being the most dangerous way to travel with far more deaths per kilometre than rail, sea or air. In fact, while road traffic injuries represent about 25% of worldwide injury-related deaths, fatalities on the road in the UK have been decreasing for some time, with last year's figure standing at 3,150. We take a look at why the number is decreasing, but why it seems impossible to eradicate fatalities completely.

Over the years, different methods of reducing the number of crashes have been tried. The Locomotive and Highways Act of 1865 introduced the idea of speed limits to the motoring world. Since then, more and more ways of controlling the behaviour of drivers have been introduced, such as one-way streets and traffic signals, as well as compulsory driver testing and licensing. These days, there are many more methods of enforcement, including speed cameras and fines for breaking motoring laws.

Another solution is to make cars themselves safer in case of an accident. This means the main focus has been on passive safety or crash survival rather than active safety or avoiding crashes. There are many innovations by motor manufacturers which have made cars safer, such as seat belts, anti-lock brakes and airbags. A lot of attention has also been paid to car interiors, as cars have got quieter, more comfortable and more luxurious. These improvements have tended to make the driver feel more in control and insulated him/her from the fast-moving and dangerous environment outside the car. It seems strange that as improvements have been made the number of pile-ups continues to increase.

Actually, it is wrong to talk about safe and dangerous cars in this way. The key to this problem is not actually the car, but the driver. In fact, making drivers feel safer is not the solution to the problem, it is the cause of the problem. As drivers feel safer, it encourages them to drive aggressively and to ignore other road users and therefore increases the number of crashes. The problem of car safety is not an engineering problem but a psychological one. Ironically, if we want cars to be safer, we need to make them more dangerous!

LISTENING

1a 2.7 **Listen to a BBC report. What exactly is the Ultra?**

1b Listen again and list the advantages of the Ultra pods. Then compare with your partner.

2 The Ultra shows us one transport development. What other transport developments will take place in the next 50 years? Why will these happen?

READING

3 Read the following introduction quickly. Find three reasons why transport will change over the next 50 years. Are they the same as your reasons in Exercise 2?

During the next 50 years, there will be great changes in our means of transport. Some of the new developments will come from our need to depend less on fossil fuels as a source of power. Other developments are likely to respond to the ever-faster pace of society by aiming to increase the speed of different means of transport, and others may pander to the thrill-seeking sections of society by introducing newer and more exciting methods of transport.

4a Work in groups of three to read the article. Read your section of the article. Which of the reasons given in Exercise 3 does your text describe?

Student A: read Text A on the right.

Student B: read Text B on page 161.

Student C: read Text C on page 167.

4b Read your text again and make notes. Tell your partners about your text.

5 In your groups, read these statements. Are they true or false? Explain why they are true or false and provide any more information necessary about them.

1 Burt Rutan owns Virgin Galactic.
2 Richard Branson was the first person to send a private spaceship into space.
3 The general public will require three weeks' training before taking a space flight.
4 Nothing will replace petrol, diesel or gas as the main fuel for cars.
5 Hydrogen cannot be used in cars because it is too dangerous.
6 Fuel cell design has made hydrogen-powered cars an alternative to fossil fuels.
7 Maglev trains do not burn up fuel.
8 There are commercially run Maglev trains in China and Germany.
9 The Maglev train accident was not due to a system fault.

A

In the field of aviation, Sir Richard Branson, the airline tycoon, attracted attention worldwide when he set up a company, Virgin Galactic, to bring space travel within the reach of the general public. When announcing his project, he said he was 'trying to make sure that, in the not too distant future, people from all over the world will be able to go into space'.

Sir Richard plans to build a fleet of five 'spaceliners' in the United States. The fleet's technology would be based on the technology developed by the famous aviation expert, Burt Rutan, for SpaceShipOne, which made history in 2004 as the first private manned craft to travel 100km (62 miles) above Earth – the official boundary of space.

While space travel might become available to all, not everyone will be able to take advantage of it. When Virgin Galactic offers its first spaceflights, the tickets will be rather expensive. A sub-orbital flight could cost about £100,000. However, Branson believes prices will eventually come down.

The Virgin Galactic spaceships will carry five passengers in luxury seats. Anyone buying a ticket will need to have about a week's initial training for the three-hour flight. Sir Richard suggested there were about 3,000 people who might be willing to sign up for the first 'wave' of flights. The plan, he says, 'will enable people to go into space, to become astronauts, to see the Earth, to enjoy weightlessness. Eventually, we want to get prices down to levels where masses of people can enjoy space.'

VOCABULARY

6a Look at the following definitions. There are three words per text. Find the words in your text.

Text A

1 someone who is very successful in business and has lots of money (paragraph 1)

2 a group of ships or vehicles owned by one company (para. 2)

3 large amounts or numbers of something (para. 4)

Text B

4 to send out gas, heat or sounds (para. 1)

5 strong smelling gas or smoke that is unpleasant to breathe in (para. 1)

6 possible and likely to work (para. 3)

Text C

7 raised off the ground, in a high position (para. 1)

8 goods carried by ships, trains or aircraft (para. 2)

9 a plane, bus or train that makes regular trips between two places (para. 3)

6b In your groups, complete the text with some of the words above.

It took millions of years for fossil fuels like coal, oil and natural gas to come about, but it only takes a few minutes for them to burn. Cars continue to burn petrol and [1]_____ harmful [2]_____. We need to look at alternative renewable energy sources as solutions to the future of transport that are [3]_____ and likely to be successful. For example, [4]_____ should be carried by rail rather than road, and companies that have a [5]_____ of vehicles should ensure they use the least damaging fuel. Currently, [6]_____ of people commute short distances by road, so we should ensure that regular rail [7]_____ become common, perhaps travelling through vacuum tubes at high speeds.

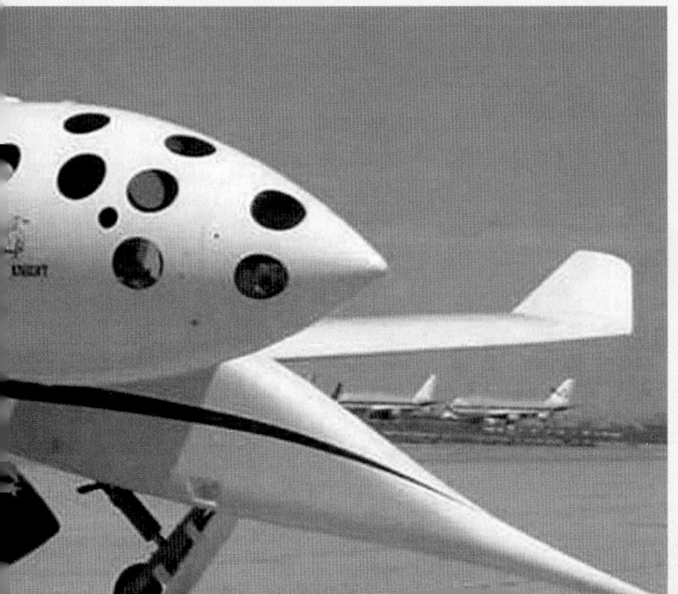

GRAMMAR: modal verbs (future)

7 Look at your texts and find ways of expressing future ability/possibility and future obligation. Complete the chart together.

	ability	possibility	obligation
Text A			*will need to*
Text B	✗✗✗✗✗	*might*	
Text C	*will be able to*		✗✗✗✗✗

➥ Language reference and extra practice, pages 142–143

8 There are grammatical errors in six of these sentences. In pairs, correct the errors and discuss what is wrong in each case.

1 Security will must improve in airports in the next 20 years.

2 Astronauts will never be able to travel to the sun.

3 We might work faster than that if we want to meet the deadline.

4 In 50 years' time, we will all have to travel in space because space travel will become much cheaper.

5 In 20 years' time, many of us can travel on magnetic trains.

6 He's had an accident so I'll be able to drive him to hospital.

7 We will need find feasible renewable energy sources in the near future.

8 We will have to apply for our travel visas before the end of the month.

9 Complete the following sentences and discuss them in pairs.

1 In five years' time, I'll be able to / I'll have to / I might …

2 In ten years' time, I'll be able to / I'll need to …

3 In twenty years' time, I won't be able to / I won't have to / I might not …

SPEAKING

10 In pairs, complete the following statements with *will have to, will be able to* or *might* according to what you believe. Then discuss them in groups.

1 Governments _____ make petrol engines in cars illegal within the next 20 years.

2 Airline companies _____ charge passengers a lot of extra money because of extra taxes on fuel.

3 City councils _____ prioritise water transport in the next ten years.

4 Space travel companies _____ lower their prices in the next 30 years.

5.3 GREAT RAILWAY JOURNEYS

READING

1a Do you know of any famous railway journeys? Use the photos to help you.

1b Look through the text quickly and find out which journeys are mentioned.

2 Now scan the article and find the following.

1 four capital cities
2 two authors
3 a Russian ruler
4 the largest freshwater lake in the world
5 the most luxurious railway in the world
6 the longest railway (and its length)
7 the highest railway (and its height)
8 the highest tunnel (and its height)

3 Read the article again and answer the questions.

1 Why did the writer's publishers finance his rail journeys?
2 Why was the toilet water heated on the Quinghai–Tibet line?
3 What did the writer like looking at most on the Quinghai–Tibet line and on the Trans-Siberian?
4 What sort of people travelled on the Orient Express?
5 What clues does the text give about the luxury of the Orient Express?

4 Find the words in the box in the text. Then complete the sentences.

era	nostalgia	gruelling	altitude
impeccable	nomads	icon	opulence

1 She was tired after the long and _____ journey.
2 We were impressed by the _____ manners of the smartly dressed porters.
3 The age of the railway brought an _____ of prosperity.
4 He was struck by the _____ of the Blue Train, with its elaborate furnishings and en-suite bathrooms.
5 Breathing becomes more difficult at high _____.
6 The _____ travelled far looking for grass for their animals.
7 The historic _____, *Mallard*, is the holder of the world speed record for steam locomotives.
8 He had always felt a certain amount of _____ for his life on the railways.

5 Which of the railways in the article would you most like to go on? Why?

The golden era of the great express trains conjures up feelings of nostalgia, romance and beautiful views. My dreams came true last year when my publishers asked me to do some research for a Great Railways travel guide. Luckily, I was able to find ten amazing journeys and managed to persuade the publishers to pay for all ten. Here are my top three.

Until recently if you wanted to go from Golmud, in western China to Lhasa, in Tibet, you had to take a gruelling 48-hour bus journey. Now you can travel from Beijing (the capital of China) to Lhasa on the *Quinghai–Tibet line*, as we did. It still isn't easy, however. We couldn't get tickets

at first because of the bureaucracy – we had to get a special permit to travel through Tibet. The line includes the Tangula Pass – at 5,072 metres above sea level the world's highest railtrack. It also includes the 1,338-metre-long Fenghuosha tunnel, which, at 4,905 metres above sea level is the highest rail tunnel in the world. On our journey extra oxygen was pumped into our carriages to counter the high altitude. Even the water in the toilets had to be heated to prevent freezing. The views of the Himalayas were absolutely breathtaking and this is a journey that will live long in my memory.

All train enthusiasts want to travel on the longest and most famous railway of all – the *Trans-Siberian Express*. It runs from Russia's capital, Moscow, to Vladivostok, on the western shore of the Sea of Japan. It is 9,198km long, spans eight time zones, and it takes about seven days to complete its journey. We took a more leisurely 14-day journey that included several stops. We succeeded in getting first class tickets: our sleeping carriages were stylish and luxurious and we had impeccable service and cuisine. For me, the highlight was skirting the scenic Lake Baikal, the largest freshwater lake in the world. We then travelled via Ulaanbaatar, the capital of Mongolia, and were able to eat in a yurt, the round felt-covered tent traditionally used by

GRAMMAR: modal verbs (past)

6a Look at the article and find different ways of talking about ability, possibility and obligation in the past.

I was able to find ten amazing journeys ...

6b Note the structures we use with each verb or phrase.

6c Look at the statements and cross out the incorrect form. (In some cases, both are possible.)

1. We use *can / could* to talk about general abilities in the past.
2. We use *must / had to* to talk about obligation in the past.
3. The past of *can* is *could / was able to*.
4. We use *managed to / could* to suggest that we had difficulty in achieving the action.
5. The verb *manage to* is similar to *must / succeed in*.
6. We use the *-ing* form of the verb after *manage to / succeed in*.

Mongolian nomads. It is amazing to think that in 1891 Tsar Alexander III had said, 'Let the railway be built.' And here I was on it. My memories of frosted plains and snowy steppes will always stay with me.

The *Orient Express* with its unmatched luxuriousness and comfort has become synonymous with stylish travel. In the past, only the richest could afford this level of luxury. The routes have changed over the years. The initial route was from the French capital Paris to Istanbul, travelling through Germany, Austria, Hungary and Romania (about 2,740km). It is an icon of passenger rail. Extravagantly elegant, it had everything – opulence, romance and fine cuisine. The train had sleeping, restaurant and salon cars with smoking compartments and ladies' drawing rooms. The Express has attracted the rich and the famous, including royalty, and has been made a household name by writers such as Agatha Christie and Graham Greene.

GRAMMAR TIP

We do not use *could* to talk about a single action that we did in the past. Instead we use *was able to* or *managed to*:

~~I could get my visa for the States yesterday.~~

I was able to / managed to get my visa for the States yesterday.

➥ Language reference and extra practice, pages 142–143

7 Choose the most appropriate alternative in the text. Sometimes both alternatives are correct.

When we read that the Quinghai–Tibet line was open, we knew we [1]*weren't able to / had to* go on it. We were so busy before we left London that we didn't [2]*manage / succeed* to organise the train journey. Once we were in China, we didn't have much access to the Internet and [3]*weren't able to / didn't have to* get much information. Still, we found a good travel agency and [4]*could / managed to* get tickets. We travelled first to Golmud and stopped there – for one day only, but we [5]*managed to / were able to* pack a lot into it.

The train journey from Golmud to Lhasa takes a day. Although most of it is really high, we didn't have any altitude problems and we [6]*were able to / had to* enjoy the fabulous scenery. Our train attendant was very helpful. Her English was not great, but she still [7]*had to / succeeded in* getting her message across and pointing out interesting sights to us, such as herds of wild Tibetan antelopes.

Before 2006, you [8]*could / were able to* travel to Lhasa from Golmud, but you [9]*couldn't / didn't have to* get there in comfort – you [10]*could / had to* take a slow, uncomfortable bus. Not any more – Lhasa is officially open to tourists!

SPEAKING

8 Think of a journey you have made that was difficult or complicated to organise. Make notes about things that you:

- had to change.
- were(n't) able to do / couldn't do.
- managed to do / succeeded in doing.

In pairs, tell your partner about the journey.

5.4 SCENARIO

SITUATION

1 **What kind of transport problems are there in your town/city? What about other major cities in your country?**

2 **Read the information about the city and look at the map. What kind of transport problems might the city have?**

Beauciel, a city in the south of France, is experiencing severe transport problems which are affecting all sections of the community. If the city council can solve the problems, it will improve the lives of everyone who lives and works there. A team of international transport consultants is working with a representative of the city council to study the problems. They will come up with an action plan to improve the transport system.

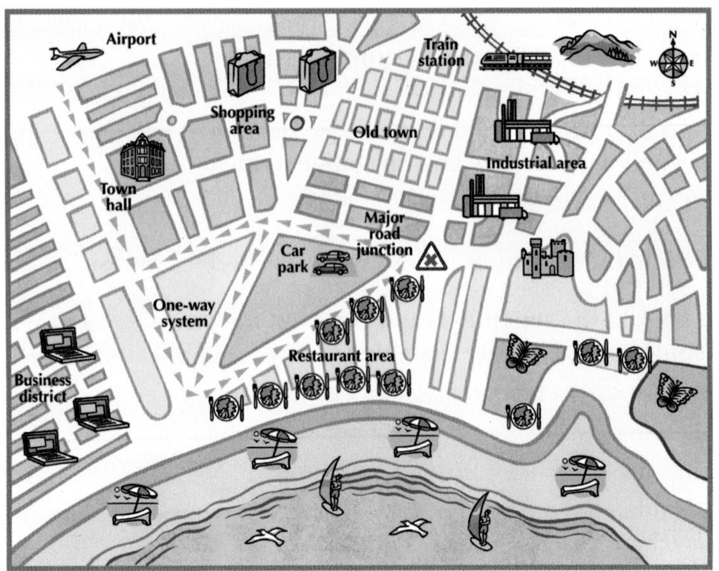

3a **2.8** **Listen to an English-language broadcast for tourists travelling in Europe. Tick the problems. Then write the percentage of residents who mentioned each problem.**

Problems relating to transport in Beauciel

- too many cars
- narrow roads
- traffic jams at peak times
- not enough car parks
- too much noise
- air pollution
- unreliable bus services
- on-street parking

3b **Compare your answers with a partner. Then listen again and check.**

4a **In small groups, brainstorm ideas for solving the city's transport problems and note them down.**

4b **The consultants are considering suggestions for improving the traffic flow in the city. Read their suggestions and do the following.**

1. Discuss the advantages and disadvantages of each suggestion.
2. Think about how expensive each project would be. Put each one into the appropriate category: cheap, reasonable or expensive.

Suggestions

1. Introduce a 'congestion charge'. Drivers coming into the city during the day would pay a certain amount of money to the city council each time, e.g. 15 euros for each visit.
2. Increase parking fines by 50% – use the money to finance wider roads.
3. Build a new subway system.
4. Rebuild the old tram system, using old lines as far as possible.
5. Have free bus transport in the city, with more bus lanes and fines for drivers of private cars who use them.
6. Put a 'park and ride' scheme into place: drivers leave their cars in car parks outside the city centre. Then they catch a special bus into the centre.
7. Build four huge underground car parks in the city.
8. Increase the road tax on motorcycles by 50%.

KEY LANGUAGE: persuading, recommending action

5a 2.9 **Listen and note down the solutions the consultants propose for the city's transport problems.**

5b Listen again. The following phrases are all used to persuade the other listeners. Fill in the missing words in each phrase.

1 OK, Luc, but I _________ we've got to do something ...
2 Surely _________ that there are just too many cars.
3 But there are other issues. I think _________ to persuade people to use smaller cars.
4 ... we also need to think about other things. _____ _____ more car parks are necessary?
5 There's _________ in my mind that the answer is to offer people a really good, cheap bus system.
6 I'm sure _________ that's the best way to get people round the city quickly ...
7 Maybe you're right, Melanie. But _________ that it's the best solution for us right now.

5c Look at Track 2.9 on page 181 and find five expressions in the conversation used to recommend action.

TASK: making an action plan

6a You are consultants working for the city council. In small groups, discuss the suggestions in Exercises 4 and 5 and choose six of the best ideas.

6b Consider the cost of each proposal. How might the city raise the money to implement the proposals?

6c Compare your ideas with another group and present the six best to the class. As a class, choose the six best ideas to recommend for action to the city council.

OTHER USEFUL PHRASES

Agreeing (strongly)

Yes, that's true.

That's a great idea.

I totally agree.

Disagreeing (strongly)

I can't agree with you.

Sorry, I don't think it'll work.

Expressing doubt

Mmm, maybe but ... (people won't accept it).

I'm not too sure about that. Don't you think ... (it could be too expensive)?

STUDY SKILLS: describing graphs, charts and tables

Euro NCAP crash test: Latest safety scores			
Car	**Class**	**Occupant**	**Children**
Skoda Roomster	Mini MPV	★★★★★	★★★★
Toyota Auris	Medium car	★★★★★	★★★★
Volvo C30	Medium car	★★★★★	★★★★
VW Eos	Medium car	★★★★	★★★★
Kia Magentis	Large car	★★★★	★★★
Chrysler Voyager	MPV	★★★	★★★★
Chevrolet Captiva	Off-roader	★★★★	★★★
Hyundai Santa Fe	Off-roader	★★★★	★★★★

table

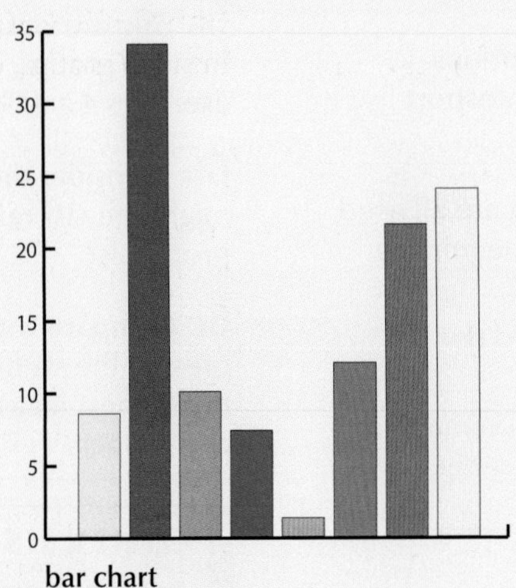

bar chart

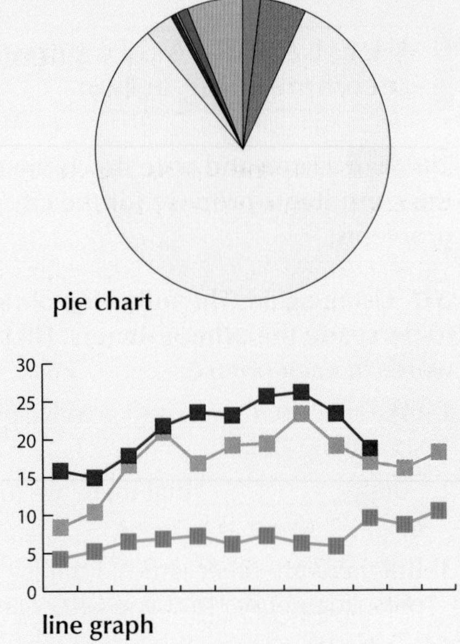

pie chart

line graph

1 Graphs, charts and tables are ways of presenting information in a form that is easy to understand. Match each type shown above with one of the descriptions.

1 A _____ shows the different parts of a total amount. For example, it could show the percentage of money that a student spends on entertainment, study materials, clothes, accommodation and food.

2 A _____ is useful for comparing things and showing amounts or quantities at specific times. For example, the percentage of people who own certain products (cars, televisions, etc.) in three different periods.

3 A _____ contains a list of numbers or facts arranged in rows and columns. It could, for example, be a list of results for football league tables.

4 A _____ is useful for showing how things change over time, and for showing two or more sets of measurements which are related to each other. For example, it might show how the number of passengers of an airline has changed from month to month.

2 Which of the above (graph, charts, table) would you use to illustrate the following information? Explain your choice to a partner.

1 the amount of rainfall falling in an area each month during a 12-month period

2 the results of a survey of 100 students giving information about the subject they chose to study in their first year

3 the increase in the sales of iPods compared with CD players in your country during the last five years

4 a comparison of the changes in population in four world regions (Africa, Europe, South America and North America) during three periods: 1900, 1950, 2000

NEWSLETTER • SUMMER

FlyAway

Last year, Spain and Italy were the most popular destinations for our customers: 45% (Spain 20%, Italy 25%) chose those countries for their holiday. This compares with 42% (Spain 20%, Italy 22%) the previous year. Similarly, North America was a popular destination: approximately 22% chose that area compared with 12% the previous year. North Africa remained stable at 10%.

Germany and France showed little change over the period. Germany attracted 4% of our customers last year in comparison with 5% the year before, while the number of customers visiting France rose from 5% to 6%.

On the other hand, results were very disappointing in the Netherlands, which was visited by only 2% of our customers, compared with 8% the previous year. However, there was a slight increase in the number of customers visiting Denmark and Sweden, 4% compared with 2% the previous year.

Other destinations accounted for only 7% of our customers last year, whereas the figure for the previous year was 16%.

3a Read the text about the FlyAway Travel Agency and create a table to illustrate the information in the text.

3b Now draw a pie chart to show last year's figures only.

3c Compare your table and chart with a partner.

WRITING SKILLS: describing information in a table

4a Underline the words/phrases used in the text to express comparison and contrast.

4b Comparison and contrast Complete the sentences with correct words or phrases from the box. Use each word/phrase once only.

compare	in comparison	on the other hand
similarly	while	

1 Twenty-five percent of our customers visited Italy, _____ only 4 percent visited Germany.
2 If you _____ Denmark and Sweden, the figures are similar.
3 _____ with the United States, our performance in the Netherlands was disappointing.
4 Our results were poor in the Netherlands. _____, sales were low in other destinations.
5 France was not a good market for us last year. _____, the United States was an excellent one.

5 Look at the table, which shows some of the world's busiest airports by cargo traffic. Which airport:

1 increased its cargo traffic the least from 2005 to 2006?
2 increased its cargo traffic the most from 2005 to 2006?
3 was the highest-ranked European airport?
4 had a decrease in cargo traffic?
5 had the second biggest increase in cargo traffic?
6 handled less than one million tonnes of cargo?

6 Read the summary of the 2006 statistics for cargo traffic. Compare it with the information in the chart. Correct the six mistakes in the summary.

The 2006 statistics for cargo traffic at international airports make interesting reading.

Memphis Airport, the top-ranked airport, increased its ranking by one place between 2005 and 2006. Hong Kong Airport, however, did not change position: it maintained its second position, handling approximately five million tonnes of cargo and increasing the volume by an impressive 51% in comparison with 2005.

Similarly, Frankfurt Airport, ranked seven, maintained its position. It transported 21,127,797 tonnes of cargo, an increase of 8.4%.

There were dramatic increases in cargo traffic at Dubai Airport (ranked 17) and Beijing Airport (ranked 21). At both airports, there was a rise in volume of over 30%.

On the other hand, Hartsfield-Jackson Airport dealt with just 746,500 tonnes of cargo. This was a disappointing performance, with freight up only 2.8% from 2005.

7 The table on page 172 contains selected rankings of the world's busiest airports by passenger traffic. Write a short description summarising the information in the table. Try to use some expressions of comparison and contrast.

FIGURE 1 (2006 statistics)

Numbers refer to freight in metric tonnes; 30 airports are included in the ranking.

Rank 2006	Airport	Location	Total Cargo	Rank 2005	% Change
1	Memphis International Airport	Memphis, United States	3,692,205	1	+ 2.6%
2	Hong Kong International Airport	Chek Lap Kok, Hong Kong, China	3,608,789	2	+ 5.1%
7	Frankfurt International Airport	Frankfurt, Germany	2,127,797	7	+ 8.4%
17	Dubai International Airport	Dubai, United Arab Emirates	1,503,696	18	+ 14.4%
21	Beijing International Airport	Beijing, China	1,028,908	24	+ 31.6%
28	Hartsfield-Jackson International Airport	Atlanta, United States	746,500	25	- 2.8%

Literature

In this unit

Grammar
- narrative tenses
- *used to, would*

Vocabulary
- literature
- people in literature
- word sets: light and dark, sounds

Scenario
- A book deal

Study skills
- improving listening skills

Writing skills
- a travel blog

6.1 THE NOBEL PRIZE

I took a speed reading course and read War and Peace *in 20 minutes. It involves Russia.*
Woody Allen, 1935–, US film-maker and actor

VOCABULARY: literature

1a What do you like reading? Do you read literature? What do you understand by the term *literature*?

1b Look at the list of types of writing in the box. Is each one fiction or non-fiction?

autobiographies biographies blogs crime stories diaries essays history memoirs novels plays poetry romances science fiction short stories thrillers travel writing

2 Which of the types of writing in the box do you consider to be literature? What makes a work of literature 'great'?

3 Discuss the following opinions about literature. Which do you agree/disagree with? Why?

1 'A work of literature is not often a bestseller.'
2 'It's well written, but often boring.'
3 'It's art, not just entertainment.'
4 'Children's books can never be considered great works of literature.'
5 'Literature should make you think.'
6 'It often makes disappointing films.'
7 'The characters should be believable and realistic.'
8 'It remains relevant to people. It's timeless, even if it was written 200 years ago.'
9 'Popular fiction is not literature.'

READING

4a Which of the following writers do you think have won the Nobel Prize for Literature?

Jane Austen	Agatha Christie	Ian Fleming
Leo Tolstoy	Vladimir Nabokov	William Shakespeare
Stephen King	J.K. Rowling	Winston Churchill

4b Read the information about the Nobel Prize. Which writers in Exercise 4a have won the prize, haven't won the prize or can't have won the prize?

5 **Read the text again. Are the statements true, false or not given in the text?**

The Nobel Prize for Literature ...

1 is only for writers who are alive.
2 is only for writers in English.
3 is only for writers who sell more than a certain number of books a year.
4 is given every two years.
5 is given for a single book.
6 has not been accepted by all recipients.

VOCABULARY: people in literature

6 **Find words in the text which mean the following.**

1 a writer
2 a writer of fiction
3 a writer of books about people's lives
4 a writer of books for other people
5 a writer of plays
6 a writer of poetry
7 a person whose job is to give their opinion of books, plays, etc.
8 a person who decides who has won a competition

7 **In small groups, discuss the questions.**

1 Why do you think so few women have won the Nobel Prize?
2 Who are the most famous writers in your country?
3 Which writers who are popular now do you think will be read in 50 years' time?

LISTENING AND SPEAKING

8a **2.10** **Listen to some members of a book group discussing the book *The Da Vinci Code*. Who liked/ disliked it? Why?**

1 Michael 2 Jenny 3 Jarvis 4 Erika

8b **Listen again and tick the adjectives they used.**

awful brilliant disturbing dreadful dull exciting gripping interesting lightweight moving overrated shocking tedious thought-provoking

9 **Complete the following expressions used by the members of the group. Check your answers in Track 2.10 on page 181. Which express a positive and which a negative opinion?**

1 It's a real _____.
2 It's not my _____ of thing.
3 I couldn't _____ it down.
4 The ending was a real let-_____.
5 I just couldn't get _____ it.
6 It's light and _____ to read.
7 It was very _____ going at the beginning.
8 It certainly lived up to all the _____.

10 **Work in small groups. Using the adjectives and expressions above, talk about a book you really enjoyed and a book you really didn't like.**

The Nobel Prize for Literature

Background

The Nobel Prize for Literature was founded in 1895 when Alfred Nobel (1833–1896), the Swedish inventor of dynamite, left much of his vast wealth to the establishment of the Nobel Prizes, including one for literature. This is an annual award to a living author from any country who has produced 'the most outstanding work of an idealistic tendency'. This refers to a body of work rather than a single work, although individual books are sometimes mentioned when the prize is awarded. The prize consists of a gold medal, a Nobel diploma and prize money which at present stands at 10 million Swedish krona (1.3 million dollars).

The winners

A wide variety of writers have won the award working in a range of fiction and non-fiction genres. Novelists, poets, dramatists and biographers have all received the award, but not ghostwriters. Perhaps one of the more unusual winners was Winston Churchill – the former British Prime Minister won the prize in 1953 for his 'mastery of historical and biographical description'. The most common language of the winners is English, although the country with the most winners is France. To date, only ten women have won the prize. Two writers have refused the award – Boris Pasternak and Jean-Paul Sartre.

Controversy

In the early years (from about 1901 to 1912), the Swedish Academy chose more idealistic writers and rejected many important and world-famous writers, such as Leo Tolstoy, Emile Zola and Henrik Ibsen, who they did not consider 'idealistic' enough. Later on, the Academy began awarding the prize for lasting literary value.

Many prominent and very popular writers have not been awarded the prize or even nominated. In 1974, for example, Graham Greene, Vladimir Nabokov and Saul Bellow were considered, but all lost when the award went to two Swedish writers, who were both Nobel judges. Bellow went on to win the prize in 1976, but neither Greene nor Nabokov won before their deaths. The 1997 award went to the Italian Dario Fo, who was felt to be rather lightweight by some critics.

6.2 CHARACTERS IN DANGER

SPEAKING AND LISTENING

1 **Have any characters in books really impressed you? Why?**

2a **2.11** **Listen to someone talking about a character that has impressed them. Was Sherlock Holmes a real person?**

2b **Listen again. Note the words and phrases you hear to describe Holmes. In pairs, decide which are positive and which negative.**

brilliant intellect (positive)

3a **2.12** **Listen to another person describing a book.**

1 Why does the speaker like the book?
2 Describe Atticus Finch.
3 What does the book teach the speaker?

3b **Listen again and match the following pairs of words.**

1 incredibly — c)	a) tale
2 moral	b) character
3 extremely	c) heart-warming
4 evocative	d) read
5 charming	e) well-written
6 child's	f) language
7 key	g) characters
8 richly-drawn	h) perspective

READING

4 **In pairs, each read an extract from a novel and answer the questions. Then ask each other the questions.**

Student A: read Text A, the extract from *The Speckled Band* opposite.

Student B: read Text B, the extract from *To Kill a Mockingbird* on page 163.

1 Who tells the story?
2 Who are the main characters?
3 Where is the extract set?
4 What happens?
5 What is / could be the danger?

A

In *The Speckled Band*, a well-known Sherlock Holmes story, a young woman's life is threatened. In the extract below, Holmes and Watson are at the house of the main suspect.

"TWO OF HIS KNUCKLES WERE BURST AND BLEEDING."

Holmes had brought up a long thin cane, and this he placed upon the bed beside him. By it he laid the box of matches and the stump of a candle. Then he turned down the lamp and we were left in darkness.

...

Suddenly there was the momentary gleam of a light up in the direction of the ventilator, which vanished immediately, but was succeeded by a strong smell of burning oil and heated metal. Someone in the next room had lit a dark lantern. I heard a gentle sound of movement, and then all was silent once more, though the smell grew stronger. For half an hour I sat with straining ears. Then suddenly another sound became audible – a very gentle, soothing sound, like that of a small jet of steam escaping continually from a kettle. The instant that we heard it, Holmes sprang from the bed, struck a match, and lashed furiously with his cane at the bell-pull.

'You see it, Watson?' he yelled. 'You see it?' But I saw nothing. At the moment when Holmes struck the light I heard a low, clear whistle, but the sudden glare flashing into my weary eyes made it impossible for me to tell what it was at which my friend lashed so savagely. I could, however, see that his face was deadly pale, and filled with horror and loathing.

He had ceased to strike, and was gazing up at the ventilator, when suddenly there broke from the silence of the night the most horrible cry to which I have ever listened. It swelled up louder and louder, a hoarse yell of pain and fear and anger all mingled in the one dreadful shriek. They say that away down in the village, and even in the distant parsonage, that cry raised the sleepers from their beds. It struck cold to our hearts, and I stood gazing at Holmes, and he at me, until the last echoes of it had died away into the silence from which it rose.

5 **Have you read the books? Which of the two books did you most enjoy / would you most like to read? Why?**

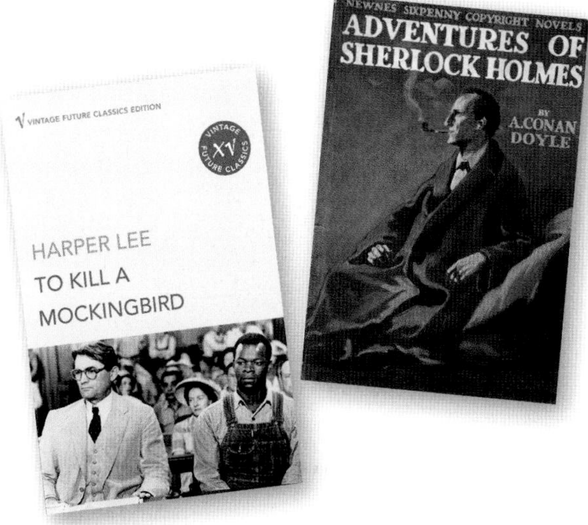

VOCABULARY: word sets

6 **Look at Text A and find words connected with light, darkness and fire, e.g. *turned down the lamp*. Compare with a partner. Together, can you find any other word sets in the text?**

GRAMMAR: narrative tenses

7a **Underline and label the tenses in these sentences from the extracts.**

1 ... Atticus was sitting propped against the front door. He was sitting in one of his office chairs, ...
was sitting = past continuous
2 We were taking a short cut across the square when four dusty cars came in ...
3 Nobody got out. We saw Atticus look up from his newspaper. He closed it, folded it deliberately ...
4 Someone in the next room had lit a dark lantern.

7b **Which tense is used to describe the following?**

a) events which took place one after the other in the story and are seen as complete actions
b) events which set the scene and provide the background against which a story happens
c) an activity that was already in progress, and which was interrupted by another action
d) events which took place in the past, before another event in the past

8 **Choose the correct form of the verb.**

1 All children, except one, grow up. They soon know that they will grow up, and the way Wendy knew was this. One day when she was two years old she *played / was playing* in a garden, and she plucked another flower and *had run / ran* with it to her mother. (J.M. Barrie, *Peter Pan*)
2 Having no near relations or friends, I *had tried / was trying* to make up my mind what to do, when I ran across John Cavendish. I *had seen / was seeing* very little of him for some years. (Agatha Christie, *The Mysterious Affair at Styles*)
3 The last minutes of the day *had been ticking / were ticking* away, and Martin Turner *could not / had not been able to* wait to be set free. The minutes dragged on as Mr Lincoln, the form tutor, lectured the class ... (Benjamin Zephaniah, *Face*)

9a **Look at the example of the past perfect continuous and complete the description of its use.**

> A lady dressed in black and heavily veiled, who had been sitting in the window, rose as we entered.
> 'Good-morning, madam,' said Holmes cheerily. 'My name is Sherlock Holmes.'

The past perfect continuous is used to emphasise the *completed / ongoing* nature of an action which happened *before / after* another action or time in the past. The action usually continues up to the second action or time.

9b **Complete the rule to show the three parts of the past perfect continuous.**

_____ + _____ + _____ form of the verb

➡ Language reference and extra practice, pages 144–145

10 **Complete this story, using the correct tense of the verbs in brackets.**

The clock struck ten. Lucien [1]_____ (sit) alone in the kitchen and he [2]_____ (shake) uncontrollably. After he [3]_____ (wait) for over an hour, he [4]_____ (hear) a key in the front door.

His parents [5]_____ (come) in. He [6]_____ (tell) them what [7]_____ (happen) earlier that evening. He [8]_____ (borrow) their car without asking, and [9]_____ (crash) into a lamppost because he [10]_____ (drive) too fast. Then the door bell [11]_____ (ring). It [12]_____ (be) the police.

WRITING

11 **You were walking in the mountains when there was a huge thunderstorm and you got lost. Write the story in three paragraphs. Use the notes on page 172 to help you.**

It was only 5 p.m. but it was getting really dark and the rain was ...

READING

1 Describe some bad characters you know from literature.

2 Read the two texts quickly and find:

1 the name of the book described.
2 the author of the book.
3 the inspiration for the book.
4 how the main character expresses his evil nature.

3 Discuss the questions in pairs.

1 Was each evil character born evil?
2 Which, in your opinion, is the more evil of the two characters?
3 Would people these days find the characters very frightening in comparison with modern characters?
4 Can an evil character be considered attractive or interesting?

It is commonly believed that the character of Dracula is based on a Romanian ruler from the 15th century, who used to inflict horrible punishments on his enemies. Vlad the Impaler, as he was known, would capture whole villages and enslave the people, or sometimes he would just burn the whole village, inhabitants and animals included.

Vlad used to sign his name Draculea or Draculya, meaning 'the devil's son'. This name was distorted into Dracula. Many of his victims were Saxons, who were horrified by his atrocities and printed books and pamphlets about Vlad's cruelty. The booklets reached Germany and Western Europe and Dracula became known as a vicious tyrant.

In 1897, the Irish writer Bram Stoker wrote his novel *Dracula*, and used Vlad the Impaler as a source of inspiration. The novel is about a mysterious and sinister nobleman from Transylvania who can turn into a wolf-like animal. He is also a vampire, who bites humans and turns them into vampires too.

Dracula is one of the most famous names in fiction. There have been more films about Dracula than about any other person in fiction except Sherlock Holmes.

B

People in the late 19th century used to be fascinated by the idea of two characters in one person. They used to be intrigued by the good and bad sides of people.

The Strange Case of Dr Jekyll and Mr Hyde was written in 1886 by Robert Louis Stevenson. Stevenson had been thinking about the duality of man's nature and he had wanted to incorporate the interaction between good and evil into a story. He had a dream that gave him the idea for the beginning of his book. The book is a dark story, showing the split personality of a kind and intelligent doctor, Dr Henry Jekyll, who turns into an evil monster.

The story tells how Dr Jekyll creates a drink in his laboratory which changes him into Mr Hyde, a man with a totally different personality. Hyde goes on to commit a number of brutal murders. He is a disgusting, depraved man, who truly is the embodiment of evil.

The book is not a detective story because we know from the outset the identity of the murderer: Mr Hyde. Instead, it is a mystery story which examines the potential for evil in all human beings.

4a Look at these words from the texts and match them with their definitions.

inflict	atrocities	tyrant	sinister	brutal

1 making you feel that something bad or dangerous is likely to happen
2 very cruel or violent actions
3 to make a person or place suffer something unpleasant
4 someone who uses their power in a cruel and unfair way
5 very cruel and violent

4b Write a short description of an evil character.

GRAMMAR: *used to, would*

5a Look at the highlighted examples of *used to* in the texts. Are the following statements true or false?

1 *used to* + infinitive can describe a habit in the past
2 *used to* + infinitive can describe a state in the past
3 *used to* + infinitive can describe a present action

5b Look at these examples. How does the form of *used to* change in the negative and question forms?

I didn't use to read books when I was young.
Did you use to read a lot when you were young?

6 Look at the highlighted examples of *would* in Text A and the ones below, and answer the questions.

1 My mother *would* often talk about her childhood.
2 When we were teenagers, we*'d* watch horror films at the cinema on Saturday mornings.

a) Do we use *would* to talk about past habits?
b) Do we use *would* to talk about past states?
c) Can we use *would* in all the cases where we use *used to*?

➡ Language reference and extra practice, pages 144–145

7 Find the mistakes of form or use in each sentence and correct them.

1 Bram Stoker would to live in Sandycove in Dublin.
2 Women of Jane Austen's time use to write anonymously.
3 Vlad the Impaler was used to sign himself Dracula.
4 George Orwell is used to work in a bookshop.
5 I use to read a lot of short stories at the moment.
6 He didn't used to read a lot as a child.
7 Did Lewis Carroll used to tell stories to young listeners?
8 The Brontë sisters all would suffer from bad health.

8 Choose the correct answer. Sometimes both forms may be correct.

The tourist guide *for* lovers *of* literature

This guide is a travel guide devoted to places connected to literature, rather than to restaurants, museums and hotels. It contains the following interesting facts.

Bram Stoker [1]*used to / would* take his holidays at Cuden Bay and used Ecclescrieg House nearby as an inspiration for Count Dracula's castle.

He [2]*used to / would* live in a house in Sandycove in Dublin.

George Orwell [3]*used to / would* sleep on insect-infested mattresses when he was down and out in Paris.

The book also answers the following questions:

Did Ernest Hemingway really [4]*use / used* to catch pigeons in the Luxembourg Gardens and cook and eat them?

[5]*Did Lewis Carroll use to / Would Lewis Carroll* go to Whitburn for his holidays?

This guide provides excellent walking tours. For example, you can take a walk through Spitalfields with a 'Jack the Ripper' tour. You can start in Dorset Street, where Miller's Court, site of the most horrific Ripper murder, [6]*used to / would* be.

pronunciation

9 2.13 *used to* Listen to two sentences from Exercise 8. Choose the correct way of saying *used to*. Then listen and repeat the sentences.

1 We pronounce the *s* in *used to* like which *s* in *says*?
2 The vowel sound in *to* is *strong / weak*.

SPEAKING

10 Discuss things you used to / didn't use to do, think or believe when you were a child.

What sort of books did you use to read as a child?
Did your parents use to tell you stories about monsters who chased naughty children?
Did you use to get frightened when your parents told you about scary characters?
Did you use to believe in giants?

6.4 SCENARIO

SITUATION

1 Read the article about Lee Hart from a music magazine. Discuss the questions.

Lee Hart to write memoirs

Great news for fans of Lee Hart, lead singer of the band Outer Edge! According to his agent, Hart will spend most of next year writing his memoirs. There is interest from a publisher to buy exclusive rights to the book.

Thirty-six-year-old Hart has led a colourful life, like all pop stars. The band had a number of hits a few years ago, but now its popularity has declined. Hart announced recently that the band would do one final tour of their favourite venues in Germany and the Netherlands, then call it a day, and split up.

Since Lee Hart has had little formal education, it seems highly likely that he will employ a ghostwriter to help him write the memoirs.

1 Why is it the right time for Lee Hart to write his memoirs, dealing with some of the events in his life?
2 What are the advantages for Lee Hart of using a ghostwriter for his memoirs?
3 Can you think of any problems or issues that might need to be resolved if Lee Hart uses a ghostwriter? For example: will the ghostwriter be able to interview all members of Hart's family? Will the pop singer have final approval of the contents of the book?

2 Read Hart's proposal for his memoirs. It contains his ideas for a bestseller.

1 Do you think Lee Hart's ideas will result in a bestseller?
2 If not, what advice can you give him to improve his proposal? Should there be more about the singer's childhood / his family / his personal life?

Proposal:
My memoirs

I think I should start with a short chapter about my family and early years, then move on quickly to how we got our first contract to perform in a club in Amsterdam. Then we could have some chapters about the band's first world tour, which was really successful. I wrote a diary at the time, so the information will be accurate about our venues and the reaction of our audiences. Then we could have a chapter about our hit records and another about our opinion of other bands. And a final chapter about our future plans. All that should make it a bestseller.

A book deal 6.4

KEY LANGUAGE: proposing, bargaining, talking about needs/ expectations

3a 2.14 **Listen to the conversation between Lee Hart and James Douglas, his literary agent. Which two topics do they discuss?**

3b Listen again. Match each sentence with its correct language function below.

1 ... if we included more chapters about your background, it'd add a lot of human interest ...
2 Why don't you talk to her?
3 If you agreed to write two or three chapters ... you'd probably double or triple sales of the book.
4 But in this case, I think 15 percent is more appropriate.
5 Really? I wasn't expecting to pay as much as that.
6 You'll find I'm good value for money.
7 Look, I'd like to make a proposal.
8 I need time to think about this and take some advice.
9 How about if I talked to him ...?
10 Could I suggest we meet towards the end of the month?

Language functions

a) bargaining
b) proposing
c) talking about what you need / expect

4 Complete the beginning of each sentence with an appropriate ending.

1 If you wrote about your father,
2 Why don't you talk to
3 The ghostwriter will need a year
4 If I find a really good ghostwriter,
5 How about if one of us
6 As this is quite complicated,
7 Could I suggest we meet
8 I'd like to make a proposal –

a) I think a 20 percent share is appropriate.
b) in two weeks' time?
c) will you contribute towards his or her fee?
d) wanted to cancel the contract?
e) it'd greatly increase our sales.
f) to write the book.
g) that you should talk to my financial adviser.
h) all the members of my band?

TASK: negotiating a contract

5a Work in pairs to role-play a negotiation between James Douglas and a publisher. Prepare to negotiate the points in Exercise 5b. Use the Key language and the Other useful phrases to help you.

Student A plays the role of James Douglas. Look at your information on page 159.

Student B plays the role of the publisher. Look at your information on page 164.

5b Negotiate with each other to reach agreement on the following points.

1 the content of the memoirs
2 the percentage of the royalty to be paid to Lee Hart
3 the deadline for submitting the final draft of the book
4 help in setting up interviews with family and contacts
5 the names which will appear on the cover of the book
6 what happens if one side wants to cancel the contract

OTHER USEFUL PHRASES

Asking for information

I'm interested in knowing ... (what kind of advance payment you want).

How much do you have in mind?

Talking about what you need/expect

He'd expect to receive ... (a generous advance payment).

It's important to have ... (several chapters about his childhood).

He'll have to / need ..., so ...

Bargaining

If you ... we might be able to ...

How about if we were to ... (deliver the final draft earlier)?

Proposing

Could I make a suggestion ... ?

I propose (that) we ...

6.5 STUDY AND

STUDY SKILLS: improving listening skills

When you listen to English, you often have to make informed guesses to understand. There are three types of guessing which you usually do:

- you predict what the speaker is going to say from your general knowledge or other clues;
- you guess the meaning of new words;
- you guess the meaning of words you did not hear clearly.

You are now going to practise each of these techniques.

1 Predicting from clues
You are going to hear extracts from a book by Paul Theroux, a well-known travel writer. Look at the cover of the book and the photo.

1 What do you think the book is about?
2 What area of the world does the book probably describe?

2a 2.15 **Guessing meaning of words**
Paul Theroux describes an experience he had at a railway station in Burma when he was offered an unusual type of food. Listen to Extract 1 and guess the meaning of the underlined words you heard in the extract.

1 a shining <u>assortment</u> of beady objects on her tray
   a) display b) choice c) mixture d) sale
2 I <u>beckoned her</u> over and had a look.
   a) asked her b) shouted out to her
   c) waved my hand at her d) ordered her

2b What do you think the 'beady objects' are? Choose the best answer.

a) grapes b) chicken c) crabs d) insects

2c 2.16 **Listen to Extract 2 to check your answer.**

3 2.17 **Listen to Extract 3. Choose the correct word/phrase in each pair.**

1 (the train) pulled away = *began to leave / was about to start*
2 bound with knotted vine = *tied / covered* with knotted vine
3 door hinge = a piece of metal to *open a door / hold a door in place*
4 skewer = a metal or wooden *box / stick*
5 lumps = *small pieces with no special shape / large pieces with a regular shape*

4 2.18 **What do you think the 'lumps of burned meat' are? Listen to Extract 4 and check.**

5a 2.19 **Extract 5 describes an incident at Tokyo Central railway station. Three words in the extract have been obscured. Listen and guess the words.**

1 A hundred Japanese men in grey suits stood watching my train. ... They had no _____.
2 The _____ was blown; the train started up, but before it moved an inch ...
3 ... and outside on the _____, the hundred men did the same.

5b Listen to Extract 5 again and answer the questions.

1 Who are the hundred Japanese men on the platform?
2 Why are they watching the train?
3 What does everyone do after the train starts up?
4 Paul Theroux comments to a Japanese man, 'It's quite a send-off.' What do you think he means?

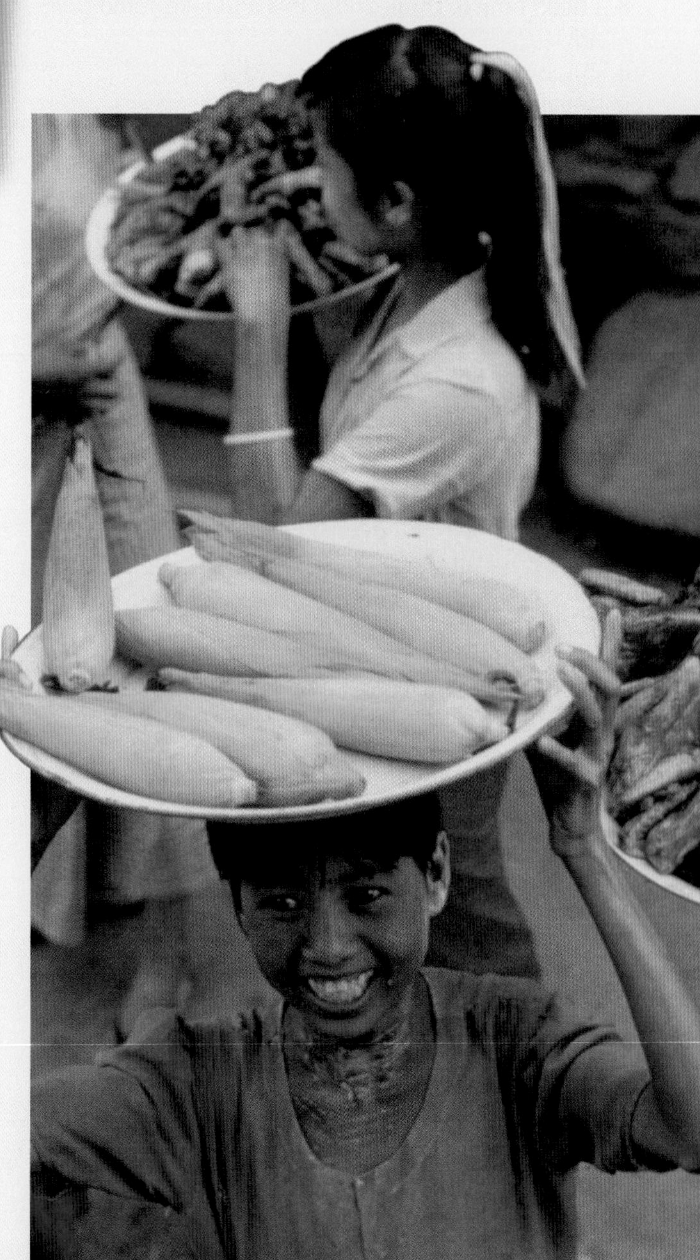

WRITING SKILLS: a travel blog

6a What is a blog? Do you read blogs? Why / Why not?

6b Read the information about travel blogs. Discuss the questions.

Travel blogs are online travel diaries or journals. Blogs are often written and published while the traveller(s) are still on their journey. They sometimes include maps and other visual effects.

1 Have you ever composed a travel blog? If so, what was it about?
2 Have you ever read a travel blog? If so, was it interesting? Why / Why not?
3 Why do people write travel blogs? Why do others read them?
4 Do you think it is better to read travel blogs or travel guidebooks before you visit a foreign country? Why?

7 You are going to read a travel blog about Havana, Cuba. What aspects of the city do you think the authors will mention (the people, shops, etc.)?

8a Read the blog and check your answers. Then discuss the questions.

1 Do the authors use a formal, neutral or informal style? Give reasons for your answer.
2 What do the following expressions mean? Try to work out their meanings from the text.
   a) choc-a-bloc
   b) drove like the wind
   c) checked out
   d) grabbed my wallet
3 What information or incident in the blog is most likely to interest readers? Explain your answer.

8b Adverbs of degree The authors use several adverbs of degree to emphasise adjectives, e.g. *extremely* old. What other adverbs of degree + adjective can you find in the blog?

9 Write a travel blog about one of these two situations. Remember, you write a blog when you are in the situation.

1 Imagine that you are in a foreign country/ place you have travelled to and know quite well.
2 Imagine that you are a foreign tourist visiting your country.

September 6, …
Havana, Cuba – first impressions

We arrived four days ago and are now staying in a four-star hotel in Vedado, close to the centre of Havana.

The journey from the airport was a bit of a nightmare. Our taxi was extremely old, it had an incredibly noisy engine and the door didn't close properly. The roads were choc-a-bloc with old American cars, huge over-filled trucks and funny-looking buses with hundreds of people in them. Our taxi driver drove like the wind, hooting his horn continually. Wow! What an unforgettable experience! But we got to the hotel in the end. It is absolutely beautiful, lots of space and really comfortable.

The next day, we strolled down the Malecon towards the centre of Havana. The Malecon's a long sea wall, by the way. In the evening, the locals go there to relax, enjoy the cool air and chat with friends. During the walk, we were able to take in the buildings in the area. The houses are worn and crumbling, but the colonial architecture is really impressive – one of the best things to see in Havana.

Yesterday, we checked out the centre of Havana, visiting the shops and bars, and wandering through the narrow, winding streets. We saw some Cuban women, sitting on the pavement, smoking huge Cuban cigars. If you want a photograph with them, you have to pay them a dollar! There are lots of beggars and pickpockets in some areas. In one street, a couple of pickpockets tried to steal my wallet. A guy pushed me hard in the back, and his partner, a young woman, grabbed my wallet. But she was pretty unlucky as my wallet was chained to my belt! The two of them ran away really quickly, so we couldn't be bothered to chase after them.

Today, we're going to visit the house of Ernest Hemingway, the famous American writer. He lived in a villa outside Havana for many years, and you can visit the building and garden. I'm looking forward to the visit, as I've read almost everything Hemingway has written. I'll report on the visit in my next blog.

GRAMMAR

1 Work with a partner to discuss the following.

1 What sort of things do you read on a computer rather than on paper?

2 How does reading a computer screen compare with reading a book?

3 What is an e-book, do you think?

2 Read the text and correct the summary for each paragraph.

1 People are surprised at how light paperback books can be.

2 The e-book can contain one book.

3 The e-book comes from established technology.

4 E-books will not be useful for many people.

3a Underline examples of the following in the text.

a form of:

1 the *going to* future (paragraph 2)

2 the past perfect continuous (para. 3)

3 the past perfect simple (para. 3)

4 the past continuous (para. 3)

5 the future continuous (para. 4)

a modal verb that describes:

6 future obligation (para. 1)

7 future possibility (para. 2)

8 past obligation (para. 3)

9 future ability (para. 4)

10 future lack of obligation (para. 4)

3b Complete the sentences with some of the phrases you underlined in Exercise 3a.

1 I find it difficult to pack because I never know what kind of clothes I _____ to wear on holiday.

2 Uncle Bill _____ from periods of back pain for several years before he eventually contacted his doctor.

3 There are no porters at that hotel so you _____ your own bags to your room.

4 When I was a child I didn't have many toys so I _____ my own games.

5 We've paid for everything in advance so we _____ any money once we get there.

6 Next year the government _____ every school with free Internet access.

7 Daniel Craig _____ as a TV actor for more than ten years before he got the role of James Bond.

8 After you put in your new contact lenses you _____ without wearing glasses.

The book is reborn

1 You are about to leave for holiday. You have two long weeks on a beach ahead of you – a chance to read all those books you've been planning to read all year. So you decide to pack a selection of paperbacks. You know paperback books are incredibly light and convenient, so it comes as rather a shock when you put four or five in your suitcase and realise they are as heavy as a brick. Suddenly the thought that you will have to carry all that weight through the airport doesn't seem quite so appealing.

2 Well, now there is a solution. Instead of carrying heavy books around you simply take an e-book. In the same way that MP3 players mean you don't have to carry around dozens of CDs, the e-book contains all the books you might want to read in one small package. So, if you're not sure whether you are going to feel like a lightweight romance or a heavyweight biography, that's no problem. You simply load all the books you might want into the memory and then make up your mind when you arrive.

3 So, how does it work? Electronics companies had been working on the e-book for years before they found the perfect combination of materials and technology. The magic ingredient was electronic paper, a US invention that is completely different from the liquid crystal display (LCD) technology used for most computer screens. Earlier versions of the e-book had suffered from the same problems as laptop computers and mobile phone screens – the screens were impossible to see in bright sunlight and people found that their eyes were getting tired after using them for any length of time. Manufacturers knew they had to invent a superior technology, and electronic paper was the result – it is flicker-free and looks exactly like real paper and ink.

4 And the e-book has many other advantages. The size of text can be changed at the flick of a switch, which means many people with poor eyesight will be able to read without needing glasses. As well as text, the e-book can display pictures and diagrams, and with an electronic pen the reader can make notes on the screen which the machine will remember, making it an ideal product for students. In fact, there are several Internet companies that will be supplying medical and scientific e-book files in the near future. So the students of tomorrow won't have to spend a fortune on those expensive university textbooks – they'll simply log on to the Internet and download everything they need to their e-book.

UNITS 4–6

VOCABULARY

4 Complete the table with the words in the box.

arthritis biography blog cancer diabetes
ferry hydrofoil memoir scooter

Medical conditions	Forms of transport	Types of writing

5 Choose the correct word in italics.

1 Aspirin is a popular form of *vaccine / painkiller*.
2 It takes years to train as a *parasite / radiologist*.
3 He *contracted / infected* malaria in Africa.
4 I don't *agree / approve* of giving drugs to children.
5 We took the *barge / cable car* up the mountain.
6 You should wear a *seat / chair* belt at all times.
7 Do you prefer novels or *small / short* stories?
8 I *shrieked / gleamed* in horror when I saw the rat.

KEY LANGUAGE

6 2.20 Listen to a conversation between two people. Decide if the statements are true or false.

1 Maria doesn't mind waiting for buses.
2 Sergei doesn't want a car.
3 Maria thinks buying a car is more important than going on holidays.
4 Sergei thinks the car insurance will be expensive.
5 Maria's friend works in a gym.
6 Dennis is a car salesman.
7 Sergei wants to spend less than £1,000 on a car.
8 Maria thinks Dennis's car is good value.

7a Complete the extracts from the dialogue with the words in the box.

agree argue be able to don't
really value wasn't way

1 I _____ think we need a car.
2 If we had a car, I'd _____ do everything much more quickly.
3 You can't _____ that we won't have money for holidays.
4 It would be good _____ for money.
5 Why _____ you talk to her?
6 That's the best _____ to find out.
7 I _____ expecting to pay as much as that.
8 Surely you must _____ that's a very reasonable price.

7b Listen again and check your answers.

LANGUAGE CHECK

8 There is one incorrect word in each sentence. Correct it, then look at the pages and check your answers.

1 We will have combining all your results to find the average speed. (page 41)
2 Will you be see the doctor tomorrow? Could you try and make an appointment for me? (page 42)
3 In a few years' time, our rivals will probably been introduced hundreds of new products. (page 42)
4 In the future people from many different countries, and even children, can to travel to other planets. (page 51)
5 I could not have time tomorrow, because I'm not sure what I'm doing yet. (page 51)
6 When we were travelling, we must to boil the water for our drinks to kill the bacteria. (page 53)
7 We managed getting our tickets for the concert last week. (page 53)
8 I had staring at the view from the window when suddenly I heard a loud noise. (page 61)
9 A young man wearing jeans, who did been sitting in the seat, got up as the old lady entered the railway carriage. (page 61)
10 Jeremy use to sign his name 'Mickey Mouse' when he was a kid. (page 62)

LOOK BACK

9 Find the exercises in Units 4–6 where you ...

- find out who discovered X-rays. (Unit 4)
- study three ways to talk about future actions. (Unit 4)
- make predictions about your own life. (Unit 4)
- learn about using modal verbs for future possibility. (Unit 5)
- read about three diffferent train journeys. (Unit 5)
- write a description of information in a table. (Unit 5)
- listen to people discussing *The Da Vinci Code*. (Unit 6)
- learn how to form the past perfect continuous tense. (Unit 6)
- write a travel blog. (Unit 6)

7 Architecture

In this unit

Grammar
- the passive

Vocabulary
- describing buildings
- idioms
- prefixes

Scenario
- On the horizon

Study skills
- identifying fact and opinion

Writing skills
- a description of a building

7.1 FAVOURITE BUILDINGS

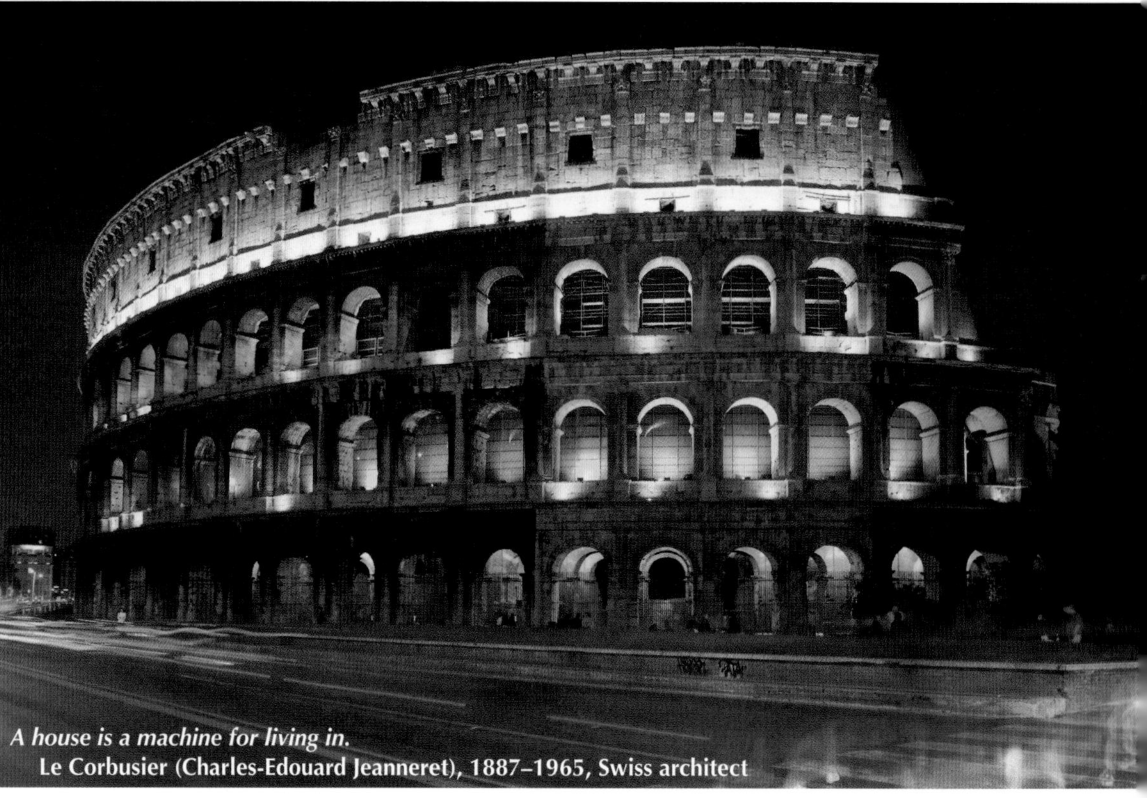

A house is a machine for living in.
Le Corbusier (Charles-Edouard Jeanneret), 1887–1965, Swiss architect

VOCABULARY: describing buildings

1 What's your favourite building? Why do you like it?

2a Are the following adjectives for describing buildings positive, negative or neutral?

ancient	dilapidated	impressive	run-down
classical	elegant	innovative	stylish
contemporary	graceful	magnificent	traditional
derelict	imposing	ornate	ugly

2b Which of the adjectives in Exercise 2a can describe a building which is:

1 not in good condition
2 not modern
3 unattractive
4 new and different
5 attractive
6 decorative
7 modern
8 important-looking

pronunciation

3 2.21 Word stress Mark the stress on the adjectives in Exercise 2a. Organise them into groups of words with first and second syllable stress. Compare your ideas with a partner, then listen and check.

4a Look at the three photos on these pages. Describe each building. Which do you like the most and why?

4b Think of a building you know. Describe it, using adjectives from Exercise 2a.

The British Museum is a very impressive building because of its magnificent dome and classical style.

5a Match the verbs on the left with their meanings.

1 damage	a) repair to put in original condition
2 rebuild	b) keep in good condition
3 construct	c) build
4 demolish	d) ask someone to build
5 maintain	e) erect again
6 restore	f) plan
7 commission	g) harm
8 design	h) knock down

5b Put the verbs into an order to show the stages in the life of a building.

READING

6a Read the following statements. Are they true or false? Guess the answers from your knowledge. Compare your ideas with a partner.

The Colosseum:

1 was built in the 15th century.
2 was a place where people watched fights.
3 is older than the other two structures.
4 is currently in very bad condition.

The Hajj Airport Terminal:

5 combines different styles of architecture.
6 keeps people cool with air-conditioning.
7 is very energy efficient.

The Eiffel Tower:

8 has always been popular.
9 was the world's tallest building.
10 was never intended to be permanent.

6b Read the texts and check your answers.

7 Find words in the texts which mean the following.

1 a circular building with seats arranged on a slope (Text A)
2 continued to exist in difficult conditions (Text A)
3 repair a building so it is in good condition (Text A)
4 scientifically advanced (Text B)
5 umbrellas that protect you from the sun (Text B)
6 a building which is easily noticed (Text C)
7 not lasting or needed for very long (Text C)
8 something ugly or very unpleasant to look at (Text C)

SPEAKING AND WRITING

8a Think of a building, in your own country or abroad, which you think is particularly:

1 impressive 2 interesting 3 ugly
4 stylish

8b Write a paragraph about a building that interests you.

A The Colosseum

I always visit the Colosseum when I'm in Rome; it's magnificent. I suppose it's what many people think of when you say classical architecture. It's an incredibly impressive building. It was opened way back in AD80. It's a vast amphitheatre and big crowds used to go there to watch gladiators and fights between wild animals. It is made of stone and concrete, and although it was damaged by earthquakes in the 15th century, the main structure has survived for almost 2,000 years. It used to look rather run-down, but recently it has been renovated and partly restored.

B The Hajj Airport Terminal

I love the Hajj Airport Terminal in Jeddah, Saudi Arabia. It's really stylish. It's a mixture of traditional architecture and high-tech materials, so it's also very contemporary. It was built to provide a meeting place for Muslim pilgrims on their way to and from Mecca. It's basically a number of huge tents, put up using some kind of innovative roof technology. It's an enormous modern airport, but it has no walls or air-conditioning. The tents are like giant parasols and their sides are open to the desert breezes. It really shows how you can design a low-energy building which both works and looks great.

C The Eiffel Tower

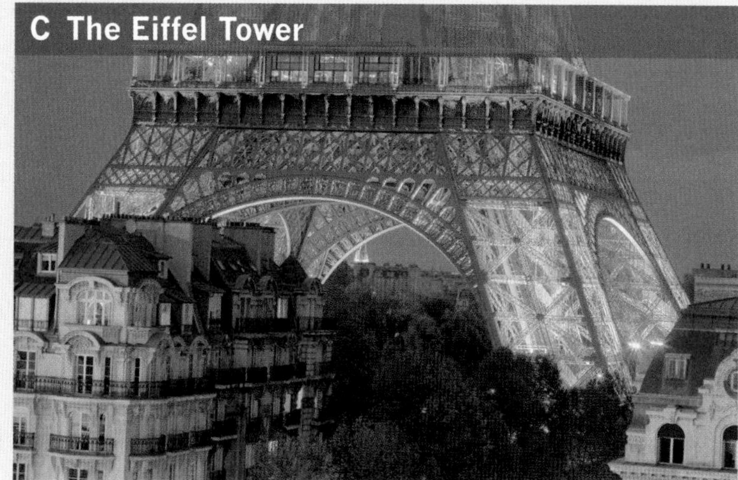

My favourite building is the Eiffel Tower in Paris. It's one of the world's best-known landmarks and it captures the atmosphere of Paris for me. It looks so elegant and graceful rising above the city. It was built as a temporary structure for the 1889 Universal Exhibition but has never been taken down, although apparently at the time there was a lot of opposition from the public to it, with many people calling it an eyesore. It's massive. I think it's about 300 metres tall – and it was the world's tallest structure until about 1930.

READING

1 Would you like to take a holiday in space? Why / Why not? What do you think a hotel in space might be like?

2 Read the description of a space hotel in the article. How similar are the features to your answer in Exercise 1?

Stranger than fiction

»Twenty years from now, where will the most innovative new hotel be built? Mainland Europe, as the UK construction industry is finally integrated into Euroland? Possibly. Africa, as developing nations look to grab their share of tourist dollars? Maybe. Or will it be, as Howard Wolff predicts, 200 miles above the Earth's surface in a space hotel?

Wolff is Vice-President of international design consultancy Wimberly Allison Tong & Goo, whose projects include the Wedding Pavilion at Florida's Walt Disney World. He is convinced the market will take off, so he is investing a substantial proportion of his company's research and development (R&D) budget into researching the needs of space tourists. 'It's important that we are in the forefront when the space race actually happens.' Wolff has one significant advantage in the race to build space hotels. He has got the second man to walk on the moon, Buzz Aldrin, working as a consultant on the project.

European and Asian companies are also becoming interested in space tourism. Last year, DaimlerChrysler and Germany's domestic space agency announced plans to build a bed and breakfast 300 miles above terra firma by 2020. In the same week, Japanese concern Shimizu announced plans for a space hotel to cater for 64 tourists at a time.

The race to create hotels in space may just be starting, but bookings are already being made for accommodation in future space hotels. What will a space hotel be like, people wonder? Howard Wolff's team envisages a resort based on a spinning wheel. The rim of the wheel will provide the hotel's accommodation pods, and the central hub will house its activities. The hotel is expected to cater for about 100 guests, as well as support staff. Guests will dine on food grown on board.

One requirement for the designers is that it allows people to experience weightlessness. But some form of artificial gravity will be required so that guests can sleep without being strapped to their beds. They will also want to eat without having to chase food around the room. Furthermore, artificial gravity is necessary to prevent space sickness, which affects more than 50% of all astronauts.

US space startup company Bigelow Aerospace has also seen the potential for hotels in space, but with a completely different design: expandable space station modules. An expandable module is a space structure that has a flexible outer shell. When it is in orbit, the module is inflated, creating a larger work, play and living area for astronauts. The expandable modules were designed by NASA (National Aeronautics and Space Administration) for a space programme. When this was cancelled, Bigelow Aerospace was given the right to commercialise some of the technology. A major advantage of inflatable modules is that the walls are flexible, which is better than rigid walls for protecting a module from the impact of space debris. The expandable modules could be used for space tourism and for orbital hotels. Bigelow plans to launch in the near future an orbital resort, which will probably be called CSS (Commercial Space Station) *Skywalker*.

3 Read the article again. Complete the sentences with no more than three words for each answer.

1 Wolff plans to spend a __________ of his R&D budget on a space project.
2 There are plans for the provision of __________ accommodation above the Earth by 2020.
3 In space hotels, there will have to be some kind of __________ so that guests can do their normal activities.
4 Bigelow Aerospace believes that the market for space hotels has a lot of __________.
5 Inflatable modules will probably not be harmed by space debris because of their __________.
6 To create a large living space for astronauts, the space modules will be __________ once in orbit.

4 Look at these expressions in the article. Choose the correct definition for the underlined part.

1 ... look to <u>grab</u> their share of ... (line 8)
a) request b) take quickly
2 ... the market will <u>take off</u> ... (line 19)
a) offer opportunities for business
b) be more difficult to enter
3 ... we <u>are in the forefront</u> ... (lines 24–25)
a) have a leading position
b) are able to take part in
4 ... has one <u>significant</u> advantage in the race ... (line 27)
a) important b) surprising
5 ... to <u>cater for</u> 64 tourists ... (line 41)
a) provide for the needs of b) offer special food for

GRAMMAR: the passive (1)

5a Look at the article again. Underline all the passive forms you can find.

5b Now circle the examples of the present simple passive and future passive (with *will*). Choose the correct words in the rule below.

We form the passive with *been / the verb be* + the *past / present* participle.

6 Look at the highlighted example of the present continuous passive and complete the rule.

We form the present continuous passive with the verb _____ + *being* + the _____ participle.

GRAMMAR TIP

We use the *-ing* form of the passive after prepositions and some verbs:

... guests can sleep *without being strapped* to their beds.

➡ Language reference and extra practice, pages 146–147

7 Complete the sentences with the correct passive form of the verb: present simple, future, present continuous or *-ing* form.

1 At present, several inflatable space modules _____ (manufacture) by Bigelow Aerospace.
2 An orbital hotel _____ (build) in space in the near future.
3 The project cannot be completed without more money _____ (invest).
4 Progress of the construction project _____ (check) each week while it is ongoing.
5 Expansion of the tourist industry will depend on more hotels _____ (construct).
6 Research _____ (carry out) by Wolff's R&D team into the needs of space tourists.
7 The project _____ (not finish) on time if we don't get the information we need.
8 She insists on _____ (include) in the team of astronauts.

8 Match these examples from the article with one of the reasons for using the passive below.

1 Where will the most innovative new hotel be built?
2 When it is in orbit, the module is inflated ...

a) The agent is unimportant or obvious from the context.
b) We don't know who/what the agent is.

LISTENING

9a 2.22 Marta Gattarosa, an architect, is answering questions from students of hotel management. Listen and write the five questions they ask. Then listen again and note the answers.

9b Listen again. Which of these statements reflect opinions expressed in the talk?

1 Architects must design buildings which meet people's needs.
2 Designing a hotel is basically a simple process.
3 For an architect, the ground floor is less important than the other floors.
4 Marta Gattarosa believes that a space hotel will be the greatest achievement in the history of humanity.
5 Architects will work on projects to build space hotels.

SPEAKING

10 'Building space hotels is a waste of time and money.' To what extent do you agree with this?

READING

1 Do you recognise the bridges in the photos? What is the most impressive bridge in your country?

2 Read the introduction to the article. Which of these reasons account for the importance of bridges?

1 They are essential for transporting goods and trade.
2 They have military significance.
3 They bring beauty into our lives.
4 They symbolise people or places.
5 They give people more belief in their ability to achieve things.

3a Read the rest of the article. Which bridge:

1 was made with soft stone?
2 was built to resist disasters?
3 changes its dimensions according to the temperature?
4 looks like a musical instrument?

3b Compare the bridges. Think about the following: age, length, appearance, use.

VOCABULARY: idioms, prefixes

4 Read the first paragraph of the introduction again. Complete these sentences with idioms from the paragraph, in the correct form.

1 I'm not leaving this job till I've got something to go to. I don't want to _____.
2 We don't need to look at the problem of falling sales yet. Let's _____.
3 Don't worry about it any more. It's _____.
4 I've had a few arguments with colleagues. If I want to get promoted, I need to _____.

5a Look at these words from the article. Underline the prefixes, then match them with the meanings below.

indisputable misplaced overcome revitalise unusual

1 again
2 not (2 prefixes)
3 wrongly
4 be too strong / too much

5b Add prefixes to these words to change the meaning.

1 important
2 understand
3 crowded
4 soluble
5 define
6 sensitive

GRAMMAR: the passive (2)

6a Look at the article again and underline examples of the past simple passive and the present perfect passive. How are these formed?

6b Look at these two sentences from the article. Match them with the forms below.

1 An earthquake added a metre to the bridge's length while it *was still being built.*
2 This work was scheduled *to be completed* ...

a) passive infinitive b) past continuous passive

➡ Language reference and extra practice, pages 146–147

7 Correct the errors *in italics* in the report.

Complaints [1]*have received* about the recent construction of the Sheridan Hotel in Main Square. It [2]*was completing* in November last year. While it [3]*was constructing*, many residents and business people of the town suffered great inconvenience. Building materials [4]*were delivering* at all hours of the day and night, and the noise level was unbearable. When the foundations [5]*were digging*, the air became polluted and the streets were very dusty. Complaints [6]*were making* daily to the Council but nothing [7]*was doing*. As a result, several shops [8]*have been closed* for some weeks during the worst period and now several claims for compensation [9]*have received* by the Council. The hotel [10]*has now built* and the Council is meeting next week to discuss the complaints and what [11]*is be done* about compensation. We expect the conclusions [12]*to publish* by the end of the week.

8a Look at these two examples of the passive. Which use, a) or b), matches each example?

1 *The 'Gherkin'* is an impressive example of modern architecture. *It* was designed by Lord Foster and Ken Shuttleworth.
2 Many tourists have been impressed by the new strange-shaped building in the City of London.

a) It is more natural to put subjects which consist of a long expression at the end of a sentence.
b) We prefer to start a new sentence with a familiar subject (something already mentioned).

8b Look at the highlighted passives in the text. Which use from Exercise 8a does each one illustrate?

SPEAKING AND WRITING

9 Work in pairs. You have a photo of one bridge and information about two. Share your information, then write a paragraph about your bridge.

Student A: turn to page 159.

Student B: turn to page 163.

BRIDGING THE GAP

Measured by the effect they have on our spirits and imagination, bridges are the highest form of architecture. They stand as metaphors for so much in life. 'Let's cross that bridge when we come to it,' I remark, when I want to put off thinking about some nasty dilemma. If I quit a secure job, I am 'burning my bridges'. If I make friends with strangers, I am 'building bridges'. If I argue with someone, but want to forget it and be friends again, I say, 'It's all water under the bridge.'

Why do we hold bridges in such regard? One reason is surely that, because of their strategic importance, they are often scenes of fierce battles and thrilling heroics. Another is that a bridge can often embody the spirit of a city, even an entire nation, as the Sydney Harbour or Brooklyn Bridges do, or the Stari Most did until it was destroyed in the Bosnian conflict. (Fortunately, it has since been rebuilt and is now listed as a World Heritage Site.)

But perhaps the chief reason is that a bridge is a leap of daring: a symbol of mankind's belief in its ability to overcome any natural obstacle, no matter how wide, deep or windswept. That belief has occasionally been tragically misplaced, but it has never been shattered.

What's indisputable is that our own age has seen one of the most innovative bursts of bridge-building ever.

▲ Built for Expo 92, the **Alamillo Bridge** across the River Guadalquivir in Seville demonstrates how a striking new bridge can revitalise an old city. The bridge is supported by a pylon and cables which form the graceful shape of a harp. It has a span of 200 metres.

▲ There has been a bridge over the River Vltava in Prague, Czech Republic for several centuries, but the now-famous **Charles Bridge** (Karlov Most) was built in the 14th century and named after the king. It is unusual because it is made of sandstone, not hard granite, which required some maintenance work in the 15th century after a flood. In 2005 further repairs started on the bridge. This work was scheduled to be completed within two years. Street vendors, street artists and tourists can always be seen along its 500-metre length.

▲ The **Akashi Kaikyo Bridge** in Japan is the longest, tallest and costliest suspension bridge ever constructed. Connecting Kobe with Awaji-Shima Island, this bridge has been built to withstand hurricanes, tidal waves and earthquakes. In 1995, an earthquake added a metre to the bridge's length while it was still being built. It has a total length of 3,910 metres.

▲ The **Golden Gate Bridge** spans the mile-wide mouth of San Francisco Bay. The total length of the bridge is 2,739 metres. The bridge expands on hot days and contracts when it is cold. On hot days the heat lengthens the cable. As a result the bridge becomes 4.9 metres lower and 1.8 metres longer. The bridge was opened on 21 May 1937 with a 'pedestrians' day', during which 200,000 people walked across the bridge. On the morning of the following day it was opened to traffic.

7.4 SCENARIO

SITUATION

1 **Discuss what facilities you would expect to find in a top-class hotel and conference centre.**

2a **Read the 'Invitation to Tender' document and answer the questions.**

1 What sort of reputation does HHCC have?
2 What will the ground floor look like?
3 What will the main purpose of the hotel be?
4 How will HHCC decide which architectural firm to choose for the design of the building?

2b **Why do you think HHCC has chosen to build the hotel and conference centre in Dubai?**

INVITATION TO TENDER

Contract for the design of a luxury hotel and conference centre in Dubai

Horizon Hotel & Conference Centre – 5 stars

www.hotelhorizon.db ◆ 320 rooms

Candidates are asked to submit their letter of intent before 24 June.

Horizon Hotels and Conference Centres (HHCC) invites the architectural firms listed below to indicate their interest in designing a Hotel and Conference Centre in Dubai.

HHCC is an international chain of high-class hotels and conference centres. It is famous for providing luxury accommodation and outstanding service. We intend the hotel to be used for conferences and congresses by a wide range of groups from all over the world.

Selected architectural firms are asked to submit a plan for the ground floor of the building, which will be L-shaped. Details of the project are as follows:

The hotel will have seven floors:
Basement – equipment and storage
Ground floor – facilities to be decided
First floor – a large conference room, three meeting rooms and a seminar room
Second floor – office accommodation
Third–fifth floors – bedrooms
Sixth floor – a large restaurant, available for guests and the general public

The contract to design the hotel and conference centre will be awarded to the architectural firm which produces the best plan for the ground floor.

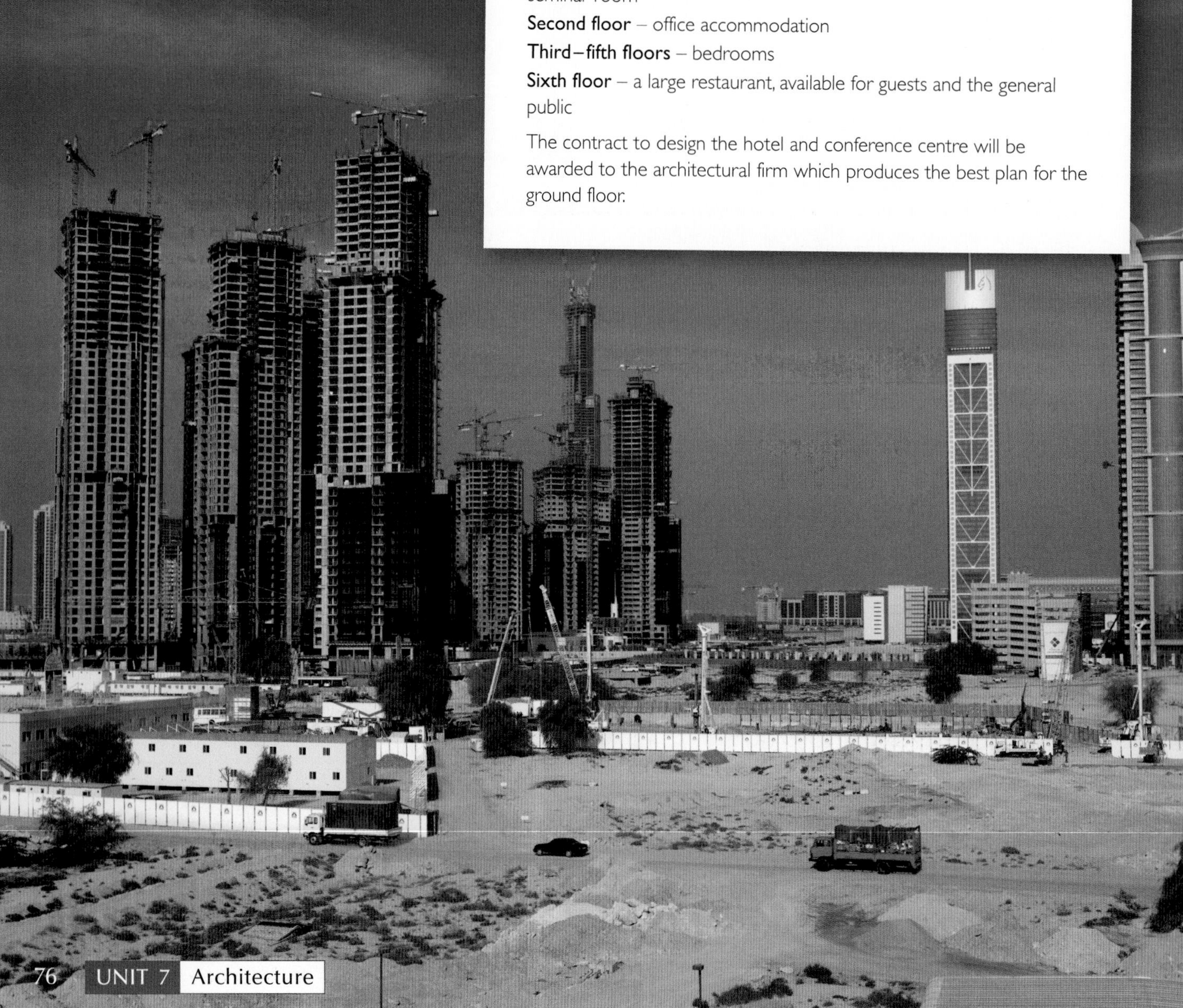

On the horizon 7.4

KEY LANGUAGE: talking about requirements

3a 2.23 Listen to three architects talking about designing the ground floor of a hotel. Answer the questions.

1 What three suggestions do the architects make to meet the needs of health-conscious guests?
2 What do the architects finally decide to do?

3b Listen again. Complete the sentences with information from the conversation.

1 ... in my opinion, *it's vital* we have some sort of __________
2 *It's absolutely essential* to offer a facility for people who __________
3 So ... *we've got to* __________
4 *We certainly need* some kind of area where __________
5 OK, maybe not a games room, but *we should offer* them __________
6 *It might be a good idea* to have an __________
7 Of course, *we'd have to* find out first if __________
8 But *we need to* __________

4a Look at the ways of talking about requirements in Exercise 3b. Which of them express strong needs?

4b 2.24 Listen to the expressions and practise saying them. Pay attention to the stress and intonation.

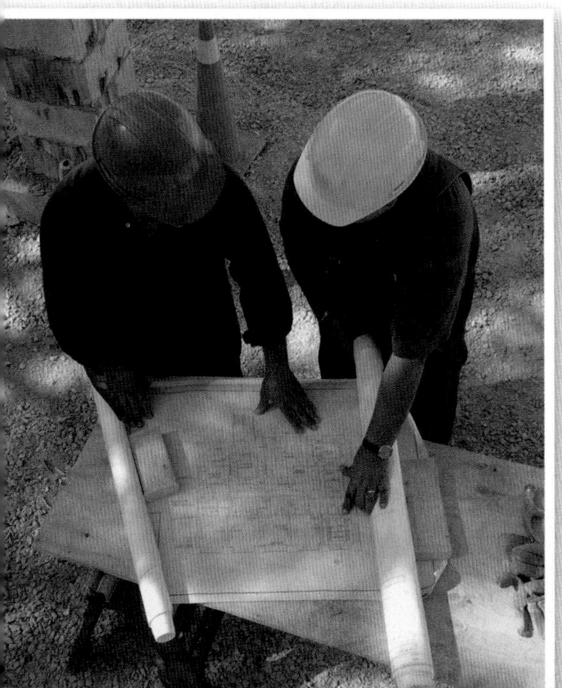

TASK: deciding on facilities in a hotel

5a Two architectural firms are going to submit a plan for the ground floor. Divide into three groups:

Groups A (Lindsay Associates) and B (Jackson and Li Consultants): you are the architectural firms. In your groups, discuss and decide what SIX facilities should be put on the ground floor and where each facility should be located. Study the diagram and draw a rough plan of the ground floor, with all its facilities.

Group C (Representatives of Horizon Hotels and Conference Centres): discuss what SIX facilities should be on the ground floor. Think about where you might locate each facility.

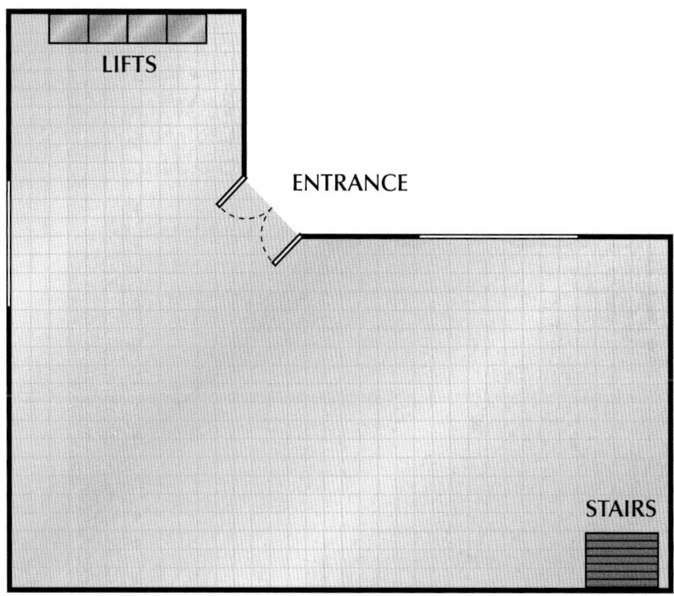

5b All groups discuss the plans and try to agree on what facilities should be on the ground floor, and where they should be located.

5c HHCC representatives decide which architectural firm should be given the contract to design the ground floor, explaining the reasons for their choice.

OTHER USEFUL PHRASES

Talking about essential requirements/needs

We really must have ... (some leisure facilities).

(A jacuzzi/gym) ... is a top priority for some people.

Talking about desirable requirements/needs

It would be really useful ... (to have some telephones there).

It's probably a good idea ... (to have a business centre).

Talking about possible requirements/needs

It might be popular to ... (provide a lot of comfortable sofas).

We could consider/think of ... (installing a fountain).

Rejecting ideas

I'm not sure that's what we want.

Maybe, but don't you think ...

7.5 STUDY AND

STUDY SKILLS: identifying fact and opinion

1 **Read the review of an exhibition. What is the writer's opinion of the exhibition? What is his opinion of Frank Lloyd Wright?**

2a **Look at these four sentences from the review. Which ones describe facts? Which ones describe opinions?**

1 It is exceptionally interesting and informative.
2 Wright learned his skills as an architect ... in Chicago ...
3 The exhibition has a number of drawings and pictures ...
4 In my view, Wright was the most important US architect.

2b **Which words in the two opinion-based sentences show that the writer is giving an opinion?**

2c **Find at least two more of the writer's opinions in the review. How do you know they are his opinions?**

WRITING SKILLS: a description of a building

3a **Avoiding repetition – nouns** **Most texts contain pronouns. These are used instead of a noun or noun phrase. Complete the lists with other pronouns that you know.**

Personal pronouns: *I, she, him ...*

Possessive pronouns: *mine, hers, ...*

Demonstrative pronouns: *that, ...*

Relative pronouns: *who, ...*

Other pronouns: *one, ...*

3b **Look at the review again. What do the pronouns in *italics* refer to?**

It (line 7) = *the exhibition*

New exhibition of Frank Lloyd Wright

THE EARLY YEARS

As a student, I was urged by my tutor to go to a Frank Lloyd Wright exhibition, and I did so when the opportunity arose in London last week. The exhibition was of his early work and it should not be missed. *It* is exceptionally interesting and informative.

Wright learned his skills as an architect and engineer in Chicago, at the offices of Adler and Sullivan. *They* created some of the finest skyscrapers in the United States. Following a fire in the city, there were great opportunities to experiment with new constructions. They did this by designing innovative structures such as the open plan office, and by breaking away from traditional rectangular rooms with doors. They were able to do it because they used leaded glass or wooden screens to partition areas.

The exhibition has a number of drawings and pictures of Adler and Sullivan's beautifully-crafted buildings, many of *which* Wright contributed to. *They* show what Wright must have learned from the firm's engineering experience and its attention to detail.

The exhibition shows the influence on Wright of European thinkers such as John Ruskin and Eugène Viollet-le-Duc. Another influence was the Art Nouveau movement. The exhibition demonstrates too the importance of the Japanese prints *which* Wright collected.

Besides constructing large buildings, Wright designed lovely houses not only to look at, but also lovely *ones* to walk into and live in. He would often design not just the house, but all its furniture, furnishings and even the dinner service to create what *he* called an 'organic unity' of materials and space.

In my view, Wright was the most important US architect. He was one of the first architects to use reinforced concrete in buildings; one of the first to use flat roofs; one of the first to design a large building to withstand an earthquake – the Imperial Hotel in Tokyo. He was truly a remarkable architect, designing over 700 buildings during his 60-year career.

WRITING SKILLS 7.5

4a Avoiding repetition – verbs It is also common in writing to avoid repeating a verb or verb phrase by using a form of *do*. What verb does the writer avoid repeating by using *do* in the example below?

They were able to *do* it because they used leaded glass or wooden screens to partition areas. (lines 23–26)

4b In paragraph 4, what verb does the writer avoid repeating by using *demonstrates*?

5 Avoiding repetition – clauses We can avoid repeating whole clauses by using the pronouns *this/that* or *so*. What do the words replace in these sentences?

I was urged by my tutor to go to a Frank Lloyd Wright exhibition, and I did *so* when the opportunity arose … (lines 1–5)

They did *this* by designing innovative structures such as the open plan office … (lines 18–21)

6 Correct the paragraph about Frank Lloyd Wright by avoiding repeating nouns, verbs or verb phrases. Check your answers on page 172.

The exhibition has a number of drawings and pictures. ~~The drawings and pictures~~ They are beautifully executed, and the drawings and pictures of large buildings are particularly impressive. Wright worked with engineers at the offices of Adler and Sullivan. He worked with them for many years and must have learned a lot from the engineers, as their attention to detail clearly influenced his work. Many European thinkers, such as John Ruskin, influenced his work as well. However, Wright also developed his own ideas. He incorporated many of his ideas into the houses he built.

7 Read the description of Fallingwater, a house designed by Frank Lloyd Wright. Number the points below to show the organisation of the text.

a) detailed descriptions of the floor, windows and stairs

b) the writer's and other people's opinion of the house

c) the exterior appearance of the house

d) the most important fact about the house

Fallingwater, Bear Run, Pennsylvania

Fallingwater (1936–1939) is the most famous house that Frank Lloyd Wright designed. It combines nature and living space in a poetic, effective manner. The building demonstrates perfectly Wright's concept of organic architecture.

The house seems to grow out of the cliff and ledges, so it fits in perfectly with the surrounding landscape. It consists of several concrete trays which project over a waterfall.

The rooms are arranged in a clever way so that the house seems very spacious. The floor of the living room is built over a natural rock, parts of which are incorporated into the interior.

The house has other interesting features. Its floor-to-ceiling windows emphasise the close connection between the inside and outside of the building, as do the stairs which lead to the water. Its rushing sound is heard constantly in the house.

In spite of its daring construction and dramatic effect, the building appears to be an integral part of the natural setting. It is admired by architects all over the world and is considered by many to be Frank Lloyd Wright's masterpiece.

8 In paragraph 3, which word is used to avoid repeating *a natural rock*? In paragraph 4, what has the writer used to avoid repeating the verb *emphasise*?

9 In paragraph 1, the writer uses the verb *combines* to describe a feature of the house. Underline all the other verbs in the text which are used to describe buildings.

10 Write about a building. Choose one of the following tasks.

Either write a description of a building you know well and whose design you admire.

Or write a description of the Ennis House in Los Angeles, which was designed by Frank Lloyd Wright in the early 1920s. Use the information on page 172, or research the building on the Internet.

Globalisation

In this unit

Grammar
- verb patterns
- *have something done*

Vocabulary
- word combinations connected with globalisation
- abstract nouns
- word set: the media

Scenario
- Supermarket superpower

Study skills
- summarising

Writing skills
- a summary

8.1 GLOBALISATION – GOOD OR BAD?

In the emerging global economy, everything is mobile.
Bill Clinton, 1946–, former US president

SPEAKING

1 What do you understand by the term *globalisation*?

2 Complete the description with the words in the box.

communications experience improvements life world

Globalisation is a term used to describe the way in which the 1_____ is developing a single economy and culture. This is as a result of 2_____ in technology and 3_____ and the influence of large multinational companies. Globalisation is changing people's 4_____ of everyday 5_____ all over the world.

3 Which of the following causes/results of globalisation are the most important for you? Why? Can you think of any others?

1 cheap air travel
2 availability of global brands and products, e.g. Sony, Adidas, Nestlé, Nokia, McDonalds
3 entertainment, e.g. music, TV, films, shows from other countries
4 communication advances, e.g. email, mobile phones
5 world events, e.g. the Olympic Games, the World Cup
6 opportunities to work or study abroad
7 international organisations, e.g. the United Nations, the World Health Organisation, the World Bank

4a Complete the sentences with the nouns in the box.

companies competition cultures environment gap industry poverty standards understanding workers

Globalisation:

1 exploits _____ in poorer countries.
2 widens the _____ between rich and poor.
3 reduces _____ and increases wealth.
4 promotes global _____ and tolerance.
5 destroys local _____ and traditions.
6 damages the natural _____.
7 improves the quality of manufacturing _____, leading to more jobs and better pay.
8 creates _____ and increases the choice of goods and services.
9 encourages better _____ for the environment, literacy, health, working conditions.
10 gives multinational _____ too much power.

4b Discuss the sentences about globalisation in Exercise 4a. Which do you agree/disagree with?

READING AND LISTENING

5a *Viewpoint* is a weekly current affairs programme. Read the opinions on the *Viewpoint* message board (right) and complete the chart for the first four messages.

Message	For or against globalisation	Reasons
1 Mike		
2 Cindy		
3 Ingrid		
4 Marco		
5 Michel		
6 Doug		
7 Astrid		
8 John		
9 Maria		

5b 2.25 Now listen to some other views from the podcast of last week's show and complete the chart.

6 Choose two of the messages and summarise each person's point in one sentence.

VOCABULARY: word combinations

7a Complete the word combinations with the words in the box.

change choice greed rights trade

1 consumer _____
2 climate _____
3 corporate _____
4 fair _____
5 human _____

child free global multinational natural

6 _____ resources
7 _____ warming
8 _____ companies
9 _____ labour
10 _____ markets

7b Now check your answers to Exercise 7a in the messages and podcasts.

Message Boards Viewpoint ▼ ▶Go

Is globalisation a good thing?

1 Globalisation is definitely about progress. It leads to better products, which are more cost effective to produce and therefore cheaper for everyone. It's about consumer choice. Globalisation also connects people by means of communication and offers them new opportunities for travel, work and education. It means a faster rate of development for the whole world. Many poorer countries have benefited from investment as a result of globalisation. *Mike, USA*

2 The global economy simply means sweatshops in poor countries so that rich countries can have cheap goods. There is a lot of inequality involved in globalisation and the desire for cheaper products. It also leads to the destruction of natural resources. Globalisation benefits the rich nations, who control prices, who influence the economies of poor countries and cause populations to migrate in order to try and improve their lives. *Cindy, China*

3 Globalisation is just another aspect of evolution. It is a new name for an old process. Surely the coming of the railways and industrialisation hundreds of years ago was globalisation. It enables products to be produced wherever it is most efficient to do so. I think it means great social and economic progress for developing countries. I don't understand this anti-globalisation movement and feeling. Surely free markets and the free movement of people, goods and services are beneficial to economies all over the world? *Ingrid, Germany*

4 Globalisation's only good for those who are already economically strong. It's the big multinational companies who really benefit, and it worries me that sometimes they seem to have more power and influence over our lives than elected governments. Some of them are actually richer than whole countries, which must be a bad thing. *Marco, Italy*

SPEAKING

8 Which of the opinions in the messages do you agree with? Which do you disagree with? Why?

9a Discuss the impact of globalisation up to now on the following:

1 your own life 2 your country 3 the world

9b Do you see globalisation as a force for good or bad? Are you optimistic or pessimistic about the future? Why?

WRITING

10 Write your opinion on globalisation for the *Viewpoint* message board.

READING

1a In pairs, discuss which of the following you have used / heard of. What kind of sites are they?

Google YouTube eBay Amazon Wikipedia MySpace Second Life

1b Read the article and check to see if you were correct.

2 Read the article again and answer the questions.

1 Why do teenagers see the world as a smaller place than their grandparents did?
2 What point does the writer make about friendships in the second paragraph?
3 What examples are given of the power of the Internet with regard to:
 a) buying and selling?
 b) getting information?
 c) social networking?
4 What warnings does the writer give about Internet sites?

3 In pairs, discuss the following questions.

1 Do people indulge in fantasy virtual life because of the disappointments of their real lives?
2 What are the advantages and disadvantages of:
 a) buying and selling over the Internet?
 b) social networking with people you have never met face-to-face?
3 Should teenagers' use of the Internet be limited?

How the Internet is changing lives forever

1 These days with inexpensive air travel, mobile phones, email and the Internet, teenagers see the world as a smaller place than it appeared to their grandparents. Of these innovations, the Internet appears to be the one with the most potential for global influence, and which will change lives the most.

2 For example, up until recently friendships developed over a lifetime but that has now changed. People often made friends locally at school and continued those friendships into adulthood, but many young people today find the majority of their friendships over the Internet. This is not restricted to teenagers. Paula Sen, who has just turned 30, says: 'I've met most of my best friends over the Internet, through common interest forums. I couldn't live without the Internet. It's my lifeline.'

3 The Internet has also greatly influenced how people buy and sell goods. International Internet shopping is now common, with people buying all sorts of goods, from sites such as Amazon, the most successful online retail site. The international auction site eBay allows millions of participants to buy from and sell to strangers, setting their own prices. But beware – there are as many unscrupulous salespeople online as on the high street.

4 One of the Internet's greatest success stories is Wikipedia, the free online encyclopaedia, which is compiled and updated by its users. It carries far more content than any other encyclopaedia and is a great starting point for research, but remember to double-check important facts as it does contain errors. If you don't have time to check your facts, consider purchasing a reliable online encyclopaedia such as the Encyclopaedia Britannica. The other major information resource on the Internet is Google, a search engine which finds and ranks web pages according to the number of links made to them.

VOCABULARY: abstract nouns

4a Match the words from the article with their definitions. Use a dictionary if necessary.

1 influence	a) talking to other people in order to share information and help each other
2 networking	b) the power to affect the way someone or something behaves or develops
3 hierarchy	c) the use of the imagination to produce new ideas or things
4 creativity	d) working together to produce or achieve something
5 collaboration	e) a system of organising people or things according to their importance

5 Probably the biggest impact that the Internet has had is the way in which it has influenced social networking. The most frequently 'googled' word in the world recently was Bebo – the social networking site – followed by MySpace. People can meet new friends through sites like these, they can renew old acquaintances through sites like Friends Reunited and they can also play games with each other in virtual worlds such as Second Life. This Internet-based, three-dimensional virtual world is 'inhabited' by more than 6.6 million residents from around the world, and global companies such as Adidas and Toyota even have outlets there.

6 It's now much easier to share experiences with others too. Sites such as YouTube allow people to upload and share videos, with unlikely clips becoming huge hits and a number of figures becoming Internet phenomena. Many people remember watching 'sabre boy' wielding an imaginary light-sabre, and laughing out loud at his antics.

7 Much of the power of the Internet lies in the fact that people are developing new ways to be creative and innovative, combining ideas and skills without an organisation or hierarchy. No one is in overall control. Collective creativity and collaboration are the key ideas. But even more powerful than this is its power to solve crimes, help change the world through giving to charities on sites like justgiving.com or find missing individuals: one website for a missing child was visited by over 40 million people within days of its being set up.

4b Use the words from Exercise 4a to complete the sentences.

1 Chad Hurley, the YouTube founder, wanted to reward _____ and imagination.
2 In the medical world we have to work in close _____ with our colleagues.
3 I'm quite shy so I find _____ difficult.
4 It took time to get used to the _____ in the army.
5 Many teachers have great _____ over their students.

GRAMMAR: verb patterns

5 Look at the highlighted sentences in the article and match these verbs with their patterns.

1 appear
2 allow
3 consider
4 remember

a) followed by the infinitive
b) followed by either the infinitive or the *-ing* form with a different meaning
c) followed by the object and infinitive
d) followed by the *-ing* form

6 Look at the following pairs of sentences and discuss the differences between the verb patterns.

1 a) I *remember watching* the first TV reports of the tsunami.
b) *Remember to lock* the door when you go out.
2 a) I'll never *forget meeting* Brad Pitt when I went to Hollywood.
b) I won't *forget to switch off* the lights when I go.
3 a) I *stopped driving* after three hours at the wheel.
b) I *stopped to have* a break for a few minutes.
4 a) I *tried sending* her flowers, but it had no effect.
b) I *tried to persuade* her to listen to me, but she wouldn't.

➡ Language reference and extra practice, pages 148–149

7 Complete the sentences with the verb in brackets in the infinitive or *-ing* form.

1 I'm sorry I forgot _____ to your email. (respond)
2 I tried _____ to the computer shop before it closed. (get)
3 I'll never forget _____ the Seattle protests in 1999. (attend)
4 I wrote this over the summer but forgot _____ it on my blog. (post)
5 I remember _____ something about how popular the movie *Titanic* was in China. (hear)
6 I stopped _____ my video clips on YouTube because my friends teased me. (put)
7 She remembered _____ her video camera to the wedding, so we've got a great film of it. (bring)

SPEAKING

8 In pairs, discuss some of these things.

- someone you'll never forget meeting
- something you stopped doing recently
- something different you should try doing next year
- something you'll never forget seeing
- something you shouldn't forget to do before going to an interview
- something you remember doing on one of your birthdays.

READING

1 Who are the people in the photos? What are they famous for? Are they global role models?

2 Scan the article quickly and find out:

1 how many children have TVs in their homes.
2 the name of the governor of California.
3 how many people watch the World Cup.
4 the names of two US TV programmes.

3 Read the article. Are the following statements true, false or not given in the text?

1 Arnold Schwarzenegger is famous mainly because he is a politician.
2 NBA basketball games are watched by two billion people.
3 David Beckham bought lots of products in Japan.
4 The foreign media attended all Beckham's news conferences in Japan.
5 Critics of the influence of US TV programmes say it is an example of a powerful country's way of life influencing a poorer country.
6 Fijian women have recently had problems with eating disorders.

4 Discuss the following questions.

1 Do you think David Beckham is the right person to be an international role model? Why / Why not?
2 Why do you think Beckham was so popular in Japan?
3 Do role models cross cultural boundaries?
4 Do you think the media are obsessed with fame and celebrity? Why / Why not?

VOCABULARY: the media

5a Underline all the words associated with the media in the article.

5b Which word or words that you have underlined mean the following?

1 to send out radio or TV programmes
2 photographers who follow famous people in order to take photos they can sell to newspapers
3 when an event or subject is reported on TV, radio or newspapers
4 collective noun for people who write reports for newspapers, radio or TV

Global role models

We all have role models when we're young, but these have changed dramatically over the last few decades. A hundred years ago, role models were respected members of the community, politicians, or maybe a local footballer who had made a name for himself. Now it's different. These days, celebrities are more famous than politicians: would you more quickly recognise a local footballer or David Beckham if you saw him on the street?

One of the main reasons for this is the spread of film and television. When the organisation UNESCO recently had a survey conducted in 23 countries around the world, it was discovered that 91% of children had a television in their home, and 88% of them could identify the Arnold Schwarzenegger character *The Terminator*. How many of those children would also know that he is the governor of California? Sports programmes on TV, especially live ones, attract global audiences. The final of the football World Cup is watched by two billion people, and the basketball games played by the NBA teams (National Basketball Association) are broadcast to many countries overseas. The popularity of football, basketball, baseball and other televised sports has led to the creation of a whole new generation of international role models for young people.

One of the most instantly recognisable faces in the world now is that of David Beckham, perhaps the most interesting example of an international role model. From the very beginning, he seemed to be aware of his potential status. He wore fashionable clothes and had his hair cut in styles which were copied by the younger generation. At the peak of his career, he was always in the limelight. Beckham had articles written about him in every newspaper and he had his photo taken by the paparazzi every time he stepped outside his house.

On his tour of Japan in 2003 he was mobbed by fans wherever he went. He made several deals there to endorse products and featured in several news broadcasts. Interestingly, though, Beckham had a clause put in his contract that media coverage should be restricted to the local press, so his appearances were mostly at local schools or at news conferences from which foreign media were banned.

Global role models are not necessarily famous people. Sometimes they are cultural images. The influence of US TV programmes has been particularly strong, and this has been widely criticised by many people who see it as a form of cultural imperialism. Critics cite a study which linked the appearance of the illness anorexia in Fiji to the popularity of American television programmes such as *Melrose Place* and *Beverly Hills, 90210*. Both series showed slim young actresses. This caused Fijian women, who are larger, to question their ideas about the ideal body. This shows that there are dangers in this global spread of role models, and we don't know yet what other effects they might have. But given the general image of politicians today, is it really any worse to look up to film stars or sportspeople? ■

GRAMMAR: *have something done*

6a Look at these two sentences from the article and answer the questions.

1 Beckham *had articles written* about him ...

2 Beckham *had a clause put* in his contract ...

a) In sentence 1, who wrote the articles, Beckham or someone else?

b) In sentence 2, who put the clause in the contract?

c) In which sentence did Beckham make the action happen?

d) In which sentence didn't he make the action happen? (It was beyond his control.)

6b Find other examples of this structure in the article. Which type are they?

GRAMMAR TIP

We often use *have something done* to talk about a bad experience that has happened to us.

He had his mobile phone stolen while he was at the match.

➡ Language reference and extra practice, pages 148–149

7 Rewrite the words in the correct order to form sentences.

1 removed the protesters had the authorities

2 we have will new phone lines three installed next month

3 at the airport the photographers searched had bags their

4 is having she her new book into Japanese translated

5 had their taken fingerprints the police by the demonstrators

6 he is to have going tested his eyes tomorrow

7 not I have had developed the film yet

8 passport last year my brother his stolen had

SPEAKING

8 In groups of three, talk about good or bad experiences you (or a friend/relative) have had.

Last year I was at a music festival, but unfortunately I had my wallet stolen. It was very crowded, and when I went to buy some food, I noticed ...

8.4 SCENARIO

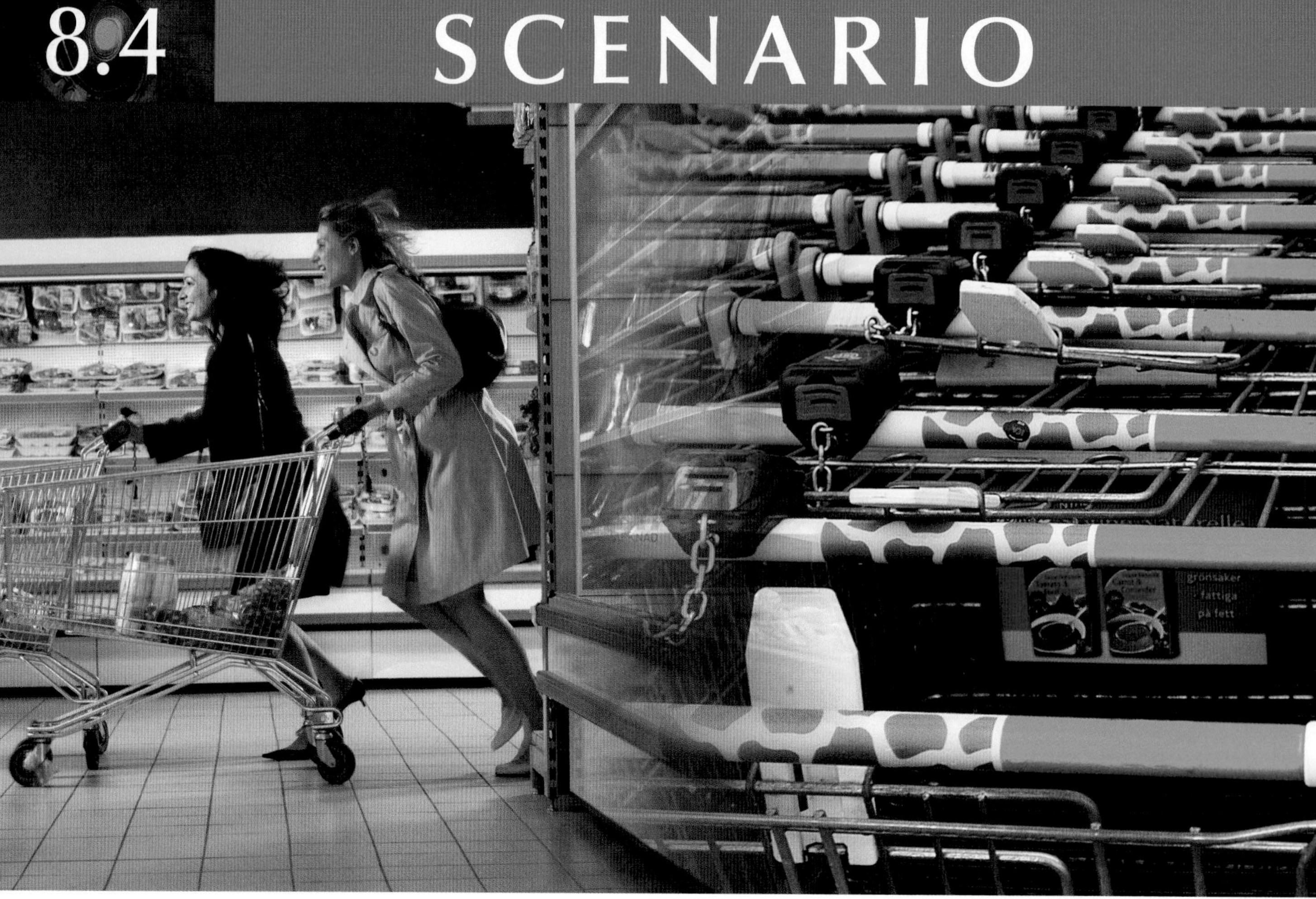

SITUATION

English language channel

Thursday 10.00

VISTA Live debate

This week the panel discusses the plans of Smithsons, the international supermarket giant, to open branches in towns and cities all over the country. Opinions on the company and its activities are sharply divided so this will definitely be one to watch.

1 Read the extract from a TV guide above and discuss the questions.

1 Do you prefer shopping in a supermarket or smaller stores? Why?

2 What do you expect to be able to buy in a supermarket? Discuss your ideas with a partner.

3 Do you think supermarkets are generally good or bad for the communities they serve?

2 Now read the newspaper report on the right and answer the questions.

1 When was Smithsons founded?

2 What does it sell?

3 Where does it sell?

4 What is happening in the near future?

5 What do you think the criticisms mentioned in the report could be?

Supermarket plans further expansion

SMITHSONS, THE SUPERMARKET giant, is on the move again. Another period of rapid expansion is underway, with entry into a number of new markets around the world. With its enormous purchasing power, analysts predict the acquisition and rebranding of established store chains in some markets, as well as direct market entry in others.

From its small beginnings as a market stall over 85 years ago, Smithsons has become one of the world's biggest companies and employers. Growing out of its bases in the USA and UK, it now has around 5,000 stores around the world. Ranging from out-of-town superstores to small city-centre convenience shops, it claims to offer something for everyone.

Today it sells a vast range of goods and has seen enormous growth since it entered the non-food area. It offers everything from books, DVDs and electrical goods to financial services, fuel, insurance and household items. The larger stores can now organise weddings and funerals. The company's slogan, 'Smithsons – for everything in life', is, it seems, becoming a reality. However, the firm continues to attract criticism from some business commentators for its policies of

3a 2.26 **Bob Craven, the chief executive of Smithsons, is on the hard-hitting radio programme *In the Hot Seat*. Listen and tick which of the following are mentioned.**

Environmental damage	Staff unions
Consumer choice	Competition
Fair trade	Treatment of staff

3b Listen again. What is said about the items you have ticked? Were the criticisms of Smithsons the same as the ones you thought of in Exercise 2?

KEY LANGUAGE: clarifying

4a Listen to the extract again and fill in the missing words.

1 ... what do you _____ by good value?
2 Basically, what I'm _____ is the customer is ...
3 Sorry, I don't _____ what you mean.
4 What I really _____ to say is ...
5 Or to _____ it another way, ...
6 Could you _____ that in more detail, please?
7 Could you be more _____?
8 Let me _____ that.
9 Could you _____ me an example?
10 To be more _____ ... we really appeal to ...

4b Divide the phrases above into two groups:

a) for making your meaning clearer.
b) asking for clarification.

TASK: a TV debate

5a Work in groups. Smithsons is planning to come to your country. You will be taking part in an edition of *Vista*, the live TV debate programme.

Student A: turn to page 159 and study your role card.
Student B: turn to page 164 and study your role card.
Student C: turn to page 168 and study your role card.
Student D: turn to page 169 and study your role card.
Student E: turn to page 170 and study your role card.

5b Hold the debate.

OTHER USEFUL PHRASES

Chairing
I'd like to ask (name) for his/her views (on this).
Thank you, (name). You've had your say. Let the others give their views now, please.
I'd like to move on now to ...

Interrupting
I'd just like to say ...
Can I just come in here?
If I can interrupt you at this point ...

Dealing with interruptions
If you could just let me finish.
Hold on a minute, please.
If I can just finish what I'm trying to say.

Getting your point across
The main issue here is ...
The really important thing is ...
Surely, the point is that ...

8.5 STUDY AND

STUDY SKILLS: summarising

1a In pairs, say whether the statements are true or false. Give your reasons.

1 A summary is a short version of the original text.
2 To write a summary, you must understand the original text.
3 You should use your own words when summarising.
4 You should never use words from the original text.
5 A summary should include important and unimportant information.
6 You do not include all the important ideas of the original text.
7 You can add information when you summarise.
8 You must not include any quotations from the original text.
9 A summary should not include your own opinions.
10 When summarising, you must not change the order of the ideas in the original text.

1b Check your answers on page 173.

Summarising

When you summarise a text, you need to select the key point in each paragraph. The main point is usually made in the *topic sentence.* This is generally the first sentence of the paragraph, though it may appear in other places, including at the end. You also need to *paraphrase* the important points to express them in a shorter, different way.

2 Topic sentences Look at paragraphs 1–3 of the article on pages 82–83. Underline the topic sentence in each paragraph, and identify one important idea that supports it.

Paragraph 1

Topic sentence: *teenagers see the world as a smaller place than it appeared to their grandparents*

Supporting idea: *this is because of cheap air travel, email, mobile phones …*

3a Paraphrasing Look at paragraph 1 of the article again and say which paraphrase below is better. Give your reasons.

Paraphrase A
For young people, the world is now much smaller because of new technology and cheap air travel. The most influential innovation is probably the Internet.

Paraphrase B
The Internet, cheap air travel, television, mobile phones, email and other things have influenced teenagers a lot. They see the world as a smaller place than their grandparents did. The Internet will probably have the most effect on the world in the future.

3b Now paraphrase paragraphs 2 and 3 of the article, then compare your paraphrases with a partner.

4 With your partner, read paragraph 4 of the article. It contains approximately 100 words. Discuss the summary below. Why is it not a good one?

Wikipedia is one of the greatest success stories. It is a great starting point for research, has a lot of interesting content and is reliable. Another major success of the Internet is Google. It is more reliable than Wikipedia, which finds and ranks pages.

WRITING SKILLS: a summary

5 Read paragraph 5 of the article. Which of the following expresses the main idea of the paragraph?

a) There are several Internet websites providing games and videos.

b) Google is having a major impact on the way people are using the Internet

c) The Internet is helping people to make contacts all over the world.

6a What is the *topic sentence* in the paragraph? Underline it.

6b What are the other key ideas in the paragraph which support the main idea in the topic sentence? Write the ideas in note form.

7a Editing to shorten One of the most important aspects of summary writing is being able to shorten text, including shortening your own text. Look at these ways of shortening parts of paragraphs 5 and 6 of the article.

a) **removing examples**
... global companies ~~such as Adidas and Toyota~~ even have outlets there. → There are even outlets of global companies.

b) **ellipsis** (cutting out repeated words)
People can meet new friends through sites like these, ~~they can~~ renew old acquaintances through sites like Friends Reunited and ~~they can also~~ play games with each other in virtual worlds such as Second Life. → People can meet new friends, renew old acquaintances and play games with each other.

c) **joining clauses**
Many people remember ~~watching~~ 'sabre boy' wielding an imaginary light-sabre, and laughing ~~out loud at his antics~~. → Many people remember laughing at 'sabre boy' wielding an imaginary light-sabre.

7b Use the techniques described above to shorten the following.

1 International shopping is now common with people buying all sorts of goods from sites such as Amazon, the online retail site, and the international auction site, eBay.

2 The Internet helps solve crimes, it helps raise money for charities and it even helps find missing children through websites designed for that purpose.

3 Google, a major source of information, finds the web pages you need and ranks them according to the number of links made to them.

8 Read the article below about eBay. Write a summary of it in approximately 90 words.

Choose A Topic

Company Overview

Executive Team

Press Releases

The eBay Company

eBay Inc. is an American Internet company. This company manages eBay.com, an online auction and shopping website where people and businesses buy and sell goods and services worldwide. Anyone can sell anything there. Millions of items are bought on eBay every day, and it is fairly easy and cheap to sell an item on the website. People have to send what they sell themselves, usually by mail. Many goods such as collectibles, appliances, computers, furniture, equipment, vehicles, and other miscellaneous items are listed, bought, and sold daily. Some items are rare and valuable, for example antique dolls, while many others are dusty articles that would have been thrown away if there were not thousands of eager bidders worldwide. Anything can be sold as long as it is not illegal. For example, large international companies, such as IBM, sell their newest products and offer services on eBay.

There have been criticisms of eBay. For instance, in late 1999 a man offered one of his kidneys for auction on eBay, attempting to profit from the potentially profitable (and, in the United States, illegal) market for transplantable human organs. The feedback system has also been criticised. After each transaction both the buyer and seller can rate each other. So if a buyer has problems, he or she can leave a comment such as 'never received product'. However, some people say the system has a number of weaknesses.

Finally, eBay is also an easy place for sellers to market counterfeit merchandise, which can be difficult for some buyers to distinguish without careful study of the auction description.

Done

Internet

9 Art

In this unit

Grammar
- ungradable adjectives
- position of adverbs

Vocabulary
- art and artists
- common adverb/adjective combinations
- order of adjectives

Scenario
- The new exhibition

Study skills
- expanding your vocabulary

Writing skills
- an online review

9.1 WHAT IS ART?

I don't know much about art, but I know what I like.
Anonymous

SPEAKING

1a Discuss the questions.

1 What sort of paintings do you like?
2 Do you have a favourite artist or painter?
3 Do you like other forms of art, e.g. sculpture, photography?
4 What sort of art don't you like?

1b Which of the following do you consider to be art? Explain your reasons.

- some graffiti on a wall
- a tattoo on someone's body
- a holiday photograph
- a pile of bricks in an exhibition
- a comic book
- a painting of a bowl of fruit
- an advertisement for a product
- a firework display

2a What is art for? Rank the following purposes 1–8 in order of importance, then discuss your ranking with a partner.

- to make people think and stimulate debate
- to communicate a political message
- to be beautiful and attractive to look at
- to entertain and make people laugh
- to show the skill of the artist
- to cause a positive or negative emotional reaction in the viewer
- to reflect society/life
- to make money

2b Can you think of any examples of works of art that achieve some of the purposes in Exercise 2a?

READING

3 Skim the leaflet opposite. What is it advertising? Who is it aimed at?

4 Read the leaflet. Which exhibition(s) is/are most suitable for a person who likes …

1 to attend talks about art?
2 art which is up-to-date?
3 paintings of the countryside?
4 to see the work of a single artist?
5 pictures of people?
6 art objects made from different materials?

5 Which exhibition would you most like to visit? Why?

INVICTA GALLERY LONDON

Future exhibitions – the year ahead

January–March
Tomorrow Now!
Contemporary painting
A selection of groundbreaking works of art by today's stars of the future. Already a hit with the critics at the preview show, this is a great way to start the New Year. With echoes of the colourful abstract action painting of the 1950s and 60s, this is sure to be popular with collectors and art lovers everywhere.

April–June
Shaping the World
An exhibition of sculpture
A retrospective of the work of the great American sculptor Cynthia Marlow, from her early ceramics to the later imposing stone statues, together for the first time with her bronze masterpiece *Woman*. Includes an opening day talk and audio guide by the artist herself.

July–September
Forever Autumn
Landscape paintings
A fascinating look at the season through the eyes of 18th- and 19th-century European landscape painters. Including works in oil and watercolour, this exhibition is all about colour and light. The very finest in romantic and realist painting.

October–December
The Start of the New
The story of Modern Art
The much talked-about and long-awaited exhibition finally arrives in this country. A sometimes controversial look at the end of realism and the beginnings of Modern Art in the late 19th and early 20th century. The exhibition brings together examples of the many movements which shocked the public and helped define the idea of 'Modern Art'. Includes a thought-provoking series of lectures on 'The origins of modernism'.

Basement bookshop and café with:
Easy on the Eye – some of the world's most famous film and TV stars feature in this permanent display of candid portrait photography.

For more information, go to: invictagallery.org.uk
Become a Friend of the Gallery. Get discounts and invitations to private views.

Be seeing you!

www.InvictaGallery/London.com

VOCABULARY: art and artists

6a Find nouns or adjectives in the leaflet which mean the following.

1 involving very new methods or ideas
2 an occasion to see something before the public
3 a show of the past work of an artist
4 a very good piece of art
5 causing a lot of disagreement
6 causing people to think

6b Read the leaflet again and find references to the words in *italics*. Choose the correct answer.

1 *Modern Art / Realism* is art which is true to life.
2 *Contemporary / Modern* Art is from the period 1890–1970.
3 *Contemporary / Modern* Art is from 1970 to the present.
4 *Abstract Art / Realism* expresses an artist's ideas or feelings, rather than showing what people and things look like.

6c List all the people connected with art mentioned in the leaflet.

sculptor, ...

LISTENING

7a 3.2 Listen to the conversation between two Friends of the Invicta Gallery. Answer the questions.

1 Which of the following exhibitions did Jane or Monica go to?
Michelangelo Monet Van Gogh Matisse Rembrandt Dada Pop Art the photo exhibition
2 Are they going to renew their membership?

7b Listen again and complete the expressions.

1 I was really _____ by it.
2 I'm not really _____ that sort of thing ...
3 ... didn't really live up to my _____.
4 ... the _____ weren't very good.
5 It wasn't worth the _____ or the entrance _____ ...
6 It was one of the best _____ I've ever seen.
7 I'd really _____ it.

SPEAKING AND WRITING

8 Think of works of art / exhibitions you have seen. Tell your partner about an exhibition, a gallery or a work of art you've enjoyed (or not enjoyed), using some of the expressions above.

9 Write an email to a friend in another country telling them about an exhibition you have seen or heard about.

READING

1 **Do you take photographs? When? Why? Do you prefer colour or black and white photographs?**

2 **Read the article and choose the best title.**

a) What makes a good photograph?

b) The best photographs in the world

c) Is photography an art form?

3 **Find arguments in the article that support the idea that photography is an art form.**

4 **Discuss the following questions.**

1 What does the article say about the difference between photography and paintings?

2 What reasons are given in the article for photography NOT being an art form?

3 Do you think photography is an art form?

Paintings are almost always considered an art form, but what about photography? The Frenchman Henri Cartier-Bresson, possibly the most famous photographer in the 20th century, emphasised the difference between painting as art and photography as art. In 1957, he told *The Washington Post* that 'There is a creative fraction of a second when you are taking a picture. Your eye must see a composition or an expression that life itself offers you, and you must know with intuition when to click the camera. That is the moment the photographer is creative.' He is, of course, referring to the immediacy of photography – the absolutely unique moment, never to be repeated, when the exposure is taken.

A further characteristic of photography, unlike painting, is that more can be captured in a photograph than was intended by the photographer. Fine details, entirely unexpected and often invisible to the naked eye, can be revealed. The photograph 'does not lie' because it has not passed through the brain of the photographer. This is completely different from the brain processes of the painter, who decides what he is going to paint, how he will make the subject interesting and how he is going to paint it.

VOCABULARY: common adverb/adjective combinations

5 **Find the following words in the article and note the adverbs that go with them.**

unexpected different wrong moving

6a **Match the adverbs in the box with the adjectives below.**

heavily	highly	~~highly~~	painfully
totally	totally	utterly	utterly

Adjectives

~~praised~~ criticised impossible qualified shy unbelievable unjustified useless

highly praised

6b **Add an adverb from Exercise 6a to the following sentences.**

1 Cartier-Bresson was praised for his coverage of Gandhi's funeral in India in 1948.

2 Mario Testino was qualified in many fields before he moved to London to train as a photographer.

3 The film was unbelievable yet strangely moving.

4 *One Hour Photo* is a film starring Robin Williams about a shy photo technician.

5 Modern Art was often criticised while it was being produced.

6 The banning of photographers from the area was unjustified.

GRAMMAR: ungradable adjectives

7a **Look at these adjectives from the article. Put them in pairs with similar meanings.**

good unique excellent essential unusual important

7b **Now put the following adjectives into pairs with similar meanings.**

angry	bad	big	cold	devastated
enormous	exhausted	fascinating	freezing	
furious	hungry	interesting	small	
starving	terrible	tiny	tired	upset

Adjectives can be gradable or ungradable. For example, *cold* is gradable (there are degrees of 'coldness') but *freezing* is ungradable – it is at the end of the scale of 'coldness'.

Some critics of photography claim that modern cameras reduce photo-taking to an automatic process. They say, 'Just point and shoot. The camera does the rest. You will get a good photo.' However, those who see photography as an art form say that the critics are completely wrong. They say that the camera cannot decide between an ordinary, functional, regular photo and a really excellent, cleverly composed photo, consciously constructed. When considering photography as art, it is the photographer who picks out the essential qualities of the subject at a particular moment. The photographer brings creativity to the process.

Millions of photographs are taken every year but very few are considered art. However, some photographs, originally taken for scientific or commercial purposes and not consciously for art, can be perceived as artistic. Very unusual photographs taken by explorers in the Antarctic for geographical purposes often reveal the wonders of nature by showing contrasts between ice and water.

Photos taken for other purposes, such as news photography, can also become iconic works of art, for example, the picture taken by Robert Capa during the Spanish Civil War of a soldier at the moment of being shot, falling backwards. This photograph is both deeply moving and historically really important.

7c What is the difference between the adjectives in each pair? Use the examples to help you.

Photos of nature can be *very unusual*.

That photo of the explosion is *absolutely unique*.

8 Write the adjectives in Exercise 7 in two columns: gradable and ungradable.

Gradable	Ungradable
angry	*furious*

9a Look at the examples from Exercise 7a in the article again, and the words before them. Underline the correct option below.

1 *Gradable / ungradable* adjectives can be made stronger or weaker with words like *very, a bit, extremely*.

2 We often use *absolutely* with *gradable / ungradable* adjectives.

GRAMMAR TIP

We can use *really* with both gradable and ungradable adjectives:

The film was ***really interesting****.*
The exhibition was ***really fascinating****.*

➥ Language reference and extra practice, pages 150–151

9b Correct the adverbs if they are wrong.

1 I thought it was a very excellent photograph.
2 We were a bit tired after our visit to the Louvre.
3 I was very devastated when they said the exhibition was closed.
4 The photographs were extremely terrible.
5 When we had finished going round the photo exhibition we were absolutely exhausted.

10 Identify the adverb–adjective combinations in this text. Are there any combinations that don't go together? Why?

The National Gallery of Ireland has a very excellent collection of European fine arts. It opened in 1854 and now has over 2,500 paintings. Admission is very cheap. It has a wonderful Irish collection, including works by Jack B. Yeats, and the Flemish and Dutch collection is very enormous. There is even a Vermeer. There are also works by Caravaggio, Picasso and Monet. We were absolutely hungry at the end of our visit and luckily the café has great food. The shop is located in the new wing, which is itself an extremely fascinating piece of architecture. For such a small country this collection is absolutely interesting and most visitors have a really wonderful day.

SPEAKING

11 In groups of three, describe one of the best photographs you have taken, and one of the best you have seen.

CONTEMPORARY SCULPTORS

READING

1 In pairs, discuss the following statement. Do you agree with it?

Modern and contemporary art is not real art. Some of it could have been done by young children.

2 Read the three profiles of artists quickly, and say what type of art each has done.

3a According to the texts, which artist:

1 still lives in his/her country of birth?
2 did not complete his/her education?
3 lived through a major conflict?
4 is influenced strongly by his/her country of birth?
5 has received criticism of his/her talent?
6 uses him/herself as a model?
7 is currently combining two artistic disciplines?

3b Which of the works of art in the photos do you like the most? Why? Would you like to go to the artists' exhibitions? Why / Why not?

VOCABULARY: order of adjectives

4a Look at the highlighted phrases in the texts. List the adjectives in them under some of these headings.

age, material, colour/pattern, opinion, nationality, function/class, size, shape, other

4b Add the adjectives from the following examples under the headings in Exercise 4a. Can you work out the order of adjectives before a noun (i.e. opinion is first)?

beautiful, antique, colourful, Japanese silk paintings

huge, well-known, dark Cubist sculpture

Check your answers in the table on page 173.

5 Rewrite the sentences, putting the adjectives in brackets into the correct order before the noun.

1 Michael Ayrton made _____ sculptures. (bronze, fabulous, large)
2 Rothko's paintings often consist of a number of _____ boxes. (coloured, large, rectangular)
3 The _____ materials date back 2,000 years. (ancient, fine, Javanese)
4 Turner is perhaps the best known of the _____ artists. (British, Impressionist)
5 Lacquer is a _____ varnish. (hard, coloured, heat-resistant)
6 Wall paintings are used to brighten up some _____ environments. (dreary, urban, modern)
7 The bird was made with a piece of _____ paper. (square, Japanese, origami)

Anish Kapoor

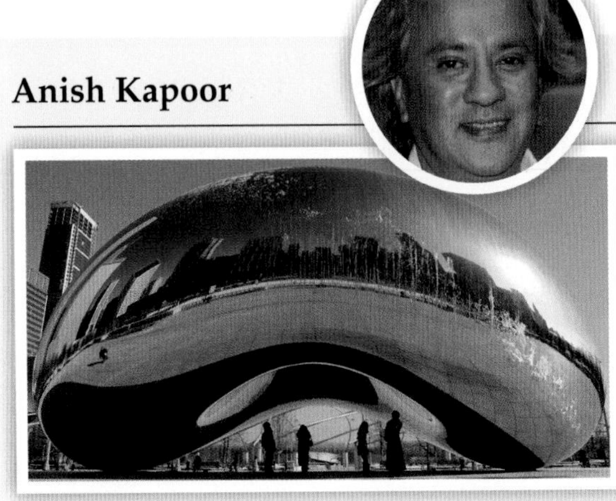

Anish Kapoor was born in Mumbai, India, in 1954 and moved to England *in 1972*. He studied at two outstanding, famous art schools in London, before starting out as a sculptor. Kapoor soon became well known because of his particular style, which, in his early works, involved the clever use of monochrome and brightly-coloured pigments surrounding the sculpture.

Although he is *mainly* resident in London, he often visits India, and Western and Eastern styles influence his work. It is said that his use of colour is *strongly* influenced by the heaps of coloured spices and powders found in Indian markets.

Kapoor's later works are *often* very large. In fact, his 110-ton Cloud Gate sculpture in Chicago is amongst the largest in the world. This sculpture is forged from a series of highly-polished stainless steel 'plates' that create an arched, highly-reflective work with Chicago's skyline and Millennium Park in the background.

Nowadays, Kapoor works on subway design in Italy and his work is becoming a mixture of art and architecture.

GRAMMAR: position of adverbs

6a Look at the adverbs / adverb phrases in *italics* in the texts. Add them to the lists.

1 Time: *then, in May*, _____, _____
2 Place: *there, at home*, _____, _____
3 Manner: *quickly, carefully*, _____, _____
4 Frequency: *sometimes, never*, _____, _____
5 Certainty: *definitely, perhaps*, _____, _____
6 Degree: *a lot, mostly*, _____, _____

6b Look at the clauses these adverbs / adverb phrases appear in and answer the questions.

1 Do groups 1–3 come at the beginning, middle or end of the clause?
2 Where do groups 4–6 come in the clause?
3 Where do the adverbs in 4–6 go in relation to the verb they modify?
4 Is this the same with all verbs? (Look at *mainly*.)

Antony Gormley

Antony Gormley was born in 1950 *in Hampstead, England*, and, like Kapoor, is famous for his very large sculptures. He studied at Cambridge from 1968 to 1971 before travelling to India and Sri Lanka to study Buddhism until 1974. On his return he studied in a number of colleges in London. His work *mainly* focuses on the human body and he uses his own body *creatively* to form metal casts for his sculptures. One of his best-known sculptures is 'The Angel of the North', an enormous metal figure, now completely rusted to a brown colour, with huge, fully-extended wings. Motorists travelling on the A1 road to the North of England and Scotland see the Angel rising above them *dramatically* as they drive closer to it. Another striking sculpture is 'Asian Field', installed in Sydney in 2006. It has 180,000 small brown clay figurines crafted by 350 Chinese villagers in five days from 100 tons of red clay. The installation is reminiscent of the terracotta warriors of Xian, China.

Yoko Ono

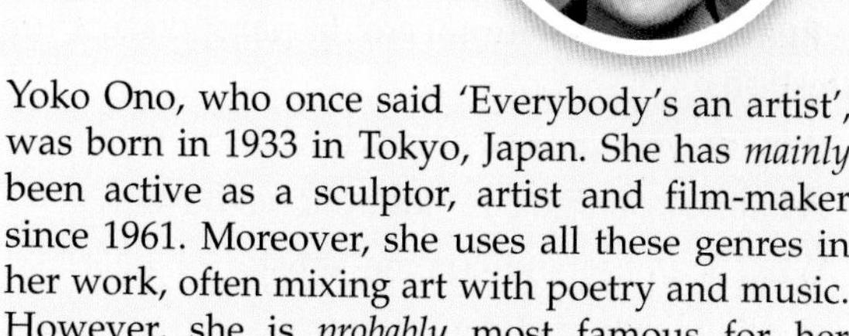

Yoko Ono, who once said 'Everybody's an artist', was born in 1933 in Tokyo, Japan. She has *mainly* been active as a sculptor, artist and film-maker since 1961. Moreover, she uses all these genres in her work, often mixing art with poetry and music. However, she is *probably* most famous for her marriage to John Lennon, of The Beatles.

In 1945, at the end of World War Two, she had to hide with her family when Tokyo was fire-bombed. Although she came from a rich, aristocratic family, she had to pawn her mother's property to obtain rice when Japan surrendered and everyone was poor. She moved with her family *to New York* when she was 18. She went to college but dropped out after two years. Her artistic work has *frequently* been criticised. Indeed, Brian Sewell, a traditional art critic, said, 'She's shaped nothing, she's contributed nothing, she's simply been a reflection of the times ...'. There is *certainly* disagreement with Sewell's views *nowadays*. In 2001, her show YES YOKO ONO received an international award.

GRAMMAR TIP

We can emphasise adverb phrases of time and place by putting them at the beginning of the clause:

***In 2001**, her show YES YOKO ONO received an international award.*

➡ Language reference and extra practice, pages 150–151

7 Rewrite the sentences with the adverb(s) in brackets in the correct place(s).

1 Van Gogh painted outdoors. (often)
2 Picasso has influenced many artists. (strongly)
3 Leonardo da Vinci sketched technical designs. (very skilfully)
4 The French post-impressionist Paul Gauguin died alone. (in Tahiti)
5 The most noticeable form of expression of art deco is in the huge skyscrapers in the USA. (probably)
6 The batik effect is produced by machines rather than being hand-made. (nowadays)

SPEAKING

8 Describe a work of art that you really like. Say why you like it, and say something about the artist.

9.4 SCENARIO

SITUATION

1 Read the information card. In pairs, discuss these questions.

1 Why do you think people will visit the exhibitions?
2 What do you think an 'institutional buyer' is?
3 What is an 'up-and-coming' artist?
4 Are there any contemporary artists you admire?

2a 3.3 The director of the gallery talks to four experts in the art world. He asks them to suggest artists for the first exhibition. Listen and complete as much of the chart as possible.

	Artist	Type of art	Best-known work of art
1	Savanna Charles		
2	Alberto Cassini		
3	Ingrid Tauber		
4	John Leach		

2b Check your answers with a partner. Then listen again and check your information.

3 From the information you have so far, which artist would you choose for the first exhibition?

MARCO GIORDANO GALLERY

Friends of the Giordano Gallery

• JANUARY UPDATE •

The gallery is planning a series of exhibitions of young, contemporary artists. The exhibitions will attract private and institutional buyers from all over the world, and will provide art lovers with the opportunity to buy the works of up-and-coming artists at affordable prices. We hope to see you all at the first exhibition, which is scheduled for the end of March. We are currently considering several artists who might wish to exhibit, and will inform you when we have made our final choices.

Marco Giordano Gallery 3–5 Bateman Square Bristol BS25 9QA

The new exhibition

KEY LANGUAGE: sequencing information, moving to a new point

4a 3.4 An employee of the gallery, Philippa Davis, is making a presentation to the director and his colleagues. Philippa thinks that the artist Marta Villanueva would be a good choice for an exhibition. Listen to Part 1 and answer the questions.

1 In what *order* does Philippa make her key points? Number the points 1–4 to show the order.
- reviews by critics ☐
- basic facts about the artist ☐
- the artist's reputation/personality ☐
- the artist's style of painting ☐

2 What basic facts do you learn about Marta Villanueva?

4b Listen to Part 1 again. Note the words she uses to sequence her information.

5a 3.5 Now listen to Part 2 of the presentation and answer the questions.

1 What subjects does Marta Villanueva paint? Fill in the missing words.
She paints mainly _____ and _____.
2 What do the critics say about Villanueva and her painting?
3 Philippa uses three adjectives to describe Villanueva's personality. Complete the words:
a) ch _ _ m _ _ g b) m _ d _ _ t c) s _ c _ _ _ _ _ e

5b Listen again. What does Philippa say to end one topic and move on to another?

6a Look at the phrases and sentences from the presentation. Match each phrase or sentence with the correct function below.

1 First, I'll give you a few basic facts ...
2 Finally, I'll describe what she's like as a person.
3 Right, I've told you a bit about her, ...
4 So, moving on now to her style of painting ...
5 OK, that's all I have to say about her style.
6 OK, that's it for the critics.
7 Let's go on to her personality and reputation.
8 Right, now you know a bit about the kind of person she is.

Functions

a) ordering information in a talk
b) signalling the end of one topic
c) changing to a new topic

6b 3.6 Listen and mark the main stress on the phrases in Exercise 6a. Then practise saying them in pairs, paying attention to the stress and intonation.

TASK: giving an informal presentation

7a Work in groups of four. Each student chooses a different artist. Prepare a presentation of your artist, using the information in Exercise 2 and these notes.

Student A: read about Savanna Charles on page 160.

Student B: read about Alberto Cassini on page 164.

Student C: read about Ingrid Tauber on page 168.

Student D: read about John Leach on page 169.

7b Make your presentation. Try to persuade the group that your artist is the best choice for the first exhibition.

8 Together, discuss the artists, including Marta Villanueva. Consider their strong and weak points, introducing any extra information you have.

9 Select two artists for the first two exhibitions. If necessary, take a vote (you may not vote for your own artist).

OTHER USEFUL PHRASES

Stating the purpose of the presentation

I'm going to talk to you about ... (a Portuguese artist).

The purpose of my talk is to ... (present an artist to you).

Summarising/concluding a presentation

To sum up, ...

Now, I'll summarise my main points.

To conclude my presentation, ...

In conclusion, I'd just like to say ... (it's been a pleasure talking to you all).

9.5 STUDY AND

STUDY SKILLS: expanding your vocabulary

1 Look at these phrases. What do you think the word *nice* means? Does it mean the same in each phrase?

1 Have a nice day.
2 Nice to meet you.
3 She's really nice.
4 That's a nice haircut.
5 Let's have a nice cup of tea.
6 It's a nice place to live.

2 Read this extract from a book about expressing yourself accurately. Is this the same as in your language?

It pays to increase your word power

Expanding your vocabulary is a sure way of improving your English and the way you express yourself in English. However, spoken and written English are often quite different.

Take a simple example – the word *nice* is very common in spoken English. It is a very general adjective, which is rather vague in meaning, as in the following examples: *Have a nice day, Nice to meet you, She's really nice, That's a nice haircut*. In this spoken context *nice* is very useful – often we don't need to be very precise because a lot of meaning is carried by our intonation and facial expression. Also, the listener and speaker can clarify what exactly is meant. In written English, these clues are absent so we need to be more precise in order to convey what we really mean.

In addition, it is good to expand your vocabulary for stylistic reasons. Your writing will be much more interesting if you avoid repeating the same words.

3 What does the word *nice* really mean in the following phrases? Choose two words from the box for each phrase.

beautiful charming delicious friendly
picturesque productive relaxing restful
stylish tasty trendy useful

1 a nice view
2 a nice meal
3 a nice holiday
4 a nice jacket
5 a nice person
6 a nice meeting

4a Look at these other common, basic adjectives. Add three more adjectives from the box below against each basic idea.

Basic idea	More precise adjectives
1 good	*excellent*
2 bad	*terrible*
3 interesting	*fascinating*
4 sad	*upsetting*
5 boring	*dull*
6 funny	*humorous*
7 exciting	*dramatic*
8 stupid	*crazy*

absorbing absurd amusing
appalling awful brilliant
compelling dreadful exhilarating
gripping heartbreaking hilarious
laughable monotonous moving
nailbiting outstanding repetitive
ridiculous tedious terrific
thrilling touching witty

Adjective–noun collocation is also important. A good thesaurus or the *Longman Language Activator* will help you to recognise collocations and find better words to express what you mean. Look up in the index the basic idea of what you want to say and you can find alternatives.

4b Collocations Which of the following can be *fascinating, absorbing, gripping* or *compelling*?

1 a book 2 a fact 3 a film

Turn to page 174 and look at the entry from the *Longman Language Activator* for *interesting*. Check your answer and decide how the adjectives can be used.

WRITING SKILLS: an online review

5a In pairs, discuss these questions.

1 What sort of films do you like?

2 What films/DVDs have you seen/bought recently?

3 Do you read online reviews before you buy/see DVDs? Why / Why not?

5b Which of the following do you think it is a good idea to have in an online review?

- information about the story
- information about the acting
- how much it costs to buy
- the genre
- whether it is a good idea to watch it or not
- the special effects
- names of the actors/director
- the music
- what happens at the end

6a Read the customer review below. Is it positive or negative?

6b In which paragraph are the following mentioned?

1 the cast	5 the writing
2 the director	6 the plot
3 the background	7 the setting
4 the music	8 the recommendation

7 Change the adjectives in *italics* in the review to improve the writing. (Use Exercises 3 and 4 to help you.)

8a Adverbs Look at the ten adverbs in bold in the review. Put them in pairs of adverbs with a similar meaning.

totally – completely

8b Match the pairs of adverbs with their meaning.

1 in every way
totally, completely

2 without doubt

3 in most cases

4 more than usual

5 extremely

9 Now write a review of a film/DVD you have seen. Use the one below as a model. Try to use some of the adjectives and adverbs you have learned.

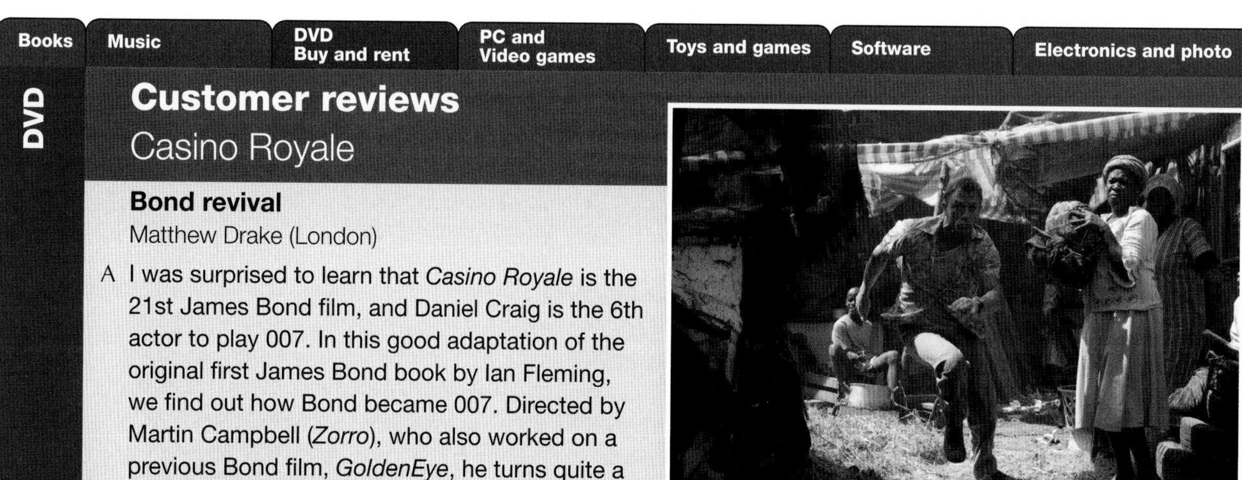

Customer reviews
Casino Royale

Bond revival
Matthew Drake (London)

A I was surprised to learn that *Casino Royale* is the 21st James Bond film, and Daniel Craig is the 6th actor to play 007. In this good adaptation of the original first James Bond book by Ian Fleming, we find out how Bond became 007. Directed by Martin Campbell (*Zorro*), who also worked on a previous Bond film, *GoldenEye*, he turns quite a *boring* story into an *exciting* film.

B The writers have created a script which is *interesting* and also *funny* in places. Of course, as you expect with any James Bond film, the action sequences are **generally** *exciting* and well done, and it's good to see there are no **completely** *stupid* special effects like in some previous Bond films. The opening chase is **particularly** *exciting*. As always with Bond, the film is set in a variety of *nice* locations such as Venice, the Bahamas, Montenegro and Africa.

C The **really** *good* thing about the film though is Daniel Craig as the new Bond. He is **definitely** the best since Sean Connery. His acting is always *good* and in some scenes he is very *funny*. His co-stars, **especially** Eva Green, are also *good*. There are some *sad* scenes between the two of them, but perhaps there is too much focus on the love story for an action film. It is very long at almost two and a half hours and some scenes are quite *boring*.

D The worst thing about the film was the title song which was **truly** *bad*. This is a shame as most Bond songs are **usually** *good*. The soundtrack is also often **totally** uninspiring. The other disappointment was the ending of the film, which was not the usual *exciting* Bond-style conclusion, but it does make you want to see the next one in the series. Overall, however, it is great cinema and I would **certainly** recommend this to any Bond fan or film lover.

REVIEW

GRAMMAR

1a Work with a partner to discuss the following.

'Seventy percent of the Earth's surface is covered in water. As the world population grows we will have to learn to live underwater.'

'As climate change makes large parts of the Earth unsuitable for food production, we will be forced to use the wealth of the oceans.'

1b Do you think people will ever live under the sea?

2a Read the text on the right quickly and choose the most suitable heading for each paragraph.

1 The site and construction team
2 The land station
3 The hotel
4 The architect
5 Life under the sea

2b Read the text again and complete the gaps with the words below.

1 a) frequently has appeared
b) has frequently appeared
c) has appeared frequently

2 a) to build b) build c) building

3 a) There will in the centre be
b) There will be in the centre
c) In the centre there will be

4 a) An absolutely
b) A completely
c) A very

5 a) will travel rapidly between
b) will travel between rapidly
c) rapidly will travel between

6 a) will be pulled
b) will pull
c) will to be pulled

7 a) add b) to add c) adding

8 a) is be built
b) is been built
c) is being built

9 a) had surveyed the land and sea bed
b) had the land and sea bed surveyed
c) the land and sea bed had surveyed

10 a) very unique
b) absolutely unique
c) a bit unique

11 a) to cost b) cost c) costing

12 a) has been designed
b) was being designed
c) designed

A holiday *in* the sea, not *by* the sea

A ________
The idea of colonising the sea has been around for centuries. It 1_____ in literature and was the inspiration for Jules Verne's *Twenty Thousand Leagues Under the Sea* in 1870. But at that time such an idea was purely science fiction. Now science fiction is about to become 'science fact'. At last a consortium of companies has decided 2_____ 'Hydropolis' – the world's first luxury underwater hotel.

B ________
Hydropolis will contain 220 rooms 20 metres below the surface of the sea. The hotel will have no foundations but will float in the sea, held down by 7,000 anchors. At sea level there will be a large circular building which will create a lagoon, containing restaurants and meeting rooms. 3_____ a ballroom with a roof that can be opened. From the ballroom, ramps and elevators will connect with the guest rooms and suites situated below the water.

C ________
4_____ long tunnel will connect the underwater hotel with the land station, a high-rise building situated on the beach. Guests 5_____ the hotel and the land station on special silent trains which 6_____ by steel cables. The land station will contain a reception area, a clinic, a marine biology laboratory and conference rooms. There are plans to build a restaurant and the company is considering 7_____ more facilities, such as cinemas, at a later stage.

D ________
Hydropolis 8_____ close to the Jumeirah beach coast in Dubai. The land belongs to the Crown Prince of Dubai, who 9_____ several years ago. The prince believes Hydropolis will be 10_____ and his enthusiasm has been crucial to its development. Covering over 260,000 square metres, the project is expected 11_____ around €550 million. The main contractors are Dutch and German but there are more than 150 different companies involved in the project.

E ________
The hotel 12_____ by Joachim Hauser. Hauser claims the design is based on the human nervous system. He wants the hotel to be a place where those that do not enjoy swimming or diving will still be able to experience life in the sea. One of his main aims is to raise awareness of the importance of marine life and the dangers of ecological destruction, such as the loss of coral reefs.

VOCABULARY

3 Read the text below and choose the correct answers.

Brad Pitt – Actor or architect?

Brad Pitt is currently one of the world's biggest international [1]*characters / celebrities*. Constantly chased by the [2]*paparazzi / programme*, he lives a life in which he is permanently in the limelight. But although acting has brought Pitt wealth and fame, it seems that his true passion is architecture.

His interest began in 2001 when he [3]*revitalised / restored* a [4]*misunderstood / run-down* mansion in Beverly Hills. He asked Frank Gehry, the Canadian architect who designed the [5]*innovative / insoluble* Guggenheim Museum in Bilbao, to help him with the design and the two became good friends.

Now Gehry has received a [6]*commission / design* to build a $250 million seafront development in the English seaside town of Hove, and he has asked Pitt to help him with the project. This [7]*networking / collaboration* between a film star and a famous architect is a new development in the world of design. The drawings produced so far show a very [8]*contemporary / derelict* structure covered in metal. Gehry's designs are always [9]*masterpiece / thought-provoking* and [10]*dilapidated / controversial*, and this scheme may not be popular with local residents who are more familiar with the [11]*retrospective / traditional* Victorian architecture of the area. But there are rumours that Pitt may buy one of the apartments in the development, which might well [12]*overcome / rebuild* the objections of the locals.

4 Match the words to make phrases.

1 highly	a) moving
2 multinational	b) choice
3 deeply	c) qualified
4 consumer	d) labour
5 heavily	e) companies
6 child	f) resources
7 painfully	g) shy
8 natural	h) criticised

KEY LANGUAGE

5 3.7 Listen to an architect talking to the directors of an art gallery about the design for an extension. Are these statements true, false or not given?

1 The architect doesn't know how many people will be visiting the art gallery.
2 The number of toilets in the new building can't be changed.
3 The gallery directors don't want exterior lighting.
4 Exterior lighting won't be expensive to run.
5 The law says public buildings must provide access for disabled people.
6 There will have to be a special entrance for disabled people.

6a Complete the extracts with the words in the box.

explain that in	be more specific	Let's go	moving on	you mean by	that's it for	be a good idea	we certainly need

1 So, _____ to the brief.
2 … I think it might _____ to have that.
3 _____ on to the planning issues.
4 So, _____ to make provision for that …
5 OK, _____ the planning issues; now I'd like to …
6 You mentioned exterior lighting. Could you _____?
7 And what do _____ disabled access?
8 Could you _____ more detail, please?

6b Listen again and check your answers.

LANGUAGE CHECK

7 There is a missing word in each sentence. Add it, then look at the pages and check your answers.

1 Reservations are being for the hotel. (page 73)
2 Don't worry – it's under the bridge. (page 74)
3 The new office was scheduled be finished within six months. (page 74)
4 It might a good idea to discuss it first. (page 77)
5 The website allows people contact their old school friends. (page 83)
6 Clare her handbag stolen on the bus. (page 85)
7 That film didn't really live to my expectations. (page 91)
8 To get this job you have to be highly. (page 92)
9 It's absolutely. There's nothing like it. (page 93)
10 OK, that's for the designs. Now … (page 97)

LOOK BACK

8 Find the exercises in Units 7–9 where you …

- learn about the present continuous passive. (Unit 7)
- study how prefixes change meaning. (Unit 7)
- write about a building that interests you. (Unit 7)
- study which verbs are followed by an object and infinitive. (Unit 8)
- learn about a structure we use to talk about a bad experience that has happened to us. (Unit 8)
- listen to people's views on globalisation. (Unit 8)
- read about Henri Cartier-Bresson. (Unit 9)
- study adverb–adjective collocations. (Unit 9)
- practise putting adverbs in the correct place. (Unit 9)

Psychology

In this unit

Grammar
- relative clauses
- reduced relative clauses

Vocabulary
- working together
- idioms with *mind*

Scenario
- Ask Vanessa

Study skills
- writing a bibliography
- referencing

Writing skills
- a discursive essay

10.1 GROUP PSYCHOLOGY

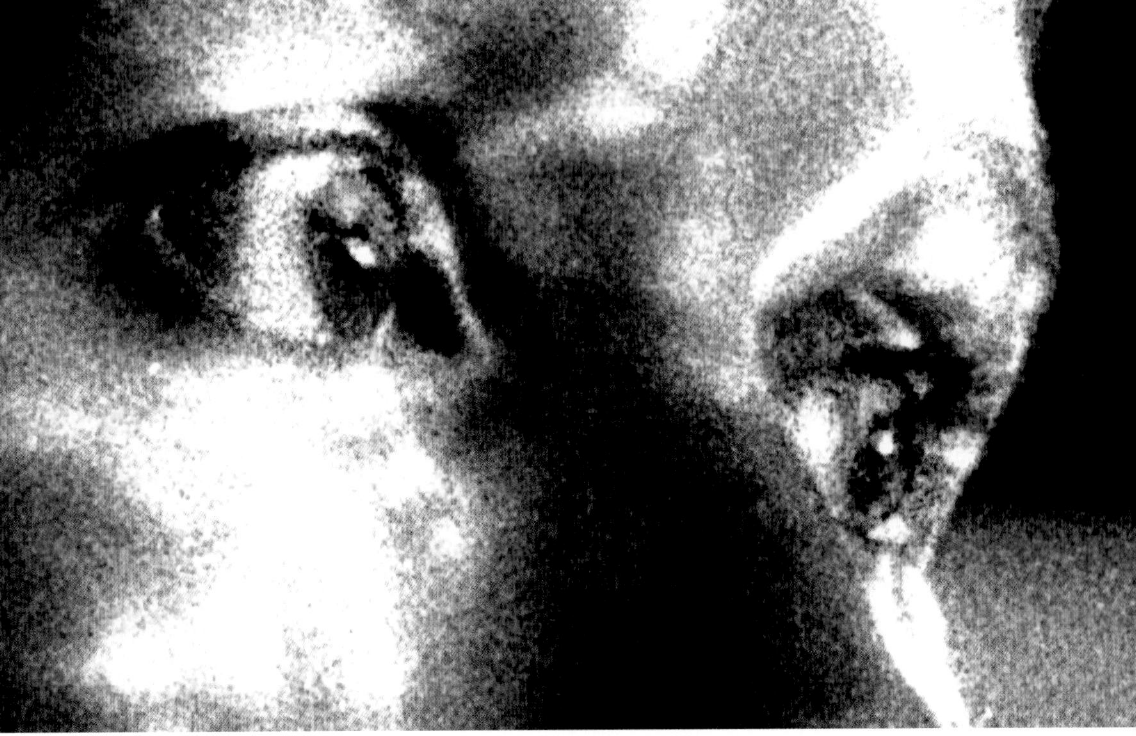

The mind is an iceberg. It floats with only 17 percent of its bulk above the water.
Sigmund Freud, 1856–1939, Austrian psychologist

SPEAKING

1 In small groups, discuss these questions.

1 What teams have you been in, e.g. playing sports, at work?
2 Describe some of the personalities in one of the teams.
3 Was it a successful team? Why / Why not?
4 What do you think makes an effective team? What sort of people do you need?

2 Look at these adjectives. Did you use any in your answer to question 2 in Exercise 1? Which do you think are the most important qualities for people in a team?

ambitious authoritative conscientious creative diplomatic energetic knowledgeable objective practical resourceful

pronunciation

3a Stress patterns Use a dictionary to find the nouns related to these adjectives and write adjective–noun pairs.

3b 3.8 Mark the stress on each word in Exercise 3a. Does the stress pattern change in any of them? Listen and check, then practise the pronunciation.

READING

4 Read the website below and on the right, which describes the Belbin model – an analysis of roles within a team. Which role(s) do you think you would be good at? Which ones wouldn't you be good at? Does your partner agree?

5 Look at the strengths column again and match the adjectives in Exercise 2 with the correct team role. Note there is one extra adjective.

plant = creative

How understanding team roles can improve team performance ▼

Belbin Model

Meredith Belbin is an expert on teams. During his research, he identified nine key roles in management teams, which are given in the table on the right. One of his most important findings was that effective teams have members covering all the roles. However, he also noted that people may have more than one role. A team does not need to be made up of nine people, but should be at least three or four.

LISTENING

6a You are going to listen to part of a lecture on group dynamics. Before you listen, look at the stages in the life of a group and decide on the order they happen in.

a) members become more familiar with each other and start to develop confidence in each other
b) the group comes together and members seem to have a friendly relationship
c) members' real personalities come out and they may argue with each other as they try to begin work
d) the group separates and members go their own ways
e) members work together well and produce good results

6b 3.9 Look at the names of the stages and match them with the definitions in Exercise 6a. Listen to check your answers.

Stages: performing storming adjourning forming norming

7 Listen again and answer the questions.

1 In which decades were a) Lewin and b) Tuckman working?
1930s 1940s 1950s 1960s 1970s 1980s
2 What does the expression *honeymoon period* mean?
3 What three practical examples of group dynamics in use does the expert give?

Home | About us | Contact us | Search

Role	Strengths	Weaknesses
Plant	comes up with ideas and solutions to problems	has difficulty communicating ideas to others
Resource investigator	enthusiastic; good at developing contacts and finding opportunities; an extrovert and networker	may perhaps lose interest towards the end of a project
Coordinator	good at leading teams and delegating; able to see the 'big picture'	sometimes can be too controlling
Shaper	outgoing and dynamic; enjoys pressure and a challenge; motivates the team to action	impatient; they tend not to be sensitive at times
Monitor-evaluator	observant; fair and has good judgement	they may lack passion or the ability to motivate
Teamworker	good listening and inter-personal skills; a peacemaker and mediator who is able to create harmony in the team	sometimes indecisive
Implementer	makes things happen; hard-working, organised and efficient	sometimes can be inflexible
Completer-finisher	a perfectionist; responsible and has a strong sense of duty	may worry too much about details; unwilling to delegate
Specialist	has special skills and expertise	can only contribute in a narrow area

VOCABULARY: working together

8a Match the verbs from the lecture with their meanings.

1 get on (with)
2 fall out (with)
3 get used to
4 get down to
5 break up
6 put up (with)

a) start work
b) tolerate
c) become comfortable with
d) separate
e) argue
f) have a friendly relationship

8b Complete these sentences so they are true for you.

1 I get on well with people who …
2 It sometimes takes me ages to get used to …
3 I find it difficult to get down to …
4 I tend to fall out with people who ...
5 A team I was in broke up because …
6 I can't put up with people who …

SPEAKING

9 Work in groups of four. You have to organise either a large surprise party for a friend's/relative's 21st/40th/60th birthday in two weeks' time, or a wedding.

1 Decide on what to do before the event, e.g. send out invitations xxx weeks/ days before.
2 Discuss what roles / multiple roles you have in your team and what roles you lack.
3 Discuss who will perform each task you have listed.

READING

1 What do you understand by peer pressure? Which of these are examples of it?

- wearing fashionable clothes
- joining in with bullying
- doing something dangerous because your friends are doing it
- going to a party when you don't feel like it
- lying about your real opinion to fit in

2 Read the leaflet quickly, then briefly answer the four questions in the text from memory.

3a Read the text again and answer the following questions.

1. What sort of people will probably give in more easily to peer pressure?
2. What example is given of giving in to peer pressure?
3. Are bullies always unpopular people?
4. How do the victims of bullying feel?
5. What advice does the writer give to parents, and to children? Do you agree with that advice?

3b Do you agree with the leaflet that peer pressure is so strong?

VOCABULARY: idioms with *mind*

4a Match the idioms on the left with their meanings. Use a dictionary to help you.

1 peace of mind	a) unable to decide what to do
2 keep an open mind	b) a feeling of calm and not being worried
3 make up (your) mind	c) decide
4 out of (your) mind	d) deliberately not form a definite opinion
5 in two minds	e) crazy, insane

4b Complete the statements with the idioms.

1. I can't _____ about what to do with the money.
2. Having insurance often gives you _____.
3. It is important to _____ when you are on a jury.
4. You must be _____ to give up such a good job.
5. I was _____ about applying for the job.

Pressure4parents.com

❶ What is peer pressure and why does it happen?

We all want to be part of a group and feel like we belong in our community. Peer pressure can happen when we are influenced to do something we would not usually do because we want to be accepted by our peers, i.e. groups of friends who are about the same age and share the same interests.

Children and young adults especially feel social pressure to conform to the peer group with whom they socialise. Conformity, which is the most common form of social influence, is usually defined as the tendency to think or act like other members of a group.

❷ How does peer pressure affect people?

Peer pressure can influence how people dress, how they talk, what music they listen to, what attitudes they adopt and how they behave. Teenagers want to belong and it is hard to belong if you are always going against the grain. They want to be liked, to fit in and to be accepted, which means peer pressure can be powerful and hard to resist. People never want to be looked down upon or made fun of. This means that people who are low on confidence and unsure of themselves may be more likely to seek their peers' approval by going along with risky suggestions. Peer pressure can lead people to do things they would not normally do on their own. In one study, a student who knew the correct answer to a question actually

GRAMMAR: relative clauses

5 Read the leaflet again. Underline all the examples of relative clauses that you can find.

6a Look at the clauses you have underlined. Identify which are defining and which are non-defining, then choose the correct words.

1. *Defining / Non-defining* relative clauses give us extra information which can be left out without affecting the main meaning of the sentence.
2. *Defining / Non-defining* relative clauses are necessary in order to complete the meaning of a sentence or identify someone or something.

Parentline 020 5320 4444
Kidshelpline 020 5320 1111

gave the wrong answer because all the others in the class gave the wrong answer and he didn't want to be different.

❸ Can peer pressure lead to bullying?

Peer pressure definitely plays a role in bullying. If a teenager is generally seen as weak or different by the majority of their peers, they can become a safe target for bullies. Bullies pick easy targets, people that the group are unlikely to defend or get upset over. Unfortunately, some bullies are popular and liked by many of their peers, which means others are less likely to call the behaviour bullying. These popular bullies can act appropriately towards teachers and adults so the problem often goes unnoticed. Many victims of bullies feel very lonely, have low self-esteem and become depressed. Understandably, parents are often deeply worried when their children are being bullied.

❹ What can parents do about it?

To achieve peace of mind parents need to know with whom their children are associating. They need to encourage children to stay out of situations in which they know they would be pressurised and uncomfortable. Children should learn to feel comfortable saying 'no', to choose their friends wisely, to talk to someone they trust, to think about the consequences of their actions and be true to themselves.

More information

You may want to check out the factsheets at the bottom of the page for more information:

Bullying • Differences and values • Finding help

6b Now complete the rules about relative clauses with some of the words from the box.

before	defining	non-defining
that	which	who	whom

1 _____ relative clauses have commas around them.
2 We use _____ instead of *who* after prepositions.
3 We use _____ (not *that*) after prepositions.
4 Prepositions come _____ the relative clause in formal English.
5 We often omit the relative pronoun _____ (or *who/which*) when it is the object of the clause.

GRAMMAR TIP

In informal English the preposition comes at the end of the sentence:

Just don't do it unless it's something that you feel comfortable with.

➡ Language reference and extra practice, pages 152–153

7a Look at the highlighted sentence in the leaflet and choose the correct answer.

Does the relative clause here refer to:

a) teenagers?
b) the fact that teenagers want to be liked?

7b This kind of relative clause adds a 'comment' to the main clause. Find another example of this in the text in paragraph 3.

8 Match the main clauses with relative clauses below. Rewrite them as one sentence. The relative clause refers to the underlined part of the main clause.

1 We are seeking a counsellor.
2 Even the bullies were crying.
3 Kurt Lewis fled to the USA from Germany.
4 Teenagers like to turn for advice to other young people.
5 People will follow someone else's lead first.
6 The type of peer pressure is never good
7 Peers are the individuals
8 We took all the teenagers to the seaside.
9 The bullying problem has now been solved.

a) about which we had a lot of discussion
b) which made a good break for them
c) that leaves you feeling confused or hurt
d) who are easily influenced
e) which was surprising
f) to whom we can refer special cases
g) with whom a child or adolescent identifies most
h) who they sympathise with
i) who many see as the father of social psychology

1–f We are seeking a counsellor to whom we can refer special cases.

SPEAKING

9 Work in groups of three. Make sentences about some of the following situations. Use the relative clauses below to make a comment on your sentence.

- a film you saw recently
- a disappointing day
- an interview you attended
- something that happened at college/work

… , which was fantastic/surprising/awful.
… , which was a huge relief / a problem.
… , which made things very difficult.

We went to see the new Harry Potter film last week, but we arrived late, which was a problem as we hadn't booked.

READING

1a Look at the following profile. In groups, brainstorm what crime the person could have committed, then check your ideas on page 173.

Caring, well-respected, but arrogant doctor with trusting patients, middle one of three children, devoted to his mother, stable marriage, successful children, helped organise charity collections and served on local committees.

1b Why are we surprised when doctors commit crimes?

2 How does a criminal profiler make a profile? Why is it useful? Scan the text on the right and check your ideas.

3 Read the text again. Which paragraph or paragraphs contain the following information?

1 how profilers work
2 a phrase for 'where people live'
3 terms for criminals who have killed lots of people
4 mention of a famous profiler
5 mention of looking at all the small pieces of information at the scene of a crime
6 types of criminals/crimes that profiling is used for
7 another name for psychological profiling

VOCABULARY

4 In pairs, complete the gaps with the words in the box. Use a dictionary to help you.

profile	psychiatrist	case file
deduce	assessment	motive

1 At first, it was difficult to find a _____ for Shipman's murders.
2 People who have memory gaps tend to fill in the gaps or _____ what has happened.
3 Two experts, a _____ and a psychologist, recommended that he should receive treatment.
4 I read a short _____ of the doctor in the local newspaper.
5 'She is also very rude,' psychiatrists noted in her _____.
6 This website is the clinician's desktop reference for psychological _____ and testing.

GRAMMAR: reduced relative clauses

5a Look at the following relative clauses. Underline two sentences in the text that mean the same.

... a number of letters *which were mailed by the suspect ...*

... the crime scene, *which enables them to describe the specific methods of operation ...*

5b What are the differences between the sentences above and the sentences in the text?

PSYCHOLOGICAL PROFILING

A This investigative technique, most commonly referred to as criminal profiling, has recently risen in popularity both in practical use and media portrayals. A quick visit to any bookstore will reveal the popularity of the true crime section, and the recent flood of novels with a likeable lead detective profiling the offender is equally popular.

B Profiling most notably can be traced back to work done in the latter part of the last century. It has become very common, especially in America, since the 1950s. It deals with methods used to detect criminals such as serial killers, and to prevent crimes such as aeroplane hijacking. Other criminals for whom psychological profiling has been used are suicide bombers and mass murderers.

C Without doubt, one of the best-known profiles performed in the last century is that of James Brussels, a New York psychiatrist, who profiled 'The Mad Bomber of New York'. Brussels was called on to help police in their search as the bomber had left about 32 explosive packages across the city over approximately eight years. Reviewing the huge case file, the photographs, and a number of letters mailed by the suspect over a 16-year period, Brussels suggested the police were looking for '... a heavy man. Middle-aged. Foreign born. Roman Catholic. Single. Lives with a brother or sister.' He also added '... when you find him, chances are he will be wearing a double-breasted suit. Buttoned.' He also deduced that the man was paranoid, hated his father, was obsessively loved by his mother and

Done

6 Look at the text again and underline at least four more reduced relative clauses.

1 Which of the underlined sentences use an *-ing* form, and which use a past participle?

2 Which type of clause is active and which is passive?

➡ Language reference and extra practice, pages 152–153

7 In each pair of sentences, write the same verb, once in the *-ing* form and once as a past participle.

1a She took a course in psychotherapy, *developing* her skills as a counsellor.

1b Psychoanalytical theory, *developed* by Freud, has been the subject of much controversy.

2a Psychology magazines _____ out of the library must be returned within one week.

2b There were paparazzi everywhere, _____ photographs and annoying the prisoners.

3a The people _____ the real decisions are not the profilers.

3b The decision to arrest, _____ by the senior detective and profiler, was correct.

4a The road _____ last year is in a shocking condition.

4b The workers _____ the road took a long time to complete it.

lived in the state of Connecticut. Brussels was so close in his assessment that the arresting officers were surprised at the similarities, even down to the double-breasted suit that was buttoned.

D What exactly is psychological profiling? Essentially, it involves investigating an offender's behaviour, motives and background to provide specific information about the type of person who commits a certain crime. This makes it possible to draw up a profile of actual or potential offenders. The investigation covers such areas as the criminal's age, sex, employment, place of residence and distinctive personality characteristics. Profilers note and evaluate minute details of the crime scene, enabling them to describe the specific methods of operation of the criminal, e.g. how he kills, where he kills, and what type of victim he selects. Profiling tries to identify potential serious offenders early; for example, in their teens they often commit petty crimes, defying authority, until they begin killing in their mid to late twenties.

E Psychological profiling helps find serial killers. However, psychology has failed to explain why some people go down this route. Similarly, it cannot work out why the public is so fascinated with serial killers, or why the media glamorises them and gives them celebrity status.

8 In this text, cross out the pronoun and auxiliary verbs and use just the present or past participle where possible.

There are several films ~~which focus~~ focusing on profilers who are investigating criminal cases. *The Silence of the Lambs* is a film which is directed by Jonathan Demme.

In it, Clarice Starling, who is played by Jodie Foster, questions a brilliant forensic psychologist and serial killer, who is named Hannibal Lecter. Lecter, who is currently serving nine life sentences in a mental institution, is charming and polite to Starling, and eventually offers her a psychological profile of the murderer Starling is trying to find. The performance of Lecter, who was played by Anthony Hopkins, is the shortest Oscar-winning performance ever by a leading actor. The most famous book series on profiling is probably the Kay Scarpetta series, which was written by Patricia Cornwell. These novels feature Benson Wesley, a criminal profiler who works for the FBI.

SPEAKING

9 In groups, discuss any books you have read or films you have seen that involve profiling or serial killers.

WRITING

10 Underline the key points in the text and write a short summary (between 150 and 180 words) about psychological profiling.

10.4 SCENARIO

SITUATION

Vanessa Cheung is an agony aunt for Metro Radio, a Manchester-based radio station. Her programme is called *Ask Vanessa*. She is highly respected for her practical advice and sensible comments. People of all ages phone in and tell her their problems. She listens sympathetically and tries to give helpful advice to her callers.

1 Read the situation and discuss the questions.

1 What exactly is an agony aunt? Where might you see an agony aunt's column?
2 Do you ever read advice columns or listen to advice phone-ins? Why / Why not?
3 Vanessa advises people of all ages. What problems do you think each age group below might wish to discuss with an agony aunt?
   a) people under 20?
   b) people 20–40?
   c) people 40+?
4 Why are advice columns and phone-in programmes so popular?
5 Do you think advice columns/phone-ins help people to lead happier lives?

2 3.10 Listen to Vanessa talking to a caller. Read the three summaries of the problem. Which one is the best summary? Give reasons for your choice.

Summary A

Michelle loves her husband but is worried because he spends too much. Early in their marriage, life was good and they had a lot of money. She was happy, but now she is confused and is planning to divorce him.

Summary B

Michelle's husband has always been a big spender. He is now retired, but has so many debts that they may have to sell their house. Michelle is very worried about their financial situation and has even considered leaving her husband.

Summary C

Since he retired, Michelle's husband has been spending too much money. As a result, he has many debts, which worries him and his wife. Earlier in the marriage, they were happy, but now Michelle has thought about leaving her husband, even though she loves him.

3a In pairs, discuss the problem. What advice would you give Michelle if you were Vanessa?

3b 3.11 Listen to the advice that Vanessa gives to Michelle. Is it the same as your advice?

KEY LANGUAGE: giving advice

4a Listen again to the phone-in conversation. Vanessa gives Michelle several pieces of advice. Fill in the gaps with correct phrases from the box.

a) I'd advise you to …	f) I think you need to …
b) Why don't you …	g) you could also …
c) You might consider …	h) if I were you, I'd …
d) it's vital that you …	i) it's essential that …
e) it might be a good idea to …	

1 OK, first of all, _____ talk to someone about the debts you have.
2 And _____ contact your local Citizens Advice Centre …
3 Well, you know, _____ have a separate bank account.
4 Great! Well, _____ check the Internet to see if there are some websites offering help …
5 And there's another thing you can do. _____ contact a finance company.
6 Mmm, it's a serious problem, _____ do something about it.
7 Or should I say, it's vital he does something about it. _____ have a serious talk with him?
8 One final bit of advice. _____ getting some counselling yourself.
9 I know you don't want to do that, … but _____ your husband changes his behaviour …

4b Check your answers with Track 3.11 on page 186.

4c Discuss whether each piece of advice is strong, neutral or tentative (not very strong).

Ask Vanessa 10.4

TASK: an advice phone-in

5a Vanessa also receives problems by email, and decides which ones to have on her phone-in. Work in pairs.

Student A: choose one of the problems below, read it and make a few notes.

Student B: choose one of the problems on page 165, read it and make a few notes.

5b Role-play the situation.

Student A: You are the caller. Describe your problem to Vanessa, and respond to Vanessa's advice.

Student B: You are Vanessa. Listen to your caller's problem and give him/her advice.

Now swap roles and Student B describes his/her problem.

Student A – Problems

Favouritism

Hi Vanessa, I'm 20, my brother Paul's 22. My problem is my mum. She's crazy about Paul, she adores him but she couldn't care less about me, and never has. But Paul's wonderful – 'why can't you be more like your brother?' – I hear it all the time.

OK, Paul's practical, thoughtful, the perfect son, fair enough. I'm a bit of a dreamer, I know I do things to get a bit of attention. Can you blame me? Mum's so unfair. Paul can borrow the car whenever he likes, but if I ask, she says 'no'. When we were younger, Paul got the new bicycle, I had to make do with his old one.

Yeah, I'm angry, bitter and rude, so what? I've no self-confidence, I know I'm not going to get anywhere in life. Lucy, my younger sister, says I'm imagining things, she just doesn't understand!

The big risk

Hi Vanessa, I want to know, am I being selfish and behaving stupidly? Or am I a brave person who wants to fulfil their dreams?

I'm American, 42, now living in England. I've got two children, both working. The oldest is married and expecting her first baby in a few months' time. Here's what I want to do. Give up my safe, well-paid job and go to study photography and film in California.

Is it wrong, Vanessa, to live out your dreams? Last year, I bought a sports car – something I couldn't afford when I was younger. That gave me the idea to do the film course.

Everyone thinks I'm crazy to give up my job. My family all think I'm having a mid-life crisis. We argue every day because none of them wants to go to the US with me. My children think I'm completely ridiculous.

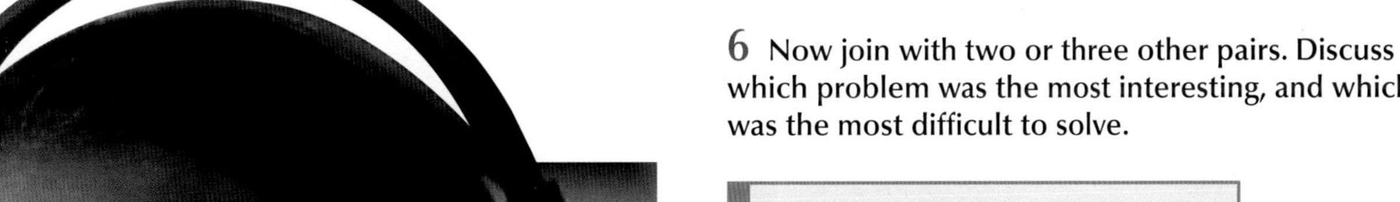

6 Now join with two or three other pairs. Discuss which problem was the most interesting, and which was the most difficult to solve.

OTHER USEFUL PHRASES

Responding to advice

Great, thanks very much.

That's very helpful. Thanks a lot.

That sounds good to me.

All right, I'll think about that.

OK, I'll think it over.

STUDY SKILLS: writing a bibliography, referencing

In academic writing, you need to put references in the text and provide a bibliography.

1 In pairs, discuss whether you think each statement is correct or incorrect.

1 You do not have to reference facts which are general knowledge or accepted beliefs.
2 Referencing is necessary because it enables the reader to understand which ideas are yours and which come from other sources.
3 Your written work looks more professional if you provide references.
4 A quotation should not be more than two sentences.
5 You do not have to reference ideas which have been very loosely paraphrased.
6 Readers are more likely to accept your ideas if you reference the source.
7 If you adapt ideas from other people's original ideas, you don't need to provide a reference to the original author.
8 You will get a better grade for an essay or report if you include a lot of references.

2 Read about the Harvard System of Referencing, and look at the extracts from a bibliography below. Find the three entries which are incorrect, and give your reasons.

1 Adler, A., (1964), *Problems of Neurosis*, New York: Harper and Row.
2 Belmont, M. & Marolla, F.A., 'Birth order, family size, and intelligence', *Science*.
3 Ernst, C. & Angst, J., *Birth Order: Its Influence on Personality*.
4 Leman, K., (1985), *The Birth Order Book: Why You Are the Way You Are*, (http://www.drleman.com), last accessed 14 April 2008.
5 Michalski, R.L. & Shackelford, T.K., (2002), *Personality and Individual Differences*, (http://www.toddkshackelford.com).

Providing references using the Harvard System

Bibliographies

A list of references must be typed in alphabetical order by surname of the author(s), or by title, if there is no author.

For a book, the order is:

Author's surname, initial(s), date of publication in brackets, title in *italics*, place of publication, publisher:

Baddeley, A.D., (1986), *Working Memory*, Oxford: Clarendon Press.

For a paper in a journal, the order is:

Author's surname, initial(s), date in brackets, title of the paper in quotation marks '', name of the journal in *italics*, volume and issue numbers, pages of journal:

MacKay, T., (2000), 'Educational psychology and the future of special education needs' legislation', *Education and Child Psychology*, vol. 17, pp. 27–35.

For a book, article or any document on the web:

The same rules as the above but the web address and the date the page was accessed are given:

(2006), *Peer Pressure*, http://www.psychology/dossier/gov.html, last accessed 7 February 2008.

References within a text

Author's surname, date of publication of the source, page numbers in brackets:

First-born children tend to have higher IQs because they receive more attention from their parents (Marzollo, 1990, pp. 59–63).

Harrigan (1992, p. 54) argues that first-born children tend to be 'perfectionist'.

WRITING SKILLS: a discursive essay

3a Read the essay title below. In pairs / small groups, think of three advantages of being an only child and three disadvantages. Note them down.

It is a big advantage in life to be an only child in a family. To what extent do you agree with this statement?

3b Compare your ideas with other pairs/groups.

4 Read the introduction to an essay on this topic. Why, in the writer's opinion, is this topic worth writing about? What is the writer's purpose in this essay?

In many parts of the world, it is becoming more common for parents to have only one child. An obvious reason for this is that many people are marrying at a later age than they did some years ago. This is an important area of discussion because many people think that being an only child is a big disadvantage in life while others take a different view. This essay presents some of the arguments and considers whether, on balance, it is truly an advantage to be the only child in a family.

5 Linking words Read the next two paragraphs of the essay. There are a number of linking words and phrases which join ideas. Underline each one and say whether it is an example of:

a) adding an important fact.

b) contrasting something with a previous statement.

c) saying that something is the result of something else.

A major advantage of being an only child is that the child gets more attention and financial support from his or her parents. They will help the child with his or her homework, so that the child achieves above-average results at school. In addition, because the only child is the sole focus of the parents' love, he or she develops more confidence and becomes more mature at an early age. Another advantage of being an only child is that they are on their own a lot more. As a result, they learn how to occupy themselves and to become more independent than other children. Furthermore, they are more able to cope with feelings of loneliness.

On the other hand, some people argue that only children miss out on brother and sister relationships as they do not have siblings to share their joys and sorrows. Moreover, it can be argued that children who have siblings are less selfish and learn at an early age how to get on with other people – an important life skill. However, it is true that brothers and sisters often quarrel a lot when they are younger, especially if they are close to each other in age. Only children, therefore, may well have quieter and more peaceful childhoods.

6 Conclusions Read the conclusion of the essay below. Which of the following does it contain?

1 a restatement of the points in the introduction

2 a summary of the main ideas in the essay

3 new evidence or ideas about the topic

4 the writer's opinion

This all suggests that there is no overwhelming argument in favour of being an only child. On the whole, it is not a big advantage in life, even though there is some evidence that only children do better academically. As far as I can see, it really does not matter a great deal whether you are an only child or were brought up with siblings. The important point, surely, is that a child has the love and support of his or her parents.

7a Read the quote and discuss it in pairs. Do you agree with the writer's point of view?

'The desire to be accepted by their peers is perhaps the strongest motivating force during adolescence.'

(Bruce A. Epstein)

7b Write a short essay on this topic, using the Internet to look up some articles or ideas. Include a short bibliography and a few references in the text.

Cultures

In this unit

Grammar
- reported speech
- reporting verbs

Vocabulary
- culture
- adjectives

Scenario
- Kaleidoscope World

Study skills
- improving reading skills

Writing skills
- a formal letter

11.1 DEFINING CULTURE

The limits of my language mean the limits of my world.
Ludwig Wittgenstein, 1889–1951, German philosopher

READING AND VOCABULARY: culture

1a What do you understand by *a culture*? What comes into your mind?

1b What do you think are the typical features of your own national culture?

2 Read the website below quickly and choose an appropriate heading for each section from the box.

Architecture	Climate	Cuisine	Customs/Traditions
Geography	Historical events	Institutions	Language
Life rituals	Religion	Rules of behaviour	The arts	Values

WHAT IS CULTURE?

The word 'culture' has a number of meanings, but in its widest sense it refers to everything that makes up the identity of a particular group of people, society or nation.

1 _____ – the general terrain and physical features such as mountains, rivers, proximity to the sea, whether there is a coastline

2 _____ – weather conditions in different seasons, length of seasons, average temperatures and types of extreme weather if appropriate, e.g. hurricanes, typhoons, droughts

3 _____ – written and spoken means of communication used by a particular group of people; this may include particular dialects, and characteristics of grammar, vocabulary and pronunciation

4 _____ – a particular style of cooking; this will include specialities, unusual dishes and staple diet of a particular area, e.g. rice, potatoes, pasta

5 _____ – things which are considered important to people and tend to guide their lives, e.g. attitudes to family, money, honesty, superstitions, nature, animals

6 _____ – characteristic styles of music, theatre, film, painting, opera, literature, etc. and their relative importance and status

7 _____ – particular faith/belief systems, e.g. Islam, Christianity, Buddhism, Judaism, including sects within a particular tradition

8 _____ – unspoken/unwritten ways of doing things, e.g. rules of etiquette and manners regarding how to eat, socialise, dress, drive, greet and address each other; punctuality, tipping, the way people treat each other (male/female/adults/children), etc.

9 _____ – particular national/public holidays, feast days, festivals (e.g. carnivals), commemorations, anniversaries and activities associated with and performed on these occasions

10 _____ – (civil) wars, invasions, revolutions, famines, natural disasters, etc.

11 _____ – birth, marriage, maturity, employment, retirement, death, and how these are treated

12 _____ – the political system and type of government and/or monarchy, the legal system, education, financial system

13 _____ – characteristic style of buildings and interior design; also common building materials used, ratio of old/new buildings, the built environment and its heritage

Professor Mancini. Institute of Cultural Studies (ICS)

Done

3a Look at these definitions for words and expressions from the website. Which section do you think you might find each of the words in?

a) kind of food eaten every day
b) particular linguistic form (often spoken)
c) ways of behaving politely
d) belief that some things are lucky/unlucky
e) particular type of land
f) a date on which we remember something special or important from the past
g) small group with particular beliefs and practices
h) traditional aspects of parts of a culture, e.g. building

3b Find the words or expressions on the website which match the definitions in Exercise 3a.

3c Select three or four of the words from Exercise 3b to discuss. Give an example from your country, or another country you know well.

4 In pairs or small groups, discuss the questions.

1 Which of the 13 factors listed in the text do you think are the most important in defining a culture?
2 Was there anything in the list which surprised you? Why?
3 Which factors do you think make your culture different from those of other countries? (Think about countries which are far away and those that are near neighbours.)
4 Are there aspects of any other cultures which you admire? What? Why?

LISTENING

5 What do/would you miss about your culture when you are abroad?

6a 3.12 Listen to six people answering the question in Exercise 5. Which person misses which of these things?

a) the sound of rain
b) expressing ideas in their own language
c) the smell of coffee
d) jokes and loud laughter
e) a special drink
f) cycling everywhere

6b Listen again. What does ...

1 Ayla say about Turkish hospitality?
2 Carola say about supermarkets in Germany?
3 Anna say about Russian friendship?
4 Danielle say about food in Cameroon?
5 Alessandra say about hearing her dialect of Italian?
6 Nancy say about making arrangements in Argentina?

7 Which of the speakers' opinions is most like yours? Is there anything which the speakers said which you thought of? Has anything you have heard changed your ideas from Exercise 5?

SPEAKING

8a In groups, agree on 12 items to be placed in a time capsule which will be opened in 200 years' time. Choose the items which you think best represent your culture as it is today.

A time capsule is a sealed container filled with objects. It is then buried in the ground and not opened until some time in the future. The idea behind this is to communicate to people in the future about what life is like now.

8b Join with another group and explain the content of your time capsule and the reasons for your choices.

CULTURE SHOCK

READING

1 Look at the quote. Do you agree with it?

'A fish only discovers its need for water when it is no longer in it. Our own culture is like water to a fish. It sustains us. We live and breathe through it.'
(Dr F. Trompenaars)

2 Skim the advice leaflet for foreign students. Choose a title for each Extract, A and B, of the leaflet.

A ______________________

Culture shock describes the impact of moving from a familiar culture to one which is unfamiliar. It is an experience described by people who have travelled abroad to work, live or study; it can be felt to a certain extent even when abroad on holiday. It can affect anyone, including international students. It includes the shock of a new environment, meeting lots of new people and learning the ways of a different country. It also includes the shock of being separated from the important people in your life, maybe family, friends, colleagues, teachers: people you would normally talk to at times of uncertainty, people who give you support and guidance. When familiar sights, sounds, smells or tastes are no longer there you can miss them very much.

3 Read Extract B again and match these descriptions with the five stages.

a) You enjoy the social, psychological and cultural differences and feel at home.
b) You can now move around the country without a feeling of anxiety.
c) You may begin to criticise the country and the values of the people.
d) You are fascinated by all the new sights, sounds, smells and tastes.
e) You may feel lonely and have a sense of loss.

B ______________________

The process (of culture shock) can be broken down into five stages:

1 The 'honeymoon' stage
When you first arrive in a new culture, differences are intriguing and you may feel excited, stimulated and curious. At this stage you are still protected by the close memory of your home culture.

2 The 'distress' stage
A little later, differences create an impact and you may feel confused, isolated or inadequate as cultural differences intrude and familiar supports (e.g. family or friends) are not immediately available.

3 The 're-integration' stage
Next, you may reject the differences you encounter. You may feel angry or frustrated, or hostile to the new culture. At this stage you may be conscious mainly of how much you dislike it compared to home. Don't worry, as this is quite a healthy reaction. You are reconnecting with what you value about yourself and your own culture.

4 The 'autonomy' stage
Differences and similarities are accepted. You may feel relaxed, confident, more like an old hand as you become more familiar with situations and feel well able to cope with new situations based on your growing experience.

5 The 'independence' stage
Differences and similarities are valued and important. You may feel full of potential and able to trust yourself in all kinds of situations. Most situations become enjoyable and you are able to make choices according to your preferences and values.

4 Discuss the following questions.

1 Have you lived in another culture, or do you know someone who has? What have been your/their experiences with culture shock?

2 What countries have a similar culture to your own?

3 What do you think reverse culture shock might be?

VOCABULARY: adjectives

5a Look at the following adjectives from the leaflet. Which are positive and which are negative?

stimulated intriguing isolated inadequate frustrated hostile

5b Check the meanings of the adjectives in a dictionary and complete these sentences.

1 It was such an _____ story, so unusual and mysterious.

2 They hope the students will feel _____ by the talk.

3 She's quite angry at the moment and feels _____ towards British culture.

4 The old people felt so lonely and _____.

5 The teacher made us feel _____ and stupid if we made mistakes.

6 I get really _____ and impatient with my computer sometimes.

LISTENING

6a 3.13 Listen to someone talking about his experience of culture shock. What were the main problems he experienced?

6b Listen again. Are the statements true or false?

1 He had culture shock all the time he was in Chicago.

2 He didn't like anything about Chicago.

3 He hated the winter but liked the summer.

4 The cafés were too hot in the summer.

5 He is experiencing culture shock in England at the moment.

6 He knows more about ice hockey than football.

GRAMMAR: reported speech

7a Look at these reported statements. Underline the actual words used in Track 3.13 on page 187.

1 He said he had emigrated to Chicago just over ten years before.

2 He said that he didn't enjoy living there.

3 He said the countryside outside the city was stunning and the people were wonderful.

4 He said that when he went outside, the cold would hit his face within minutes.

5 He said he is just not fitting in at the moment.

7b Look at sentences 1 and 2 in Exercise 7a. What changes do we make when we report speech?

8a What is different about sentences 3–5 in Exercise 7a?

8b Here are three reasons for not changing the direct speech verb in reported speech. Match the reasons with sentences 3–5.

a) The action or situation in the indirect speech is still happening/ true.

b) The reported verb expresses a fact or situation that cannot or is unlikely to change.

c) The verb comes immediately after a time conjunction, e.g. *when, after*.

➡ Language reference and extra practice, pages 154–155

9 Susan has recently returned to England from Japan. Report the following things she said. Change the tense of the verb only if necessary.

1 I studied the language before I went.

2 I lived in a tiny studio flat while I was there.

3 The trains were crowded, but were always on time – as they still are.

4 I gave chocolates to my boss once – and he was really surprised.

5 I really miss Japan and would love to go back.

6 I often go to Japanese restaurants to eat Japanese food.

7 Yesterday, I bought a ticket for a holiday in Japan.

8 I can't wait to get back there!

SPEAKING AND WRITING

10 You are going to read two blogs about studying in a foreign country, to discuss with your partner.

Student A: turn to page 159.

Student B: turn to page 165.

11 Write a letter to a pen friend who is coming to study in your country. Give him/her advice on how to cope with culture shock.

LISTENING

1 **Have you ever made any cultural mistakes? What were they?**

2a **3.14** **Listen to two people talking about mistakes they made when visiting other countries. Where were they and what mistakes did they make?**

2b **Listen again and complete these sentences.**

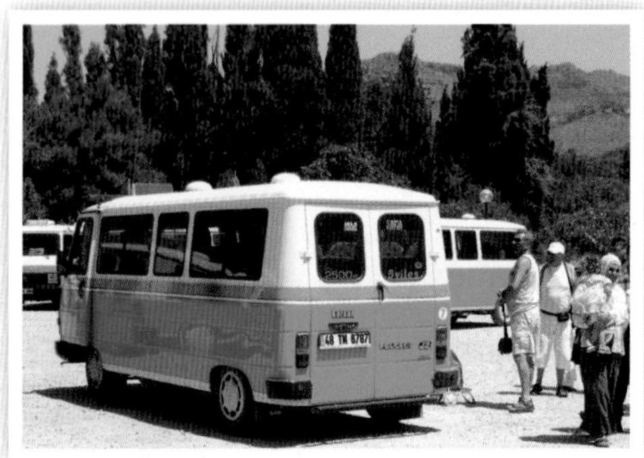

1 My wife __________ there by *dolmus*.
2 I __________ the money and __________ it to him.
3 He __________ not to get on his bus again. I __________ by *dolmus* ...
4 I'd __________ the orientation programme because I'd been to Malaga ...
5 ... my hosts had __________ me up at nine o'clock and that I'd __________ them ...
6 They __________ lots of different dishes.
7 They nearly fell off their chairs laughing and __________ forget about eating any more food.

GRAMMAR: reporting verbs

3 **Look at the verbs you have written in Exercise 2b and add them to the chart.**

verb + *to* + infinitive	*offer*
verb + object + *to* + infinitive	*invite*
verb + *-ing* form	*consider*
verb + preposition + *-ing* form	*insist on*

➡ Language reference and extra practice, pages 154–155

4 **We often use verbs like the ones in the chart to report speech. Report the underlined parts of the sentences, using some of the verbs from the chart.**

1 '<u>You should study your heritage</u>.'
2 'Yes, I think <u>I did sound a bit rude</u>.'
3 '<u>We really must treat everyone equally</u>. It's really important.'
4 '<u>You really should think about it for a few more days</u>.' 'OK, I will.'
5 '<u>Don't come into my shop again!</u> I'll phone the police next time!'
6 '<u>I shouldn't have left university early</u>. It was a stupid move.'
7 'I haven't done anything wrong. <u>I'm not going to resign</u>.'
8 '<u>I'm sorry I was so late</u>.'

1 She encouraged me to study my heritage.

5a **In groups of three, look at your prompts and make sentences.**

Student A: turn to page 159.
Student B: turn to page 165.
Student C: turn to page 167.

5b **Now tell and report your sentences. Student A reads a sentence to Student B, who reports it to Student C. Then change roles.**

Student A: *I'll take notes and photocopy them for you.*
Student B: *Henri offered to take notes and photocopy them for me.*

READING

6a **What other cultures are you aware of in your country?**

6b **Read texts A and B opposite. What are the main differences between the opinions of the two writers?**

7 **Choose the most appropriate answer.**

1 Text A argues for the following.
   a) Doctors should treat symptoms of illness.
   b) We should all understand the causes of illness.
   c) We should all be culturally aware.
2 Text A argues that
   a) thinking about other people's behaviours and beliefs is strange.
   b) it is very easy to describe what other people believe and how they behave as strange.
   c) our own ways of behaving are perfectly normal.

3 Text B states that
   a) small differences don't get into the newspapers.
   b) it is important to know how close you should get to someone on public transport.
   c) small cultural differences are unimportant.

4 Text B states that
   a) multiculturalism can work in certain circumstances.
   b) multicultural communities should be easy to establish.
   c) your kids' education is more important than being able to find a job.

8a Which of the words below suggest a style closer to Text A and which closer to Text B? You may choose more than one word to describe each text.

textbook blog email essay formal informal chatty distant

A

Cultural differences

A knowledge of differences between cultures, in an ever-shrinking globalised world, is becoming one of the essential key skills that modern 'citizens of the world' need to possess in order to work and learn effectively. At a superficial level this involves knowing about food or body taboos. For example, some cultures don't eat meat, cows can be sacred, the head must not be touched. But while it is important to know about these things, if this is where your intercultural knowledge stops, you will still end up offending people or being misunderstood.

More important than superficial behaviour is the value system of a culture. In the same way that a good doctor needs to understand underlying causes rather than just treat symptoms, the culturally aware individual needs to have not only a knowledge of publicly visible behaviours and stated beliefs, but also an awareness of the underlying value systems of cultures that shape those behaviours and stated beliefs.

Of course, these belief systems can be very different from one's own, and it is very easy to label other people's behaviours and beliefs as strange. It is more difficult to accept that one's own ways of behaving, which seem perfectly normal, can be seen as strange and even rude in another culture. But unless one tries to observe one's own culture objectively and have an understanding of why other cultures do things differently, it is inevitable that cultural mistakes will be made.

Done

8b What examples of differences in style can you find between the two texts? Think about:

- the pronouns that are used.
- the formality of the vocabulary and grammar.
- questions in the text.

9 Look at the texts on page 173 and say whether each is closer in style to Text A or Text B.

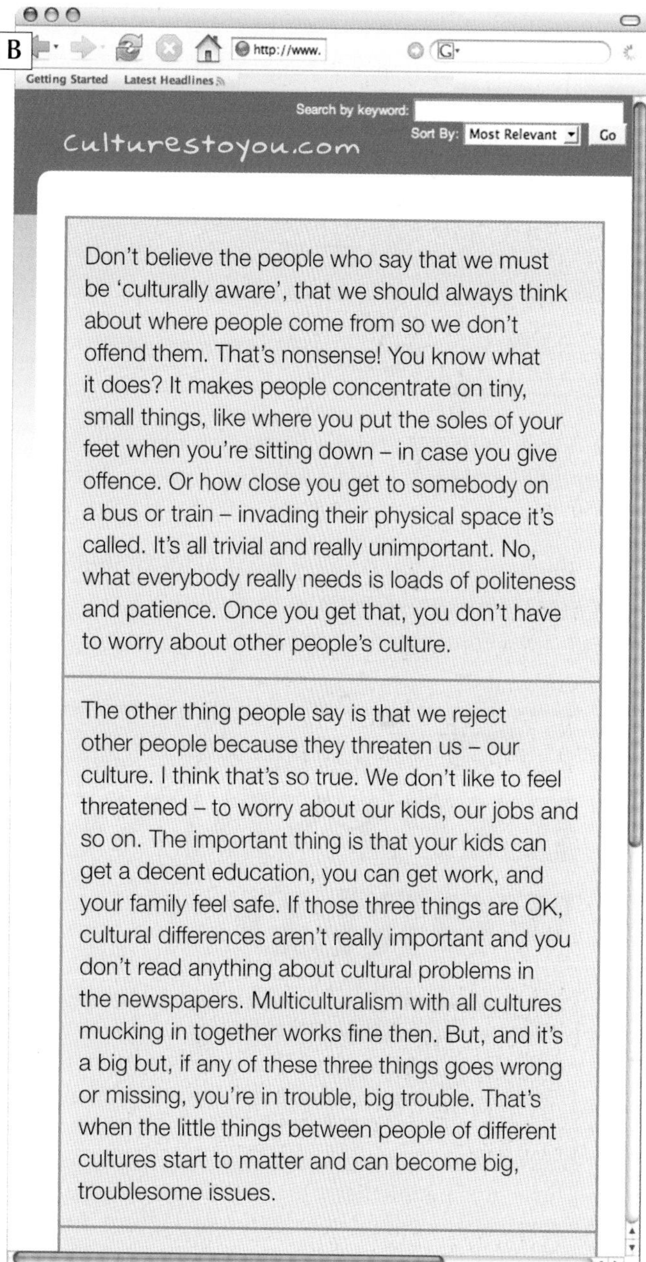
B

http://www.

Getting Started Latest Headlines

Search by keyword:

Sort By: Most Relevant Go

Culturestoyou.com

Don't believe the people who say that we must be 'culturally aware', that we should always think about where people come from so we don't offend them. That's nonsense! You know what it does? It makes people concentrate on tiny, small things, like where you put the soles of your feet when you're sitting down – in case you give offence. Or how close you get to somebody on a bus or train – invading their physical space it's called. It's all trivial and really unimportant. No, what everybody really needs is loads of politeness and patience. Once you get that, you don't have to worry about other people's culture.

The other thing people say is that we reject other people because they threaten us – our culture. I think that's so true. We don't like to feel threatened – to worry about our kids, our jobs and so on. The important thing is that your kids can get a decent education, you can get work, and your family feel safe. If those three things are OK, cultural differences aren't really important and you don't read anything about cultural problems in the newspapers. Multiculturalism with all cultures mucking in together works fine then. But, and it's a big but, if any of these three things goes wrong or missing, you're in trouble, big trouble. That's when the little things between people of different cultures start to matter and can become big, troublesome issues.

Done

SPEAKING

10 Work in groups of four to have a debate on the motion *Cultural differences are important*. Students A and B are for the motion; Students C and D are against.

11.4 SCENARIO

SITUATION

1 **Work in pairs to think of a foreign country you would like to visit. Explain why the country interests you.**

2 **If you visited the country, what kinds of things would you do to learn about its culture?**

visit a museum, do an official tour, ...

28 **News**

EXPANDING WORLD

KALEIDOSCOPE WORLD, the prestigious cultural exchange organisation, is set to expand its network of destinations. Founded back in the 1960s, it has been operating cultural exchange programmes with the involvement of about 30 countries around the world for the past 40 years. These give people aged 18–25 the opportunity to experience a completely different culture from their own for a short time. These visits have been highly praised for their benefits by academics and writers. Some governments however have been critical of the organisation and its aims. Funding comes partly from government grants and partly from donations. A spokesman explained, 'In these troubled times Kaleidoscope World has decided to step up its activities and reach out to young people all across the world.'

3 **Read the newspaper article and the advert, and answer the questions.**

1 What is the purpose of Kaleidoscope World?
2 Where does it get its money from?
3 What do you think are the benefits mentioned in the text?
4 What do you think are the criticisms mentioned in the text?
5 What change is taking place?

Calling all TOURIST BOARDS

- Are you proud of your culture and heritage?
- Do you think people in other countries misunderstand your way of life?
- Do you want to improve your country's image around the world?

If you answered YES to any of the above, read on.

KALEIDOSCOPE WORLD

invites presentations in English from tourist boards around the world wishing to become destinations for our popular and successful cultural exchange programmes.

For further details go to: www.kaleidoscopeworld.com

Kaleidoscope World 11.4

4a 3.15 **Listen to Part 1 of a presentation made by a representative of the Toronto tourist board to the Kaleidoscope World organisation. Answer the questions.**

1 How many sections are there in the presentation?
2 What does the presenter say about questions?
3 Which of the following are mentioned in the first part of the presentation?
population climate location type of city

4b 3.16 **Listen to Part 2 and answer the question: what three sights are recommended? Why?**

4c 3.17 **Listen to Part 3 and answer the question: what three activities are suggested for visitors to try and do?**

KEY LANGUAGE: creating impact in a presentation

5a 3.18 **Listen to part of the presentation again. Complete the examples of the techniques.**

Tripling (saying things in threes)

1 ... it's an important industrial, _____ and _____ centre.
2 ... they help to create the _____, friendly, _____ atmosphere the city is famous for.

Repetition

3 Toronto's getting _____ and _____ these days, as _____ and _____ people come from all over the world ...

Rhetorical questions

(These help to create anticipation in the minds of the audience.)

4 So, _____ are the main _____ of the city?
5 OK, _____ is the CN Tower _____ seeing?

5b **Now look at Tracks 3.15–3.17 on page 188 and find other examples of the techniques described in Exercise 5a.**

TASK: giving a formal presentation

6a **You work for the tourist board of your home town (or city/region). You are going to prepare and deliver a five-minute presentation to Kaleidoscope World. Use the notes below to prepare your presentation.**

- The purpose of the presentation is to persuade the Kaleidoscope World agents to include your town/city/region in their list of destinations for cultural visits.
- The presentation should have an introduction and conclusion.
- The main body of the presentation should be structured in the following way:

  A three key pieces of background information, e.g. location, climate, population, history

  B three places to visit / main sights

  C three other things a visitor should try/do, e.g. special food, sporting events, customs, traditions, festivals.
- Try to use some of the techniques for creating impact in your presentation.

6b **Students give their presentation to other groups. Choose the best presentation(s).**

OTHER USEFUL PHRASES

Starting

Good morning everyone. I'd like to talk to you today about ...

Signalling structure

The presentation is organised into three sections.

I'll begin with ... Next, ... and lastly, ...

Moving on

Turning to the next part, ...

Let's now look at ...

Summarising

In conclusion I would just like to say ...

To summarise ...

Inviting questions

Now if there are any questions, I'll be happy to try and answer them.

Please feel free to ask any questions and I'll do my best to answer them.

11.5 STUDY AND

STUDY SKILLS: improving reading skills

1a What sort of reader are you? Work in pairs to discuss which of the following techniques you use when you read in English. Do you …

1 focus on headings and subheadings?
2 only look at summaries and conclusions?
3 read every word very carefully?
4 predict what comes next?
5 ask yourself questions about what you are reading?
6 use your finger to help you follow what you read?
7 have questions to which you want to know the answers before you read?
8 read aloud?
9 focus on the unknown vocabulary?

1b How important are the techniques? Decide on the three or four most important ones for you.

2a 3.19 Listen to part of a radio programme on the subject of reading and answer the questions.

1 Who is the guest and what has she written?
2 What does she say about the benefits of reading?
3 What advice does she give?

2b Listen again. Tick the techniques in the list in Exercise 1a that the guest mentions.

3 Ways to improve your reading There are different techniques for improving reading speed and ability. Do the exercises to try them out.

a Reading and chunking

If you want to improve reading speed, it's important to look at groups of words rather than individual words. You can read the sentence below one word at a time:

All / cultures / develop / from / a / range / of / diverse / influences.

However it is better to 'chunk' groups of words as below:

All cultures / develop from / a range of / diverse influences.

The cosmopolitan atmosphere / of many world cities / is a result of / centuries of immigration.

How are the sentences above chunked? Do you notice any patterns?
Divide these sentences into appropriate chunks.

1 He wrote a brief history of Western culture.
2 Many people argue that American culture will soon take over the world.
3 Cultural Studies is becoming an increasingly popular university course.

b Reading and vocabulary: guessing unknown words

Often identifying the type of word can help with meaning. The context will help you decide if the unknown word is a verb, noun or adjective. Prefixes and suffixes can also be very helpful.

Match the prefixes below with their meanings.

1 **pre**date	a) after
2 **inter**national	b) before
3 **post**war	c) between
4 **multi**cultural	d) many
5 **sub**culture	e) opposite
6 **mis**understanding	f) bad or wrong
7 **anti**social	g) against
8 **counter**culture	h) under

Identify the suffixes in the words below. Decide if they are noun or adjective suffixes.

1 sociology	5 responsible
2 sexism	6 development
3 timeless	7 communication
4 valuable	

Add some more words with the same suffixes.

Look back at the texts on page 117 and identify as many prefixes and suffixes as you can (look for verbs, nouns and adjectives).

c Reading and understanding: linkers

Focusing on linking expressions will help you to understand how the ideas in a text are connected.

Match the common formal linking expressions with their functions to make sentences.

1 alternatively	a) adds something
2 on the contrary	b) introduces a result
3 provided that	c) gives the purpose of something
4 in addition	d) introduces a surprising piece of information
5 similarly	e) introduces another choice
6 nevertheless	f) suggests a condition
7 in order to	g) makes a comparison
8 therefore	h) makes a contrast

4a Work in pairs. You each read a different text, then summarise your text orally for your partner. What ideas are similar in both texts?

Student A: turn to page 160.

Student B: turn to page 166.

4b Identify the prefixes, suffixes and linking phrases in your text. How did you chunk the text as you read? Discuss with your partner.

WRITING SKILLS 11.5

WRITING SKILLS: a formal letter

5 Letter layout Match 1–12 below with A–L on the diagram of a formal letter.

1 greeting (*Dear Sir/Madam* or *Dear Mr/Mrs/Miss/Ms* + name)
2 main message of letter
3 writer's address
4 subject heading (where appropriate)
5 date
6 writer's name and position
7 ending (*Yours faithfully* or *Yours sincerely*)
8 signature
9 reference to previous contact or reason for contact
10 address of recipient
11 reference to future contact
12 closing remarks

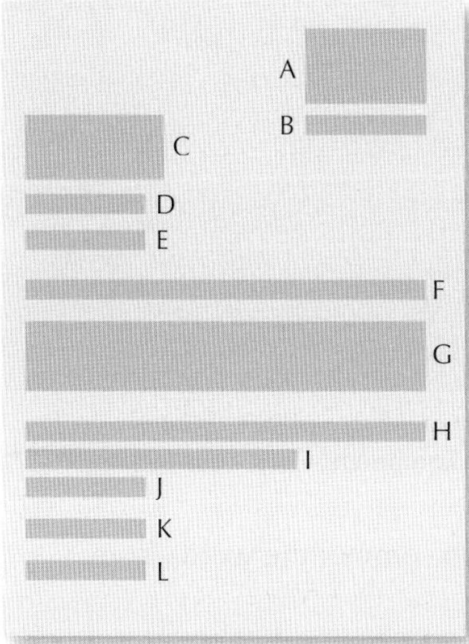

6a Formulaic language The language of formal letters is very formulaic, i.e. we tend to use the same expressions again and again. Complete the expressions below with words from the box.

assistance contacted enclosed forward future hesitate information question reference writing

1 I look _____ to hearing from you in the near _____.
2 I am _____ with _____ to (your advertisement).
3 If I can be of any further _____, please do not _____ to contact me.
4 Please find _____ a copy of my (CV) for your _____.
5 Regarding the _____ of (the conference dates), I think …
6 I can be _____ at the above email address at any time.

6b Match the sentences in Exercise 6a with their functions.

a) reason for contact
b) how to get in touch
c) including something with your letter
d) reference to the future
e) closing remark
f) reference to an issue

7 In small groups, read the advertisement and discuss the questions in it.

UNICORNTELEVISION

Unicorn Television is commissioning a series on the history and influence of youth cultures around the world, to be called 'Street Styles'.

We would like to hear from people all over the world who would be willing to be interviewed on any of the following points:

1 Do youth cultures give young people a sense of identity?
2 Are youth cultures a problem for parents?
3 What are your personal experiences of youth cultures?
4 Are youth cultures a normal part of growing up?
5 What are the main youth cultures in your country?
6 Are youth cultures simply a way for business to exploit the young?
7 Do youth cultures pose a danger to society?

Please write to the following address stating your age, availability, and include a recent photograph.
The Commissioning Editor
Unicorn Television
Forest Lane
London W1
All replies will be acknowledged.

8 Write a letter in reply to the advertisement. In your letter you should do the following:

- refer to the advertisement
- give the topic you would be willing to answer questions on
- briefly state your views/experience of youth cultures
- say when you will be available
- make a closing remark
- refer to the future

12 Technology

In this unit

Grammar
- conditionals

Vocabulary
- technology
- opposites (prefixes)

Scenario
- Computer crash

Study skills
- plagiarism – what it is and how to avoid it

Writing skills
- an article

12.1 DEVICES AND GADGETS

There is no reason anyone would want a computer in their home.
Ken Olsen, 1926–, Chairman, Digital Equipment Corp. (quote from 1977)

VOCABULARY: technology

1 Discuss these questions.

1 What are the three items of technology you use most often?
2 Are you technologically minded or are you a technophobe?
3 What do you think is the greatest technological innovation? Give your reasons.

2a Look up the following words in a dictionary. Check if they are countable or uncountable. What are the common collocations?

apparatus appliance device engine equipment gadget machine

2b Complete the questions with some of the words from Exercise 2a.

1 How many household _____ can you name?
2 How often should you upgrade your computer _____?
3 How often do you use a cash _____ to get money?
4 What do you think is the most useful labour-saving _____?
5 What other clever _____ can you think of, e.g. satellite navigation system, compass, can opener, MP3 player?
6 What is the name of the breathing _____ which divers use so they can stay underwater?

2c Work in pairs to ask and answer the questions.

3a Find two adjectives in the box which match each of these concepts.

1 non-polluting　2 very new　3 old-fashioned
4 simple to operate　5 long-lasting　6 useful

cutting edge durable easy to use environmentally friendly green handy hard-wearing obsolete out-of-date practical state-of-the-art user-friendly

3b Look at the objects below. Use some of the adjectives to describe them.

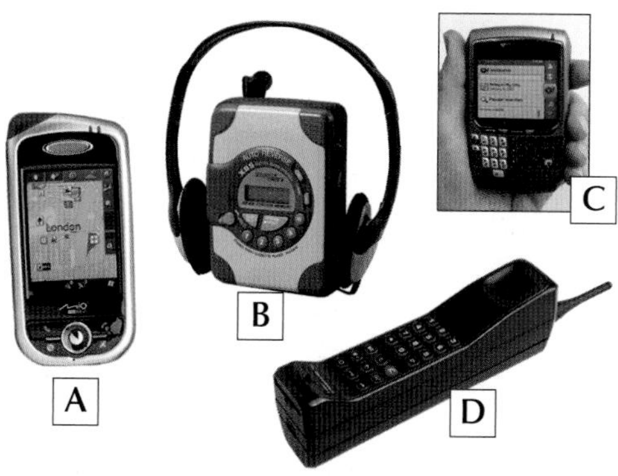

3c Think about some items of technology you own. Which of the qualities listed in Exercise 3a does each one have?

LISTENING

4a 3.20 Listen to three people describing technological equipment and answer the questions.

1 What piece of technology is mentioned by each speaker?
2 What do they like/dislike about the technology they mention?

4b Discuss a piece of technology you like or dislike, giving your reasons.

READING

5 What inventions do you associate these names with?

Alexander Graham Bell W.H. Hoover
King Camp Gillette Lazlo Biro
John Boyd Dunlop Elisha Otis
Orville and Wilbur Wright (the Wright brothers)

6a Work in groups of three. Each of you reads the introduction and one of the texts on this page or on pages 166 and 168. Answer the questions.

1 Who is the text about?
2 What did the person do?
3 When did they do it?
4 Why did they fail?
5 What recent developments have there been?

6b Exchange information about your texts.

The Nearly men

Technological advance is not a smooth process. Often the pioneers don't get the credit they deserve, or they pay the price for being first. Sometimes they fail to protect their ideas by taking out a patent. In this short article our correspondent celebrates three of these unsung heroes responsible for some of the most important pieces of communication technology.

Up in the air

Percy Pilcher was an English engineer and pioneer aviator. In the 1890s he built and flew a glider called 'the Hawk'. However, Pilcher's dream was to achieve powered flight. He built another 'soaring machine', this time with an engine. In September 1899, he was ready to make his first test flight. Unfortunately, the engine broke, and not wanting to disappoint the audience, he decided to fly his 'Hawk' glider instead. Tragically, he crashed and died of his injuries two days later. As there was no one to carry on his work, his designs were lost. The American Wright brothers were to achieve the first powered flight four years later on 17 December 1903. In 2003, at the time of the centenary of powered flight, a replica of Pilcher's plane was built and flown, achieving a controlled flight of one minute and 26 seconds, significantly longer than the Wright brothers' first flight of 59 seconds.

SPEAKING AND WRITING

7 Work in small groups to discuss the following statements. Think of arguments for and against each one.

1 People rely on technology too much these days.
2 The pace of technological change is too fast in some countries.
3 Inventors of new technology should share ideas, not protect them.
4 Technology can solve all the world's problems.
5 Technology often leads to social and environmental problems.

8 Write a short text (100–150 words) giving your opinion (for or against) about one of the above statements.

READING

1 Look at the photos on these pages which were taken recently. What is unusual about them? Why?

2a Look at these questions from a website about the Amish community in North America. Read the website and match the questions with the answers.

1 I'm going to Pennsylvania next month and may meet some Amish. Why do people say they are so different?
2 Is there any way I can find out more about them?
3 Do they ever use modern technology? I mean, imagine one of them had to go to hospital for an operation – would that be OK?
4 Why do they live in such an old-fashioned way?

2b Answer the questions in Exercise 2a.

3 Read the website again. Do the Amish value or reject the following ideas?

simplicity self-sufficiency equality close-knit community privacy independence from the outside world material comforts modern technology

4 What do you think of the Amish's attitude to modern technology?

VOCABULARY: opposites

5a Find the opposites in the text of these words.

appropriate convenient efficient equality like likely trust

5b What other opposites can you think of beginning with *in-*, *dis-*, *mis-* or *un-*?

6 Complete the following text using the opposites of the words in the box.

able accurate ~~effective~~ efficient equality management necessary sensitive

Various problems have been found in the US health service in a recent report. It stated that US citizens spend around $300 billion on [1]*ineffective*, inappropriate and [2]_____ treatments. It suggested that the failure to use information technology properly was due to [3]_____ administration, poor coordination and [4]_____. It is [5]_____ to say the expertise in health information technology is not there. The US health care system leads the world in innovation. However, the system has been accused of [6]_____, with some people [7]_____ to afford private health care insurance. Patient feedback, however, is more concerned with over-long waiting times, customer service and [8]_____ staff.

Lancaster County, Pennsylvania

Amish FAQs • Amish-made furniture • Amish quilts

Amish: Frequently

A ____________________

People say they are different because of their plain style of dress, limited use of technology, such as cars and electricity, and their simple way of life. If you visit an Amish area, you'll see women in long dresses and people travelling in buggies drawn by horses. And if you pass an Amish farm, you'll notice farm equipment being pulled by horses. You're unlikely to get to know any of the Amish, but if you were invited into an Amish home, you'd find no televisions, no telephones and no kitchen appliances run by electricity. The Amish are different and wish to separate themselves from mainstream society. They do not join the military, pay social security or accept financial assistance from the government.

B ____________________

The Amish value simplicity and self-sufficiency. They are not inefficient. They just do not wish to depend on the outside world or on modern technology. The conveniences that we take for granted, such as electricity, television, cars and tractors are thought to create inequality and to lead the Amish away from their close-knit community. They are considered inappropriate and are not encouraged or accepted. The Amish believe in equality and they are not attracted by material comforts. They live in a separate world, with its own values, the most important of which is a mistrust of anything modern, especially modern technology.

GRAMMAR: conditionals (1)

7a Complete the following sentences, then check them in the text.

1 If you visit an Amish area, you _____ women in long dresses ...

2 If you _____ invited into an Amish home, you _____ no televisions ...

7b Which of these is a first conditional? Which is a second conditional? Find other examples of these two conditionals in the text.

7c Which conditional describes an imaginary or unlikely situation? Which describes a future possibility?

➡ Language reference and extra practice, pages 156–157

Amish faith • History of the Amish • Amish videos

Asked Questions

C ____________________

The Amish do compromise with the modern world, as long as it is strictly necessary. They dislike the telephone as it interferes with their separation from the world. It brings the outside world into their home and is an intrusion into their privacy. But, supposing that an Amish had to make an important telephone call, they would go to a small outbuilding usually located at an inconvenient distance from their home. And, to answer the second part of the question, if they had to go to hospital, they would be able to ride in cars and travel in planes. One final example: the Amish will even allow the use of modern farm equipment, provided that it is pulled by teams of horses and not tractors.

D ____________________

You can search the Internet. But another way to find out more about the Amish is to watch the film *Witness*, starring Harrison Ford. Many think the film portrayed Amish lifestyle fairly accurately, although it showed a limited segment of Amish lifestyle. A lot of Amish had reservations about the film because it was filmed in the geographical area of the Amish but not on a real Amish farm, and obviously the actors were not Amish.

8 Put the verbs into the correct conditional form according to the likelihood of the condition.

1 He's always late. If he _____ (be) late again this week, I _____ him (fire).

2 If you _____ (wait) a moment, I _____ the technician (call). He'll come immediately.

3 If I _____ (have) enough money, I _____ (buy) a Ferrari – what a dream!

4 Look, if you _____ (buy) this computer now, I _____ (give) you a free MP3 player.

5 Are you around later? If I _____ (have) enough time, I _____ (call) you.

6 If I _____ (know) the answer, I _____ (tell) you, but I don't.

9a Find the following conjunctions in Part C of the website (including the question). Which word can they all replace in conditional sentences?

as long as imagine provided that supposing that

9b Which two of the conjunctions introduce a strict condition (*only if X happens ...*)? Which two introduce imaginary situations?

10 Correct the following sentences. (Some can be corrected in two ways.)

1 I'd buy you an MP3 player as long as you agree to study harder.

2 Would you be interested in investing in more technology, if you have the chance?

3 If I start this technology course again, I think I'd do it differently.

4 Imagine you had a million pounds – what will you do with it?

5 Supposing that the computer crashed, who will you phone?

6 You can borrow my MP3 player provided that you would bring it back tomorrow.

11 In pairs, write sentences based on the following prompts. Think about whether the situation is possible or unlikely.

1 ice cap melt / next 20 years / coastal towns / flood

2 scientists find / cure for cancer / people / live longer

3 government / not invest in medicine / patients / suffer

4 computer games / ban / children / happier

5 fewer people drive / roads / safer

6 sun / get much hotter / Earth / in danger

SPEAKING

12 In small groups, discuss how you would manage without technology. What would you miss? What would you find most difficult?

READING

1 What is your opinion of genetically modified food? What about the use of chemicals in food production?

2a Read the first paragraph of the article. Which statement is closest to the author's opinion, do you think? Which is what many other people think?

a) Technical innovation is frightening and goes against human nature.
b) The technological rate of change is different now from 40 years ago.
c) Technological innovation is good news for human development.

2b Now read the whole article and check your answers.

3 Read the article again and answer the questions.

1 What took half a century to be used by 25 percent of people in the US?
2 What are commonly used in computers nowadays?
3 How big is the gadget that destroys cancer cells?
4 What would be the advantage of removing gossypol from cotton?
5 What is 'golden rice'?
6 When would it be impossible to regulate certain technologies?

4 Look at the article and find an example of the following ways the author shows his opinion.

The author:

1 uses an imperative to appeal to the reader to agree with him (paragraph 2) ... *imagine that now.*
2 asks a rhetorical question which he immediately answers (para. 2)
3 states his opposition to others' opinions and gives a reason for it (para. 3)
4 comments forcefully on the call to reject new technologies (para. 4)
5 uses an inclusive pronoun to draw the audience in (para. 5)
6 uses a negative modal verb to show his strength of feeling (para. 5)

5 Look at the text again and find sentences that are pro-technology and anti-technology.

GRAMMAR: conditionals (2)

6 Look at the following example and complete it. Check your answers in the text, then answer the questions.

If these groups _____ not opposed its development so strongly, it _____ _____ been produced ...

1 Did the groups oppose the development?
2 Did scientists produce 'golden rice'?
3 Which conditional is this?
4 When do we use it?

7a Look at these sentences from the article and answer the questions.

1 If [these groups] *had been* less critical, thousands of children in poorer areas *would not be* blind today.
2 If we *devoted* more resources to modern technology, we *could have avoided* many modern-day problems.

a) Which conditional sentence looks at a present condition with a past result?
b) Which conditional sentence looks at a past condition with a present result?

No going back to nature

Ray Kurzweil

1 The times, they are a-changing – and a lot more quickly today than when Bob Dylan sang those words 40 years ago. We are doubling the rate of technological innovation every ten years. Great news for human development, you'd have thought. Not everyone thinks so. Many people are fearful of this pace of progress in science and technology, and the way it is challenging basic ideas about the nature of human life. As a result, they are doing their best to hold it up.

2 The modern world must be an alarming place for anti-technology movements, given the extraordinary pace of development. Whereas the telephone took 50 years to be adopted by a quarter of the US population, the cellphone did that in just seven. Five years ago most people didn't use search engines; imagine that now. Greater changes are on the way, such as the use of RNA interference, which can turn genes off, and gene therapy, which can add new ones. Scientists at the Massachusetts Institute of Technology have designed a device the size of a blood cell that can find and destroy cancer cells in the bloodstream; within 20 years, each of us could have millions of them in our bodies keeping us healthy. By the 2030s, we will be more non-biological than biological. Will that make us less human? I don't believe so. We have always extended our mental and physical reach with technology in a way no other species has.

7b Now complete the formation rules.

In sentence 1 we use *if* + ______, + *would/should/might/could* + infinitive.

In sentence 2 we use *if* + ______, + *would/should/might/could* + *have* + ______ participle.

➡ Language reference and extra practice, pages 156–157

8 Match the parts of the conditional sentences, 1–7 with a–g. Some are third conditional, some mixed (both types).

1 If Sir Alexander Fleming hadn't discovered penicillin in 1928,
2 If we didn't like the professor,
3 If he didn't believe in his research proposal,
4 If I had studied harder,
5 If we'd bought a satellite navigation system for the car,
6 If I'd wanted to,
7 If Sir Tim Berners-Lee hadn't invented the Internet,

a) we would know where we are now.
b) he wouldn't have started his doctorate.
c) we'd find it difficult to treat infections.
d) I could have gone to university to study technology.
e) I might have passed the technology exam.
f) we would find it much more difficult to get information.
g) we wouldn't have invited him to lecture here.

9 Complete the prompts, in more than one way if possible, then discuss them with a partner.

1 If I had won the lottery last week, ... *I'd be rich now. / ... I'd have bought a Ferrari.*
2 If I'd told my friend the truth, ...
3 If we hadn't gone to live abroad, ...
4 If we wanted to have solar panels, ...
5 If we had had more money when we were growing up, ...
6 If we didn't take life so seriously, ...

SPEAKING

10 Hold a class debate on the motion: ***The rapid rate of technological development has improved our lives.*** **Discuss the motion first in two groups.**

Group A: you are for the motion; turn to page 160.

Group B: you are against the motion; turn to page 165.

3 Anti-technology groups do not think this way. For an example of why they are dangerous, consider their opposition to the genetic engineering of cotton to remove the toxin gossypol from the seeds so that they can be eaten. This advance could help feed millions of people in climates where other food is hard to grow. A similar example is 'golden rice': a variety of rice produced through genetic engineering to be used in areas where there is a shortage of dietary vitamin A. Some groups have been against the use of 'golden rice' and it is currently not available for consumption. If these groups had not opposed its development so strongly, it would have been produced in many countries. And if they had been less critical, thousands of children in poorer areas would not be blind today. Such attitudes are unfortunate because they are a major obstacle to relieving suffering.

4 The democratisation of technology and its inevitable consequence – giving anyone the means to find the equipment and know-how to produce bio-weapons – has encouraged the call to reject technologies such as biotechnology, nanotechnology and artificial intelligence. This is a bad idea: if we didn't develop such technologies, we would not receive the important benefits they will bring. Also, most importantly, it would drive these developments underground, where they would be impossible to regulate.

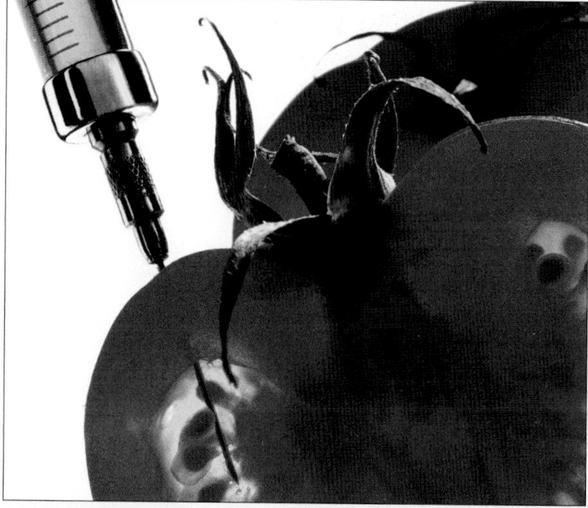

5 Rather than stop this kind of research, we need to speed it up. If we devoted more resources to modern technology, we could have avoided many modern-day problems. We need to reassure people of the profound benefits that today's rapid advances in technology will bring, while developing defences against their abuse. We should not let anti-technologist groups hold us back.

Adapted from *New Scientist*, March 2007

19

SITUATION

1 Read the article from a newspaper about European Breakdown Services (EBS) and discuss the questions.

1 How serious is the situation? Explain your answer.
2 What do you think Richard Makepiece means by the phrase 'intelligent building'?
3 If you were head of EBS, what action would you take after reading the newspaper article?

2a 3.21 Listen to some comments by staff about the building and working conditions. Which comment is about each of these complaints?

a) the area provided for food and drink
b) a piece of equipment which is too complicated for its purpose
c) a problem concerning insufficient space
d) the temperature inside the offices at different times of the year

2b Listen again and note down the details of each complaint.

34 **Business**

Is EBS a falling star?

What's going wrong at EBS? Consumer magazine *On the Watch* reports that European Breakdown Services (EBS) has fallen from first place to fourth place in terms of customer satisfaction. EBS's services are rated as 'poor' and 'not value for money'.

EBS operates a vehicle breakdown service. Based in the UK, they provide support and help for drivers throughout Europe. Twelve months ago, they moved to a new state-of-the-art building, and introduced a new computer system which controls the building facilities, such as the heating and lighting, the fire prevention devices, and car parks. It also controls the databases, allowing office staff to deal with new subscribers, customer records, billing and other administrative matters. When staff moved into their new premises, the head of EBS, Richard Makepiece, said, 'The building's ahead of its time. It's a truly "intelligent building". It will greatly benefit our staff and customers.'

Unfortunately, this has not been the case. At present, the staff are extremely unhappy and demotivated because the computer systems are not working properly. Some key staff have already left the company, customer complaints have risen sharply and many have switched to rival firms. EBS is clearly facing a crisis.

Computer crash

3a A number of problems affect the admin staff and patrolmen/women (who deal with car breakdowns on the road). Work in pairs to rank the problems below in order of their importance. (1 = the most serious problem.)

1 Staff are often unable to find customers in the database system.
2 Bills have been sent late to some customers. Other customers have been overcharged.
3 Details of subscribers are often incorrect.
4 The computer crashes at least once a month.
5 There have been over 45 minor problems with the computer system since it was introduced, causing work to be delayed.
6 Staff are not confident about using the computer because there was a gap of five months between their training and the introduction of the new system.
7 The patrolmen/women often cannot locate drivers who have broken down. This is either because the computer doesn't work properly or because the Satellite Navigation System (installed in all vans and trucks) is not reliable.

3b Discuss and compare your ranking with another group.

KEY LANGUAGE: reassuring and encouraging

4a 3.22 Listen to a director talking informally to one of the office staff and answer the questions.

1 What is Rosa worried about?
2 What is she unhappy about?
3 What happened to the computer system last week?
4 How did the team leader react to the incident?
5 What's going to happen on Wednesday evening?

4b Listen again and fill in the gaps with words/phrases from the conversation.

1 You can be frank with me, Rosa. I __________, it won't go any further.
2 Look, I __________ you feel.
3 But I can __________, we're going to put things right.
4 Mmm, that doesn't sound __________ to me.
5 Anyway, __________, Rosa, we know you're one of the best workers in the company.
6 And I __________ sort out the problems.
7 You won't be out of a job, you __________ that.
8 I can see __________ and we're going to do something about it, I promise.
9 And stop worrying about your job. Things'll get better, __________.

4c Check your answers by looking at Track 3.22 on page 189.

TASK: problem-solving meeting

5 Work in groups of four. Choose one of the following roles. Read the role card and prepare to hold the meeting between the staff listed below.

Head of Human Resources: turn to page 160.
Representative of admin staff: turn to page 166.
Representative of the team leaders: turn to page 168.
Representative of the patrol staff: turn to page 170.

6 The Head of Human Resources leads the meeting. Discuss what needs to be done to improve customer service and staff morale. Note down any decisions.

7 Compare the results of your discussions as a class. Agree on which decisions should be put into practice and which require further research. Are there any decisions which should NOT be implemented?

OTHER USEFUL PHRASES

Asking for more information
Can you tell me a little more about that?
Can you give me an example?

Asking a polite question
Do you mind if I ask you something?
Could I (just) ask you … (how do you feel about …)?

STUDY SKILLS: plagiarism – what it is and how to avoid it

1 In groups, discuss which of the following is plagiarism.

1 Quoting from a text without acknowledging the author
2 Rewriting a sentence from another text in your own words
3 Including someone else's ideas in your own work without acknowledging the source
4 Copying material from another student for an essay or report
5 Downloading text from the Internet and inserting it in a written assignment
6 Rephrasing an idea from another source without acknowledgment

2a 3.23 Listen to part of a lecture about plagiarism. Check your answers to Exercise 1.

2b 3.24 Listen to Part 2. Tick the correct points the lecturer makes about quotations.

1 You should not use too many quotations.
2 Lecturers value the ideas of other writers more than your own ideas.
3 You should usually paraphrase a quote.
4 Always use quotation marks to identify a quote.

2c Listen again and answer the questions.

1 What three reasons does the lecturer give for people plagiarising?
2 Why is it likely that a lecturer will find out if you have plagiarised material?

3 These examples show the difference between acceptable paraphrasing and plagiarism. In pairs, discuss whether each version on the right is an example of plagiarism.

Original

Both movements are anti-technology so the modern world must be an alarming place for them. There is no denying the extraordinary pace of development. Whereas the telephone took 50 years to be adopted by a quarter of the US population, the cellphone did that in just seven. Five years ago most people didn't use search engines; imagine that now.

(R. Kurzweil, (2007), 'Let's not go back to nature', *New Scientist*, March 2007, page 19)

Version A ▼

The modern world is a frightening place for opponents of technology because of the extraordinary pace of development. The telephone took 50 years to be adopted by 25% of people in the US, but the cellphone took just seven. In the past, most people didn't use search engines; imagine the situation now.

Version B ▼

Technology has grown at a very fast rate in recent years, which is unsettling for a lot of people. Examples of this include the speed at which the cellphone came into common use, and the fact that we can't imagine living without search engines now.

Version C ▼

R. Kurzweil (*New Scientist*, March 2007, page 19) points out that it took 50 years for the telephone to be used by a quarter of the US population. However, the cellphone achieved the same use in just seven years. Furthermore, the use of search engines has become common after only five years. These examples illustrate the very fast growth of technology in recent times.

Version D ▼

Technology is developing so fast now that it isn't surprising to find people taking stands against it. Even everyday gadgets are developing faster: 'Whereas the telephone took 50 years to be adopted by a quarter of the US population, the cellphone did that in just seven. Five years ago most people didn't use search engines; imagine that now.'

WRITING SKILLS: an article

4 A friend is asked to write an article for an academic journal on technology. What advice would you give him/her?

Do some research and quote your sources.

5a The magazine *Science Today* has invited articles on the question *Has technology improved human life or made it worse?* In pairs, think of the following and note your arguments.

- three arguments that technology has improved human life
- three arguments that technology has made human life worse

5b What examples can you think of to illustrate both viewpoints? Compare your arguments with other students.

6 The article on the right appeared in *Science Today*, vol. 10/4, page 118. Read the article and answer the questions.

1 Which statement indicates the writer's purpose?

2 What is the writer's opinion regarding the issue?

7 Identifying the writer's position The writer shows his position concerning the issue by using the techniques below. Find other examples in the article which show the writer's position.

emphatic statements, e.g. 'it is important also to be aware ...' (paragraph 1)

strong adverbs, e.g. 'Surely' (para. 3)

strong adjectives, e.g. '*dangerous* effects' (para. 4)

strong language/images, e.g. 'like zombies' (para. 3)

rhetorical questions, e.g. 'does the technology benefit people in those countries?' (para. 5)

8 Write your own article on the above topic. It should be between 250 and 300 words. Use information from this article and from the one on pages 126–127. Use at least two references in your text and include a short bibliography.

Technology:

always a force for good?

FRANCIS NOBLE

1 Technology has undoubtedly brought great benefits to human beings. However, it is important also to be aware of the dangers of technology. This article will present some of the disadvantages of technological advances.

2 People often mention the social benefits of the Internet. For example, users can communicate with people from all over the world and make friends with them. But what is the result of 'chatting' with friends over the Internet for hours? People lose opportunities of meeting real people and having face-to-face contact.

3 Technology such as television, the Internet, mobile phones and email speeds communication but also creates isolated people who interact with machines rather than with other human beings. Young people sit for hours in front of their computers, like zombies, playing Internet games. Surely they could find a more useful and rewarding way to spend their time.

4 One of the most dangerous effects of technology is that we have no privacy any more. Big Brother is constantly watching us and recording what we are doing. For example, CCTV (closed circuit television) is ubiquitous – it tracks our movements everywhere these days. In addition, many companies nowadays check up on their employees to find out what they are uploading on websites such as YouTube. Someone is always spying on us.

5 Throughout the world, rich countries are using technology to dominate poor countries. Multinational companies introduce advanced machines and computers into poor countries. However, does the technology benefit people in those countries? Often the result is that many workers lose their jobs and slip into a life of extreme poverty.

6 In conclusion, technology is developing at much too fast a pace. It should be our servant rather than our master. It is essential to control technology before it is too late – before it controls us.

REVIEW

3-D is back!

Although the filmed or photographic image has come a long way, it is still constrained by two dimensions – the height and width of the flat screen 1_____. But humans do not see things in two dimensions. Because we have two eyes we see everything from two slightly different viewpoints. For us the real world is not flat, it has depth. In other words we see the world in three dimensions or 3-D.

For years film-makers have longed to be able to recreate that feeling of depth in movies but have been frustrated by the lack of technical progress. We would all now be watching 3-D films, even on our own televisions, if camera technology had developed at the same rate as computers. In fact, the first 3-D system was developed in the 1950s. If it 2_____ more sophisticated it might have been more popular, but the quality of the images was poor and audiences had to wear special glasses which were uncomfortable and could cause headaches. Now, developments in the field of digital imaging have made high-quality 3-D films a practical possibility, at least in cinemas fitted with the latest state-of-the-art equipment.

In the last few years many movies 3_____ 3-D technology have appeared around the world. Some of the biggest studios in Hollywood have begun to release 3-D versions of their hit films, including Disney's *Meet the Robinsons* and *Journey 3-D*, a spectacular new version of Jules Verne's *Journey to the Centre of the Earth*, 4_____ Brendan Fraser. The rock band U2 has made a film of their latest tour of South America called *U2 3D*, 5_____ on nine special cameras. More than 700 US cinemas have invested in the technology and hundreds of other cinemas have 6_____ the equipment.

But the existing technology is not sufficient for everyone. James Cameron, 7_____ is best known for directing *Titanic*, has actually made his own cameras for his latest film, *Avatar*. He 8_____ fed up waiting for the latest technology to be incorporated into cameras and insisted on 9_____ his own 3-D cameras for the film. If *Avatar* makes as much money at the box office as *Titanic* did, then 3-D movies 10_____ here to stay.

GRAMMAR

1 **What have been the most important changes in technology in film-making and cinema, do you think? How do you think things might change in future?**

2 **Read the article quickly. Who or what are the following?**

1 James Cameron
2 *Journey 3-D*
3 *U2 3D*
4 700
5 *Meet the Robinsons*

3 **Choose the correct option(s) for each gap in the text. Sometimes two options are possible.**

1 a) which on it appears b) on which it appears c) which it appears on
2 a) had been b) was c) would be
3 a) which feature b) featuring c) featured
4 a) which stars b) starred c) starring
5 a) recording b) recorded c) which was recorded
6 a) said to buy b) promised to buy c) promised buying
7 a) that b) who c) whom
8 a) told he had become b) said he has become c) said he had become
9 a) making b) to make c) him to make
10 a) would be b) would have been c) will be

VOCABULARY

4 **Complete the crossword using the clues.**

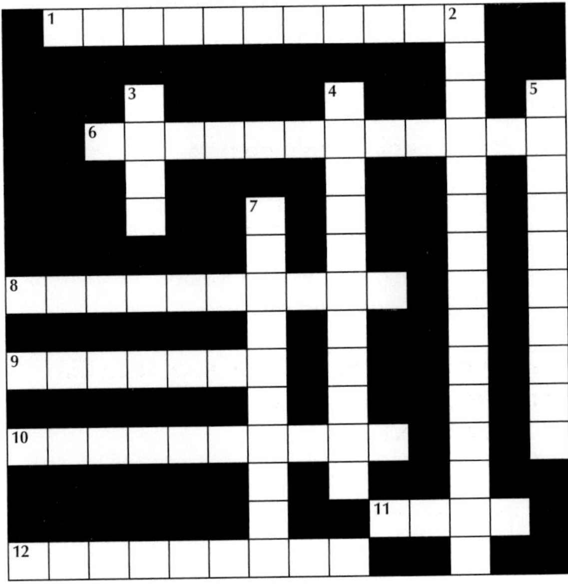

Clues Across

1 Ellie's a _____ – she's terrified of new technology.
6 A _____ helps people who are mentally ill.
8 I get _____ when people don't listen to me.
9 I've never tried Korean _____ – is it spicy?
10 The story is really _____ – it's full of surprises and you never really know what's happening.
11 You should never _____ out with your friends.
12 You need a lot of _____ for camping – tents, sleeping bags, etc.

Clues Down

2 I try to be _____ friendly – I recycle what I can.
3 I can't get _____ to living here – it seems strange.
4 This coat is really _____; it's ten years old and as good as new.
5 My interest in the Romans was really _____ by that film.
7 If you want to learn to drive, three or four lessons are _____ – you need at least ten or twelve.

5 Complete the second sentence so that it has a similar meaning to the first, using an idiom with *mind*.

1 My brother can never decide what to do.
My brother can never __________.
2 Elizabeth was crazy with grief.
Elizabeth was __________ with grief.
3 Try not to form a definite decision too quickly.
Try to __________.
4 I don't know whether to buy it or not.
I'm __________ about whether to buy it or not.
5 Now I've got my results I feel calm and relaxed.
Now I've got my results I have __________.

KEY LANGUAGE

6 3.25 Listen to Tara talking to Henry, her student advisor, about problems she is having. Are these statements true or false?

1 Tara's course is too difficult.
2 Tara's flatmates play music every evening.
3 Tara usually does her coursework in the evenings.
4 Tara has complained to her flatmates several times.
5 Tara hasn't told her landlord about this problem.
6 Henry thinks things will improve.

7 There is one incorrect word in each sentence. Correct it, then listen to the conversation again and check your answers.

1 You can be frank of me, Tara.
2 Why don't you say me all about it?
3 Look, I understand how you feel it.
4 That isn't sound very fair to me, I must say.
5 It might be a good idea to explain them how you feel.
6 If I be you I'd just ask them to …
7 You might consider talking to your landlord for this.
8 Stop worry about it. Things'll get better, …

LANGUAGE CHECK

8 There is one missing word in each sentence. Add the missing words, then look at the pages and check your answers.

1 William Shakespeare is a playwright about historians know very little. (page 105)
2 Justice is something in we all believe. (page 105)
3 There was a strange man pictures of us as we left. (page 107)
4 He said he never been to that place before. (page 115)
5 The woman insisted inviting us into her house. (page 116)
6 The student apologised not finishing her essay on time. (page 116)
7 The security guard warned us not go into the building. (page 116)
8 I'm sure you enjoy it if you go there. (page 125)
9 If you went into their homes, you be offered food and drink. (page 125)
10 If agricultural production had been increased, many children not be suffering now. (page 127)

LOOK BACK

9 Find the exercises in Units 10–12 where you …

- read about the nine key roles in management teams. (Unit 10)
- complete the rule about when we can omit *that* in relative clauses. (Unit 10)
- study the phrases which we use to give advice. (Unit 10)
- decide on items to put into a time capsule. (Unit 11)
- listen to someone talking about life in Chicago. (Unit 11)
- learn about reporting verbs followed by the infinitive with *to*. (Unit 11)
- study examples of the first and second conditional. (Unit 12)
- practise talking about past conditions with present results. (Unit 12)
- listen to a lecture about plagiarism. (Unit 12)

Language reference

GRAMMAR

G1 The continuous aspect

Use the continuous aspect to talk about:

- an action which is in progress.
  Answer the door! **I'm watching** something.
- an unfinished action.
  She **was working** on a new novel when she died.
- a temporary action.
  I'm using Jo's laptop while mine is being repaired.
- a trend, changing action or situation.
  Scientists say the weather **is getting** hotter.

Compare the present simple and continuous:
I **live** in a small flat. (permanent situation)
I'**m living** with a host family for six weeks. (temporary situation)

We can also use the present continuous for repeated actions which are happening around now.
I'**m watching** the new series of *The Sopranos*. It's fantastic. (I watch it every Thursday evening.)

We often use the past continuous and the past simple to talk about a longer background action in the past when a shorter action happens during it or interrupts it.
I was washing the car **when the phone rang**.

We can also use the present continuous to describe future arrangements.
We're collecting our new car **at the weekend**.

G2 State verbs

Some verbs describe something passive or a state. Examples of these verbs are: *agree, believe, belong, depend, hate, hear, know, like, love, prefer, see, understand, want*.

We rarely use state verbs in the continuous:
~~I'm not understanding~~ this word. ✗
I don't understand this word. ✓

G3 The perfect aspect

Use the perfect aspect to look back from one time to another.

Present perfect

The present perfect looks back from now to a time before now. There are four main uses.

- a state that started in the past and is still continuing
  I've lived here all my life.
- a completed action in the past which has some relevance to the present (e.g. a present result)
  There **has been** a severe storm and the airport is now closed.
- finished actions in a period of time that is still continuing
  I've been there once already today.
- actions in the past which may happen again
  Deborah Tannen **has written** several books on communication. (She could write more books.)

! Use the past simple, not the present perfect, when talking about a definite time in the past.
Our lesson ~~has finished~~ at four o'clock. ✗
Our lesson finished at four o'clock. ✓

Past perfect

The past perfect looks back from a time in the past to another time before that.
She'**d applied** for ten jobs before she got this one.

We can use the past perfect to describe a sequence of events. The past perfect describes the first action.
When we arrived, the train **had left**. (First the train left, and then we arrived.)

We can use *just* or *already* to show that the first action happened recently or earlier than expected.
We arrived at six but the train **had just left**.
When they arrived, the film **had already started**.

We can use the past perfect for repeated earlier actions.
By 2006 Deborah Tannen **had written** 20 books.

KEY LANGUAGE

KL Outlining problems and offering solutions

Outlining problems

The problem is, …
The trouble with that is …
It's a very tricky situation.
It's a vicious circle.
It's a rather difficult situation.

Offering solutions

I think the best solution is …
I agree we should …
We can sort it out.
The best way to deal with this is …

Reacting to suggestions

That might well solve the problem.
That seems to be the way forward.

VOCABULARY

V1 Communication

appearance, body language, charisma, cultures, digressions, eye contact, listener, nerves, pace, rambler, sense of humour, vocabulary

V2 Idioms to do with communication

actions speak louder than words, (can't) get a word in edgeways, get straight to the point, have a quick word with, hear it on the grapevine, be on the same wavelength, think before you speak

V3 More idioms

burst into laughter, hold centre stage, run out of things to say, the life of the party

Extra practice

G1 1 Read the sentences and choose the best explanation.

1 We were quite poor when I was growing up.
   a) I'm an adult now.
   b) I'm still a child.
2 She's on a diet so she isn't eating any ice cream.
   a) She ate ice cream in the past.
   b) She never eats ice cream.
3 By the end of the day we were feeling quite tired.
   a) We got more tired as the day went on.
   b) We felt tired all day.
4 I was checking my emails when my computer stopped working.
   a) I managed to check all my emails.
   b) I only managed to check some of my emails.
5 Michael's doing a project on wind farms.
   a) Michael has finished the project.
   b) Michael has not finished the project yet.
6 The family was living in a caravan at that time.
   a) The family lived there for a temporary period.
   b) The family always lived there.

G2 2 Make questions from the prompts. Use a continuous form if possible.

1 you / prefer / chicken or fish ?
2 you / read / anything interesting at the moment ?
3 this mobile phone / belong / to you ?
4 your course / get / more difficult ?
5 anyone / know / the answer to this question ?
6 you / agree / with him ?
7 the students / learn / about / pollution this week ?
8 your parents / know / how to send emails ?

G3 3 Complete the text with a), b) or c) on the right.

John Gray is a famous US psychologist and author. His best-known work is *Men Are from Mars, Women Are from Venus,* which he [1]_____ in 1992. By 2007 the book [2]_____ over six million copies.

For over 20 years he [3]_____ seminars and courses on relationships and communication, and he [4]_____ frequently on television shows including *Oprah* and *The Today Show*.

Gray was born in Houston, Texas, in 1951. He [5]_____ high school and the University of Texas, but instead of completing his degree he [6]_____ to move to Switzerland. After he [7]_____ in Switzerland for nine years Gray decided to return to the USA, where he [8]_____ a doctorate in Psychology at Columbia Pacific University. The research for his PhD formed the basis of *Men Are from Mars, Women Are from Venus*.

Following the success of that book, Gray [9]_____ several more best-selling guides to relationships and communication. He now [10]_____ in California with his wife and three children.

1 a) has written b) had written c) wrote
2 a) had sold b) has sold c) was selling
3 a) is leading b) had led c) has led
4 a) appeared b) has appeared c) is appearing
5 a) attended b) had attended c) was attending
6 a) has decided b) was deciding c) decided
7 a) had been b) has been c) was being
8 a) has completed b) completed c) was completing
9 a) had written b) was writing c) has written
10 a) had lived b) lives c) has lived

KL 4 Complete the dialogue with one word in each gap.

A: What's the problem?
B: Well, it's a [1]_____ difficult situation. My boss keeps asking me to work late. And the more I do, the more she expects – it's a [2]_____ circle.
A: Don't worry. I'm sure you can [3]_____ it out. Why don't you just say 'no'?
B: The [4]_____ with that is that then she'll think I'm lazy and I might lose my job …
A: I think the best [5]_____ is to explain your situation to her. I'm sure she'll understand.
B: I'm not sure. It's a very tricky [6]_____.
A: Well, maybe the best way to [7]_____ with this is to talk to the area manager. He's very helpful.
B: OK. That might well [8]_____ the problem.

V1 5 Replace the words in *italics* with words from V1 with a similar meaning.

1 You speak very slowly. Try to talk at a faster *speed*.
2 A smart *look* is very important at a job interview.
3 I'm very interested in other *customs and lifestyles*.
4 To be a successful film star you need to have *charm and appeal*.
5 English has an amazing *number of words*.
6 I get *anxious feelings* when I meet new people.

V2,3 6 Choose a–g to continue the sentences.

1 Carol and Jim always have very different ideas.
2 I can't get a word in edgeways.
3 They spend ages talking about irrelevant things.
4 Rachel is always the life of the party.
5 Can I have a quick word with the manager?
6 It's important to see what they've actually done.
7 John burst into laughter when I told him that story.

a) I'm glad she's coming tonight.
b) After all, actions speak louder than words.
c) They're just not on the same wavelength.
d) They should get straight to the point.
e) But it wasn't really that funny!
f) They never stop talking.
g) It won't take very long.

Language reference

GRAMMAR

G1 Present perfect simple and continuous

Form the present perfect continuous with *has/have* + *been* + *-ing*.

John's **been telling** us about climate change.
Have you been watching that new series on global warming?

Use the present perfect continuous to talk about an ongoing situation or action that started in the past and is still continuing.

Sea levels **have been rising**.
The climate **has been getting** warmer.

Compare this use of the present perfect continuous with the present perfect simple.

We've been painting the house. (continuing action)
We've painted the house. (completed action)

We also use the present perfect continuous to talk about the reason for something in the present. We are more interested in the activity than the result.

Why are you wet?
Because **I've been washing the car**. (This is the reason I'm wet.)

With the present perfect simple the focus is on the result, not the activity.

Is the car ready?
Yes, **I've washed** it. (So now it is ready.)

! To describe repeated actions we use the present perfect simple, not the present perfect continuous.
I've watched that film ten times. ✓
~~I've been watching~~ that film ten times. ✗

since, for and other time expressions

We often use *since* or *for* and expressions such as *recently, over the last …*, etc. with the present perfect continuous to talk about an ongoing situation or action that started in the past and is still continuing.

We've been studying climate change **since the 1980s**.
Recently, I've been thinking about changing jobs.

With *since* and *for* and some verbs that describe continuous actions or states (e.g. *live, stay, work, study, teach*) we can use the present perfect simple or continuous with little difference in meaning.

I'**ve waited** for ages. / I'**ve been waiting** for ages.
He'**s worked** there since 1995. / He'**s been working** there since 1995.

G2 Indirect questions

An indirect question is a question inside another question or statement.

What is the answer? + Do you know …?
→ Do you know what the answer is?

There are a number of introductory phrases that can be used to begin an indirect question. For example:

I'd like to know …   Do you know …?
Can/Could you tell me …?   I wonder …

Use indirect questions in formal situations or to be tentative.

Could you tell me if it's OK to use mobiles here?
I wonder if she likes me.

! In indirect questions use statement word order (subject before the auxiliary), not question word order (subject after the auxiliary).
Do you know where the post office is? ✓
Do you know ~~where is the post office~~? ✗

But with an indirect subject question (when we use *who, what* or *which* to ask about the subject of a sentence), do not change the word order.

Who knows him? → I wonder **who knows him**.
What made it go wrong? → Do you know **what made it go wrong**?

We use *if* or *whether* to introduce *yes/no* questions.

Are they expensive? → I wonder if/whether they are expensive.

! We only use question marks if the introductory phrase itself is a question.
I'd like to know how much it costs. (not a question)
Do you know how much it costs? (a question)

KEY LANGUAGE

KL Being polite

Asking polite questions
I'd like to know …
I'm interested in knowing …

Agreeing
You're absolutely right, because …
That's very true, because …
I'd go along with you there, because …

Being diplomatic
That's one way of looking at it, but …
You have a point, but don't you think …

VOCABULARY

V1 Word combinations (local environment)

abandoned cars, apartment block, cosmopolitan atmosphere, crime rate, detached house, mindless vandalism, noise pollution, open spaces, rush hour, stunning views, traffic congestion, transport connections

V2 Word combinations (weather patterns)

climate change, false impression, global warming, satellite image, scientific journal, significant effect

V3 Adverbs with similar meanings

comparatively – relatively, generally – normally, intentionally – deliberately, mostly – mainly, possibly – perhaps, thoughtfully – slowly/pensively

Extra practice

G1 1 Choose the best answer to complete the dialogues.

1 Why are you so out of breath?
 a) I've run.
 b) I've been running.
2 Are the exam results ready?
 a) Yes, our teacher's put them on the wall.
 b) Yes, our teacher's been putting them on the wall.
3 Did my mother contact you?
 a) Yes, she's phoned three times.
 b) Yes, she's been phoning three times.
4 Is the computer working now?
 a) Yes, I've just repaired it.
 b) Yes, I've been repairing it.
5 What a mess!
 a) I know, we've cleared out the cupboards.
 b) I know, we've been clearing out the cupboards.

2 Complete the email extracts with either the present perfect simple or continuous form of the verbs in brackets. Use at least one form of the present perfect continuous in each extract.

I 1_________ (look at) the website you recommended but I didn't really understand the information. I 2_________ (read) the chapters in our coursebook but I still don't really understand them. I 3_________ (worry) about it all day.

Although I 4_________ (live) here for three years I still can't get used to the climate. Right now we're in the middle of the monsoon. It 5_________ (rain) for days! I 6_________ (buy) a new air conditioner but it doesn't seem to be very effective.

G2 3 Choose the correct answer.

1 I wonder where *he works / does he work*?
2 Can you tell me *are they / if they are* for sale?
3 Do you know how much *is it / it is*?
4 Could you tell us where *we can get / can we get* application forms?
5 Do you know whether *it is / is it* expensive?
6 I'd like to know what *does she do / she does* for a living.

4 Put the words in the correct order to make indirect questions.

1 it me could how much you costs tell ?
2 I'd starts the film like when to know
3 coming you know she's whether to the party do ?
4 this model can if you me is available tell ?
5 put I where the keys wonder they
6 what earthquakes to know like I'd causes

KL 5 The residents of an apartment block are discussing the budget for roof repairs. Complete the dialogue with five of the phrases below.

A: OK. Any more questions before we vote?
B: Yes. I'm 1_____ knowing how much this is going to cost.
A: Well, I think that depends on the damage.
C: That's 2_____ because we don't know how much work is needed yet.
B: OK. You 3_____, but we can't just sign a blank cheque. We need to get an estimate of costs.
D: You 4_____ right, because we only have a limited budget for next year.
C: Yes. I'd 5_____ you there.

a) very true
b) one way of
c) are absolutely
d) don't you think
e) interested in
f) have a point
g) go along with

V1 6 Complete the text with words from V1.

Are you fed up with life in the inner city? Do you want to escape from mindless 1_____ and the rising 2_____ rate? Come to Lensford Green, the new town just outside Birmingham. We have a range of affordable properties available, from spacious 3_____ houses to flats in smart apartment 4_____. There are plenty of 5_____ spaces for children to play in. And with our excellent transport 6_____ you can be in Birmingham in 20 minutes. Who wants to look at 7_____ cars and busy streets when they can have 8_____ views of unspoilt countryside?

V2 7 In each sentence two words are in the wrong order. Put them in the correct order.

1 Have you seen the images satellite? They're great!
2 Do you read any journals scientific?
3 This has had effects significant on the climate.
4 There are many effects of warming global.
5 Statistics can sometimes give a impression false.
6 Did you see that documentary about change climate on TV last night?

V3 8 Choose the correct adverb.

1 Mobiles are *pensively/relatively* cheap these days.
2 I think the factory owner started the fire *deliberately/thoughtfully*.
3 There are plenty of car parks in the city centre, but elsewhere there are *possibly/comparatively* few.
4 Poisonous insects are *mainly/relatively* found in tropical countries.
5 The professor nodded *generally/pensively* and told us she would think about it.
6 The weather is *normally/intentionally* warmer at this time of year.

3 Language reference

GRAMMAR

G1 Quantifiers

Use quantifiers to describe the quantity of something. We use different quantifiers with plural countable nouns and uncountable nouns.

+ plural countable noun	+ uncountable noun	+ countable or uncountable noun
few, (too) many, several	little, (too) much	hardly any, a lot of, some, all

To talk about things in general use quantifier + noun.
Many people prefer football.

To talk about something specific use quantifier + *of* + *the* / *my* / *our* / *these,* etc. + noun.
Some of the people in the survey prefer golf.

little / few / a little / a few

Little and *few* have a negative meaning similar to 'not much / not many / almost none'.
There's **little** food in the house. We'll have to do some shopping.

But *a little* and *a few* have a positive meaning similar to 'a small quantity / some'.
There's **a little** food in the fridge if you're hungry.

some/any

We usually use *some* in positive statements and *any* in questions and negatives.
We are playing **some** games next month but there aren't **any** at the weekend.

G2 Definite and zero articles

Use the definite article (*the*):

- when referring to something that is already known to the listener because it has been mentioned before.
  So I showed **the** photos to the police. (I've mentioned these photos before.)
- when referring to something that is already known to the listener because it is obvious from the context.
  I forgot to give **the** cat her supper. (It is obvious I'm talking about *my* cat).
- when something is unique (including superlatives and *first, last, next, only*).
  She is **the** greatest sportswoman.
- when a defining or prepositional phrase makes the noun specific.
  It's **the** house at the top of the street.
- before the names of some geographical features, buildings and places.
  I live in **the** countryside, not **the** town.

Use the zero article (no article):

- before abstract nouns.
  You can't stop **time**.
- before general plural nouns.
  Computers are very powerful now.

! But if the abstract or plural noun is made specific by a defining phrase we use an article.
The computers we've just bought are fantastic.

- before people's names and the names of most companies, materials, countries, mountains and lakes.
  Alexandra lives in **Italy**. She lives near **Lake Como**. She works for **Deutsche Bank**.
- before the names of types of institutions, for example *school, hospital, university*.
  My brother is about to start **school**.

! But if we are referring to a particular building we use the definite article.
Excuse me. Is **the school** near here?

KEY LANGUAGE

KL Emphasis and comparison

Emphasising adjectives

an *amazing* achievement
an *incredible* achievement
tremendous determination

Emphasising adverbs

extremely hot weather
really impressive
truly remarkable
definitely the greatest modern sportsperson …
were *particularly* impressed with …
The journey back was *incredibly* hard …
She was *totally* exhausted …
She's *undoubtedly the greatest sportsperson* of …

Emphasising expressions

But, *most of all*, she's famous …
But *above all*, she's a great person …
She's a great competitor, *there's no doubt about that,* …
What's extraordinary, also, about her is …

VOCABULARY

V1 Idioms

a level playing field, score an own goal, a whole new ball game, start the ball rolling, be on the ball, take your eye off the ball, move the goalposts

V2 *Self-*

self-confidence, self-control, self-defence, self-development, self-discipline, self-respect

V3 Abstract nouns from adjectives

agility, calm, coordination, courtesy, flexibility, tolerance

V4 Adjectives

aggressive, disgusted, dramatic, expert, illegal, phenomenal, professional

G1 **1 Choose the correct word or phrase.**

1 Borrow one of my pens – there are *few* / *a few* in the cupboard.
2 Hardly any *students* / *of students* passed the test.
3 There's *few* / *hardly any* music on my MP3 player.
4 Almost *none* / *none of* our photos came out well.
5 *Several* / *Several of* my friends are at university.
6 I need *a few* / *a little* help with my homework.
7 There's *a little* / *little* furniture in the flat so we'll have to buy some.
8 You should invest your money with my bank. *Few* / *A few* other banks offer such good interest rates.
9 There's far too *much* / *many* rubbish on the streets.

G2 **2 Read the text and add six definite articles.**

Quidditch is a fictional sport invented by the author J.K. Rowling for best-selling Harry Potter books. It is a ball game in which players try to score goals. There are four balls and two teams of seven players. Usually players are wizards and witches and play game by flying on their broomsticks. The goals are ring-shaped and are above the ground. The object of game is to score more goals than opposing team.

3 Complete the sentences with either the definite article or a blank space if no article is needed.

1 How far is it from _____ capital city?
2 Did you see _____ last episode of *Heroes*?
3 I've bought a new phone. _____ phone's got a fantastic camera.
4 Who is _____ best singer at the moment?
5 All children should do _____ sports when they are at _____ school.
6 Is that _____ house where you grew up?

KL **4 Two managers are discussing job applicants they have just interviewed. Complete the dialogue with the phrases below.**

A: Well, Caroline and Toby were [1]_____ in the group – they both have lots of experience.
B: You're right, [2]_____ that.
A: So, Caroline or Toby? Who do you prefer?
B: Well. I was [3]_____ with Caroline.
A: I don't know. I thought she was a bit direct.
B: Well, she's certainly got [4]_____ determination.
A: Toby's CV is [5]_____, don't you think?
B: Yes, it is. And [6]_____, also, about him is that he knows so much about finance.
A: Yes, he does. And he'd [7]_____ get on well with the rest of the team.

a) really impressive
b) particularly impressed
c) definitely
d) undoubtedly the best
e) tremendous
f) there's no doubt about
g) what's extraordinary

V1 **5 Read the summary of a business meeting and use the information to complete the sentences below with the names in *italics*.**

Once everyone had sat down, *David* started the meeting by making some suggestions and asking everyone for their ideas. *Steve* made sure everybody had a chance to speak. *Lucy* said she wanted to talk about the marketing campaign, but then she realised she had left her notes behind, which made her look foolish. But of course *Walter* remembered that he had a summary of the campaign on his laptop, so he was able to help her with the details. We then asked *Miranda* to give a summary of the situation, but she hadn't been listening so she couldn't say much. Then *Caroline* said she wanted to discuss everybody's opinions on the new US office, but then suddenly decided she wanted us all to write our opinions in a report, which was rather annoying.

1 _____ tried to create a level playing field.
2 _____ moved the goalposts.
3 _____ scored an own goal.
4 _____ started the ball rolling.
5 _____ took her eyes off the ball.
6 _____ was really on the ball.

V2 **6 Match the sentences.**

1 I'm always nervous at interviews.
2 I never lose my temper.
3 I want to improve my skills and understanding.
4 I find it difficult to make myself work hard.
5 I'm not really happy with my personality and behaviour.

a) I lack self-discipline.
b) I have a lot of self-control.
c) I don't have much self-respect.
d) I don't have any self-confidence.
e) I'm interested in self-development.

V3,4 **7 Complete the gaps in the text with words from the box. There are two extra words.**

courtesy	dramatic	agility	expert
illegal	coordination	disgusted	

Capoeira is a combination of fighting and dancing. The aim of the game is not to hurt your opponent, but to demonstrate your skill and physical [1]_____. The game originates from the black slaves who were brought to Brazil from Africa. It was [2]_____ until 1937. Success in the game depends on [3]_____ between all parts of the body. [4]_____ fighters show incredible skill – their amazing movements and lightning speed make the games very [5]_____ to watch.

Language reference

GRAMMAR

G1 Future continuous, *going to*, present continuous

Future continuous

Form the future continuous with *will/won't* + *be* + *-ing* form of the verb.

I **will be working** from home tomorrow, so I **won't be meeting** any clients.

Use the future continuous to talk about a temporary action in progress at a particular time in the future.

They**'ll be opening** the new hospital next Tuesday.
I **won't be working** on Wednesday. It's my day off.

We can also use the future continuous to ask tentative questions about people's plans, especially if we want them to do something.

Will you **be coming** to the party? (I want you to come.)
Will you **be using** your car this evening? (I'd like to borrow it.)

We can also use this form to give reasons for refusing something.

I'm afraid I can't come to the party – I**'ll be working**.

going to

Use *going to* to talk about intentions (things you plan to do).

I'm **going to get** a new computer. (I want to get one, but I haven't ordered it yet.)
We're **going to work** much harder next term. (We want to do this, but we may not.)

Present continuous

Use the present continuous for fixed arrangements (things that have already been planned and organised).

I**'m getting** a new computer tomorrow. (I've already ordered it.)
Jane**'s working** at the supermarket next week. (It's organised.)

We normally use a time reference (or the speakers know what time is being referred to) with the present continuous for fixed arrangements.

I'm starting my degree course **this September**.

G2 Future perfect, *will*

Future perfect

Form the future perfect with *will/won't* + *have* + past participle.

He **will have arrived** home by the time you phone.
We **won't have done** the work in time for the meeting.

Use the future perfect to talk about an action you expect to be completed by a time in the future.

By this time next year I **will have finished** all my exams. (My exams will finish before this time next year.)

We usually use a time expression (*soon*, *by then*, *by* + date, *in* + date).

Don't worry – we'll have finished the project **by then**.
They will have completed the stadium **in time for the Olympics.**

will

We use *will* + infinitive to make predictions about the future.

They **will** lose the next election.

Use adverbs of certainty (*probably*, *possibly*, *definitely*, *certainly*) to make the predictions more or less certain. In affirmative sentences, the adverbs come after *will*, before the main verb.

The old hospital will **probably** close down in the next few years.
He'll **definitely** call you if he's interested in coming.

In negative sentences, the adverbs come before *will not*.

I **probably** won't come to the lecture tomorrow.

KEY LANGUAGE

KL Predicting

But it'll probably …
It'd probably …
They'll want us to …
If we …, I don't think …
They think it'll …
It could …
What angle do you think …
It might …
I'll be … (talking to Diana).

VOCABULARY

V1 Medical terms

Alzheimer's, anaesthetist, antibiotic, arthritis, cancer, chest infection, diabetes, heart disease, injection, midwife, morphine, painkiller, pharmacist, physiotherapy, psychiatrist, radiologist, surgeon, transplant

V2 Illness and medicine

contract, fever, infection, parasite, symptom, vaccine

V3 Dependent prepositions

adjust to, approve of, consent to, participate in, relate to, succeed in

Extra practice 4

G1 1 Match the sentences 1 and 2 with the explanations/continuations a) or b).

1 1 We're seeing Swan Lake tonight.
2 We're going to see a ballet soon.
a) We haven't bought the tickets.
b) We've bought the tickets.

2 1 I'm going to do some exercise.
2 I'll be doing lots of exercise.
a) I'm spending two weeks at a health spa next month.
b) I'd like to get fit.

3 1 I'll be speaking to the manager.
2 I'm going to speak to the manager.
a) We always have a meeting on Wednesday.
b) I want to make a complaint.

4 1 I'm going to do a yoga course.
2 I'll be doing a yoga class on Tuesday.
a) I enrolled for it last week.
b) I think there's one at my local gym.

5 1 We'll be repainting the house.
2 We're going to repaint the house.
a) We haven't decided when to do it yet.
b) We've arranged to take a week off work to do it.

G2 2 Read the itinerary for a day trip to the Tower of London. Complete the sentences to talk about what the tour group will or will not have done by certain times in the day. Use the future perfect.

8:30	Collection from your hotel
9:15	Arrive at main gate
9:30–11:00	Lecture on history of the Tower
11:00–11:20	Coffee
11:40–12:25	Visit to the White Tower
12:30–13:30	Lunch
13:45–14:45	Visit the Crown Jewels
15:00–15:40	Tour of Traitor's Gate
16:00	Depart from main gate
16:45	Arrive at your hotel

1 We __________ the Crown Jewels before lunch. (see)
2 By 2 p.m. we __________ lunch. (have)
3 We __________ seeing Traitor's Gate by 3.30 p.m. (finish)
4 By 9.30 a.m. we __________ at the main gate. (arrive)
5 We __________ the Tower by 3 p.m. (leave)
6 By 5 p.m. we __________ to our hotel. (return)
7 We __________ to a lecture before having coffee. (listen)
8 By the time we leave we __________ over six hours in the Tower. (spend)

3 Complete the dialogue with the phrases below. There are two extra phrases.

A: Sorry, I can't meet you on Monday. I'm still working on my project and I [1]_____ it by then.
B: OK. Well what about Tuesday?
A: I'm not sure. I [2]_____ most of the work by Tuesday evening. What are your plans?
B: I [3]_____ Sara then, but it depends on her.
A: [4]_____ your car with you?
B: No, it's being serviced and the garage [5]_____ it by Tuesday.
A: That's a pity. Well, look, I [6]_____ you on Tuesday afternoon and we can talk then.

a) will have had
b) 'll probably visit
c) won't have finished
d) 'll phone certainly
e) 'll definitely phone
f) 'll have done
g) won't have returned
h) Will you have

KL 4 There is one word or phrase missing in these sentences. Complete them with words or phrases from the box. There are three extra words or phrases.

angle	could	it'll	be talking	want
probably cost	spend	impact	greatly	

1 If we the money on the buildings, I don't think we'll have enough for the equipment.
2 I'm not sure about that. It'd quite a lot of money.
3 We'll have to think about that; it have an effect on other projects.
4 I'll to the manager later, so I'll ask her then.
5 I'm not sure about that. What do you think the local press will have on it?
6 We need to be careful. That might have a big on our sales.

V1,2 5 Find 20 words connected with medicine in the word square.

V P R R U M I D W I F E N L T
T F J K T R A N S P L A N T D
A E N X S U R G E O N I S Y A
F V P A I N K I L L E R P N R
S E P J R J S P Z M A A I O T
Y R E H T W X L I S R D V I N
M V A N A E S T H E T I S T U
P L A H I R J H H T H O M C C
T A R C H C M T P E R L O E A
O Q R N C T O A S B I O R F N
M I R A Y I F H C A T G P N C
O F I D S O N N L I I I H I E
O M Y Y P I F E M D S S I J R
E Y H Y C I T O I B I T N A T
I P N O I T C E J N I F E X D

Language reference

GRAMMAR

G1 Modal verbs: future ability, possibility and obligation

Use *will/won't be able to* to talk about future ability.

After I pass my driving test I'**ll be able to** drive a car on my own.

She's going on holiday so she **won't be able to** see you next week.

! Don't use *can* for future ability. Use *will be able to* instead.

~~Can~~ I type by the end of the course? ✗

Will I **be able to** type by the end of the course? ✓

Use *may, might* or *could* to describe future possibilities.

In the future cars **might** contain high pressure hydrogen tanks.

We **could** go to Greece next summer.

They **may** be able to help you with your problem.

! To describe a negative possibility in the future we use *might not*; we don't use *could not*.

The weather forecast is good so we ~~could not~~ need our umbrellas tomorrow. ✗

The weather forecast is good so we **might not** need our umbrellas tomorrow. ✓

Use *will have to* or *will need to* to describe future obligation.

There's an admission charge so we'**ll have to** take some money with us.

Use *will not have to* and *will not need to* to describe a lack of obligation in the future.

They're going to give us lunch so we **won't need to** take any food.

Use *can't* to talk about a prohibition (a negative obligation) in the future.

We should eat something now. You **can't** take food into the theatre.

G2 Modal verbs: past ability, possibility and obligation

Use *could* or *was/were able to* to talk about a general ability/possibility in the past.

When I was young I **could** run for miles without getting tired.

Years ago people **were able to** drive without taking a test.

! But to talk about a single action in the past we only use *was able to*, not *could*.

There was a bus strike, but I ~~could~~ get a lift with a colleague. ✗

There was a bus strike, but I **was able to** get a lift with a colleague. ✓

Use *manage to* or *succeed in* to talk about something you did that was difficult. Use the *-ing* form of the verb after *succeed in*.

Our flight was cancelled but we **managed to** get seats on the next one.

After several phone calls we **succeeded in** speaking to the manager.

Use *couldn't* or *wasn't/weren't able to* for a negative possibility in the past.

I lost my key and I **couldn't** find it.

When I was young I **wasn't able to** stay out late.

Use *had to* to talk about obligation in the past.

I **had to** get a visa when I went to the US last summer.

Use *didn't have to* to talk about a lack of obligation in the past.

At my old school we **didn't have to** wear a uniform.

Use *couldn't* to talk about a negative obligation (a prohibition) in the past.

We **couldn't** use calculators in class when I was at school.

KEY LANGUAGE

KL Persuading, recommending action

Persuading

I really think …

Surely you must agree that … ?

I think it's essential to …

Don't you think that … ?

There's no doubt in my mind that …

I'm sure you can see …

… you can't argue that …

Recommending action

The best solution would be to …

It's the way forward for us.

… the answer is to …

… that's the best way to …

We need action now to …

VOCABULARY

V1 Methods of transport

balloon, barge, cable car, coach, ferry, glider, helicopter, hovercraft, hydrofoil, lorry/truck, Maglev train, motorbike, quad bike, scooter, submarine, tram, van

V2 Transport problems

fogbound runway, lane closure, low tide, platform alteration, puncture, rough weather, signalling problems, tailback, turbulence

V3 Safety features

airbag, anti-lock brakes, one-way street, seat belt, speed cameras, speed limit, traffic signals

V4 Words connected with transport

elevated, emit, feasible, fleet, freight, fumes, masses, shuttle, tycoon

G1 1 Match the sentence halves.

1 We'll have to go by train
2 We could go by train
3 We won't be able to go by train
4 We might not go by train
5 We won't need to go by train

a) because Uncle Jim's going to give us a lift.
b) if the bus fare is a lot cheaper.
c) as it's more relaxing than flying.
d) because my car isn't working.
e) because there's going to be a rail strike.

G2 2 Choose the correct answer.

1 A: Did you fix the car?
B: Yes, I *could* / *managed to* repair it.
2 A: Did you get lots of homework last term?
B: No, we *mustn't* / *didn't have to* do much.
3 A: Was the Maths test very difficult?
B: Yes. We *couldn't* / *didn't able to* use calculators.
4 A: Did you speak to the manager?
B: Yes. We succeeded *in getting* / *to get* a refund.
5 A: Did you pay for the meal by credit card?
B: No, we *didn't able to* / *couldn't* use it.
6 A: I thought you lost your front door key.
B: Yes, but we managed *finding* / *to find* it.
7 A: What did you do about that broken camera?
B: I *could* / *was able to* get a replacement.
8 A: Were your parents strict when you were small?
B: No, we *didn't have to* / *could* do whatever we liked.

3 Complete the second sentence so that it has a similar meaning to the first, using a form of *could*, *able to*, *have to*, *manage* or *succeed*.

1 It wasn't possible to repair your computer.
I __________ repair your computer.
2 I had the ability to sing well when I was a child.
I __________ sing well when I was a child.
3 It wasn't necessary for Juan to wear a suit.
Juan __________ wear a suit.
4 We had no problem getting tickets for the show.
We __________ get tickets for the show.
5 It was necessary for me to pay a €20 fine.
I __________ pay a €20 fine.
6 It was possible for me to borrow the money from the bank, although it was extremely hard.
I __________ in borrowing money from the bank.

KL 4 Complete the sentences with the words in the box.

agree answer mind need really sure that way

1 John, I _____ think we've got to do something about the amount of traffic.
2 Surely you must _____ that there aren't enough buses.
3 There's no doubt in my _____ that the answer is more bus lanes.
4 I'm _____ you can see that's the best solution.
5 Don't you think _____ more trains are necessary?
6 Building more roads is the _____ forward for us.
7 The _____ is to offer the public cheaper fares.
8 We _____ action now to improve the situation.

V1 5 Match the words on the left with the descriptions on the right.

1 submarine
2 motorbike
3 barge
4 quad bike
5 cable car
6 glider

a) doesn't have an engine
b) carries freight on water
c) hangs from a steel cable
d) travels under water
e) has four wheels but isn't a car
f) has two wheels

V2 6 Choose the correct answer.

1 The flight was delayed because of a *tailback* / *fogbound runway*.
2 The only time I hate flying is when you are going through *turbulence* / *signalling problems*.
3 The *low tide* / *rough weather* made us seasick.
4 Can you repair a *lane closure* / *puncture*?
5 It took us hours to get here; there was a massive *tailback* / *turbulence* on the motorway.
6 There's been a *platform alteration* / *lane closure* so we'll have to cross to the other side of the station.

V3 7 Complete the table with words from V3.

something inside or part of a car	something on the road	a law

V4 8 Complete the sentences with words from V4.

1 As well as being prime minister of Italy, Silvio Berlusconi was a famous media _____.
2 The Skytrain system in Bangkok is _____ above the streets.
3 A lot of _____ is carried by rail.
4 There's a _____ to the centre every five minutes.
5 United Airlines has a _____ of 460 aircraft.
6 Electric cars don't _____ any harmful gases.

6 Language reference

GRAMMAR

G1 Narrative tenses, past perfect continuous

Past simple

Use the past simple for single finished actions.

He **closed** his newspaper.

We also use it for a sequence of single actions (to say that one action was followed by another one).

I **turned** the knob, **opened** the door and **walked** into the room.

Past continuous

Use the past continuous for an ongoing action which sets the scene or background for a story.

The rain **was falling** as we left the house.

Use the past continuous and past simple in the same sentence to talk about a longer background action in the past when a shorter action happens during it or interrupts it.

I **was washing** the car when the phone **rang**.
Picasso **was living** in Paris when the war **began**.

Past perfect

The past perfect looks back from a time in the past to another time before that, so we can use it to describe an earlier action in a sequence of events.

It was dark. Someone **had turned off** the light.
When we arrived, the train **had left**. (first the train left, then we arrived)

Past perfect continuous

Form the past perfect continuous with *had* + *been* + *-ing* form of the verb.

A lady **had been sitting** in the chair.

Use the past perfect continuous to describe an ongoing action which continued up to or finished just before another action or time in the past.

Karl realised he**'d been waiting** for over an hour.

We often use the past perfect continuous to explain a past result.

I was angry because **I'd been waiting** so long.

We often use the past perfect continuous with *before*, *after* and *when*.

Carol **had been working** there for a year **before** they gave her a pay rise.

G2 *used to* and *would*

Use *used to* + infinitive without *to* to talk about states that existed in the past, but no longer exist, and for actions that were repeated in the past but don't happen now.

We **used to live** in the suburbs. (past state)
I **used to read** a lot but I don't have enough time now. (past repeated action)

! Note the spelling changes for statements, questions and negatives.
I **used to** be a student.
Did you **use to** be a student?
We didn't **use to** be students.

Use *would* + infinitive without *to* to talk about things that happened regularly in the past.

When I was a child we **would spend** every summer by the seaside.

! We never use *would* to talk about states in the past:
Summers ~~would~~ be cooler here in the past. ✗
Summers **used to** be cooler here in the past. ✓

We usually use a time expression with *would*.

She would spend each evening reading **when she was a child**.

KEY LANGUAGE

KL Proposing, bargaining, talking about needs/expectations

Proposing

Why don't you …?
Look, I'd like to make a proposal.
Could I suggest we meet towards the end of the month?
How about if I talked to him …?

Bargaining

If you included more chapters about your background, it'd add a lot of human interest …
If she agreed to let you write two or three chapters … you'd probably double or triple sales of your book.
You'll find I'm good value for money.

Talking about needs/expectations

I need more time to think about this and take some advice.
But in this case, I think … is more appropriate.
Really, I wasn't expecting to pay as much as that.

VOCABULARY

V1 Types of writing

autobiographies, biographies, blogs, crime stories, diaries, essays, history, memoirs, novels, plays, poetry, romances, science fiction, short stories, thrillers, travel writing

V2 People in literature

author, biographer, critic, dramatist, ghostwriter, judge, novelist, poet

V3 Light, darkness and sound

candle, lamp, darkness, silent, gleam, lantern, strike a match, glare, flash, straining ears, audible, whistle, silence, cry, yell, shriek, echoes

Extra practice 6

G1 **1 Read the sentences and choose the best explanation.**

1 We were cooking dinner when there was a power cut.
   a) We finished cooking dinner.
   b) We didn't finish cooking dinner.

2 Darlene stood up, walked to the window and put on her glasses.
   a) She walked to the window before putting on her glasses.
   b) She put on her glasses and walked to the window at the same time.

3 When we arrived, we realised it had been raining.
   a) It stopped raining before we arrived.
   b) It was still raining when we arrived.

4 Although I knew his name, I'd never actually met him before.
   a) I met him. b) I didn't meet him.

2 Complete the text with the words in the box.

brought had brought looked was looking sat was sitting had been sitting had hadn't had was went had been working

Joe 1_____ on the balcony when he suddenly felt his arms burning. He 2_____ down and noticed his skin was red and felt hot. It wasn't surprising as he 3_____ in the sun all day. He knew he 4_____ some after-sun cream, but he wasn't sure where it 5_____ – he 6_____ so hard in the few days before leaving home that he 7_____ time to pack everything properly. Firstly, he 8_____ into the bathroom but it wasn't there. He 9_____ his bag into the bedroom and 10_____ at the desk, trying to think. He 11_____ through the bag again when he remembered that he 12_____ a tube of shaving cream – it was probably just as good!

G2 **3 There are two mistakes in each extract. Correct them.**

A

When I was a child I use to read lots of adventure stories at night. I would lie in bed and pull the sheets over my head. Then I would to read by the light of a torch.

B

Years ago I would live in a house by the sea. Every day we would go down to the beach and spend hours swimming. It would be such good fun.

C

Don't I know you? Didn't you used to live in Dorking Street? Do you remember me? I would live in number 16 – the house with the blue front door.

KL **4 There are mistakes in six of the sentences below. Add or delete a word to correct them.**

1 Oh, I wasn't expecting for to pay so much.
2 How about I talked to her?
3 If they agreed to let us buy a new computer system, we'd increase sales.
4 You'll find I'm good for money.
5 Look, I'd like make a proposal.
6 Could I suggest we to meet in November?
7 But in this case, I think ten percent is more appropriate.
8 I need more time think about this and take some advice.

V1 **5 Complete the word puzzle with the eight different types of writing.**

1 B □ O □ □
2 P O □ □ □ □
3 B □ O □ □ □ □ □ □ □ □
4 H □ □ □ O □ □
5 M □ □ O □ □ □
6 A □ □ O □ □ □ □ □ □ □ □ □ □ □
7 R O □ □ □ □ □ □
8 N O □ □ □ □

V2 **6 Which person in V2 is described in each sentence?**

critic novelist judge biographer poet dramatist

1 Jeremy chose a popular writer as the winner.
2 Cindy has just published a book of poems.
3 Has Joe completed his book on Nelson Mandela?
4 They're putting on Debbie's play at a local theatre.
5 I've just read Henry's review of the play.
6 Janet has just published her second novel.

V3 **7 Find the following words in V3.**

1 four nouns for something that produces light: _____ _____ _____ _____
2 four verbs that mean to make a loud noise: _____ _____ _____ _____
3 three nouns that describe a particular type of light: _____ _____ _____
4 two abstract nouns that describe the lack or absence of something: _____ _____
5 two adjectives that describe whether a noise can be heard or not: _____ _____

Language reference

GRAMMAR

G1 The passive: present simple and continuous, *will* future and *-ing* forms

Form the present simple passive with *am/is/are* + past participle.

The castle **is protected** by high walls.

Form the present continuous passive with *am/is/are being* + past participle.

We'**re being watched**.

Form the future simple passive with *will be* + past participle.

The new bridge **will be opened** next year.

! The form of *be* agrees with the subject of the passive verb.

A bag was stolen.
Ten bags were stolen.

Form the passive of *-ing* forms with *being* + past participle, for example after prepositions.

The children **insisted on being taken** to the zoo.
I don't **like being watched**.

! Intransitive verbs (verbs which don't have an object) cannot be made passive.

~~The train was arrived on time~~. ✗

We often use the passive when:

- the agent is obvious from the context.
  The man was arrested yesterday. (obviously by the police)
  I'm going to be given a promotion. (obviously by my boss)
- the agent is unknown or isn't important.
  My watch has been stolen.
  The house has been demolished.

G2 The passive: past simple and continuous, present perfect, infinitives

Form the past simple passive with *was/were* + past participle.

The building **was demolished** in 2005.

Form the past continuous passive with *was/were being* + past participle.

The rooms **were being decorated** so we couldn't go in.

Form the present perfect passive with *has/have been* + past participle.

The factory **has been designed** by a Spanish architect.

Form the past perfect passive with *had been* + past participle.

The flight **had been cancelled** because of fog.

Form the passive of infinitives with *to be* + past participle.

The builders are scheduled **to complete** the work within two years. → The work is scheduled **to be completed** within two years.
I wanted somebody **to help** me. → I wanted **to be helped**.

G3 Use of the passive

In English we prefer to start a new sentence with a familiar subject (something that has already been mentioned). The passive can help us do this.

The house is in Illinois. Frank Lloyd Wright designed **it**. ✗
The house is in Illinois. **It** was designed by Frank Lloyd Wright. ✓

We usually prefer to put short subjects at the beginning of a sentence and longer expressions at the end. The passive helps us do this.

An engineer who had previously worked on a bridge in Spain designed the new bridge. ✗
The new bridge **was designed by an engineer who had previously worked on a bridge in Spain.** ✓

KEY LANGUAGE

KL Talking about requirements

… it's vital we have …
It's absolutely essential to offer …
We've got to offer them …
We certainly need …
… we should offer them something …
It might be a good idea to have …
… we'd have to find out …
But we need to think this through …

VOCABULARY

V1 Adjectives for describing buildings

ancient, classical, contemporary, derelict, dilapidated, elegant, graceful, imposing, impressive, innovative, magnificent, ornate, run-down, stylish, traditional, ugly

V2 Verbs used with buildings

commission, construct, damage, demolish, design, maintain, rebuild, restore

V3 Idioms

build bridges, burn one's bridges, cross a/that bridge when we come to it, water under the bridge

V4 Prefixes *in-, mis-, over-, re-, un-*

indisputable, insensitive, insoluble, misplaced, misunderstand, overcome, overcrowded, redefine, revitalise, unimportant, unusual

Extra practice 7

G1,2 **1 Complete the second sentence so that it has a similar meaning to the first. Do not include the agent (the person or thing that does the action).**

1 Someone has stolen my dictionary.
My dictionary ________.
2 A security guard was watching the building.
The building ________.
3 Something is keeping me awake at night.
I ________.
4 They gave my father a watch when he retired.
My father ________ when he retired.
5 We require a large deposit.
A large deposit ________.
6 We can't explain it.
It ________.

2 Complete the text with a passive form of the words in brackets.

The Parthenon was commissioned while democracy [1]________ (establish) in Athens in the 5th century BC. Many of the old buildings in Athens had been burnt down by the Persians and Phidias, a sculptor, [2]________ (give) the task of rebuilding them. The Parthenon [3]________ (build) to house the statue of Athena. Phidias insisted on [4] ________ (allow) to use only the most expensive and beautiful materials. Ever since ancient times architects all over the world [5]________ (influence) by the Parthenon. Over the years a number of exact copies [6]________ (construct) in different parts of the world. Even the Capitol building in Washington DC [7]________ (inspire) by it.

At the moment the Parthenon [8]________ (damage) by pollution, but it is expected [9]________ (restore) to its former glory in the years to come.

G3 **3 Choose the best way to follow the sentences.**

1 Jane's lived in that house by the river all her life.
a) It was built by Don Baum, who was a famous architect.
b) Don Baum, who was a famous architect, built it.
2 The bridge only lasted 20 years.
a) The terrible earthquake that damaged much of the city destroyed it.
b) It was destroyed by the terrible earthquake that damaged much of the city.
3 I've always enjoyed talking to my grandmother.
a) Great stories about her life are told to me by her.
b) She tells me great stories about her life.
4 The film has received five Oscar nominations.
a) It was directed by James Cameron, who also directed *Titanic*.
b) James Cameron, who also directed *Titanic*, directed it.

KL **4 Complete the sentences with the words in the box.**

absolutely	find	need	got
offer	vital	idea	through

1 We've _____ to offer good value for money.
2 But we need to think all the problems _____.
3 It's _____ we have plenty of time to discuss this.
4 It's _____ essential to offer leisure facilities.
5 It might be a good _____ to have a sauna.
6 We'd have to _____ out how many rooms we need.
7 We should _____ them something, that's for sure.
8 We certainly _____ parking spaces.

V1 **5 Circle the odd one out in each group.**

1 derelict dilapidated ornate run-down
2 elegant innovative graceful stylish
3 ancient imposing impressive magnificent
4 classical ugly contemporary traditional

V2 **6 Replace the phrase in *italics* with the correct form of a verb from V2.**

1 After the fire many buildings had to be *made again*.
2 The earthquake *harmed* large areas of the country.
3 We decided to *ask* a German construction company to build our new company headquarters.
4 They plan to *knock down* the dangerous building.
5 Who *planned* the Sydney Opera House?
6 This building is hard to *keep in good condition*.
7 We'd like to *repair* all the original decoration.
8 They plan to *build* a new library here.

V3 **7 Match the sentence halves.**

1 We should forgive that past mistake. It's
2 You don't need to deal with that now – you can
3 If you do that, you'll never be able to work there again, so don't
4 After their past disagreements, they all need to

a) cross that bridge when you come to it.
b) build bridges.
c) burn your bridges.
d) water under the bridge.

V4 **8 Choose the correct word.**

1 We'll never know the answer to that question – it's *misplaced / insoluble*.
2 Some of the old houses in the city are terribly *insensitive / overcrowded*.
3 Investment in industry has *revitalised / misplaced* the town.
4 I'm sorry – I obviously *misunderstood / overcame* what you said.
5 Don't worry about that – it's *indisputable / unimportant* right now.

8 Language reference

GRAMMAR

G1 Verb + *-ing*/infinitive

When one verb follows another, it may appear in the infinitive or *-ing* form. The form depends on the first verb, and the following structures are possible:

- verb + infinitive, e.g. *appear, attempt, decide, manage, need, offer, promise, seem, want.*
  Globalisation **appears to be** a serious political issue these days.
- verb + object + infinitive, e.g. *advise, allow, encourage, invite, persuade, remind, request, tell.*
  The Internet **allows people to communicate**.
- verb + *-ing* form, e.g. *consider, deny, dislike, enjoy, feel like, finish, practise, suggest.*
  Would you **consider giving** us a refund?
- verb + *-ing* or infinitive with different meanings:

remember

Remember to bring the tickets. We need them for our flight. (+ infinitive: thinking about a future action)

I **remember watching** the Olympics in 2004. (+ *-ing* form: thinking about an earlier action)

forget

Don't **forget to bring** your passport. (+ infinitive: thinking about a future action)

I won't **forget eating** my first Thai curry. (+ *-ing* form: thinking about an earlier action)

stop

I **stopped to have** a break. (+ infinitive: stop one action in order to do something else)

They **stopped making** them in 2002. (+ *-ing* form: finish an action)

try

Carla's **trying to** lose weight. (+ infinitive: make an effort to do something difficult)

Why don't you **try cooking** it in olive oil? It might taste better. (+ *-ing* form: do something as an experiment – you don't know if it will work or not)

G2 *have something done*

Use this form when an action is done for you by somebody else.

I **had my suit cleaned**. (The shop did it.)

He **had his mobile phone repaired**. (An engineer did it.)

Use a form of *have* + object + past participle:

- present simple
  Claire **has her hair cut** every month.
- present continuous
  Dave and Bill **are having their hair cut.**
- past simple
  Claire **had her hair cut last week.**
- present perfect
  Claire **has had her hair cut.**

! Do not confuse this form with the past perfect.

We **had a new computer system installed.**

The technician **had installed a new computer system**. (past perfect)

We can make questions and negatives.

Are you **having your car serviced** this week?

I **haven't had the windows cleaned** for ages.

In spoken or informal English, we can also use *get* + object + past participle.

I **got my eyes checked** last week because I've been having headaches.

We also use this form to talk about something that happens to us that we have no control over.

In this street we **have our rubbish collected** once a week.

We often use the form for unexpected or unpleasant things that happen to us.

To our great surprise, we **had our money refunded.**

He **had his mobile phone stolen**.

KEY LANGUAGE

KL Clarification

Asking for clarification

What do you mean by … ?

Sorry, I don't know what you mean.

Could you explain that in more detail please?

Could you be more specific?

Could you give me a specific example?

Clarifying (making your meaning clearer)

Basically what I'm saying is … the customer is …

What I really want to say is …

Or to put it another way …

Let me rephrase that.

To be more precise … we really appeal to …

VOCABULARY

V1 Word combinations (globalisation)

child labour, climate change, consumer choice, corporate greed, fair trade, free markets, global warming, human rights, multinational companies, natural resources

V2 Abstract nouns

collaboration, creativity, hierarchy, influence, networking

V3 Media words

broadcast (n/v), celebrity, character, coverage, newspaper, paparazzi, press, programme, televised

G1 1 **There is a missing or incorrect word in each sentence. Find the mistakes and correct them.**

1 Our teacher allowed us use calculators.
2 We stopped the car look at the beautiful view.
3 Would you consider give us a larger room?
4 I'm afraid I forgot locking the door before I left.
5 The door seems be locked. Do you have the key?
6 There's no answer. I'll try send him a text message.
7 Did you remember turning off the lights?
8 I always try stay in touch with my old friends.

2 **Complete the gaps with the appropriate phrase below each sentence pair.**

1 1 They _____ sugar in those drinks years ago.
  2 We _____ some petrol in the car.
  a) stopped to put   b) stopped putting
2 1 Don't _____ eggs when you go shopping!
  2 I'll never _____ only 10 percent in my final university exam. It was so embarrassing!
  a) forget to get   b) forget getting
3 1 I _____ my first girlfriend to meet my parents.
  2 I must _____ some warm clothes with me.
  a) remember to bring   b) remember bringing
4 1 I _____ the door but it was stuck.
  2 She _____ a shop but it never made a profit.
  a) tried to open   b) tried opening

G2 3 **Complete the second sentence so that it has a similar meaning to the first, using a form of *have something done*.**

1 The police have searched the suspect's house.
  The suspect __________.
2 The children are washing my car.
  I __________.
3 The jeweller repaired Uncle David's watch.
  Uncle David __________ by the jeweller.
4 Janice cuts my hair once a month.
  I __________ by Janice.
5 The company has cancelled Danielle's contract.
  Danielle __________ by the company.
6 They searched our bags when we arrived.
  We __________ when we arrived.

KL 4 **Match the sentence halves.**

1 Could you explain that	a) to say is …
2 Could you be more	b) rephrase that.
3 What I really want	c) what you mean.
4 What do you	d) in more detail, please?
5 Let me	e) another way …
6 Could you give me	f) specific?
7 Or to put it	g) a specific example?
8 Sorry, I don't know	h) mean by globalisation?

V1,2 5 **Complete the crossword using the clues.**

Clues Across

6 _____ companies have offices and factories in many different countries.
8 In some countries human _____ are not respected.
10 _____ greed means some companies do anything to make a profit.

Clues Down

1 The media has a huge _____ over public opinion.
2 Artists need _____ in order to think of new ideas.
3 The United Nations is a good example of _____ between people from different countries.
4 Jack does a lot of _____ – he has lots of contacts.
5 There's always a _____ in animal groups, ranging from the leader down to the least important member.
7 Russia has plenty of natural _____ like coal and gas.
9 Some say _____ trade lifts people out of poverty.

V3 6 **Complete the text with words from V3.**

Victoria Beckham is an international [1]_____ and is often seen as a role model for young people. She is constantly in the [2]_____, especially women's magazines, and is followed around by dozens of [3]_____ desperate to get pictures of her. She has been really famous since she married England footballer David Beckham. Whenever they make public appearances the couple are mobbed by fans, and a number of TV stations have [4]_____ several documentaries about them.

Victoria first became famous with the pop group the Spice Girls and one British [5]_____ gave her the nickname *Posh Spice*. At the peak of their success in 1994 the Spice Girls had number one hits in both the US and UK. The group split up in 2001 and the announcement that they would re-form in 2007 led to enormous press [6]_____ throughout the world.

GRAMMAR

G1 Gradable and ungradable adjectives

Adjectives describe a quality that something possesses. To describe, for example, variations in temperature we can use *hot* or *cold*, which are gradable adjectives. But to describe the limits (the maximum or minimum level) of temperature we use *boiling* or *freezing*, which are ungradable adjectives.

limit ← amount of a quality → limit

ungradable	gradable		gradable	ungradable
tiny	small	**size**	big	enormous
excellent	good	**good/bad**	bad	terrible
boiling	warm/hot	**temperature**	cold	freezing

Some other common gradable and ungradable forms are *tired → exhausted, angry → furious, hungry → starving, interesting → fascinating, upset → devastated, unusual → unique* and *important → essential.*

Adverbs make adjectives stronger or weaker. Some adverbs can only be used with gradable or ungradable adjectives.

used with gradable adjectives	used with ungradable adjectives	used with both gradable and ungradable adjectives
very extremely a bit slightly	absolutely completely totally	really

The water was **very cold**.
By the end of the day I was **extremely hungry**.
The water was **absolutely freezing**.
We were **really hungry** and **really exhausted**!

! Don't use comparative or superlative forms of ungradable adjectives. Use gradable adjectives instead.

~~This water is **more freezing** than the water in the sea.~~ ✗

This water is **colder** than the water in the sea. ✓

With some adjectives we don't use *very, absolutely,* etc., but instead we use other adverbs, e.g. *highly qualified, completely wrong.*

G2 The position of adverbs / adverb phrases

Adverbs / Adverb phrases of time, place and manner

We usually put adverbs of time (e.g. *then, in 1972, nowadays*), adverbs of place (e.g. *there, at home, to New York*) and adverbs of manner (e.g. *quickly, carefully, creatively, dramatically*) at the end of a clause.

The last invasion of England took place **in 1066**.
When did you live **there**?

We can emphasise adverbs of time and place by putting them at the beginning of the clause:

In 2001 I decided to give up my job and go back to college.
At home I always feel calm and relaxed.

Adverbs of frequency, certainty and degree

We usually put adverbs of frequency (e.g. *never, often, usually, frequently*), adverbs of certainty (e.g. *definitely, probably, certainly*) and adverbs of degree (e.g. *completely, mostly, mainly*) in the middle of a clause, between the subject and the verb.

We often take the train to college.
You probably left your mobile phone in the taxi.
His work mainly focuses on the human body.

With the verb *to be,* we put the adverb after the verb.

She **is probably** the best person for the job.
His later works **are often** very large.

With auxiliary verbs, we put the adverb between the auxiliary and the main verb.

We **have often laughed** at his jokes.
She **was definitely staying** in the big hotel.

KEY LANGUAGE

KL Sequencing information, moving to a new point

Ordering information in a talk

Firstly, I'll (give you a few basic facts).
Finally, I'll (describe what she's like as a person).

Signalling the end of one topic

Right, I've told you a bit about (her).
OK, that's all I have to say about (her style).
OK, that's it for (the critics).
Right, now you know a bit about (the kind of person she is).

Changing to a new topic

So moving on now to (her style of painting) …
Let's go on to (her personality and reputation) now.

VOCABULARY

V1 Art and artists

abstract, artist, art lover, collector, contemporary, controversial, critic, groundbreaking, masterpiece, modern, painter, preview, realism, realist, retrospective, sculptor, thought-provoking

V2 Adverb/adjective combinations

completely different, completely wrong, deeply moving, entirely unexpected, heavily criticised, highly praised, highly qualified, painfully shy, totally different, totally unbelievable, totally unjustified, utterly impossible, utterly useless

Extra practice 9

G1 1 Choose the correct adjective or adverb. Sometimes both choices are possible.

1 Let's stay at home; it's *very / absolutely* freezing outside!
2 I was *really / absolutely* devastated when I heard the news.
3 This work of art is *absolutely / a bit* unique.
4 It's *really / very* important to have good friends.
5 Her new mobile is *slightly / extremely* unusual.
6 Be careful. The boss is *very / absolutely* angry.
7 These photographs are very *good / excellent*.
8 Mike's new house is really *enormous / big*.
9 Her latest book is extremely *interesting / fascinating*.
10 In August, Madrid is *hotter / more boiling* than Paris.
11 I'm absolutely *hungry / starving* – can we get something to eat?
12 Maria was a bit *devastated / upset* by her exam results.

G2 2 There are seven adverbs / adverb phrases in the wrong position in the text. Find and correct the mistakes.

Bridget Riley probably is the most famous living painter of op art (optical art). These are works which feature usually patterns that create illusions of movement and colour in the viewer's mind.

Riley studied in London and then had a number of jobs in art colleges and in the art department of an advertising agency. Her most famous works were painted in the 1960s. In these large paintings she used skilfully black and white lines to create amazing illusions. Her in London first big exhibition was in 1962. The paintings on display were so powerful that viewers complained frequently of seasickness or headaches.

In the 1970s and 1980s Riley became inspired by Egyptian art. In the paintings from this period she used imaginatively colour. She in the late 1980s began to experiment with diagonal patterns.

3 Choose the correct answer.

1 He *is mainly / mainly is* a singer, but he occasionally writes songs too.
2 Michaela *opened carefully the envelope / opened the envelope carefully*.
3 *In 2004 I / I in 2004* moved to Birmingham.
4 They *get home usually / usually get home* at 4 p.m.
5 You *certainly know / know certainly* lots about art!
6 We *often have seen / have often seen* foxes in our garden at this time of year.
7 What time *there did you get / did you get there*?
8 Jack was in a rush so he *finished his essay quickly / finished quickly his essay*.

KL 4 A tour guide is telling a group about a trip. Complete the talk with the phrases below. There is one extra phrase.

1_____ I'll give you some basic information about today's trip. Then I'll tell you about some of the paintings we'll be looking at. 2_____ I'll give you your tickets for the exhibition.

3_____ the details of tomorrow's trip. We'll be leaving the school at 9 a.m., so please all be here by 8.45.
4_____ the timetable I'll tell you about the paintings. So, Lucien Freud is one of our greatest living painters. I want you to notice his very distinctive use of colour.
5_____ I have to say about the exhibition. 6_____ to organising the tickets …

a) Let's go on
b) So, moving on to
c) Finally,
d) OK, that's all
e) Right, I've told you a bit
f) Firstly,
g) Right, now you know

V1 5 Find the following in V1.

1 six people connected with art
2 four styles or periods of art
3 three adjectives describing opinion
4 two types of exhibition
5 the word for the best example of an artist's work

V2 6 Choose the correct word in italics.

1 The funeral was deeply *different / moving*.
2 Jo is *completely / painfully* shy so she hates parties.
3 Sorry – I'm utterly *useless / wrong* at Mathematics.
4 The model's behaviour was heavily *criticised / praised* in the press.
5 Although she is *highly / totally* qualified, she doesn't earn much money.
6 The sudden change in the weather was *heavily / entirely* unexpected.
7 A lot of people think the book's plot is *totally / deeply* unbelievable.
8 Jemma's painting was *highly / utterly* praised by the critics.
9 Your comments are *heavily / totally* unjustified.
10 The two works of art were totally *criticised / different*.
11 His answer was completely *qualified / wrong*.
12 It's *utterly / highly* impossible to live without food or water.

10 Language reference

GRAMMAR

G1 Relative clauses

Relative clauses give us information about something or someone in a main clause.

Defining relative clauses

Use defining relative clauses to identify or define things, ideas, places, time and possessions.

Mr Carson is the man **who taught us geography**.

Without the relative clause, the main clause doesn't have a clear meaning.

~~Mr Carson is the man~~. ✗

Use a relative pronoun or adverb to introduce the relative clause. Use *that* for things and people, *which* for things, *who* for people, *where* for places, *when* for times, *whose* for possession.

! Don't repeat the noun from the main clause or introduce a personal pronoun to replace it.

Mr Carson is the man who ~~he~~ taught us geography. ✗

In formal English we prefer to put prepositions before the relative pronoun. In informal English we normally put the preposition at the end of the clause.

Parents need to know **with whom** their children are associating. (formal)

Parents need to know who their children are mixing **with**. (informal)

Use *whom* instead of *who,* and *which* instead of *that* after prepositions.

Children feel social pressure to conform to the peer group **with whom** they socialise.

Parents need to encourage children to avoid situations **in which** they could be pressurised.

! Don't use prepositions with the relative adverbs *when* and *where*.

2005 was the year when she left home ~~in~~. ✗

This is the school where I studied ~~at~~. ✗

If the relative pronoun is the object of the clause we can omit it.

Karl is the person (that) I told you about. (I told you about **him**.)

! We can't omit the relative pronoun if it is the subject of the clause.

I'd like you to meet Steve, who used to be my boss.

~~I'd like you to meet Steve, used to be my boss~~. ✗

Non-defining relative clauses

Non-defining relative clauses give us extra information which can be left out without affecting the main meaning of the sentence. They are more common in written English.

The author lives in the countryside.

The author**, who is quite elderly,** lives in the countryside.

These clauses have a comma before the clause, and after it if necessary.

! Don't use *that* in non-defining relative clauses.

~~My new TV, **that** I bought last week, is broken~~. ✗

My new TV, **which** I bought last week, is broken. ✓

! We never omit the pronoun in non-defining relative clauses.

~~My new car, I bought last week, has already broken down~~. ✗

In both spoken and written English we can use a non-defining clause to add a comment or opinion about the action or situation in the main clause.

We took all the teenagers to the seaside, **which was a good break for them**.

Everyone failed the test, **which was really unfair**.

G2 Reduced relative clauses

We can often replace a relative clause with a participle phrase (a phrase beginning with the past participle or *-ing* form of a verb).

We looked at the letters **which had been posted by the suspect**.

= We looked at the letters **posted by the suspect**.

He arrived late, **which made us miss the train.**

= He arrived late, **making us miss the train.**

In these clauses the *-ing* form has an active meaning and the past participle has a passive meaning.

There was a huge storm, **causing** serious floods. (The storm caused floods. = active meaning)

We saw the famous picture **painted** by Picasso. (The picture was painted by Picasso. = passive meaning)

We can't replace the relative clause like this if the relative pronoun is the object of the relative clause.

~~Karl is the person telling you about~~. ✗

~~Karl is the person told you about~~. ✗

KEY LANGUAGE

KL Giving advice

I'd advise you to …	You might consider …
I think you need to …	If I were you, I'd …
Why don't you …?	It's vital that you …
You could also …	It's essential that …
It might be a good idea to …	

VOCABULARY

V1 Verbs connected with working together

break up, fall out with, get down to, get on with, get used to, put up with

V2 Idioms with *mind*

be in two minds, be out of your mind, keep an open mind, make up your mind, peace of mind

V3 Psychology

assessment, case file, deduce, motive, profile, psychiatrist

Extra practice 10

G1 1 Combine the information to make one sentence using a relative clause. If possible, do not include a relative pronoun.

1 That's the man. I met him yesterday.
That's __________.
2 This is the DVD player. It doesn't work very well.
This is __________.
3 Janine is the woman. Her house was destroyed in the earthquake.
Janine __________.
4 My sister lives in an old house. She's a doctor.
My __________.
5 This is the computer game. I told you about it.
This is __________.
6 The course is very difficult. It began in September.
The __________.

2 Rewrite the sentences in more formal English.

1 I don't fully understand the problem that he's working on.
2 Protecting the environment is a cause that she really believes in.
3 This is the bill that we disagreed about.
4 This is the course which they applied for.
5 That hotel is the one that we often stayed in.
6 Constance is the architect who I work for.
7 That's the team that my brother plays football for.
8 Do you remember the project that we used to work together on?

3 There is a mistake in each sentence. Correct it.

1 Do you know the person about who I am talking?
2 This phone, that was very expensive, has never worked properly.
3 I'm visiting the place where I grew up in.
4 Michael who is very intelligent, isn't very good at solving puzzles.
5 The students, are from many different countries, are learning English.
6 She's a woman that she never admits she's wrong.

G2 4 Choose the correct answer.

1 This is one of the houses *designing / designed* by Le Corbusier.
2 There was a lot of rubbish *leaving / left* by the previous residents.
3 We noticed a girl *standing / stood* on the corner.
4 I always do the exercises *recommended / recommending* by my personal trainer.
5 We arrived early, *giving / given* us plenty of time to check in.
6 We live in a house *buying / bought* by my father in 1992.

KL 5 Complete the sentences with the phrases below.

1 It might be _____ to speak to a lawyer.
2 Why don't you _____ your boss?
3 If I were you, _____ get some counselling.
4 It's essential _____ tell somebody about it.
5 I'd _____ you to ask for a refund.
6 You might _____ contacting a lawyer.
7 I think you _____ to see a doctor.
8 It's _____ that you talk to him

a) consider
b) vital
c) a good idea
d) I'd
e) need
f) advise
g) talk to
h) that you

V1 6 Replace the phrases in *italics* with the verbs in V1.

1 I *have a friendly relationship with* my neighbours.
2 It's hard to *become comfortable with* a new home.
3 My parents *separated* when I was quite young.
4 It's important not to *quarrel with* your colleagues.
5 My father won't *tolerate* bad behaviour.
6 Have you managed to *start* work on that project?

V2 7 Match the sentences.

1 Carol deliberately doesn't form a definite opinion.
2 Michaela is crazy.
3 Now she's finished, Isabel feels calm and relaxed.
4 Cristina knows what she wants to do.
5 Serena can't decide what to do.

a) She's in two minds.
b) She's out of her mind.
c) She keeps an open mind.
d) She's made up her mind.
e) She has peace of mind.

V3 8 Complete the text with the correct form of words in V3.

Speakers at next month's conference for the world's leading criminal profilers will include police officers, psychologists and [1]_____ from all over the world. Participants will be able to examine [2]_____ from a number of well-known criminal investigations. Presentations include lectures on psychological [3]_____ and the use of [4]_____ in terrorist cases. There will also be discussions on the analysis of [5]_____ and whether we can [6]_____ future criminal activity from youthful behaviour.

11 Language reference

GRAMMAR

G1 Reported speech

Use reported speech to report someone's words.

'I'm hungry.'
She said **she was hungry**.

We use statement word order in reported questions. We don't put a question mark at the end.

'How much is it?'
She asked **how much it was**. ✓
~~She asked how much was it?~~ ✗

To report a *yes/no* question we use *ask* + *if* or *whether*.

'Is it expensive?'
She asked **if it was expensive**.

When we use reported speech, we often make changes to the tense of the verb, to pronouns and to time adverbs. The table shows the most common changes:

Direct speech	Reported speech
tenses:	
present simple	past simple
present continuous	past continuous
present perfect	past perfect
past simple	past perfect
will	*would*
can	*could*
pronouns:	
I	he/she
we	they
my	his/her
our	their
time adverbs:	
today	then / that day
yesterday	the day before
tomorrow	the next day / the day after
last week	the week before

! The past perfect simple and continuous, and the modal verbs *could*, *would*, *might* and *should* do not change.

In some situations we can choose NOT to change the tense in reported speech. This can be because:

- the action or situation in the statement is still happening/true.
  'I'm expecting a baby.'
  She said she'**s expecting** a baby. (She's still expecting a baby.)
- the verb expresses a fact or situation that cannot change or is unlikely to change.
  'The city is beautiful.'
  He said the city **is** beautiful. (It's still true.)
- the verb comes after a time conjunction, e.g. *when*, *after*.
  'I started my job after I finished university.'
  He said he had started his job **after** he **finished** university.

! We do not change the tense or time adverbs if the reporting verb is in the present tense.
He **says** he **is working** very hard **this year**.
She **tells** us she **isn't earning** very much money **at the moment**.

G2 Reporting verbs

We often use particular verbs to report speech. The verbs show the attitude of the person speaking so they give a lot more information than *say*.

'I think you really should apply for the job.'
He **encouraged** me to apply for the job.

Different reporting verbs are followed by different structures.

infinitive with *to*	*offer, refuse, agree, promise*
object + infinitive with *to*	*advise, invite, warn, tell, encourage, persuade*
-ing form	*admit, regret, consider, deny* all verbs followed by a preposition, e.g. *insist on, apologise for*

KEY LANGUAGE

KL Creating impact in a presentation

Tripling (saying things in threes)

... an important **industrial**, **commercial** and **cultural** centre.

... they help to create the **lively**, **friendly**, **cosmopolitan** atmosphere the city is famous for.

Repetition

Toronto's getting **better** and **better** these days, as **more** and **more** people come from all over the world.

Rhetorical questions

So, **what** are the main sights of the city?

OK, **why** is the CN Tower worth seeing?

VOCABULARY

V1 Aspects of culture

architecture, climate, cuisine, customs, geography, historical events, institutions, language, life rituals, religion, rules of behaviour, the arts, traditions, values

V2 Adjectives

frustrated, hostile, inadequate, intriguing, isolated, stimulated

V3 Prefixes

anti-, counter-, inter-, mis-, multi-, post-, pre-, sub-

V4 Suffixes

-able, -ible, -ism, -less, -logy, -ment

Extra practice 11

G1 1 Complete the reported statements. Make changes to tenses, pronouns and time adverbs.

1 'I'm working in a café.'
She said she ________ in a café.
2 'I lived in Berlin for three years.'
He said he ________ in Berlin for three years.
3 'You should see a doctor.'
She said I ________ a doctor.
4 'We'll see you here tomorrow.'
They said they ________ us ________.
5 'I've been abroad with my wife and our children.'
He said he ________ abroad with ________ wife and ________ children.
6 'My father received a tax bill yesterday.'
He said ________ father ________ a tax bill ________.

2 Complete the reported statements. Do NOT change the tense if it is not necessary.

1 'I don't have a job at the moment.'
This morning Caroline said ________.
2 'The weather here is always cold in the winter.'
This afternoon the receptionist told us ________.
3 'We're going to France when we finish the course.'
They said ________.
4 'I went to a terrible school when I was a child.'
Michaela said she ________.
5 'We watched the final episode of *ER* last night.'
Last Wednesday my friends said ________.
6 'Pollution from cars causes global warming.'
We want to buy a smaller car because the scientist said ________.

G2 3 Choose the correct answer.

1 The driver *warned* / *refused* me not to jump off the bus while it was moving.
2 Carol *refused* / *regretted* to pay the bill.
3 Our teacher *apologised for* / *offered* being late.
4 They've *offered* / *invited* to give me a trial.
5 My friends *persuaded* / *agreed* me to go to the park with them.
6 I'm afraid she didn't *agree* / *advise* to lend it to me.

4 Complete the sentences to report the statements.

1 'I'll carry your case.' He offered ________.
2 'I was really stupid to get married so young.'
She regretted ________.
3 'Don't buy anything in that shop.' Mike warned ________.
4 'I'm really sorry that I shouted at you.' She apologised ________.
5 'We really think you should learn the guitar.' My parents encouraged ________.

KL 5 Use the notes to write sentences for a presentation about Cambridge. Use the techniques of tripling, repetition or rhetorical questions.

1 why / Cambridge / seeing?
2 it / important educational / cultural / business centre
3 facilities / tourists / better each year
4 its buildings / parks / countryside / make it / beautiful place / live
5 the university / becoming / more popular / international students
6 what / main historical sights / city?

V1 6 Complete the sentences with words in V1.

1 Most children learn a foreign _____ these days.
2 The financial and legal systems are vital _____.
3 I'm not keen on Indian _____ – I find it too spicy.
4 Buddhism is a popular _____ in Asia.
5 I love _____ in general, but my favourite is opera.
6 She loves the _____ of 16th century Italy, especially Michelangelo's buildings.
7 Having a formal dance at the end of the year is one of the _____ of high school life in the US.
8 I love places with a warm _____ – I hate the cold!

V2 7 Match the sentence halves.

1 I'm a happy person, but I live alone
2 My neighbours hate me – they shout at me
3 I feel frustrated when
4 Being surrounded by very intelligent people
5 We were really stimulated by
6 I couldn't work out who the murderer was

a) and can be quite hostile.
b) can make me feel inadequate.
c) so it was very intriguing.
d) so I sometimes feel isolated.
e) I can't find the answer to a problem.
f) all the exciting possibilities ahead of us.

V3,4 8 Complete the gaps with a suitable form of the word in brackets.

1 She owns a very _____ watch. (value)
2 It's OK – my children are very _____. (responsibility)
3 Budget airlines have made _____ travel much more affordable. (nation)
4 There are 20 different nationalities here – it's a very _____ area. (culture)
5 We had a fight over a stupid _____. (understand)
6 We will not tolerate _____ behaviour here. (social)
7 The castle is very old. It _____ the surrounding buildings. (date)
8 Really good music is _____ – it appeals to people just as much today as it did in the past. (time)

12 Language reference

GRAMMAR

G1 First and second conditionals

First conditional

Form the first conditional in the following way:

if-clause +	main clause
if + present simple	*will/may/might/should,* etc. + infinitive without *to*

Use the first conditional to talk about real possibilities.

If you **ask** him, he'**ll be** happy to help you.

As long as and *provided that* mean *only if*. We often use these expressions to talk about rules or to make a bargain or promise.

We will give you a refund **provided that** you produce a valid receipt. (= We will give you a refund only if you provide a receipt.)
You'll be able to take photographs **as long as** you don't use a flash.

Second conditional

Form the second conditional in the following way:

if-clause +	main clause
if + past simple	*would/could/might,* etc. + infinitive without *to*

Use the second conditional to talk about an unreal situation in the present or future.

If you **had** good eyesight, you **wouldn't need** glasses. (= You don't have good eyesight.)
If you **were** invited to the party, **would** you **go**? (= You are unlikely to be invited to the party.)

We can introduce the condition with *supposing (that)* or *imagine*. We often use these expressions to talk about an imaginary situation.

Supposing you won the lottery, what would you buy?
Imagine you were a film star, how would it feel?

G2 Third and mixed conditionals

Third conditional

Form the third conditional in the following way:

if-clause +	main clause
if + past perfect	*would/could/might + have* + past participle

Use the third conditional to talk about unreal situations in the past, i.e. situations that are contrary to the facts.

If you'**d been** there, you **would have seen** her. (= You weren't there so you didn't see her.)
If I **hadn't been** to university, I **wouldn't have got** this job. (= I did go to university so I did get this job.)

We often use the third conditional to talk about regrets or to criticise.

If I'**d studied** harder, I **could have gone** to university. (= I regret that I didn't study harder.)
If you'**d listened** to me, this **wouldn't have happened.** (= You should have listened to me.)

Mixed conditionals

We can combine the clauses from the second and third conditionals to talk about the present or past results of unreal situations.

- second + third conditional: past condition with present result

if-clause +	main clause
if + past perfect	*would/should/might/could,* etc. + infinitive without *to*

If you'**d brought** a map, we **wouldn't be** lost **now.** (= You didn't bring a map so now we are lost.)

- third + second conditional: present condition with past result

if-clause +	main clause
if + past simple	*would/might/could + have* + past participle.

If you **paid** attention in class, you **would have got** higher marks. (= You don't pay attention in class. You didn't get high marks.)

KEY LANGUAGE

KL Reassuring and encouraging

I promise you, it won't go any further.
Look, I understand how you feel.
But I can assure you, we're going to put things right.
Mmm, that doesn't sound very fair to me, I must say.
Anyway, don't worry …
And I guarantee we'll sort out the problems.
You won't be out of a job, you have my word for that.
I can see how you feel.
Things'll get better, I guarantee that.

VOCABULARY

V1 Technology

apparatus, appliance, device, engine, equipment, gadget, machine, technological, technology, technophobe

V2 Technology adjectives

cutting edge, durable, easy to use, environmentally friendly, green, handy, hard-wearing, obsolete, out-of-date, practical, state-of-the-art, user-friendly

V3 Prefixes (opposites)

dislike, **in**accurate, **in**appropriate, **in**convenient, **in**effective, **in**efficient, **in**equality, **in**sensitive, **mis**management, **mis**trust, **un**able, **un**likely, **un**necessary

Extra practice

G1 1 Complete the sentences with the correct form of *buy*, a), b), c) or d).

a) buy b) bought c) will buy d) would buy

1 I _____ you a new TV if you really needed it.
2 If you _____ me an expensive ring, I'll marry you.
3 I _____ lunch if you buy dinner.
4 If that phone isn't too expensive, I _____ it.
5 Joe _____ us a camera provided he can borrow it.
6 Supposing you _____ a big car, would you use it?
7 I _____ you a pet as long as you look after it.
8 Imagine you _____ a flat abroad – it'd be great!

2 There is a mistake in each sentence. Correct it.

1 If I'll go tomorrow, I'll call you.
2 Supposing we are rich, wouldn't it be fantastic?
3 I'd be much happier if I can play the piano.
4 As long as you would look after it, I'll let you borrow my dress tonight.
5 Jane will be able to take photos of the party tomorrow if she would bring her camera.
6 Imagine you lived to 100, won't it be amazing?

G2 3 Match the sentence halves.

1 If my mobile phone battery hadn't run out,
2 If the Internet hadn't been invented,
3 If I hadn't found the tickets under the sofa,
4 If I hadn't bought a laptop computer,
5 If France hadn't had a revolution,
6 If airlines hadn't introduced cheap flights,
7 If we had invested in renewable energy sources,
8 If the shops had been open,

a) we wouldn't be able to travel so often.
b) I would have to go to Internet cafés.
c) we wouldn't be able to send emails.
d) she would have bought you a present.
e) we wouldn't have lost so many natural resources.
f) we wouldn't have been able to go to the concert.
g) it would have a king now.
h) I would have sent you a text message.

4 Complete the sentences with a suitable verb form to make sentences using the third conditional or mixed conditionals.

1 If I'd seen you, I _____ to you. (I didn't talk to you.)
2 If I _____ more revision, I wouldn't have failed so many tests. (I don't do much revision.)
3 We would have visited our friends if we _____ time. (We didn't have time.)
4 Clare _____ the manager now if she hadn't lost that client. (She isn't the manager now.)
5 If I _____ to college, I would have a better job now. (I didn't go to college.)
6 There _____ so many wars if governments talked to each other more. (There have been a lot of wars.)

KL 5 Choose the best explanation for each phrase.

1 We'll sort out the problem.
2 It won't go any further.
3 Things'll get better.
4 That doesn't sound very fair.
5 You won't be out of a job.
6 We're going to put things right.
7 I can see how you feel.
8 I guarantee that.

a) I'm sure this will happen.
b) We won't fire you.
c) I won't tell other people.
d) We'll find a solution.
e) We're going to resolve the problem.
f) The situation will improve.
g) I understand your feelings.
h) That's not reasonable.

V1 6 Choose the correct word.

1 We sell a full range of domestic *apparatus* / *appliances*, from washing machines to cookers.
2 I've just bought an XJ56 – it's a *device* / *technology* for measuring distances between two points.
3 Did John get the *appliance* / *apparatus* he needs for his scientific experiments?
4 What *device* / *equipment* do you need for camping?
5 I've just found this little *engine* / *gadget* that helps you peel vegetables.

V2 7 Match the words and phrases in the box with the definitions below.

durable	environmentally friendly	obsolete
user-friendly	state-of-the-art	handy

1 easy for people to use
2 uses the most recent technology
3 will last for a long time
4 so old-fashioned that you can't use it any more
5 very useful and convenient
6 doesn't harm the planet

V3 8 Complete the words in the sentences with the prefixes *dis-*, *in-*, *mis-* or *un-*.

1 Since the operation I've been _____able to walk.
2 Our party fights _____equality in society.
3 Eleanor _____likes spicy food – she never eats it.
4 The report is full of _____accurate information.
5 I _____trust politicians – they never tell the truth.
6 Don't bring a gift – it's completely _____necessary.
7 That company is very _____efficient.
8 He wore a dirty T-shirt to my wedding. I think that's very _____appropriate behaviour.

COMMUNICATION

INFORMATION FOR STUDENT A

Lesson 1.4 Exercise 6a (page 13)

Martin came to see you last week and told you the following. Note down the key points.

He wants to have a system for buying food – the fridge is full of bottles of milk and packets of butter. There are four jars of coffee on the shelves. It's a waste of money, in his opinion.

He wants a rota for cleaning – the flat is always in a mess. 'I can't live like that any longer.'

Stewart's friend is still in the flat. He must leave – he uses too much electricity (without paying) and eats too much food.

Martin wants the flatmates to go out together at least twice a week for a meal or to a club, so that they can develop a friendlier relationship.

Lesson 2.1 Exercise 7a (page 17)

Look at the information from a survey (below) and answer the questions.

1 Where does the information come from?

2 What does it show?

3 Are there any trends? What are the main changes?

4 Is there any unusual or surprising information?

Cost of living (CoL) survey – Worldwide Rankings 2007/2006
Base city: New York, USA (=100) Rank 2007= 15 Rank 2006= 10

Rankings				CoL Index	
March 07	March 06	City	Country	March 07	March 06
1	1	Moscow	Russia	134.4	123.9
2	5	London	United Kingdom	126.3	121.74
3	2	Seoul	South Korea	122.4	119.1
4	3	Tokyo	Japan	122.1	116.3
5	4	Hong Kong	Hong Kong	119.4	110.6
6	8	Copenhagen	Denmark	108.3	108.3
7	7	Geneva	Switzerland	109.8	103
8	6	Osaka	Japan	108.4	101.1

Scores are based on *Mercer*'s cost of living database and include housing and basket items.

Source: *Mercer*

Lesson 2.4 Exercise 5 (page 23)

Environmentalist

You want the wind farm to go ahead as soon as possible.

You are a member of an environmental pressure group 'Lovers of the Land' (LoL).

Your group is keen on renewable energy sources and supports the building of wind farms.

You think:

- there is an urgent need for sources of renewable energy.
- nuclear power is dangerous.
- the wind has been used as a clean and efficient source of power for centuries.
- the latest wind farms are much more efficient.
- the proposed wind farm is environmentally friendly.
- the wind farm sets a good example for other areas and countries.

You want to know what the disadvantages of wind farms are.

Lesson 5.1 Exercise 8a (page 49)

Read this quote from a representative of the Campaign for Better Driving. Discuss the points in it with your group.

'I agree that we need to do something about the number of accidents and injuries on the roads today, but I don't agree with all these restrictions and safety features that the police want to introduce, you know, like speed cameras. They affect everybody and penalise the good drivers as well as the bad ones. It's a fact that driving fast doesn't cause accidents – it's driving badly that causes them, so I think we should be looking at bad drivers. Now, most crashes are caused by young men, so why don't we raise the age for learning to drive, say to 20 for women and 22 for men? Another possibility is to retest young drivers every two years until they're 30 – make sure they're driving well. I firmly believe that educating and monitoring young people is the way to solve this problem.'

Lesson 6.4 Exercise 5a (page 65)

JAMES DOUGLAS (literary agent)

You will negotiate with the publisher on the points below. You want:

- the book to have 15 chapters. The first six will deal with the singer's childhood and family background. The next six will present his professional life and achievements. The last three will deal with his mental illness, depression, which he has suffered from throughout his adult life.
- Lee Hart to receive an advance payment from the publisher of £100,000.
- the fee for the ghostwriter to be paid by the publisher.
- Lee Hart to be paid a royalty of 12 percent on the price the publisher receives for each book.
- Lee Hart and the ghostwriter to submit the final draft of the book to the publisher in 15 months' time, i.e. in March of next year. You think that the book will sell better after the band does a farewell international tour at the end of the year.
- the publisher to help set up interviews with family members, friends, etc. and to record the interviews.
- the name of Lee Hart to be on the front cover of the book in large letters, with the name of the ghostwriter in smaller letters on an inside page.
- the ghostwriter and Lee Hart to receive financial compensation if the publisher cancels the contract. The amount should be decided by an independent lawyer.

Lesson 8.4 Exercise 5a (page 87)

Chairperson

You will chair the debate about supermarket growth. You need to make sure everyone speaks and to stop people dominating the discussion. You may need to clarify points.

Begin by welcoming the participants and the audience at home to the programme.

Introduce the topic, which tonight is 'Supermarket superpower? The continued growth of a supermarket giant'.

Ask the panel the following general questions to start the debate.

- Should Smithsons come to your country?
- What effect will its arrival have on the economy? / employment? / other retailers? / shopping habits?

Bring the debate to an end and thank the guests and the audience at home for watching.

Lesson 7.3 Exercise 9 (page 74)

Read the information below and decide which points you think refer to the Millau Viaduct (above). Use the photo to help you. Then discuss with your partner the information you think refers to his/her bridge. Use the information to write a paragraph about the Millau Viaduct.

- Spans the River Tarn in the Massif Central mountains, France.
- Construction of the bridge started in 2001.
- It stretches from Karkoy Square in Istanbul to the Old Town.
- The New Bridge replaced the Old Bridge in 1992.
- It is the tallest car bridge in the world. At its summit, it is 343 metres.
- The landing stage is used by steamboats and ferryboats every day.
- It is considered to be one of the engineering wonders of the world.
- It is located over an earthquake fault.

Lesson 11.2 Exercise 10 (page 115)

Read the blog of a student who is studying in a foreign country. Make notes on what he/she says and then report it to your partner.

Before I came here I read up about the country and its culture – I learned that it's really important not to get offended easily, even though there are different rules about manners here. Culture shock is a normal experience and I think I just need to take advantage of all the help that the university offers. Oh, one more thing. I'm looking for a supplier of my favourite food – so get in touch if you can help me out.

Lesson 11.3 Exercise 5a (page 116)

Make sentences from these prompts.

Offer to take notes and photocopy them.

Warn your partners not to be late for the cinema this evening.

Insist on buying your partners a coffee.

Lesson 9.4 Exercise 7a (page 97)

Use the information in Exercise 2 and some of the following facts for your presentation.

SAVANNA CHARLES

Age: 32

Nationality: American – living in London

Artwork: makes huge constructions mainly from different metals. They usually represent giant insects or women. Has exhibited only in Britain and the United States. Her creations are breathtaking. They have great impact on spectators.

Reputation: becoming well known, but few galleries have the space to show her enormous creations. The Giordano gallery could only show photos of her structures and one piece of her work in the gallery's largest room.

Personality: very shy person. Does not like to appear in photographs. Does not give talks about her work.

Here you have two facts about another artist who will be presented. You can use this information in the discussion in Exercise 8.

You know that Alberto Cassini has been in prison twice for violent behaviour. People say he is moody and difficult to talk to.

Lesson 12.4 Exercise 5 (page 129)

Head of Human Resources

You hope to:

- find out how staff feel.
- learn what they want the directors to do.
- get suggestions for improving the situation.

You won't accept:

- proposals to bring back the old computer system.
- any suggestion to pay staff a bonus or pay increase.

You want to:

- spend five million pounds to upgrade the present computer system. That might mean that the company will have to cut office and patrol workers by 20%.
- spend as little money as possible on new facilities for staff.
- get useful, cheap suggestions for improving the situation.

Warning! The other members of the meeting will expect you to be cooperative and to spend money on them.

Lesson 11.5 Exercise 4 (page 120)

What is a subculture?

A subculture is a group of people with a particular set of beliefs, ideas and behaviour, which makes them different from a larger culture. They may be different due to their race, gender or ethnic background. Subcultures are often defined by their opposition to the values of the larger culture to which they belong, although not all writers agree on this. Members of a subculture will often show their membership through a distinctive and symbolic use of style and dress. Therefore, the study of a subculture often consists of the study of the clothing, music and other visible signs used by members of the subculture to identify it. In addition, the ways in which these same symbols are interpreted by members of the dominant culture are important. Provided that the subculture is characterised by a systematic opposition to the dominant culture, then it may be described as a counterculture.

It may be difficult to identify subcultures because their style (particularly clothing and music) may often be adopted by mass culture for commercial purposes, as business is always looking for opportunities to make money. This process of cultural absorption may result in the death or evolution and development of the subculture, as its members adopt new styles.

A common example is the punk subculture of the United Kingdom, whose distinctive (and initially shocking) anti-fashion style of clothing was swiftly adopted by mass-market fashion companies once the subculture became a media interest. Nevertheless, many subcultures do constantly evolve, as their members attempt to remain one step ahead of the dominant culture. This process provides a constant stream of styles and ideas which can be commercially adopted by the mainstream culture. This activity seems to stimulate rather than kill the development of youth cultures.

[adapted from *Wikipedia*]

Lesson 12.3 Exercise 10 (page 127)

Work out and note down all possible arguments to support the motion and include defences against points that might be brought up by the opposition. Decide who will say what, and in what order. Think of your own ideas but the following may help.

- People learn new skills.
- There are more advances in medical treatment.
- Housework is more convenient.
- Communication is easier.
- Modern technology can lead to future improvements in pollution.
- Most people have a higher standard of living than 20 years ago.

Lesson 1.4 Exercise 6a (page 13)

Paul came to see you last week and told you the following. Note down the key points.

He thinks the other flatmates don't understand his problems – they don't realise that law is very competitive. He must study day and night to keep up with the other students.

He sends emails to the other flatmates if he studies late in the library – he likes to keep in touch with them that way. But it seems to annoy Carlos and Martin as they think it's too formal.

He does not like Martin very much – Martin often makes fun of his American accent. Also, he puts up notes everywhere in the flat, telling people what to do. 'Martin is a real dictator!'

He is thinking of leaving the flat because of the unfriendly atmosphere, but he would have to pay to get out of the contract.

Lesson 2.1 Exercise 7a (page 17)

Look at the information from a survey (below) and answer the questions.

1 Where does the information come from?

2 What does it show?

3 Are there any trends? What are the main changes?

4 Is there any unusual or surprising information?

Quality of living survey – Worldwide Rankings 2007/2006
Base city: New York, USA (=100) Rank 2007= 48 Rank 2006= 46

Rank 07	Rank 06	City	Country	Index 07	Index 06
1	1	Zürich	Switzerland	108.1	108.2
2	2	Geneva	Switzerland	108.0	107.1
3	3	Vancouver	Canada	107.7	107.7
3	4	Vienna	Austria	107.7	107.5
5	5	Auckland	New Zealand	107.3	107.2
5	6	Düsseldorf	Germany	107.3	107.2
7	7	Frankfurt	Germany	107.1	107.0
8	8	Munich	Germany	106.9	106.8

Overall scores are based on an evaluation of 39 criteria, including the following environments: political and social, economic, natural, socio-cultural as well as medical and health considerations, public services and transport, recreation, consumer goods, housing.

Source: *Mercer*

Lesson 2.4 Exercise 5 (page 23)

Local resident 1

You are very much in favour of the wind farm.

You live in the area and own some of the land needed for the wind farm. You represent a number of farmers. You will receive money because the wind farm will be built on your land.

You think:

- wind farms are beautiful structures.
- the wind farm will attract visitors to the area. It will be the biggest in the country.
- the wind farm will provide cheap power for the local community.
- building the wind farm will create jobs for local people.
- the wind farm will attract international interest and publicity.

You want to know what the disadvantages of the wind farm would be.

Lesson 5.2 Exercise 4a (page 50)

B

What about road vehicles? How will they change in the next 50 years? It is obvious that we will have to find an alternative to petrol soon. Many experts think hydrogen could replace petrol, diesel and natural gas as the main fuel for cars, buses and trucks in the years to come. Cars run on hydrogen have enormous advantages: they do not emit exhaust gases or carbon dioxide fumes which contribute to global warming. Furthermore, they are not affected by worries about diminishing oil supplies and rising prices.

There are, however, technical difficulties to be overcome when using hydrogen as a source of power. It is difficult to store enough of it, in a compact space, on board a car to travel hundreds of miles. Also, there might be a huge explosion if a car crashed. This problem could perhaps be overcome if cars could store hydrogen in high pressure tanks similar to those used for natural gas. If hydrogen is handled properly, many experts believe it will not be any more dangerous as a fuel than petrol.

Recent technological advances, particularly in fuel cell design, have made hydrogen-powered cars a feasible alternative to petrol-driven ones. In the not-too-distant future, many of us could be driving non-polluting cars fuelled by hydrogen.

Lesson 4.1 Exercise 5a (page 39)

ASPIRIN

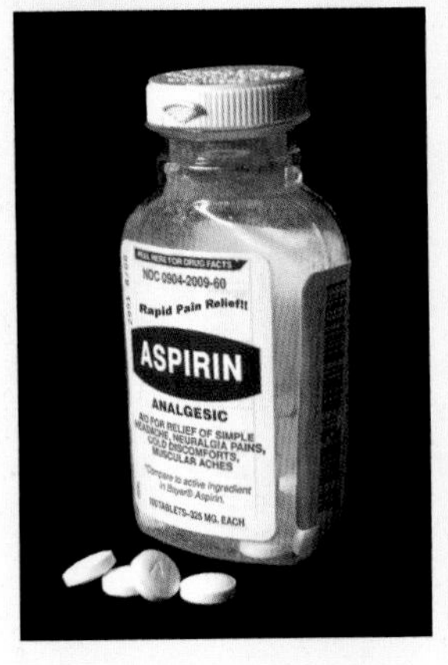

Aspirin is one of the most effective painkillers in the world. Hippocrates, a Greek physician, wrote in the 5th century about a powder made from the willow tree, which could help aches and pains and reduce fever. However, it was not until 1897 that Felix Hoffman, a German chemist, synthesised the ingredient *acetylsalicylic acid* to treat his father's arthritis. This was the first synthetic drug, which means it was a copy of something already existing in nature. Aspirin was patented on 6 March 1899. It was marketed alongside another of Hoffmann's products, a synthetic of morphine, called heroin, which he invented 11 days after aspirin. To start with, heroin was the more successful of the two painkillers and was thought to be healthier than aspirin. However, aspirin took over and has become the world's best-selling drug. In 1969, it even went to the moon with Neil Armstrong. Today, it is still one of the most effective painkillers, despite having a number of side effects. Aspirin is also effective against many serious diseases such as heart disease, diabetes and arthritis.

ANAESTHESIA

Anaesthesia is a way of preventing patients from feeling pain during surgery. Crawford Williamson Long was the first person to use ether as an anaesthetic during operations in 1842. Then on 30 September 1846, in Boston, Massachusetts, William Morton, an American dentist, performed a painless tooth extraction after giving ether to a patient. He also gave the first public demonstration of the use of ether to anaesthetise a patient on 16 October 1846. Following the demonstration, Morton tried to hide the identity of the substance as he planned to patent it and profit from its use. However, it was quickly shown to be ether, and it was soon being used in both the US and Europe. It was soon discovered that ether could catch fire easily, so in England it was replaced with chloroform. Nevertheless, Morton's achievement was the key factor in the development of modern surgery.

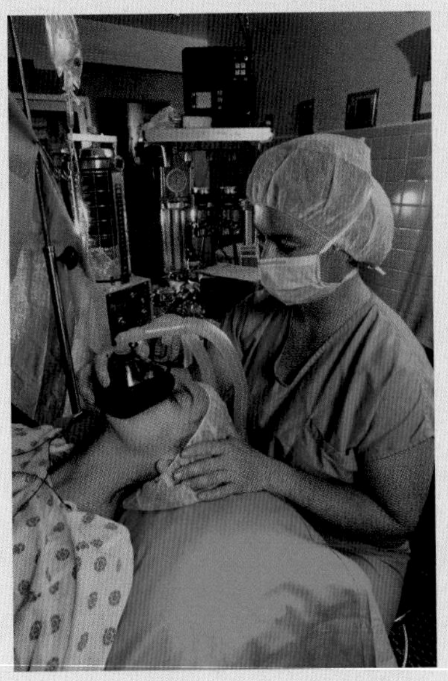

Lesson 5.1 Exercise 8a (page 49)

Read this quote from a car manufacturer. Discuss the points in it with your group.

'A lot of people talk about understanding why crashes happen and educating people to stop them happening, but I don't agree with that. It just isn't possible to change people's behaviour – put some people behind the steering wheel of a car and you've got an accident waiting to happen. A car is a dangerous machine for everyone – the driver, passengers in the car and other road users, I mean other drivers, cyclists and pedestrians. I'm a great believer in using technology to solve problems, and we can certainly make cars safer. For example, we can have automatic speed limiters in cars so that the driver can't go above, say, 100km per hour. You can get better computer systems – we're trying to look at a system where the car senses how close it is to other vehicles, and it increases the distance. Another possibility might be making cars softer with external airbags to protect people both inside and outside the car if there's a crash. So, you see, there are lots of options. Engineering is the way to solve this problem.'

Lesson 6.2 Exercise 4 (page 60)

B

To Kill a Mockingbird was written by Harper Lee, who was born in Alabama, USA. The book tells the story of Scout Finch (aged 6) and her brother Jem (aged 10). In the story, Scout looks back as an adult to the two years of her life when she learnt courage and kindness and the importance of doing what is right.

Scout's father is Atticus, a highly respected lawyer in a small Alabama town. Atticus agrees to defend a black man, Tom Robinson, against the charge of attacking a white woman.

In this extract, some of the townspeople come to the prison where Tom Robinson is being kept before the trial. They want to take Robinson from the jail and deal with him themselves, rather than wait for the court case. But Atticus is waiting there to stop them …

As we walked up the sidewalk, we saw a solitary light burning in the distance. 'That's funny,' said Jem, 'jail doesn't have an outside light.'

'Looks like it's over the door,' said Dill.

A long extension cord ran between the bars of a second-floor window and down the side of the building. In the light from its bare bulb, Atticus was sitting propped against the front door. He was sitting in one of his office chairs, and he was reading, oblivious of the nightbugs dancing over his head.

I made to run, but Jem caught me. 'Don't go to him,' he said, 'he might not like it. He's all right, let's go home. I just wanted to see where he was.'

We were taking a short cut across the square when four dusty cars came in from the Meridian highway, moving slowly in a line. They went around the square, passed the bank building, and stopped in front of the jail.

Nobody got out. We saw Atticus look up from his newspaper. He closed it, folded it deliberately, dropped it in his lap, and pushed his hat to the back of his head. He seemed to be expecting them.

'Come on,' whispered Jem. We sneaked across the square, across the street, until we were in the shelter of the Jitney Jungle door. Jem peeked up the sidewalk. 'We can get closer,' he said. We ran to Tyndal's Hardware door – near enough, at the same time discreet.

In ones and twos, men got out of the cars. Shadows became substance as light revealed solid shapes moving towards the jail door. Atticus remained where he was. The men hid him from view.

'He in there, Mr Finch?' a man said.

'He is,' we heard Atticus answer, 'and he's asleep. Don't wake him up.'

In obedience to my father, there followed what I later realized was a sickeningly comic aspect of an unfunny situation: the men talked in near-whispers.

'You know what we want,' another man said. 'Get aside from the door, Mr Finch.'

'You can turn around and go home again, Walter,' Atticus said pleasantly.

Lesson 7.3 Exercise 9 (page 74)

Read the information below and decide which points you think refer to the New Galata Bridge (above). Use the photo to help you. Then discuss with your partner the information you think refers to his/her bridge. Use the information to write a paragraph about the New Galata Bridge.

- Spans the Golden Horn in Istanbul.
- Designed by British architect Norman Foster and French bridge engineer Michel Virlogeux.
- It was built to clear traffic jams round the town.
- It is over 300 metres high – taller than the famous Eiffel Tower in Paris.
- Its total length is 2,460 metres. Width: 32 metres.
- It is made with concrete and steel pillars.
- It was finished in 1994.
- The bridge was described as 'delicate as a butterfly' by its architect.

Lesson 6.4 Exercise 5a (page 65)

THE PUBLISHER

You will negotiate with the literary agent on the points below. You want:

- the book to have 12 chapters. The first chapter will deal with Lee Hart's childhood and family background. The rest of the book will focus on the singer's professional career: how the band got together; their achievements and popularity; their international tours and future plans.
- Lee Hart to receive a small advance of £10,000. He is known as a volatile person who suffers from depression. In your opinion, he is quite likely to lose interest in the book and cancel the contract.
- the cost of the fee for the ghostwriter to be shared between your company and Lee Hart. A 50/50 deal would be fair for both parties.
- Lee Hart to be paid a royalty of 10 percent on the price you receive for the sale of each book. It is the standard royalty for new writers.
- Lee Hart and the ghostwriter to submit the final draft of the book in nine months' time, i.e. by September 1 of this year. If the book is published later, there will be fewer sales because the band is becoming less popular.
- Lee Hart and the ghostwriter to be responsible for organising all interviews with family members, friends and other contacts.
- the name of Lee Hart to be on the cover in large letters with the name of the ghostwriter in smaller letters.
- to receive financial compensation if Lee Hart or the ghostwriter decides to cancel the contract.

Lesson 8.4 Exercise 5a (page 87)

Labour relations expert

You need to listen carefully to the chairperson and other guests. Ask them to clarify anything you are not sure about. You also need to make the following points.

You are worried about the following:

- low wages
- rival businesses closing and unemployment
- poor working conditions, e.g. no breaks, overtime, etc.
- anti-union policies
- high staff turnover

Lesson 9.4 Exercise 7a (page 97)

Use the information in Exercise 2 and some of the following facts for your presentation.

ALBERTO CASSINI

Age: 28

Nationality: Argentinian, living in Florence

Artwork: an abstract painter. Uses dark colours, makes small dots and splashes of paint on his canvases. Has an aggressive style of painting. Often seems as if he has thrown paint at the canvas. His paintings reflect his moody, volatile character.

Reputation: art critics' opinion – some think he will be a very important painter in the future. Plans to change his style. This worries many professional buyers.

Personality: a difficult person, often bad-tempered. Bitter because of a handicap – he limps badly as a result of a childhood injury. No social skills.

Here you have two facts about another artist who will be presented. You can use this information in the discussion in Exercise 8.

People have told you that Savanna Charles is mentally unstable. They also say she is not very sociable.

Lesson 10.4 Exercise 5a (page 109)

Student B – Problems

Bullying at work

Hi Vanessa, I really need your help and advice.

I'm 30. I've just got a 'dream' job working in the clothing department of a large store. I'm good at the job, but maybe I'm too good; it certainly hasn't made me popular. My problem is, the younger staff don't like me and make nasty comments about me. They say I need to lose weight, and they criticise the way I dress and talk.

The manager's no help. She'll do anything to be popular with her staff. So when I complained the staff were making fun of me, she just said, 'Can't you take a joke?'

A couple of weeks ago, she said my timekeeping was bad. What did she expect? I live a long way from the store, and also I'm depressed and not sleeping properly. I don't want to leave this job, Vanessa. I just wish they'd stop bullying me.

How can I deal with this situation, Vanessa?

An adopted child

Hi Vanessa, I hope you can help me with my problem.

I got married when I was young, much too young. We didn't last very long, but, unfortunately, when we split up, we had just had a little baby boy. We didn't have much money at the time and neither of us had a job. Life was really hard, so we decided to have the baby adopted. That was 18 years ago.

Recently, I got a letter from my biological son. He said he'd often thought about his birth parents and wanted to meet us. I can't tell you how shocked and upset I was. It was so hard to give up my child for adoption. I've felt so guilty over the years.

Vanessa, I don't want to upset my son's adoptive parents by meeting him. I'm sure they're very hurt because he wants to get in contact with me. Anyway, he won't be very impressed when he sees me. I live in a small apartment with my two children. We don't have much money – I live on welfare payments – but we're happy. My sons don't know they have another brother – the news will be a big shock for them.

I don't feel I'm strong enough, emotionally, to meet my adopted son. What do you think I should do, Vanessa?

Lesson 11.2 Exercise 10 (page 115)

Read the blog of a student who is studying in a foreign country. Make notes on what he/she says and then report it to your partner.

Before I came here I studied the language. That was really helpful. Another thing I did before I left was I surfed the Internet for lots of information about the culture.

Now that I'm here … well … I keep in touch with home by telephone. I ring my mum once a week. I have lots of familiar things around me in my room, such as photos. I'm making friends with lots of other international students. And I also take regular exercise. That keeps me happy.

Lesson 11.3 Exercise 5a (page 116)

Make sentences from these prompts.

Invite your partners to dinner on Saturday evening.

Apologise for interrupting too much.

Refuse to share your sandwiches with your partners.

Lesson 12.3 Exercise 10 (page 127)

Work out and note down all possible arguments to oppose the motion and include defences against points that might be brought up by the opposition. Decide who will say what, and in what order. Think of your own ideas, but the following may help:

- People lose their jobs.
- People basically do not like change.
- Medical advances only help the rich.
- Modern technology has led to more pollution.
- Children cannot communicate as well as they could before.
- People may be richer but they are not happier.

Lesson 11.5 Exercise 4 (page 120)

What is youth culture?

With the development of post-World War Two affluence and the subsequent baby boom in the United States and Europe, young people began to gain considerable influence and buying power. Throughout the 1950s, the growing numbers of young people in the USA and Europe began to greatly influence music, television and cinema, spurring the explosion of rock and roll in the late 1950s and a full-blown youth culture by the mid-1960s. Examples of the new youth cultures included mods, rockers and hippies. As teenagers and adolescents created their own identity and their disposable income increased, marketing companies focused their efforts on this emerging subset of society. Given this commercialisation, it is perhaps surprising that this activity did not kill off youth cultures. On the contrary, in the 70s and 80s new youth cultures from the UK such as punk and goth developed and travelled around the world.

The tastes of young people began to drive fashion, music, films and literature. Corporations and businesses quickly took note and adapted to the shift by devising new marketing strategies. For young people, being more open to change and challenge, technology came more easily and their fashions changed more quickly than their adult counterparts. Baby boomers began to enter the workforce in the 1970s, and thereby had even greater influence, helping to innovate the computer revolution. Their children similarly provided the next generation of youth cultures. In the 90s and beyond, grunge style and hip-hop culture from America became popular around the world. Despite the fact that we live in an age of instant communication, it is still very difficult to predict what the next youth culture to sweep the world will be.

[adapted from *Wikipedia*]

Lesson 12.1 Exercise 6 (page 123)

Call waiting

Antonio Meucci was an Italian inventor living in New York. In 1860, he demonstrated a device he called the *teletrofono*, for electronic voice communication. He had a description of it printed in New York's Italian newspaper. Between 1856 and 1870, he developed more than 30 different prototype telephones. He filed a caveat (a kind of intermediate patent) in 1871, a full five years before Alexander Graham Bell. After being injured in an accident, Meucci became ill and was unable to work so he did not have enough money to renew his caveat in 1874. When Bell registered his own patent in 1876, Meucci sued, but died before the case was finished. Bell won and was credited with the invention of the telephone. Finally, in 2002, the US House of Representatives passed a resolution that 'the life and achievements of Antonio Meucci should be recognised, and his work in the invention of the telephone should be acknowledged.'

Lesson 12.4 Exercise 5 (page 129)

Representative – admin staff

You hope to:

- persuade the directors to bring back the old computer system.
- get a bonus of 1,000 pounds at the end of the year for the stress and inconvenience you have suffered.
- get a gym built on company premises.

You won't accept:

- long working hours without overtime payments.
- the present attitude of the team leaders – they always blame admin staff for mistakes.

You want to:

- have more training if they keep the new computer system.
- be paid more money if you have to use the new, more sophisticated computer system.
- feel more valued by the team leaders and directors.

Warning! If the directors have to spend more money, they will probably want to cut admin and patrol staff by 10–20 percent.

Lesson 1.4 Exercise 6a (page 13)

Stewart came to see you last week and told you the following. Note down the key points.

He is unhappy with the other flatmates, especially Martin and Paul – they don't like his friend Tom staying with him. They want Tom to leave the flat, but Stewart feels happier with a friend from home around.

He thinks Martin and Paul are very unfair and insensitive – Tom is unemployed and has no money.

He does not like Martin – Martin makes fun of him. He says Stewart is mean about money and 'eats like a little bird'.

He finds Carlos very annoying – Carlos never stops talking. He's always inviting friends to the flat. They play Brazilian music very loudly and it stops Stewart studying. Carlos telephones his family in Brazil late at night. It disturbs everyone in the flat.

Stewart just wants to be left alone. He doesn't really like the other flatmates and is happy as long as he stays in his room and studies.

Lesson 2.4 Exercise 5 (page 23)

Local resident 2

You are completely opposed to the wind farm.

You live in the local area and run a hotel. The area is popular with tourists who want relaxing walking holidays.

You think:

- the wind farm will damage the tourist industry and affect local property prices.
- the machinery used creates a lot of noise pollution and wind farms are not as efficient as other ways of producing electricity.
- wind farms are ugly and ruin the landscape.
- the flashing lights on the towers and the shadows from the blades can disturb and upset people.
- it will take five years to build the wind farm. There are certain to be traffic problems.

You want to know what the advantages of the wind farm would be.

Lesson 11.3 Exercise 5a (page 116)

Make sentences from these prompts.

Admit making a lot of mistakes in your life.

Tell your partners to phone you at the weekend with any news.

Encourage them to buy some designer clothes.

Lesson 5.1 Exercise 8a (page 49)

Read this quote from the head of a traffic police unit. Discuss the points in it with your group.

'I obviously think that we can help to solve the problem of deaths and injuries on the road by changing the law. Sure, you can make cars safer, and you can educate people, but I think the only way to make a difference is to hit people where it hurts – fine them or take away their licence. So, I think we should have tougher penalties for drivers who break the law, so maybe they should automatically lose their licence for a year for speeding, or they should be given a really large fine for driving carelessly, something like that. Of course, we can try to change the way drivers behave by having lower speed limits and using more speed cameras. We could then use the money we get from the fines for more road safety classes, and advanced driving courses. But you've got to make people see that breaking the law when they drive is very serious.'

Lesson 5.2 Exercise 4a (page 50)

C

Finally, rail transport could be revolutionised in the next 50 years with the development of Maglev technology. Maglev is short for MAGnetic LEVitation. Maglev trains are lifted by magnetic power and propelled along an elevated guideway by powerful magnets attached to the trains. They do not have any contact physically with the guideway, do not need engines and burn no fuel.

A Maglev train will be able to move passengers and freight at higher speeds than at present, using less energy. By 2020, it is predicted that Maglev trains will reach a speed of about 800km per hour. By 2050, they will run through vacuum tubes and reach speeds of 3,000km per hour. Thus, people will be able to go by train from England to the US in less than two hours.

At present, the only Maglev train running commercially is a shuttle from the Shanghai city centre to its new international airport. However, different types of Maglev trains are currently being developed in Germany and Japan.

The safety of Maglev trains has become a concern, however. When a Maglev train crashed into a maintenance wagon in northern Germany while on a test run, 23 people were killed and around ten were injured. It appears to have been the result of human error, not a technical fault.

Lesson 8.4 Exercise 5a (page 87)

Government representative

You need to listen carefully to the chairperson and other guests. Ask them to clarify anything you are not sure about. You also need to make the following points.

You think Smithsons will bring the following benefits:

- an overall benefit to the economy
- lots of new jobs (it's a big employer)
- improvement in the environment in some areas through Smithsons' community work
- increased competition, which will encourage other retailers to do better
- up-to-date retail methods

Lesson 9.4 Exercise 7a (page 97)

Use the information in Exercise 2 and some of the following facts for your presentation.

INGRID TAUBER

Age: 30

Nationality: German – living in Hamburg

Artwork: takes portraits all over the world. Her best photos are of ordinary people showing extraordinary emotions on their faces. Recently, takes mainly photographs of famous people (makes more money selling them). Only works in black and white – no colour photos.

Reputation: becoming well known. Some critics think the subjects of her photos are too limited. She does not pay attention to critics.

Personality: a strong but stubborn person. Often criticises other photographers. People say she is too egotistic and boastful. Other people, especially women, admire her a lot.

Here you have two facts about another artist who will be presented. You can use this information in the discussion in Exercise 8.

You know that John Leach, the British graffiti artist, upsets audiences when he gives talks. He often argues aggressively with his audience. People say he loves the sound of his own voice and is not a good listener.

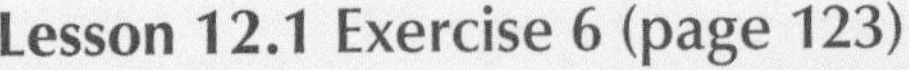

Lesson 12.1 Exercise 6 (page 123)

The write man

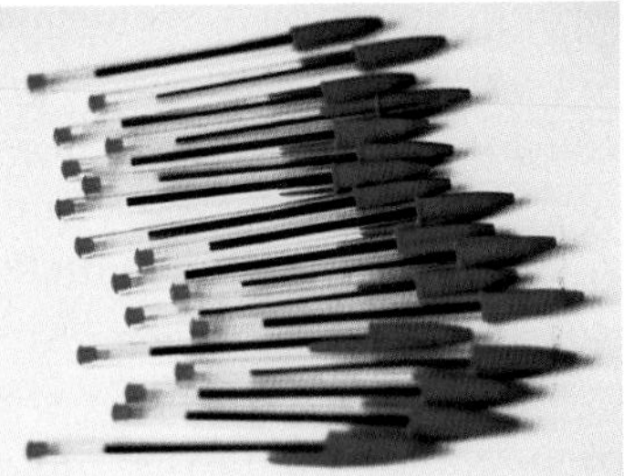

The problems of writing with a pen and ink were that they often leaked and ink was slow to dry on the page.

John J. Loud, an American leather tanner, recognised this problem and invented a new gadget for writing – a pen with a small rotating ball instead of a nib. He patented his invention on 30 October 1888. Although it still leaked, it could be used to mark rough surfaces such as leather. Loud, however, failed to exploit his patent commercially and it was left to the Hungarian Lazlo Biro, working with his brother, to patent the ballpoint pen between 1938 and 1943. Biro later licensed his pen to the Frenchman Marcel Bich, who called his company BiC. This is today the market leader in ballpoint pens, with annual sales of 1.38 billion euros. The company sells 14 million per day of the Bic Cristal.

Lesson 12.4 Exercise 5 (page 129)

Representative – team leaders

(A team leader is responsible for a group of about eight admin workers.)

You and the other team leaders hope to:

- work fewer hours.
- keep the present computer system.
- be paid more money (5–10 percent) for the extra responsibility and stress you have (leading de-motivated workers is very difficult).

You won't accept:

- the suggestion that you blame staff all the time for errors. They need to learn the new computer system properly.
- any responsibility for the present problems.

You want to:

- persuade the other representatives that your job is very difficult and stressful in the present situation.
- keep your present job, but with better pay and working conditions.
- help the admin staff and patrolmen/women to enjoy their job more.

Warning! If the directors have to spend a lot of money, you may lose your job because they will want to cut costs.

Lesson 1.4 Exercise 6a (page 13)

Carlos came to see you last week and told you the following. Note down the key points.

Carlos quite likes Martin – Martin is friendly and sociable. He's a nice person, except he likes to put notes everywhere and he bosses everyone too much.

Carlos doesn't like Stewart – Carlos asked Stewart to go to a club with him. Stewart refused, saying, 'Sorry, but I don't have enough money to go with you.' He thinks Stewart doesn't like him.

Carlos thinks Paul is boring – Paul spends all his time studying. He emails them a lot when he's late in the library. Carlos can't understand why Paul bothers to do that.

Carlos would like the flatmates to have more fun and to get to know each other better. They never have parties in the flat or go out anywhere together. Carlos thinks that university should be fun and social as well as hard work.

Lesson 2.4 Exercise 5 (page 23)

Wildlife group representative

You are very hostile to the wind farm.

You are a member of a radical wildlife group: Flora and Fauna Protection (FFP). You are strongly against the building of wind farms in areas of natural beauty.

You think:

- wind farms are dangerous to all wildlife.
- birds and bats are often killed when they fly into the blades of wind turbines.
- the habitat of many birds, animals and plants will be destroyed during the building of the farm.
- the proposed site is home to several rare species of butterfly.
- the area currently attracts a large number of scientists and naturalists who study the wildlife of the area.
- wind farms are an expensive and wasteful way of producing electricity.

You want to know what the advantages of wind farms are.

Lesson 8.4 Exercise 5a (page 87)

Opposition party representative

You need to listen carefully to the chairperson and other guests. Ask them to clarify anything you are not sure about. You also need to make the following points.

You think Smithsons will have the following negative effects:

- be bad for the economy
- destroy jobs and small businesses
- use foreign suppliers, which is bad for local suppliers
- cause damage to the environment

Lesson 9.4 Exercise 7a (page 97)

Use the information in Exercise 2 and some of the following facts for your presentation.

JOHN LEACH

Age: 26

Nationality: British – living in Birmingham

Artwork: his graffiti are in many European and South American cities. Shows the dark side of life. Horrible, frightening images, especially for children – but very powerful impact on all who see them.

Reputation: some say he's a genius. Others say he just likes to shock people. Some cities ban his graffiti, other cities protect his artwork.

Personality: volatile person. Rather insecure, perhaps because he never knew his parents and grew up in an orphanage, then spent a year in a young offenders' institute when he was 16 (continual shoplifting). But enjoys giving talks. Willing to give three talks at any exhibition.

Here you have two facts about another artist who will be presented. You can use this information in the discussion in Exercise 8.

You know that Ingrid Tauber did not get permission to photograph some of her 'ordinary' people. She is involved in two court cases with people asking for compensation. You met her recently and she talked about herself all the time.

INFORMATION FOR STUDENT D

Lesson 12.4 Exercise 5 (page 129)

Representative – patrol staff

You hope to:

- get a new system of navigation for your vehicles. Approximate cost: 150,000 pounds.
- be given the most up-to-date mobile phones – the present ones don't work well.
- receive training in communication skills – customers have been very difficult to deal with recently.

You won't accept:

- the present situation – you have had job offers from other breakdown firms.
- directors' excuses that there is no money to spend on staff or facilities.

You want to:

- change your job if the situation doesn't improve. The other breakdown companies are looking for staff.
- have more free days. At present, you are working six days a week.
- make it clear to the directors that the patrol workers make the money for the company. They need to be valued and should be paid more.

Warning! The directors may not want to spend much money at the moment.

INFORMATION FOR STUDENT E

Lesson 2.4 Exercise 5 (page 23)

Government representative

You are a government minister in the Energy Department. You will welcome people to the meeting and lead the meeting.

You think:

- wind farms are a good idea and building new ones is a government policy.
- it is important, however, to listen to the opinions of local people. There is an election next year and you do not want to upset too many potential voters. As Sparrow Hill would be a very big wind farm it is important to make the right decision.

You want to know what the feelings of local people about the proposed wind farm are.

Lesson 8.4 Exercise 5a (page 87)

Consumer group representative

You need to listen carefully to the chairperson and other guests. Ask them to clarify anything you are not sure about. You also need to make the following points.

You think Smithsons will:

- benefit the consumer by lowering prices, which is good for poorer sections of society
- give consumers a greater range of products at affordable prices
- bring general improvement in quality
- provide more international and up-to-date products

SUPPLEMENTARY INFORMATION

Lesson 4.5 Exercise 8a (page 46)

Herbal medicines

Information sources

4,500 members surveyed (2,815 completed / sent back)

Articles from well-known medical journals

Facts

- use plant extracts for remedies/ medicines
- herbs have been used for thousands of years – ancient remedy
- three types of medicines: western, Chinese, Indian
- safety: users need to take care. Side effects from some herbs. Also, they can interact badly with other drugs
- members found herbs very effective for a wide range of illnesses; 55 percent would recommend herbal medicine to friends

Summary

Some herbal medicines have a harmful effect on the body.

But many benefits from herbs as well.

Recommendations

- must be used with great care – get advice from a herbalist
- absolutely essential to tell your doctor if you are using herbal medicine
- make sure the herbal remedy is the correct product for you
- good idea for a herbalist to make a remedy specially for you
- don't believe all the claims you read on the packaging of a herbal product

Lesson 3.4 Exercise 8a (page 33)

Zinedine Zidane Former footballer

Born France, 1972. Parents immigrated to France from Algeria

Achievements Starred in the French national team and played for four top European club teams, including Real Madrid.

Helped France to win the World Cup final in 1998 when the team beat Brazil.

Also contributed to his team's victories in European championships.

Elected FIFA World Player of the Year three times (equalling the record).

In the 2006 World Cup, he was an inspirational figure, helping France to reach the Final.

Was named Outstanding Player of the tournament.

Contribution to the sport Has raised interest in football among young people.

A modest, quiet and shy man, but with a quick temper on the pitch.

Michael Schumacher Former Formula 1 racing driver

Born Germany, 1969

Achievements Formula 1 driver, seven times world champion. Holds very nearly every record in Formula 1, e.g. most drivers' championships, race victories, fastest laps and most races won in a single season.

Joined the Ferrari team in 1996. They had not won a drivers' championship for 15 years. Schumacher won five consecutive drivers' titles with the team, from 2000 to 2004.

First German to win the world championship.

World's first billionaire athlete.

Contribution to the sport Helped to make Formula 1 racing popular in Germany; it had been a minor sport before he appeared.

Likes to protect his family life; does not like the celebrity spotlight. Gave huge donation of $10 million for aid after the 2004 Indian earthquake. Donates generously to many other charities.

Martina Navratilova Former tennis player

Born Prague, Czech Republic, 1956

Achievements Generally considered one of the greatest women tennis players of all time.

Played well on all surfaces, especially grass.

Won 18 Grand Slam singles titles and 41 doubles titles.

Won the women's singles title at Wimbledon a record nine times.

In her career, won 167 top-level singles matches, more than any other woman player in modern times. In 2002, she won the mixed doubles title at Wimbledon. This made her the oldest ever Grand Slam champion (aged 47 years and 8 months).

When young, she was overweight for a tennis player. A journalist, Bud Collins, called her the 'Great Wide Hope'. A determined person, she became very strong and fit.

Contribution to the sport Raised the women's game to a new level with her power and aggressive play.

A role model for many young sportswomen.

Tiger Woods Golfer

Born California, USA, 1975

Achievements One of the most successful golfers of all time.

Highest paid professional athlete.

In 2006, aged 30, he won his 12th major golfing championship. He has more wins on the PGA Tour (Professional Golf Association) than any other active player.

In 2001, he held all four major PGA championship titles, an achievement known as the 'Tiger Slam'.

Woods is one of only five golfers who have won the four major championships.

He had victories by record margins in two championships: the Masters 1997 and in the US Open 2000.

A consistent, cautious player. He rarely has a bad game. He has excellent all-round skills. Hits the ball powerfully, trains more hours than almost all other golfers.

Contribution to the sport He has promoted great interest in golf among minority groups and young people in the US.

Responsible for higher standards of athleticism among professional golfers.

He has talent, looks, youth appeal and charisma. He has a $100 million endorsement contract with Nike and is a role model for young golfers.

Lesson 5.5 Exercise 7 (page 57)

Rank	Airport	Location	Total passengers	Rank	Change
2006				2005	
1	Hartsfield-Jackson International Airport	Atlanta, US	84,846,639	1	-1.2%
2	O'Hare International Airport	Chicago, US	76,248,911	2	-0.3%
3	London Heathrow Airport	London, UK	67,530,223	3	-0.6%
7	Paris Charles De Gaulle Airport	Roissy, France	56,808,967	6	+5.6%
9	Beijing International Airport	Beijing, China	48,501,102	15	+18.3%
15	Suvarnabhumi Airport	Racha Thewa, Thailand	42,799,532	18	+9.8%

Lesson 6.2 Exercise 11 (page 61)

You should structure your story in this way.

Paragraph 1: Set the scene. Describe the weather, the time of day, how much light there was, how you felt and what you were doing (use the past continuous for some verbs).

Paragraph 2: Write about what happened before the thunderstorm. Use mainly the past perfect.

Paragraph 3: Write about what happened next and your rescue. Use mainly the past simple.

Lesson 7.5 Exercise 6 (page 79)

Model answer

The exhibition has a number of drawings and pictures. They are beautifully executed and the ones of large buildings are particularly impressive. Wright worked with engineers at the offices of Adler and Sullivan. He did so / this for many years and must have learned a lot from them, as their attention to detail clearly influenced his work. Many European thinkers, such as John Ruskin, did so as well. However, Wright also developed his own ideas, and incorporated many of these / many of which were incorporated into the houses he built.

Lesson 7.5 Exercise 10 (page 79)

The Ennis House

- designed by Frank Lloyd Wright in 1923, for Mabel and Charles Ennis
- situated on a hill
- design based on Mayan temples
- constructed from concrete blocks
- very large building – 10,000 square feet
- glass windows and doors darker at top, lighter at bottom
- dining room elevated, with large fireplace and beautiful mosaic above
- house sold to media personality John Nesbitt in 1940 – added swimming pool and heating system
- house badly damaged in 1994 by earthquake and later by heavy rain
- needed to be restored at cost of $15m
- Ennis House used as location for many Hollywood films (*Blade Runner, House on Haunted Hill*) and for advertising and promotional events
- one of California's most historic landmarks

Lesson 8.5 Exercise 1b (page 88)

Answers

1 True. Most summaries should be about a third of the original length.
2 True. If you do not understand the text, your summary will not be accurate.
3 True. If you do not use your own words, you could be accused of plagiarising.
4 False. You may have to use certain technical words in your summary. It may be more convenient to do so.
5 False. It should only include important information, i.e. the key points.
6 False. A complete summary will include all the important points.
7 False. A summary does not include additional information.
8 False. You may include a limited number of quotations.
9 True. It is the original writer's opinion which is important.
10 False. You may change the order of ideas if this makes the summary clearer or more readable.

Lesson 9.3 Exercise 4b (page 94)

The table below shows the order of most adjectives before a noun. (We don't usually use more than about three adjectives before a noun.)

Adjectives									Noun
opinion	**size**	**shape**	**most other qualities**	**age**	**colour/ pattern**	**nation-ality**	**material**	**function/ class**	
beautiful				antique	colourful	Japanese	silk		paintings
	huge		well-known		dark			Cubist	sculpture
outstanding			famous					art	schools
			stainless				steel		plates
	enormous						metal		figure
	huge	fully-extended							wings
	small				brown		clay		figurines
			rich, aristocratic						family

Lesson 10.3 Exercise 1a (page 106)

Harold Shipman appeared to be a caring, well-respected doctor. Actually, he was an arrogant drug addict and mass murderer who killed approximately 236 people between 1971 and 1998. The people he killed were his elderly patients, so their deaths did not at first seem too suspicious. He was tried and imprisoned, but he hanged himself in prison in January 2004. A possible reason for his crimes was this: Shipman was devoted to his mother, Vera, who became ill with lung cancer when Shipman was very young. The family doctor injected Vera with morphine and she died aged 43. Shipman was only 17 years old.

Lesson 11.3 Exercise 9 (page 117)

A

Local cultures reflect ordinary people's feelings of appropriateness, comfort and correctness. Given the strength of local cultures, it is hard to argue that one global culture exists.

B

Look, everyone's basically the same. I mean at work nearly everyone wears the standard man's business suit with a coloured tie and a buttoned shirt. It's worn just about everywhere.

C

Those who deny the importance of cultural diversity may refer to the universal business suit. But local variations have appeared. Iranian parliamentarians do not wear ties and Saudi diplomats alternate the business suit with traditional robes.

D

You can see that most hotels in the world have become standardised. I mean, they now have western-style beds, toilets and showers. A lot of them have fitness centres and restaurants. They all fit a sort of global standard.

E

The Davos group is an elite group of highly educated people operating in finance, media and diplomacy. They share common beliefs about individualism and market economy. However, they are too small a group to count as a coherent cultural system.

Lesson 9.5 Exercise 4b (page 98)

interesting

RELATED WORDS

opposite: —— **boring/bored**

▸ *see also* **interested, excited/exciting**

1 something that makes you feel interested

- ▸ interesting
- ▸ fascinating
- ▸ intriguing
- ▸ be of interest
- ▸ stimulating
- ▸ hold your attention
- ▸ absorbing

interesting /ˈɪntrɪstɪŋ/ **[adj]** if something is **interesting**, you give it your attention, because it is unusual or exciting or because it is something that you want to know about: *We saw an interesting film about African wildlife.* | *The most interesting thing about dinosaurs is the fact that they all died out so suddenly.* | *Michael's new job sounds really interesting.* | *There's a course in English business law at King's College that looks interesting.* | **find sth interesting** (=think something is interesting) *I found the book quite interesting even though it's not the sort of thing I'd normally read.* | **find it interesting (that)** *I find it interesting that no one has yet mentioned the President's appalling record on the economy.* | **it is interesting (that)** *It is interesting that the present recession is much deeper in the south than in the north.* | **it is interesting to do sth** *It would be interesting to know how much he earns.*

fascinating /ˈfæsɪneɪtɪŋ/ **[adj]** extremely interesting: *Singapore's exotic mix of cultures – mostly Chinese, Indian, and Malay – makes it a fascinating holiday destination.* | *The programme focuses on the fascinating story of Mary Shelley, the woman who, at just 18, wrote the horror masterpiece Frankenstein.* | **find sth fascinating** (=think something is fascinating) *We went round Chesmore Zoo the other day and found it fascinating.* | **it is fascinating to do sth** *It's fascinating to imagine what might have happened if the US had stayed out of World War II.*

intriguing /ɪnˈtriːɡɪŋ/ **[adj]** if something is **intriguing**, you want to know more about it because it is unusual or difficult to understand: *Taylor's latest CD presents the listener with an intriguing mixture of musical styles.* | **it is intriguing to do sth** *It is intriguing to note that only one of his books was published during his own lifetime.*

be of interest /biː əv ˈɪntrɪst/ **[v phrase]** if something **is of interest** to someone, they want to know more about it because it is related to a subject or activity that they are interested in: *Finally, in the last section of the talk I will cover a few miscellaneous topics which I think may be of interest.* | **+to** *Pull your chair over. I heard something today that might be of interest to you.* | *It is expected that the results of the research programme will be of interest not only to academics, but also to the government.*

absorbing /əbˈsɔːʳbɪŋ, -ˈzɔːʳ-/ **[adj]** something that is **absorbing** holds your attention for a long time because it is very interesting and enjoyable: *Developing your own photographs can be an absorbing hobby.* | *In an absorbing book about how she learned to fly, Diane Ackerman tells why she chooses to risk her life.*

2 so interesting that you cannot stop watching, reading etc

- ▸ riveting/gripping
- ▸ I couldn't put it down
- ▸ compelling
- ▸ engrossing
- ▸ mesmerizing/enthralling
- ▸ spellbinding
- ▸ page-turner

riveting/gripping /ˈrɪvɪtɪŋ, ˈɡrɪpɪŋ/ **[adj]** a film, book etc that is **riveting** or **gripping** is so interesting or exciting that you do not want to stop watching it, reading it etc: *The novel is absolutely riveting from start to finish.* | *The story is a riveting one about two children who find an adventure game which becomes real as they are playing it.* | *Hitchcock's film 'The Birds' is a brilliant psychological thriller with a gripping climax.* | *The play is never quite interesting or gripping enough in the right places despite the considerable efforts of the actors.*

I couldn't put it down /aɪ ˌkʊdnt pʊt ɪt ˈdaʊn/ **spoken** say this about a book that was so enjoyable that you did not want to stop reading it: *What an amazing book! I just couldn't put it down.*

compelling /kəmˈpelɪŋ/ **[adj] written** a film, book etc that is **compelling** is so interesting that you feel you must keep watching or reading it: *The film was so compelling I could scarcely take my eyes off the screen for a second.* | *Orwell's 'Burmese Days' is a compelling account of life under British Colonial rule.*

4 an interesting city, building, work of art etc

- ▸ interesting
- ▸ fascinating
- ▸ unusual
- ▸ have character

interesting /ˈɪntrɪstɪŋ/ **[adj]** a building, work of art, object etc that is **interesting** is unusual or special in some way: *The exhibition includes some interesting old musical instruments.* | *What makes San Francisco so interesting is its architecture, which is completely different from that of other American cities.*

fascinating /ˈfæsɪneɪtɪŋ/ **[adj]** extremely interesting: *London is one of the most exciting and fascinating cities in the world.* | *It was a fascinating painting, with clever use of colour and light.* | *The Scottish Craft Centre has a fascinating range of pottery, jewellery and textiles for sale.* | *Alice Thornton's autobiography provides a fascinating account of family life in seventeenth-century England.*

unusual /ʌnˈjuːʒuəl, -ʒəl/ **[adj]** different in style from other buildings, cities, or works of art, and therefore interesting: *Louise makes hats that are eye-catching and unusual.* | *Yuri invited me to sample some of Osaka's more unusual restaurants.*

have character /hæv ˈkærɪktəʳ/ **[v phrase not in progressive]** if a place or a building **has character**, it is old and has a lot of unusual features which make it interesting and special: *The hotel has character and charm, and is ideal as a base for exploring the city.*

From *Longman Language Activator*, second edition 2002

Lesson 1.1 Track 1.2

1

The most important thing for me is that someone doesn't talk in a boring way. I can't stand people who go on and on for ages without saying anything at all. Good communicators stick to the point and don't lose their train of thought.

2

I hate it when people stop me speaking all the time when I'm trying to tell them something. You know – just let me finish!

3

I think good communicators anticipate when a listener doesn't understand something – you know, if they use an unfamiliar word or phrase, or some kind of jargon, they give an example of what they mean.

4

Well, for me, good communicators don't make things complicated or difficult to understand for their listener. They talk in a logical way, so what they say is easy to follow.

5

I don't like it when people get off the point and start talking about an unrelated subject, and don't tell you that's what they're doing. I find it really annoying when someone starts doing it and you don't know what they're talking about. Some people do it all the time.

6

The key point for me is simple – do they actually pay attention to what someone else is saying, or are they already thinking about what they want to say?

7

I think the best communicators are people who make things easy to understand by giving reasons – they don't assume too much knowledge. I hate people who think you know what they're talking about all the time.

Lesson 1.3 Track 1.4

We're starting today by discussing the work of Deborah Tannen. Many of you will have heard of Deborah – she has become famous through her research into male and female communication and has written several books on interpersonal relations and communication. Her most famous book, *You Just Don't Understand*, was published in 1990 and it spent nearly four years on the *New York Times* bestseller list. Deborah had already written a book on conversational styles, which contained just one chapter on gender differences. But after receiving a huge popular response to that chapter, she decided to focus more of her research on the subject – and the result was *You Just Don't Understand*. In 1994 she wrote the highly successful *Talking from 9 to 5*. Deborah has written for most major newspapers and magazines. In addition to her academic research and writing, she has published poetry, short stories and essays. In fact, by 2006, she had published 20 books and had written over 100 articles. She's also become a bit of a celebrity and has appeared on the Larry King show, and on Oprah. Deborah has been in the Linguistics Faculty at Georgetown University since 1979 and has lectured all over the world. … Let's start with one of Deborah's most interesting quotes: 'Saying that men talk about baseball in order to avoid talking about their feelings is the same as saying that women talk about their feelings in order to avoid talking about baseball.' Jeremy, can I ask you first, what's your interpretation …

Lesson 1.4 Track 1.5

Carol, Jean

C: I saw Marco in your office again this morning, Jean. What did he want this time?

J: He needs money. He shares a flat with a couple of other students, as you know. The problem is that he's been spending too much recently and he can't pay this month's rent. The others aren't happy as they'll have to pay more than usual.

C: Well, we can sort it out, can't we? The best way to deal with it is to tell him to get a loan from the student union.

J: Yeah, it's the obvious solution, but the trouble with that is that it's the third time he's run out of money. There's a pattern: he spends too much money, he can't pay the rent, and then he gets a loan from friends or the student union. It's a vicious circle – he can't escape from it.

C: Mmm, I see what you mean.

J: It's a very tricky situation because it's not just about the rent. They have a lot of parties in the flat and once again they've broken something – a really expensive lamp. And the landlord wants to charge them a lot of money to replace it. Marco just doesn't have any money to pay his share of the cost.

C: Mmm, he's really got problems, hasn't he? It's a rather difficult situation, isn't it? If I remember, Marco comes from a poor family and he has to work part-time to pay for his studies. He's really struggling. Oh, I must say, I feel a bit of sympathy for him.

J: Me too. I think we should both have a chat with him. Give him some advice about managing his money. That might well solve the problem – at least in the future.

C: Yes, that seems to be the way forward, but will he listen to us?

J: He has to. It's his last chance. Let's do that. And now we need to think about how we can get some money for him to pay this month's rent. Oh, and for the lamp they broke, of course.

Lesson 1.4 Track 1.6

Martin, Carlos, Paul, Stewart

M: OK, guys. I wanted us to meet because there are a few issues with the flat. The problem is, we don't have any rules.

C: Rules? What do you mean? We're all adults, Martin, we're not at school any more. We don't need any rules. What do you think, Paul?

P: Well … I don't know. What have you got in mind, Martin?

M: OK, we need a rule about buying food, don't we? It'd be much cheaper for us if we bought in larger quantities – that's why we need a rule.

C: I don't think so, Martin, it's much better if we each buy the food we want, and just put it in the fridge or on the shelves. It's simpler that way.

P: Yeah, I think Carlos is right, Martin. Anyway I don't eat much food here, and Stewart eats hardly any food at all.

S: Yeah, it's true, Paul, I'm not a big eater. I'm trying to save money, so I don't spend much on food. Personally, I think we should just carry on buying our own food.

M: OK, forget about food, but what about washing up and cleaning? I come down each morning for breakfast and there's always a load of dirty dishes to wash up. And it's me who usually does it. I put up notices about it, but no one pays any attention. It's the same thing with cleaning. The place is a dump, we need to clean it much more often.

C: Martin, really, you're exaggerating, it's not as bad as that.

M: Exaggerating? I don't think so. Look, why don't I make out a rota with set times when we do the washing up and cleaning? Paul, what's wrong?

P: I don't know, Martin. I don't like rotas, and, actually, I'm getting fed up with your little notes and messages everywhere. What do you think, Stewart?

S: Er … no, no, a rota isn't necessary.

M: Well … OK, we'll leave things as they are. But there's one thing I do feel strongly about and I want us to have a rule about it. It's people staying for long periods. Stewart, your friend Tom's been staying here for days now. He just sits around in the living room, bothering the rest of us. I want him to leave. Right away.

S: Oh? I thought you liked him. Actually, he's just staying until he finds a job. What's wrong with that? I pay the rent, so surely I can have friends to stay if I want to.

M: Sorry, I don't agree. What do you think, Paul?

P: Well, to be honest, I'm not keen on people staying. I need to study during the day, not chat to Tom. How about you, Carlos?

C: Well, I love having friends in our flat. We don't want to study all the time. We want to have some fun as well. We don't need a rule about that, Martin.

M: Actually, Carlos, we do. Paul and I are here to study. You should respect our opinion. The best way to deal with this is to have a rule. It's quite simple, 'no long-term visitors'.

P: You know, you may think this is stupid, but I think the way to sort out our problems might be to go to the Student Advice Centre – they deal with all sorts of things …

Lesson 1.5 Track 1.7

Part 1

Good evening everyone.

Did you know that in many surveys the worst phobia for many people is public speaking? Not spiders or rats or heights, but having to face an audience and talk to them.

How do people react when put into this situation? Well, there are a number of things which happen to our bodies when we are put in stressful situations, and making a speech is no different. Basically, your body goes into the classic 'fight or flight' response. In other words, your hands may sweat and your mouth may go dry. Your heart may beat faster and you may start feeling sick. Your voice may be strained – for instance, the audience will probably notice that you are speaking fast and that your voice sounds weak and with a higher pitch than normal. You will want to rush to the end of the talk and may even ignore the audience. There is a strong feeling of wanting to run away.

But making a speech to a group of people is in fact a great opportunity to impress them and really show what you can do, so why do so many people have a phobia about it?

Well, there are several reasons. Firstly, people feel they'll make mistakes and lose their way. Secondly, the speaker may worry that the audience will not like the speech or him or her, and finally, they may fear that the audience will not really understand what they're trying to say. All of these fears create a sense of looking a fool in front of other people, which is the main reason for all of our worries and fears – no one wants to look a fool.

This response is more than just nerves. That's normal, and it would be strange not to feel nervous. Nerves will keep you alert and stop you feeling too relaxed. If controlled well, nerves can make the difference between an average speech and one which keeps people listening and wanting to hear more.

Lesson 1.5 Track 1.8

Part 2

So how can we control our nerves and become more confident about making a speech? Well, the most important thing is to get your nerves to work for you rather than against you.

I intend to discuss a number of things you can do to help. First of all, I can say that rehearsal is essential. Nerves are caused by fear and being unfamiliar with things, so take time to practise your speech to feel comfortable with what you're going to say. Secondly, it's a good idea to know your introduction by heart. You'll feel most nervous at the beginning and may stumble over words. If you learn the beginning, this will become second nature and help you get into the main part of the speech more comfortably. Another good thing to do is to begin with some kind of interest hook, such as an anecdote, or a diagram or photo. This will engage the audience and help you get over the beginning of the speech.

Take some deep breaths before you start. This'll help control your nerves. Breathe in slowly, count to three and then breathe out slowly. Finally, remember, you will always be more nervous than you look. You can 'trick' your mind in a few simple ways to help you – try and look confident and you'll become more confident. Stand in a relaxed way, hold your head up and smile. Look happy and enthusiastic, even if you're not!

One other thing is to focus on something other than yourself. Pay attention to the environment you're in to distract yourself. Notice the audience. For example, how are they dressed? Who's wearing glasses? Who's the most attractive? All of this will help to trick your mind into not noticing the situation you're in. The less you concentrate on how you're feeling, the more confident you'll become.

You should use plenty of eye contact, change the pace of your delivery, change the volume of your voice, and perhaps move around a bit. Don't worry too much about mistakes. A few mistakes are all right, they show the audience you're human. One way you can really engage with your audience is humour – tell a joke! If you aren't good at jokes, tell a story, or draw on your personal experience again to try and connect with your audience.

The main rule about public speaking is that there are no rules! This seems a strange thing to say, but it's true – everyone is an individual and so you have to find what works for you in terms of delivering a speech. The most important thing is to control your nerves, build your confidence and learn to enjoy it!

Lesson 2.1 Track 1.9

1

Well, I live in a detached house in a suburb of a major city. What do I like about it? Mmm, well, I like the access to all the cultural events and shops, but I also like the fact that my local area is very green – you know, lots of parks and open spaces for the kids. The public transport connections are very good too, so I can be in the city centre in a very short time if I avoid the rush hour, so I guess you could say I have the best of both worlds! The only real problem, I think, is the mindless vandalism that goes on, you know, damage to cars and bus stops, which we all have to pay for in the end. It's bored young people with nothing to do. I suppose it's the price you pay for living in a city.

2

I live in a farm cottage on the edge of a very small village, almost a hamlet really, in the countryside. It really is very rural – about 25 kilometres to the nearest town. It's the peace and quiet I like really, and the fresh air. There aren't many vehicles on the roads – so no traffic congestion … the air's very clean, and there's very little noise and light pollution. The whole pace of life is much slower – no one rushes anywhere. Oh yes, and the stunning views, I'm surrounded by magnificent scenery. One problem we're having at the moment is abandoned cars. People are dumping old cars they don't want any more in the village at night. We then have to wait for ages before they're taken away.

3

I live in an apartment block in the city centre. It's the cosmopolitan atmosphere I like. There's always plenty to do, and such a wide range of shops. I can go out at any time of the day or night and get whatever I want, either food and drink or entertainment. I love the liveliness of the city and being surrounded by people all the time – you know, that constant buzz of activity. People talk about the crime rate in the city, but where I live there always seem to be loads of police so I feel very safe. The one thing that gets me down is the amount of litter people drop on the streets. It's so unnecessary and just makes me feel depressed. I sometimes feel like saying to them, 'I have to live here with all your rubbish'. The council could do more to keep the streets clean as well, I suppose, but we all have to pay for it in higher taxes.

Lesson 2.3 Track 1.11

Professor, Students

P: Finally, to check you've all been listening, I'm going to ask you a question. So, what is a volcano? Yes, the young man in the red shirt.

S1: Erm … volcanoes are a natural way that the Earth has of cooling off … well, the Earth and other planets.

P: Yes that's right. OK. Do you have any questions for me? Yes, the woman in the green jacket.

S2: Professor, can I ask what the biggest volcano in the world is?

P: Right, that's easy. The biggest volcano on Earth is Mauna Loa in Hawaii and it's about 8.5 kilometres high – that's from the bottom of the ocean to its top. It's interesting that most of the volcanoes on Earth are found around the rim of the Pacific Ocean. But there are volcanoes around the coastline of Antarctica and there are even volcanoes underwater. There are probably more volcanoes and eruptions than people think. Between 1975 and 1985 there were 376 reported eruptions – so that's about 35 to 40 volcanoes erupting every year. Another question, … yes, you.

S3: Do you know whether people can go inside volcanoes?

P: That's an interesting question. Obviously, you can't go inside an erupting volcano. As I told you, extremely high pressures under the Earth cause volcanoes to erupt – the pressure forces very hot lava up out of the volcano. Lava flows can have temperatures up to 1,250 degrees centigrade. But, actually, the answer to your question is yes. You can go inside volcanoes. Some people live inside volcanoes as some of them don't erupt for long times. In the USA people live in three volcanoes, the most famous being the large volcano under Yellowstone National Park, which, incidentally, has been showing a lot of activity recently. Yes, the young man with the beard.

S4: Could you tell me if Vesuvius is an active volcano?

P: Well, an active volcano is one that has erupted in historical time. Vesuvius, which is east of Naples in Italy, famously destroyed Pompeii in AD 79 and it is the only volcano on the European mainland to have erupted within the last hundred years – I think it was 1944. So yes, it is an active volcano ... and a lot of people live near it. In fact, one in ten of the world's population live within volcanic danger zones. Last question ... yes?

S5: I'd like to know why volcanoes stop erupting.

P: That's a good question to end on. There are three possible reasons. Maybe the heat runs out when the rocks are melted. Or the hot rocks – which, if you remember, we call magma, solidify on their way up, or the magma can't generate enough pressure to crack the rock above it.

Lesson 2.4 Track 1.12

Switchboard, Deborah Rydell, John Reynolds

S: Good morning, Power Gas and Electricity, how can I help you?

DR: Good morning. Can I speak to John Reynolds, please?

S: Certainly. Who's calling, please?

DR: It's Deborah Rydell, from the Department of Energy.

S: Putting you through now.

DR: Hello, is that John?

JR: Speaking.

DR: Hi John, it's Deborah from the Energy Department. I wanted to have a chat with you about the wind farm proposal, you know, the one at Sparrow Hill.

JR: OK, Deborah. You're still in favour of it, I hope. You're not going to cancel it, are you?

DR: Well, it's not really my decision, John. Personally, there's no doubt in my mind that wind farms are the future, although some of my colleagues seem to think we should be doing more with nuclear power. It's much more cost effective at the moment, they say.

JR: Well, that's one way of looking at it, but we need to think long term. We just can't go on in the same old way.

DR: You're absolutely right, because oil and gas will run out eventually. Well, really, my reason for calling, John, is that I'd like to know if you think we should have a public meeting about Sparrow Hill. You know, to stop any rumours.

JR: No, it's much too early. I'm totally convinced that we should wait until we get the approval, as there's likely to be a lot of trouble about this.

DR: You have a point, but don't you think we should have a meeting and put our case? I mean, I'm sure we'll be able to get some supporters to attend.

JR: Mmm, I'm just worried that it could get out of hand – you know a lot of people feel strongly about this sort of thing. Though ... thinking about it, I'm interested in knowing what sort of local support we're likely to get, and perhaps it could be a chance to see how people who live in the area really feel.

DR: Yes, exactly. I just think if we want it to get public approval, we need to persuade people it's right for the area, and this would be a good opportunity.

JR: That's very true, because without local support we're probably not going to get much further.

DR: OK, I'll sort out a venue for some time in July and organise some publicity and security. I think that's important in case things get out of hand.

JR: I'd go along with you there, because some of these environmental groups can get quite violent. But, don't worry, I'm sure it will be OK. Remember, all the really great ideas are unpopular at first.

DR: Yes, OK, John. Goodbye.

JR: Goodbye.

Lesson 2.5 Track 1.13

Lecturer, Student

L: It's not easy to design a good questionnaire, Paula. I'm not surprised you're having problems. How can I help?

S: Well, a few tips would be useful. I mean, what are the key points?

L: Erm, OK, when you design your questionnaire, remember two things. Firstly, you need to ask the right questions so you get the information you're looking for. And secondly, you want to make sure you get enough data to analyse. You need as many questionnaires as possible to be completed and returned to you. OK?

S: OK, so I have to choose good questions and get as many responses as possible.

L: Exactly. Now would you like me to give you a few tips about the wording of questions? Of course, the type of question depends on what the aims of the questionnaire are, but there are certain rules, I'd say ...

S: Oh, yes?

L: Mmm, first of all, use simple, short sentences. And avoid questions which are too long. Some people just won't bother to answer them if they're long, and other people just won't understand them.

S: OK, short and snappy questions, I've got it.

L: Another thing, Paula. Try to use open and closed questions in your questionnaire. Mix them if possible.

S: Hold on, can you explain, erm, open and closed questions?

L: Sure. Open questions, well, they allow people to answer as they wish, for example, if you ask people, 'How do you feel about the quality of the teaching you received?' it's an open question. You'll probably get a variety of answers. But closed questions are questions to which the answers are given, so the person answering has a limited choice. For example, a question like, 'How satisfied are you with your course? a) satisfied b) not satisfied c) don't know. Circle the appropriate answer.' Well, that's a closed question; the choices are given to you. OK?

S: Right. I suppose you get more information with open questions.

L: Yes, you do, but it takes a lot longer to analyse all the answers!

S: Yeah, I can see that.

L: A word of warning about open questions. Ask for only one piece of information at a time. For example, if you ask, 'What is your opinion of the course materials and teaching method', that's not really a good question. It's really two questions, and it would be better to use two separate questions, not one, to get your information.

S: I see, OK.

L: Another thing about questions. All questions should be clear and well structured. In other words, respondents should be able to see the point of the question; they shouldn't be thinking 'what on earth does it mean?' Also, it's good to start with fairly simple questions which people can answer easily. This encourages them to complete the questionnaire.

S: Yes, I see! OK, I've got all that.

L: One final piece of advice. Before designing your questionnaire, you need to look ahead and think carefully about how you're going to analyse the data you get. People often forget to do this when they design a questionnaire, and they find out they can't analyse the data very easily. It's too late then!

Lesson 2.5 Track 1.14

Donna, Eduardo, Sophie

Part 1

D: OK, let's talk about the questions we'll put in our questionnaire. Eduardo, you've done some work on this, what have you come up with?

E: OK, well, I think we all agree that we need to get some basic data about the respondents in our sample. You know, we'll need to know their age, sex, marital status, that sort of thing. And their educational qualifications, of course.

D: Yes, and also get something about their current employment situation. Are they employed or still students?

E: Exactly. And I'd add a question about their nationality – that could be very useful for us to know.

D: True, let's get that as well. OK, the next thing is ... what issues do we want to include? Sophie, I think you've got some ideas about that.

S: Yeah, I've done a bit of research, the key issues are ... let's see ... in no particular order: nuclear power; climate change; air pollution; real food, in other words, there's a lot of concern about genetic engineering of food products – GMOs. Those are the four key issues. OK?

D: It's a good list. How about protecting rainforests?

S: It's an important issue, I agree, but I think four issues are enough.

D: OK, we'll go with those. Now, what other questions ...

Lesson 2.5 Track 1.15

Donna, Eduardo

Part 2

D: Now, what other questions shall we include? Any suggestions, Eduardo?

E: Yes. We'll need to know how important each issue is for our respondents; that'll be the first question. So, I think we should ask them to rank the issues in order of importance, with 1 being the top issue. And then we should have a second question asking them to give reasons for their choice. Of course, that would be an open question, and the answers might be more difficult to analyse.

D: Yes, but it'd be a useful question, so let's include it. Anything else?

E: We'll need to find out how *aware* they are of all the issues, and how *worried* they are about them. Those could be questions three and four. Probably for question four they could fill in a chart with headings like 'very worried', 'fairly worried', 'not worried at all', and they put ticks in the appropriate boxes to show their opinion.

D: Great idea. Just one final point. I'd like to have a question asking if they're prepared to help us, you know, by working in the office, interviewing people, taking part in campaigns, or raising money for us – that's very important. Let's put one in – a final question – to find out if they want to join us. Right, time to get started writing the questionnaire.

Lesson 3.2 Track 1.16

Interviewer, Mr Cole

I: How long have you been doing karate?

C: OK. My time in karate is just over 25 years now. I started back in 1981 in my final year at university down in Bath and I've been training ever since on the basis of something like between two and five times a week. So, 25 years in karate. Like, we say it takes about five to six years to get to black belt – that's what we say is the beginning of karate. So I achieved my black belt in 1987 and since then I've been working my way as a black belt through the various levels and I'm now at the fifth level of black belt.

I: What gives you most satisfaction in teaching karate?

C: Well, I think I'm going to sum it up with one word. Impact … having an impact on people – our students – students who now these days range from four to … I was going to say 64, but we've had someone of 73 in one of our clubs.

We can measure progress through different belts – something which was introduced in the West. These days people need to measure their achievement and that's good. It's a way to distinguish different levels. And when students achieve their new belt … I take tremendous joy in seeing their reaction, you get smiling faces, you get some children coming up and saying, 'Wow, it's the best day of my life.' I mean, for the adults it may be simply an expression of relief – the fact that they've got through an exam 20 years after having left school and not taking anything of this like before.

But I'd like to take that a step further. I take greatest satisfaction from witnessing the change in a student's approach and attitude. When I see students who cross a barrier from just doing movements to feeling or living their karate, then I feel great – we've made a change somewhere, and I can think of a number of incidences where I've had, say, children who are floppy and not really with it, and after a certain level something snaps – all of a sudden they are down in their stances, they're breathing, they're concentrating, they're looking, things are working, and for me that's a case of … well, between us, them and me, we've made a change.

Lesson 3.2 Track 1.17

Interviewer, Mr Cole

I: Is it a hobby or is it more of a way of life?

C: Yeah, this is a classic question, really. I mean, for most people who do it these days it's undoubtedly a hobby. Mmm, for some, lessons learnt in karate can be part of their life, it can become part of their life if they do it for longer and longer.

But for me, you see, I mean, it took like I said, it took six years to get to black belt. So, after the six years we say it takes to start karate, to some extent when you get to black belt, you kind of come down from a high of training a good number of times during the week, you've had extreme effort and concentration, and it's a case of 'Can you survive to the next level?' as we say, … and really after black belt, we say you just have to keep training, which is very hard for some people to accept. So, for them it's not a way of life, it's become more than a hobby, it's become a goal in their life to achieve black belt and a very admirable one, and we've had people who've achieved black belt and said, 'That's my lot', and that's fair enough, as long as they admit that to me and to themselves. But for others it's a case of, they've become disillusioned, it's black belt and where do I go now? And it almost just stops, and sometimes that's a bit of a shame if they can't accept that.

I: Why do people start karate?

C: The majority of the new starters these days are children and either they are attracted themselves by the glamour and excitement of karate, the martial arts, they've seen it on TV, they've enacted it on their Playstation games, they see the noise, the excitement, they see the fast-flowing kicks and so on. Or it may be because their mum or dad has encouraged them to attend. And there could be the twin attractions there of karate instilling discipline and control in their children. As is increasingly the case these days, maybe things don't work at home, parents are out at work more often. Maybe the school doesn't instil discipline. Very often these days teachers are restricted in terms of what they can say and can do and parents bring their children and say 'sort them out'. And the kid can also, from a parent's perspective, their child can also learn stuff which enables them to look after themselves, and that's an admirable aim in itself because everyone's fearful of their child being out of their sight.

Lesson 3.3 Track 1.18

1 I studied sports psychology as part of my course at university.
2 We can meet outside the university at six o'clock.
3 Did you see the game where the captain broke his ankle?
4 Tennis players tend to suffer a lot of wrist injuries.
5 We saw all the tennis players who had arrived early at the courts.

Lesson 3.4 Track 1.19

Ellen MacArthur was born in England in 1976. She's a *truly* remarkable person. In my opinion, she's *definitely* the greatest modern sportsperson. Let me tell you why.

She first came to people's attention when she took part in a famous yachting race, the Vendée Globe. It's a round-the-world solo yacht race, which takes place every four years, and the competitors are top-class yachtsmen and women. Ellen MacArthur came second in the race, and was the fastest woman competitor. It was an *amazing* achievement, and the French were *particularly* impressed with her performance. In fact, she became a heroine in France – they just love her there.

But, *most of all*, she's famous because in 2005, she broke the record for sailing non-stop around the world. Her voyage took 71 days. The record was previously held by a Frenchman, Francis Joyon. It was an *incredible* achievement, especially as the seas were very rough in the South Atlantic area, and in other parts of the world, she was sailing in *extremely* hot weather. The journey back was '*incredibly* hard', she said, and she was *totally* exhausted at the end of the trip.

She's a great competitor, *there's no doubt about that*, but *above all*, she's a great person, a really fine human being. And that's why people admire her so much. For example, during the Vendée Globe race, she stopped sailing at one point to help another yachtsman who was in difficulties. It was a marvellous, unselfish act.

What's extraordinary, also, about her is that she's a small woman, without obvious physical advantages, but you need to be very strong to take part in round-the-world races. Like many other top sportspeople, she's got *tremendous* determination and courage. But compared to people like Tiger Woods, the golfer, she doesn't attract a great deal of financial support, you know, endorsements from businesses, that sort of thing. Some sportspeople make a fortune that way. Another thing, sailing around the world is actually very dangerous. If Ellen fell overboard, she could easily drown. And unlike other top sportspeople, erm, footballers, golfers, tennis players and so on, she doesn't make a lot of money from her sailing. She just loves the sport. Oh, I forgot to mention, she often beats male competitors – not many women can do that! *It's really impressive*, don't you think?

I'd like to stress that she's both a fantastic competitor and a wonderful human being. She's a role model for all sportspeople. She's *undoubtedly the greatest sportsperson* of the modern era. Please vote for me and my choice, Ellen MacArthur.

Lesson 3.5 Track 1.20

Lecturer, Students

L: Right, thank you very much for coming and I hope you found the session useful. Now, if there are any questions, I'll be here for a few minutes if anyone wants to discuss anything.

S1: I have this essay to write and I'm finding it a real struggle. Could you give me a few tips?

L: Sure. Gosh, where do I start? OK, well, a common mistake new students often make is about the purpose of an essay. An essay is basically a question which needs an answer. Erm, I mean, it isn't an opportunity for you to show how much you know about a particular subject, so, if you don't actually answer the question, you'll fail the task, however good your writing is. A lot of people forget this.

S1: I see, that makes sense. So what's the best way of preparing to write an essay, do you think?

L: Well, the first thing I would do is analyse the title. I think it's helpful to underline any key words and work out what you're actually being asked to do. Then decide if ... whether the title indicates a clear structure to you. For example, is it a, a for-and-against essay or are you being asked to compare and contrast, or even offer solutions to a problem?

S1: OK, thanks. That's good. Then, what do you recommend I do next?

L: Well, then I think you should make some notes. Start by writing the exact title at the top of a new sheet of paper to focus your attention, and then brainstorm your ideas. I find it's helpful for students to get into the habit of starting with the topic area and just noting down any topic vocabulary which comes to mind.

S1: Oh, OK. That's a good idea. What next?

L: Well, I suggest that you ask yourself questions such as, what do I already know? What do I need to find out? Get all your ideas down on paper, however crazy they may seem. Then, organise your notes – it's really important that you have a clear and logical structure in your mind before you start writing.

S1: Yeah, I think that's one of my problems, getting to that. Thank you very much.

L: That's OK.

S2: I was wondering if you could give me some advice on how I should go about actually writing the essay?

L: Sure ... a good approach to writing is what I call the beginning, middle and end approach. I think that good essays tend to follow this.

S2: Oh, right. What does that mean?

L: Right, I'll explain. I think at the beginning or in the first paragraph you should restate the question in your own words and introduce the topic. The next two, three or four paragraphs are the middle or main part of the essay where you state the arguments for and against the proposition, or offer solutions to the problem. The third part and final paragraph is a conclusion where you should refer back to the question and offer your own opinion if that is appropriate.

S2: That's useful, thanks very much. Is there anything special about academic writing that we should think about?

L: Mmm, let's think. Yes, firstly, most questions involve some kind of comparison and contrast, if only looking at the for and against of something, or assessing which solution to a problem is better. Secondly, good academic writing will have a logical argument and guide the reader through the argument, using examples and supporting ideas with examples where necessary and appropriate. You should also put similar ideas in a single paragraph, you know, all the reasons for a particular thing, that sort of thing.

S2: OK, great, thanks.

S3: Could I ask about the language itself?

L: Mmm, good point. Most important – academic writing tends to be neutral in tone.

S3: Neutral? What exactly do you mean?

L: Well, you need to stand back and to appear to look at the question from a distance – to be emotionally detached. A good way of achieving this is to leave yourself out of your writing – don't keep writing 'I think', but instead use phrases like 'it is clear that' and 'it is obvious that', 'this shows that', 'it is true that' and so on. You can put in your own experience, but it's often better to make this sound more general by introducing personal opinions and experiences with phrases like 'for many people', and 'a lot of men, women, younger people find ...'. Passive structures are often used because they help to give that distance and objectivity. Finally, you should avoid abbreviations and contractions if it's a formal academic essay.

S3: Well, thanks very much. You've really been helpful. I think I'm ready to make a start now.

L: No problem, I hope it helps.

Review 1–3 Track 1.21

Kenny, Chloe, Vince

K: Right, I think we need to talk about the line-up for next week's match. Chloe, what's the situation with injuries?

C: Not too bad, but Marek definitely isn't going to be fit by Saturday.

V: What about Steve?

C: Well, it's a very tricky situation, Vince. He's still suffering from that knee injury. I just don't know if he'll be well enough to play on Saturday.

V: Let's get Patrice in to replace him.

K: The trouble with that is we'll be very weak in defence. Patrice is really more of a striker.

C: That's very true.

V: OK. You have a point. We could try out Sinan. I know he hasn't played for the first team before, but he did incredibly well in the trials last month.

C: Yes. That could solve the problem.

K: I'm not so sure. Perhaps we should give Giancarlo a chance. I've been watching him recently. Compared to Sinan, I think he's got a lot more potential.

V: OK Kenny. You're the manager. It's your decision.

Lesson 4.2 Track 2.3

Professor John Dodge

The pharmaceutical industry has a problem at the present time because the very common diseases throughout the world such as high blood pressure, asthma, diabetes and so on have huge markets with potentially very large profits for successful drugs, but the people who are paying for the drug, such as insurance companies and state health services, do not wish to pay more than they have to for an effective treatment. That is why so much money goes into marketing as well as into development and testing of drugs.

There are still very large areas of medicine where new drugs are desperately needed. For example, it would be wonderful if we had more anti-malarial drugs because many of the existing preparations have become less effective as time has gone on and the malaria parasite has become resistant to them. Ideally, we need a vaccine against malaria so that all the people in a particular malarial country can be immunised and thereby protected. This of course needs to be combined with measures to reduce mosquitoes and so on. But these countries where there are huge needs for effective new treatment are generally poor and can't afford the huge cost of new drugs. So the pharmaceutical companies are less keen to develop new treatments which will not be very profitable. This type of development really depends upon support from international agencies such as the World Health Organisation, the World Bank, the European Union and similar organisations. Working in partnerships with university departments, the agencies can try to produce treatments and develop them to a stage where a pharmaceutical company would be interested in bringing them to the market.

Lesson 4.4 Track 2.4

Medical Director, Nursing Director

MD: Let's talk about the Goldwater grant, Jenny. Everyone seems to have different ideas about how to spend the money. What's your opinion?

ND: Well ... I'd like to do something about the gardens. They're in a terrible mess at the moment – a real eyesore. And they're the first thing people see when they visit the hospital. It doesn't make a very good impression. We need to get an expert to landscape the gardens, then employ full-time gardeners to look after them.

MD: You're right, of course, the gardens are in a dreadful state. But it'll probably cost quite a lot to have them landscaped and then employ gardeners. I don't have precise figures, but I'd say it'd probably use up over half of the grant.

ND: Maybe, but the gardens are very important for patients. It's where they go to recuperate from operations, and where they take their friends and relatives for a chat. It's important to have beautiful, well-cared-for gardens. When you're sick, you appreciate that sort of thing, and when you're getting better, you spend a lot of time in them.

MD: I think we need to look at the implications of that choice, Jenny. If we spend the money on the gardens, I don't think the Boston Medical Foundation will be very pleased. They'll want us to spend the grant on up-to-date equipment. They're very keen for us to get a new scanner. They think it'll greatly improve our treatments.

ND: Mmm, I see what you mean.

MD: Another thing to think about, if we spend the money on the gardens, is that it could have an effect on other projects …

ND: Ah, you're thinking of research, I imagine.

MD: Exactly. It might have a big impact on research. We wouldn't have enough money to hire a new research assistant – and that's something we've wanted to do for a long time.

ND: That's a thought, I must say. What angle do you think the local newspaper would have, if we spent some money on the gardens?

MD: My guess is that they wouldn't like it. They'd say we were betraying the principles of the hospital, you know, that money should be spent on low-income patients.

ND: Well, we have to make a choice, that's for sure. Talking of principles, I wonder what Edgar Dowling would have done with the money.

MD: Somehow, I don't think he'd have spent it on the gardens. He preferred to spend money on medical care and the latest equipment! You know, Jenny, I think we need to think this through. We need to listen to people, get their opinions, then make up our minds. Our decision must be in the interests of patients and the hospital.

ND: Absolutely. That's the best way forward.

MD: I'll be talking to Diana Marsden some time this weekend. She's chief surgeon at Boston State. I'll see what she has to say. I respect her opinions a lot.

ND: Good idea.

MD: And next week, say Wednesday or Thursday, we can meet, look at the options and make a decision.

Lesson 4.5 Track 2.5

Part 1

When you're looking at websites for research, you must trust the source of your information and get the very best quality of information you're searching for. Now, there are two points which I consider to be very important.

Firstly, it's essential to know who's responsible for the site and its information. A good site will tell you that, usually at the bottom of each page, or you can generally find it out in the 'About us' section. Government websites are usually excellent sources of information.

Secondly, you must know the purpose of the site. It should be clear what the purpose is, and when you know that, it should help you to evaluate the site. For example, you need to ask yourself if the aim of the website is to inform or educate you, or if it is trying to persuade you or sell you something.

If the site is trying to get you to buy something, either directly or indirectly, you need to be careful. Commercial sites may not give you objective information; the sites are often biased in some way and give you misleading or inaccurate information. They're there to sell things and often exaggerate the qualities of their products.

Lesson 4.5 Track 2.6

Part 2

What are the websites you can rely on? Well, of course, government-sponsored sites, educational sites run by universities or medical schools, and websites of well-known professional organisations, they're usually non-profit-making and should be trustworthy, you can rely on them. By the way, government agencies in the UK usually have the suffix *.gov* in the address, and educational bodies have *.ac*, though in the United States *.edu* is more commonly used for academic sites. Professional organisations and charities sometimes have *.org* and commercial organisations often finish with *.com*.

A word about health and medical information you find on the net. Any statement or evidence should be supported by well-established research or medical institutions. Or, if the material you find has been reviewed by an expert, that's a good sign. We call that 'peer reviews'. If the material has not been reviewed, then be careful. Check other sources, other websites, to see if they support the statement or evidence you have found. The material should be up-to-date – medical sites should really be updated weekly or monthly – well that's the ideal.

I think one other point is worth mentioning. It's important the website separates opinion from research results. Research results are based on evidence, and you need to know what the evidence is. It's OK for opinions to be included in the website, as long as it's clear they are opinions, and not scientific facts. Oh, yes, and by the way, a good website will provide links with other sources of information so you can check if these back up the findings or research results.

Well, I hope these tips will help you to evaluate information you get from Internet websites. You're lucky to have this source of information. When I was studying medicine, the library was the main source of information for me. Nowadays, I use the Internet a lot in my research, but I'm very careful what websites I use. I'm sure you will be too.

Lesson 5.2 Track 2.7

No fumes and no driver.

Could this really be the future of urban public transport? The battery-operated pods travel at up to 25 miles an hour, computerised sensors making sure they keep to a strict route. And because you travel in relative privacy, the inventors hope the pods will appeal to passengers who don't like sitting with strangers.

'You have private space in here. It's as low cost as anything else, and it's as cheap as a bus ride. You share with your friends. You are not sharing with anyone else and it takes you straight to your destination within a matter of minutes.'

The Ultra has been designed for towns and cities – places like Swindon and Daventry are seriously interested. But the first contract has gone to Heathrow Airport. In two years' time a fleet of pods will carry passengers from the car parks to Terminal One.

…

And if the Heathrow scheme is successful, the pods will then be taken up by other UK airports.

Lesson 5.4 Track 2.8

… And now some news for all you tourists who are planning to go to the beautiful city of Beauciel for a vacation. The results of a survey about the transport system in the city have just been published by the newspaper, *Echo de France*. It reveals some interesting information.

As many people know, Beauciel has serious problems concerning transport. The main problems, according to the survey, are too many cars in the city, huge traffic jams at peak times, not enough car parks, too much noise and slow, unreliable buses.

The residents also mentioned on-street parking and the fact that the city had no underground, unlike some major European cities.

For most people in the survey, over 80%, traffic congestion was the biggest problem. At peak times, 8 to 10 in the morning and 4 to 6 in the evening, there are usually serious traffic jams when people enter and leave the city. It's a nightmare for drivers at these times.

Over 75% of the residents in the survey considered that there were just too many cars in the city. According to them, it was vital to reduce the number of cars.

Many residents, about 70% of those surveyed, felt that the city needed more car parks. There's only one car park in the centre of the city, and that's always full, according to them. The other car parks, dotted around the city, are generally small and inadequate for the number of cars.

Many residents, roughly 60% in the survey, spoke of the unacceptable noise levels, especially in the morning and evening, and not just from cars but also from motorcycles.

According to them, this has a bad effect on their quality of life.

Just over 45% drew attention to the problem of on-street parking. According to them, there are too many private cars parked on the road. This caused problems for people who had an essential need to park on the road, such as ambulance drivers, taxis, school buses, and so on.

Other problems mentioned were the unreliable bus services, criticised by 40% in the survey and the length of time it took to travel by bus from the centre of the city in the west to the old town and port in the east. The bus journey was usually over an hour – far too long, according to the residents.

The survey results have come at the right time. They'll no doubt be studied carefully by the group of international consultants who are at this very moment trying to sort out the city's transport problems. That's all from me. I'll be back again tomorrow morning at 11 o'clock.

Lesson 5.4 Track 2.9

Luc, Melanie, Jim

L: So, what do you think can be done about our transport problems? You know, it took me over an hour to get to the centre, and another 20 minutes to park. I was tired out before I even started work.

M: The first thing, Luc, is that I'm convinced there are too many cars in the centre. I think the best solution would be to have a pedestrian mall there. Close the area to cars completely – that'd be a good idea.

L: Maybe you're right, Melanie. That would be good for shoppers, but what about people who would still have to come into the centre – business people, traders, you know?

J: OK, Luc, but I really think we've got to do something about the number of cars in the city. Surely you must agree that there are just too many cars – that's the heart of the problem. We've got to reduce the number somehow.

L: Well, I suppose you're right, Jim. But there are other issues. I think it's essential to persuade people to use smaller cars; there just isn't the space here for big cars. It makes me angry when I see a huge four-wheel drive with just one person in it.

M: I'm not too sure about that. A lot of people have families, they need big cars.

J: OK, but I strongly believe we need to sort out the main problem first, I mean, too many cars in the city.

L: I agree, but we also need to think about other things. Don't you think that more car parks are necessary? I mean, parking is one of our issues.

J: No, I disagree. It's not the answer to build loads of car parks. That'll just bring more cars into the centre and increase the traffic jams. No, I heard of a good idea recently, it's the way forward for us, in my opinion. The Council should sell permits to people who want to use cars here. Maybe 10,000 euros for a large car and 5,000 euros for a small car. The money could go to improving the roads and bus service.

M: No, I don't think that'd work, Jim. People would be very upset if that was proposed. There's no doubt in my mind that the answer is to offer people a really good, cheap bus system, and get some of the cars off the roads. I'm also very much in favour of building a tram system. I'm sure you can see that's the best way to get people round the city quickly and efficiently – and we can build on the old system that closed down years ago.

L: Maybe you're right, Melanie. But you can't argue that it's the best solution for us right now. It would be very expensive, take years to finish and be very disruptive for businesses. It's a very long-term solution. We need action now to improve things. I recommend some simple solutions, like, er, building more bicycle lanes. Now that wouldn't be too expensive and it would be something we can put in place quite quickly. We need to think in terms of both short- and long-term solutions. OK, can you do a report on where we are for my next council meeting? It would be very useful to have some costings ...

Lesson 6.1 Track 2.10

Jenny, Michael, Erika, Jarvis

J: Now, if everyone's got a coffee, I think we should begin. Has everyone read this month's book?

M/E/JA: Yes, sure.

J: Well, Michael, I suppose as you chose this book for us to read you should start us off. Why did you choose it?

M: Yes, well ... OK. I chose it because of all the publicity really. I thought we should all see what all the fuss was about. So, *The Da Vinci Code* by Dan Brown. What can I say? I really thought it was brilliant! It's a real page-turner. I read the whole thing in a day.

JA: Really??!! I thought it was dreadful! ...

M: Oh come on Jarvis!

JA: All that stuff about the Louvre being a museum, which is in Paris, which is in France. I felt insulted. And what was all that romantic stuff in the middle? No, I'm sorry, it's not my kind of thing. Jenny, what did you think?

J: OK Jarvis, I agree that was a bit odd, but you must agree the plot was exciting, all those twists and turns? I couldn't put it down.

JA: Really, Jenny, I'm surprised at you. It was really tedious. And the ending was a real let-down. After 500 pages nothing really happened. I found that Stephen King book we read last month much more interesting, and at least the characters were written with some imagination.

E: I agree with you, Jarvis – I just couldn't get into it. It was really dull and just not thought-provoking, which I was surprised about, considering the subject matter.

M: Come on, Erika, it's a thriller. It's light and easy to read, just a good story.

E: Well, not for me. It was very hard going at the beginning and then I just gave up. There were just too many people in it for me. And all those really short chapters about the different people – I suppose that was to make it easier to follow, except that for me it didn't work. I don't know if it was the way it was written.

J: Well, for me it certainly lived up to all the hype – I'd definitely read one of his others now. I agree with Michael. It was really gripping. I couldn't wait to see what would happen next.

JA: Not me. I mean, I like a good mystery but this was definitely overrated.

E: Yes, just awful ... anyway, let's agree to differ on this one, but it's my turn to choose for next month and it's going to be something a bit less lightweight. How about a classic, perhaps something by Charles Dickens, you know, with interesting characters?

J: Great.

M: Yes, I've never read any of his.

J: Sounds good.

Lesson 6.2 Track 2.11

The Sherlock Holmes stories made a huge impression on me when I first read them, and the reason's simple. Sherlock Holmes himself is a fascinating person ... someone we can all admire. He's got a brilliant intellect and incredible analytical powers. He's also got amazing powers of observation – just by looking at people, he can deduce all kinds of things about them and their lives. He's supremely talented as a detective and can solve the most difficult cases.

But he has human failings as well. He has character flaws, like he can be very arrogant – especially in his relations with his sidekick, Dr Watson. Watson accompanies him on most cases, and he isn't stupid, but Holmes is so brilliant! And he's a very courageous person, especially when dealing with some very dangerous men. He's knowledgeable and he's talented musically. He often plays the violin when he's in an unhappy mood.

He's very believable as the main character in the stories. A lot of people think he really exists. Tourists come to England and go to Baker Street to see where he lived; some don't realise he's a fictitious character. And I suppose I think of him as a real character too. I feel I know him well. When I was young, my uncle used to read extracts from the stories to me, and he could quote pages of the stories by heart. I love Sherlock Holmes and re-read the stories many times.

Lesson 6.2 Track 2.12

One book that's made a huge impression on me is *To Kill a Mockingbird* by Harper Lee – so much so that it's a book I always buy for people as a present. The reason I like it so much is that it's incredibly heart-warming and it's a moral tale. Also, it's extremely well written and in a subtle way it's a page-turner. You want to know what happens to all the characters in the story.

As well as that, the language is very evocative. It's a charming read. You really get the feel of a sleepy town in a hot summer during the great Depression in the United States. Something that's special about the book is that in a way it's written from a child's perspective. This gives a revealing view of the adult world; in particular, it shows the absurdity of racism but we also get an insight into the world of the child, especially the world of games and adventures during the summer.

A key character in the book is Atticus, Atticus Finch – he's the father of the child and he provides the moral centre of the book. He's an incredibly fair, wise person. And from him we get the main lesson, as does young Scout, the child in the book. The main lesson from this book, I think, is that we need to learn to see from other people's perspectives – that we need to sympathise with their position and try to understand them. So, all round I think it's a marvellous book – the characters are richly drawn and it's a book that can teach us something in our own lives. It's certainly a lesson I learnt and an attitude of fairness that I try to carry with me through life.

Lesson 6.3 Track 2.13

1 Bram Stoker used to take his holidays at Cuden Bay.
2 He used to live in a house in Sandycove in Dublin.

Lesson 6.4 Track 2.14

Douglas, Hart

D: There are one or two points I'd like to discuss with you, Lee, before I contact a publisher.

H: OK. What do you want to talk about?

D: Well, you said you'd like to start with a short chapter about your family.

H: Yeah, it'll bring back some bad memories, so I don't want to make it too long.

D: I can understand it'll be difficult for you to talk about your childhood, but if we included more chapters about your background, it'd add a lot of human interest to the book. Readers would like to know about your childhood, your parents and your two sisters. I believe your father left home when you were eight, didn't he? It must have been very difficult ...

H: Yeah, it was. He was a terrible man, my father, violent, unstable, he made our lives a misery. I was really happy when he walked out on Mum. We all were. I don't want to upset her now by writing about that time.

D: I know how important your mother is to you, Lee. Why don't you talk to her? If you agreed to write two or three chapters about the family, you'd probably double or triple sales of the book. It's a long time since your father left home: maybe you can persuade her that readers would be really interested in that part of your life.

H: OK, I'll try. If she and the rest of the family don't object, perhaps we can have more chapters about my family background.

D: Good, let's hope there's no problem there. Now, there's another important matter to discuss with you. Money! It's how I'll be paid for being your agent. As you know, agents are usually paid 10 percent of the money the writer receives from a book. That's 10 percent of the royalties you receive.

H: OK.

D: But in this case, I think 15 percent is more appropriate.

H: Fifteen percent? Really? I wasn't expecting to pay as much as that.

D: Well, it's a little bit above the market rate, but I'm very experienced in this kind of work. You'll find I'm good value for money. You see, I'll have more expenses than agents normally have. I'll have to go to a lot of international book fairs, set up interviews to promote the book, spend a lot of time negotiating with publishers, discussing TV and film rights and so on. The contract will be very complex and time-consuming.

H: I see.

D: There's going be a lot of interest in the book. Once it's launched, it'll be a full-time job for me to deal with everything ...

H: OK, I get your point, but 15 percent still seems too high. Look, I'd like to make a proposal. I need time to think about this, and take some advice. I'm seeing my financial adviser at the end of the week. How about if I talked to him, and after that we set up another meeting to discuss the financial details? If we agree, we can draw up a contract.

D: Fine, let's do that. Could I suggest we meet towards the end of the month? I'll be at the Cannes Film Festival for the next few days, and I'll be pretty busy for a while.

H: Yeah, I'm sure that'll be OK.

Lesson 6.5 Track 2.15

Extract 1

The Local to Maymyo

At the early sloping stations, women with trays were selling breakfast to the passengers: oranges, sliced pawpaws, fried cakes, peanuts and bananas. One had a shining assortment of beady objects on her tray. I beckoned her over and had a look.

Lesson 6.5 Track 2.16

Extract 2

They were fat insects skewered on sticks – fried locusts. I asked the old man next to me if he'd like some. He said politely that he had had breakfast already, and anyway he never ate insects. 'But the local people are quite fond of them.'

Lesson 6.5 Track 2.17

Extract 3

Paul Theroux meets a Burmese man. They go in search of food and drink at the station. He describes what happens next.

Back on the train I couldn't find the Burmese man, and it was not until after the train pulled away that he appeared, out of breath, with two palm-leaf parcels, bound with knotted vine. We uncapped the bottles on the door hinge, and, elbow to elbow at the end of the coach, opened the palm leaves. There was something familiar in the contents, a wooden skewer with three blackened things on it – lumps of burned meat. It wasn't that they were irregularly shaped, but rather that they were irregular in exactly the same way. The skewers lay half-buried in beds of rice.

'In Burmese we call them –.' He said the word.

I peered at them. 'Are these wings?'

Lesson 6.5 Track 2.18

Extract 4

'Yes, they are birds.'

Then I saw the little heads, the beaks and burned-out eyes, and dark singed claws on feeble feet.

'Maybe you call them sparrows,' he said.

Maybe we do, I thought ...

Lesson 6.5 Track 2.19

Extract 5

Back in Tokyo Central, on Platform 18, a hundred Japanese men in grey suits stood watching my train. There was a melancholy reverence in their faces. They had no (*beep*); they were not travellers. Grouped around one car in a respectful semicircle, they stared, their eyes fixed to one window. Inside the train, at that window, a man and woman stood next to their seats, their chins just showing below the window frame. The (*beep*) was blown; the train started up, but before it moved an inch the man and woman began bowing at the window, again and again, and outside on the (*beep*), the hundred men did the same – quickly, because the train was speeding. The bowing stopped: the hundred men burst into applause. The man and woman remained standing until we were out of the station and then they sat down and each opened a newspaper.

I asked the Japanese man next to me who they might be.

He shook his head. For a moment I thought he was going to say, 'No Engrish' – but he was thinking. He said, 'Offhand, I would say a company director. Or it could be a politician. I do not know him.'

'It's quite a send-off.'

'It is not unusual in Japan. The man is important. His employees must show some respect, even if' – he smiled – 'even if they do not feel it in their hearts.'

Review 4–6 Track 2.20

Maria, Sergei

M: I really think we need a car, Sergei.

S: Are you sure? What's wrong with the bus?

M: I'm fed up spending hours waiting at the bus stop. If we had a car, I'd be able to do everything much more quickly.

S: But I like the bus. It's cheap.

M: Well, we could get a cheap second-hand car.

S: Yes, but if we spend the money on a car, we won't be able to afford other things, like holidays.

M: You can't argue that we won't have money for holidays. I mean, we could use the car for our holidays instead of going on the train. So it would be good value for money.

S: OK, Maria, but it's not just the cost of buying it. It'll probably cost quite a lot to insure.

M: Oh, I hadn't thought of that. How much is that going to be?

S: I don't know, but that friend of yours from the gym works for an insurance company, doesn't she? Why don't you talk to her? She'd probably know how much car insurance costs these days.

M: Oh yes, that's the best way to find out.

S: Anyway, we haven't even seen a car we want to buy yet.

M: Erm, you remember Dennis from the dry cleaner's?

S: I think so.

M: He's selling his old car. He only wants £1,000 for it.

S: £1,000! I wasn't expecting to pay as much as that.

M: But it's only five years old. Surely you must agree that's a very reasonable price …

Lesson 7.2 Track 2.22

Students, Marta

S1: What do architects find interesting when designing buildings?

M: A good question. I'd say the most interesting thing relates to our role as an architect. In most cases, what are architects trying to do? Well, we're trying to design an ideal place to meet human needs. That's really our main motivation. It's our 'duty' if you like, to create a place that integrates interior design with the needs of the people who'll be using the building. It's, how can I say, a relationship in which the individual and the place are integrated. They depend on each other.

S2: What do architects take into consideration when designing a hotel?

M: When you think about the concept of a hotel, it's important to consider the area it'll be located in and what kind of people the hotel's designed for. You'd have to check if it'll be near a business or resort centre. You'll have to consider issues like, erm, the budget, access to the hotel, the facilities and of course, who'll use the hotel, what kind of people will be staying there and so on. In general, hotels are aimed at people who have two different purposes – business or leisure. However, in both cases, it's essential that guests can find a relaxing and cosy atmosphere, so they enjoy the time they spend there. If someone's purpose is business, the hotel project needs to be focused on events that companies may be interested in, like conferences, congresses, trade exhibitions, and so on. There are a lot of things to be taken into account when planning a hotel. It's a complicated process.

S3: What factors would influence an architect when designing the ground floor of a hotel?

M: OK, for a start, you have to bear in mind that the ground floor of a hotel is its 'visiting card'. When planning this floor, you've got to take into account the aesthetic appearance of the interior and the function of the ground floor. It's crucial to integrate the facilities and leisure areas when welcoming guests. A spacious lounge is really important, and it should have a cosy atmosphere. It must be in harmony with the décor. Another point, the lounge is sometimes used as a waiting room. So, the ground floor should have a small cafeteria or brasserie as well as a TV room. Of course, toilets and elevators shouldn't be forgotten. And there should be good access to all the rooms and facilities in this part of the hotel.

S4: What do you think of having hotels in space?

M: I like the idea. Architects are professionals. We're responsible for creating spaces that shelter people, and for buildings which change the environment. I believe space hotels would be an example of human progress, they'd be a huge challenge for human beings. Actually, that phrase of Neil Armstrong comes into my mind, you know, when he first stepped on the moon. Didn't he say something like, erm, 'One small step for man, one giant leap for mankind'? Well, I'd say, for space hotels, it'll be a giant step for technology and also a really big leap for mankind. Yes, as an architect, I'm excited by the prospect of hotels in space. They can't come soon enough for me.

S5: Would an architect be involved in designing space hotels?

M: Yes, in my opinion, definitely, an architect would be involved. I'm sure we wouldn't miss the opportunity to be part of such an amazing scientific breakthrough. You know, if you think back, architects have been present at most of the big moments of social and historical change. We don't just reflect cultural changes but also represent the progress made by societies. I believe a space hotel will be a landmark in the history of mankind. And architects will be fully involved in the process, there's no doubt about that. We'll be designing hotels that are fit for space tourists to stay in. So, to answer your question, I feel we'll play a vital role in the planning process.

Lesson 7.4 Track 2.23

Fatima, Yasmin, Richard

F: Let's talk about our plans for the ground floor, Yasmin. What ideas do you have?

Y: Well, I need a little more time to think about it, but seeing that space won't be a problem, in my opinion, it's vital we have some sort of sports facility on the ground floor. That's a priority, I think. Also we'll need an area where people can relax.

F: How about you, Richard? What do you think?

R: I agree, Yasmin's right. It's absolutely essential to offer a facility for people who want to forget work for a while, just chill out, and the ground floor's the best place to provide it. But I'm not sure what sort of facility it should be.

F: So, Yasmin, any ideas?

Y: Mmm, well, people are health conscious, they do want to relax, they're often very stressed. So … we've got to offer them something, that's for sure. Off the top of my head, I suggest we have a games room on the ground floor – you know, table tennis, snooker. It'd be very popular with some of our guests.

F: Mmm, I don't know, Yasmin. We certainly need some kind of area where people can take it easy, let their hair down a bit. But I'm not sure a games room is the answer. I mean, is it really the right choice for a business hotel?

Y: OK, maybe not a games room, but we should offer them something to help them relax, maybe a sauna, a jacuzzi, that sort of thing. Don't you agree, Richard?

R: Yeah, a sauna, why not? And, erm, I've just thought of something. It might be a good idea to have an aerobics and dance studio. Of course, we'd have to find out first if our guests really wanted that kind of facility.

F: Mmm, I like that idea, Richard. It would probably appeal to all age groups. I think most people would enjoy doing aerobics and dance. But we need to think this through. There are plenty of options to meet the needs of groups who want to keep fit, and others who'll want to wind down. Let's talk about it tomorrow and get ideas from the rest of the team.

Y: Yes, they'll have plenty of ideas. Let's see what they come up with.

Lesson 8.1 Track 2.25

5

I'm Michel, from France. Globalisation's definitely made the world smaller, but I don't think it's a fairer place. I think it has benefits for developed world consumers, but not for workers in poorer countries. It often means things like child labour and other abuses of human rights. There are some benefits but they're not evenly distributed. It's contributed to the gap between the rich and poor countries. Globalisation exploits the poor and has no respect for local cultures.

6

Hi, I'm Doug from Australia. Globalisation has been a force for change in so many ways for so many people. It has given them access to information and improved their lives, and has given global mobility to skilled workers. Fair trade has the ability to lift people out of poverty. It creates a level playing field and allows countries across the world to share their best products, goods and services. Many workers in developing countries now have employment because of globalisation. Globalisation benefits all nations by increasing competitiveness and efficiency.

7

This is Astrid, from Sweden. I think it's true that globalisation has connected the world with great technological advances in communications. Television and the Internet have improved people's lives all over the world. For me personally, globalisation is a good thing but it has also pushed rich and poor further apart. Globalisation is basically an economic movement. Manufacturing goes to the cheapest places. Companies maximise profits by exploiting workers as a way of reducing costs. Globalisation is mostly about corporate greed.

8

John, from the UK. Globalisation benefits everyone, including people in developing countries. It allows me personally to work from home in the UK with clients and colleagues all over the world. Globalisation isn't just benefiting big corporations. It also benefits small businesses like my own. Technology and cheaper transport mean I can compete with large corporations who used to have a monopoly on faraway markets.

9

I'm Maria, speaking from Colombia. You know, when the result of globalisation is damaging the environment, it's a bad thing. It's clear to me that global warming and climate change are the direct results of globalisation. Industry and big business have no respect for the environment – they're only interested in making money. I don't see any benefits for workers in poor countries who are just exploited by globalisation.

Lesson 8.4 Track 2.26

Presenter, CEO

P: Good evening everyone and welcome to this week's edition of *In the Hot Seat*, with me, Louise Falcon. Tonight my guest is Bob Craven, chief executive of the supermarket giant Smithsons.

CEO: Good evening, everyone.

P: Welcome to the programme, Bob. It's good to finally have you on the show to answer a few questions.

CEO: It's my pleasure, Louise.

P: Could I start off by asking you about the success of Smithsons – why do you think it's so successful?

CEO: Well, Louise, I think it's because of our range of products and because we have always meant good value for money.

P: Yes, but what do you mean by good value? Surely in some markets, and for some people, you are very expensive?

CEO: Well, I don't think so actually. Basically, what I'm saying is the customer is at the heart of our business. We always charge lower prices than our competitors.

P: Ah, yes, but some people accuse you of using low prices to force the competition out of business.

CEO: Sorry, I don't know what you mean, Louise.

P: Well, there've been examples where you have destroyed small businesses by keeping prices low, which of course you can do because of your size.

CEO: That's ridiculous, Louise. What we're doing is offering the consumer a choice … and part of that choice is lower prices. And we're proud of that. Now, you could force people to use higher-priced competitors to keep them in business, but that doesn't seem right to me. What I really want to say is that we believe in the customers' right to choose where they shop.

P: I see, but …

CEO: Or to put it another way, businesses come and go. The world changes. Nothing lasts for ever.

P: OK, but that's a very arrogant thing to say when you consider the impact on people's lives. If you don't mind, I'd like to move on now to your staff. There have been criticisms of the fact that as a company you pay low wages and also, there are accusations that some of your clothing suppliers may use child labour and sweatshops.

CEO: Right, well, I can't comment on our suppliers, but what I can tell you is that in many markets our workers are paid over the minimum wage and as a company we do a lot for charity.

P: Could you explain that in more detail, please? What do you actually do for charity?

CEO: Certainly. I can tell you that Smithsons gives about 2.5 percent of its profits to local community projects.

P: Could you be more specific? Because many people have claimed they haven't seen the results of these community projects.

CEO: Yes, well, er, for example, if we build a new store, we, er, also, er, set aside money for a community centre or park. People like Smithsons, Louise. We do a lot for people.

P: Yes, but what about the negative impact of Smithsons?

CEO: Sorry, I don't follow you.

P: OK. Let me rephrase that. What I'm talking about is economic and social damage which big multinational companies like yours can do around the world.

CEO: Could you give me an example?

P: Yes, the fact that as a company you are anti union. You don't let employees join workers' organisations.

CEO: Yes, that's true. We don't think that unions are a good idea for staff or the company as a whole.

P: But why not? What I mean is … what are you worried about?

CEO: I don't think we're worried at all. I'm sorry, I don't see what you mean by all this damage you talk about. I see only benefits. Perhaps in some ways we are victims of our own success. We are almost too successful, but that's down to our customers. Statistics show that in the markets we have entered recently it is actually the poorest sections of society who benefit most. To be more precise … we really appeal to everyone and alienate no one.

P: … Right. Another question for you now …

Lesson 9.1 Track 3.2

Monica, Jane

M: So Jane, do you think you'll renew your membership? I was just looking at the programme for next year.

J: I'm not sure really. I didn't get to see as many exhibitions as I'd hoped to last year. I only went to a couple. I saw the Matisse exhibition. It was fantastic – so inspiring. I was really impressed by it.

M: I didn't get to see that. I'm not really into that sort of thing, but I heard it was something special, though. I also heard the Monet one was excellent, but I didn't see it.

J: No, neither did I. The only other one I got to was the Pop Art one which didn't really live up to my expectations. How about you? Did you see it?

M: No, I didn't actually, but the reviews weren't very good.

J: Well, you didn't miss much at all. It wasn't worth the effort, or the entrance fee for that matter. Yeah, it was very expensive, now I think about it.

M: Oh, I'll tell you what I really liked – the Rembrandt exhibition at the start of the year. It was excellent, although it was really packed. I even had to queue up for half an hour. It was one of the best exhibitions I've ever seen. But I think the other thing I really enjoyed last year was the portrait photos exhibition in the café, which is free anyway.

J: Mmm. The thing is, the membership is expensive if you don't go to most of the exhibitions. So, how about it then? Are you going to rejoin, or what?

M: I don't know. What are you going to do? What's on that looks interesting?

J: The 'Tomorrow Now' exhibition in January looks fab! If it's anything like the exhibition I saw in Paris last summer – I think some of the works on show will be the same – it should be wonderful. I'd really recommend it.

M: What about the Cynthia Marlow exhibition?

J: Oh, let's give that a miss – she's boring.

M: Well, I think we should rejoin, but make sure we go to almost everything next year.

J: OK, then, that's what we'll do.

Lesson 9.4 Track 3.3

Experts, Director

1

E1: I recommend Savanna Charles. She's an American sculptor living in London.

D: What is she? I mean, what sort of thing does she do?

E1: Difficult to describe really. She's got such an original style. She makes huge figures out of glass, aluminium and other metals. They're mostly exhibited in large halls or open spaces. They're amazing. Absolutely breathtaking.

D: Sounds interesting. What's she best known for?

E1: She did something called 'Spiderwoman'. It was exhibited recently at the Rockefeller Centre in New York. It's over 30 metres high.

2

E2: There are several artists I could mention. The best is probably Alberto Cassini. He'd be a very good choice. He's from Argentina, still young, about 28, living in Florence at present. He's an abstract painter, a bit similar to Kandinsky, but with his own style.

D: OK, tell me a bit about his style.

E2: Well, the shapes on the canvas have a lot of movement and drama, like Kandinsky. But Alberto likes darker colours, and he doesn't use as many geometric shapes. His best-known work is called 'Chaos'. That's the normal English spelling, C-H-A-O-S.

D: Mmm, I'd like to look at a few photos of his work.

E2: By all means, I've brought some along for you to see.

3

E3: For your first exhibition, why not be a bit different? How about showing the work of a photographer?

D: OK, who do you have in mind?

E3: Well, how about Ingrid Tauber, a young German photographer?

D: Tell me about her.

E3: She's based in Hamburg. Married, husband also a photographer. Erm ...

D: What sort of photos does she take?

E3: She's fascinated by faces. So she takes lots of photos of people's faces, showing different emotions, happiness, sadness, loneliness, despair, that sort of thing. People of all ages, anyone, not just celebrities.

D: Mmm, I think I've seen some of her photos. Didn't she do one of an old woman – I saw it in a magazine, I think?

E3: Yes, that's right. Her most famous photo is called 'Homeless Woman'. It's a compilation of about 50 shots of a very old woman, showing all kinds of emotions. It's incredibly moving.

D: I must look at more of her work. She could be the artist we're looking for.

4

E4: I can suggest a very interesting artist. How about John Leach – that's L-E-A-C-H, by the way? He's British, a graffiti artist, you can see his work all over Europe.

D: A graffiti artist, now that would be interesting. What sort of stuff does he do? Is it very abstract?

E4: Not at all. He does murals, usually images of war, starving children, crowds out of control, that sort of thing. There are a lot of walls in Berlin, Paris and Amsterdam covered with his art.

D: What's his most famous mural, or should I say, piece of graffiti?

E4: When he went to Brazil, he did an astonishing piece of graffiti in one of their cities, maybe São Paulo or Rio, it's over 20 metres long, let's see, it's called 'Battleground', you must have seen it on postcards.

D: Yes, it rings a bell. I think I know who you mean.

Lesson 9.4 Track 3.4

Part 1

Hello everyone, I hope you enjoyed your lunch. I'm going to talk to you now about Marta Villanueva, as I think she could be the artist we're looking for for one of our exhibitions. First, I'll give you a few basic facts about her. Then, I'll talk about her style of painting. After that, I'll mention some reviews she's received. Finally, I'll describe what she's like as a person. I've got some photos of her work. You can look at them after I've finished. One other thing, please feel free to interrupt me at any time, if you have questions.

OK, I take it not many of you have heard of Marta Villanueva. Right? Well it doesn't surprise me really, but she is an up-and-coming artist, and that's why she's so exciting. Let me give you a few facts about her: she's Portuguese, 28 years old, living and working in Paris. She's married to a French businessman. At the moment, she paints in her spare time. She's got a full-time job working in a United Nations organisation. By the way, she speaks fluent Portuguese, English, Spanish and French – quite a linguist. OK?

Lesson 9.4 Track 3.5

Part 2

Right, I've told you a bit about her, I've given you a few basic facts. So, moving on now to her style of painting; she paints mainly landscapes and cityscapes, using bright colours and light and shade to create the mood of her paintings. Her paintings are really beautiful. Many of her landscapes and scenes of everyday life remind me of Monet and some of the other French Impressionist painters.

OK, that's all I have to say about her style. What do the critics say about her? Well, *Art World*, a magazine you all know, described her as 'an artist worth watching'. And the *Modern Art Review* said recently, 'Her colours are amazing. They explode from the canvas. Collectors are beginning to take a great interest in Marta Villanueva.' Need I say more?

OK, that's it for the critics. Let's go on to her personality and reputation. Well, I've met her several times. I think I know her quite well now. She's charming, modest and sociable, and she can talk intelligently about a wide range of subjects. She's extremely knowledgeable, not just about art. Right, now you know a bit about the kind of person she is.

To conclude now. Let me remind you of my main points. Marta Villanueva's paintings are eye-catching and colourful. There's a lot of interest in her work. She's a linguist, and she's got a friendly personality and good communication skills. Just what we need for our first exhibition.

Review 7–9 Track 3.7

Architect, Directors

A: Good morning everyone. I'm here to talk about the plans for extending the gallery. First I'd like to talk about some queries we have with your brief. Then I'd like to go through one or two of the planning issues. Finally, I'll be asking for your contributions to the discussion. So, moving on to the brief. I'm not exactly clear on the number of visitors you expect each day. This has quite a big impact on the provision of toilet facilities and cloakroom space. So perhaps you could give us a more precise indication, so we can make the necessary changes. We also need to know if you want any exterior lighting on the building – I think it might be a good idea to have that. OK, that's all I have to say about the brief. Let's go on to the planning issues. I've noticed that you haven't mentioned disabled access in your brief. Perhaps you aren't aware that it is now a legal requirement to provide disabled access in public buildings? So, we certainly need to make provision for that – I don't think it's going to be a problem but I just wanted to make you aware of it. OK, that's it for the planning issues; now I'd like to invite any questions or comments.

D1: Yes. You mentioned exterior lighting. Could you be more specific?

A: Of course. It's absolutely essential to make the public aware of the extension and having a building lit up at night does attract a lot of attention. There are several new types of spotlight that are very effective but have low running costs.

D1: I see.

D2: And what do you mean by disabled access? Could you explain that in more detail, please?

A: Sure. Basically, what I'm saying is that we need to provide a lift for wheelchair users near the entrance area and the bookshop ...

Lesson 10.1 Track 3.9

Good morning, everyone. Our topic today is group dynamics. I want to talk about how groups develop over a period of time. So I'll describe the stages that groups often go through.

Erm, first of all, I'd like to mention an academic who did some interesting early work on groups. His name's Kurt Lewin, you spell Kurt, K-U-R-T, by the way. Lewin was one of the first researchers to study groups scientifically, so he's important. He published his results during the 1940s and 1950s. And he created the term 'group dynamics' to describe how groups and individuals act and react in changing situations.

OK, the next really important contribution came from a researcher, Bruce Tuckman. Tuckman developed a theory about groups in 1965. He argued that groups went through four stages.

Now I'd like to look briefly at each of the stages in turn.

First, 'Forming'. This is the stage when the group pretends to get on well with each other and everyone seems to be happy. It's a kind of honeymoon period.

Next is the 'Storming' stage. As the name suggests, at this stage, members of the group are less polite to each other and they try to resolve their issues, even if they lose their tempers at times. Individual group members may fall out with each other as the true personalities of group members become clearer at this time.

'Norming' is the stage after that. Members get used to each other at this stage. They begin to trust each other, share information and are much more productive as they get down to the job of working together.

The final stage is 'Performing'. The members of the group have common goals. The atmosphere in the group is good. They work efficiently together and cooperate effectively with each other.

Those are the four stages in the development of the group. Maybe I should say too, Tuckman added a fifth stage. He called it 'Adjourning'. That's the stage when the group breaks up. Of course, some groups never even reach the 'Norming' stage. If they don't trust each other, and members find they cannot put up with each other, the group may break up early, before the 'Norming' stage.

Tuckman's theory is useful and of practical value. Think for a moment about pop groups you know, the Beatles, for example. They went through all five stages. During the 'Performing' stage, they were very effective, and wrote and performed some of their best songs, but eventually John Lennon moved away from the group and after Paul McCartney left, the band began to break up. You can also think of successful football teams which go through those stages. After early struggles, they have a period of success, they win championships, and then the team breaks up – for whatever reason. Finally, a very contemporary example would be in reality TV shows such as *Big Brother*, where the way the group works is actually the most interesting part of the programme. So Tuckman's model is a good one, and it's useful for analysing group dynamics.

Now are there any questions so far …

Lesson 10.4 Track 3.10

Vanessa, Michelle

V: OK, let's go to my next caller, who's in Preston.

M: Hello Vanessa, my name's Michelle.

V: Hi Michelle. How can I help?

M: It's about my husband, you see, he's retired now, he hasn't worked for over a year. And the problem is, he's got nothing to do all day except spend money and, well … he's spending an awful lot of money.

V: Oh dear! That must be worrying.

M: Yes it is. You see, he's run up a lot of debts, he owes people money all over the place, and if he goes on like this, well, we'll have to sell our house.

V: Michelle, I can see you're very upset. Can you tell me a little bit more, what's he spending his money on?

M: Well, you see, he spends a lot of time on the Internet. He's bored I suppose, and then he continually buys things. Usually it's really expensive stuff, top-brand clothes, designer sunglasses, that sort of thing. A few weeks ago, he bought a Rolex watch on eBay, it cost a fortune, over £7,000.

V: Mmm, I'd say he's addicted to spending money.

M: Yes, you're right, he is. We just can't afford that level of spending. He's already up to the limit on three credit cards, we've no savings left in the bank, and he's just taken out a personal loan.

V: And doesn't this level of debt worry him?

M: Well, no. It doesn't seem to, no.

V: Well, you can't go on like that. What was he like before he retired, Michelle? Was he always a big spender?

M: Yes, he was. He always loved giving parties, going out on the town, helping his friends if they needed money – that sort of thing. Actually, early on in our marriage, he went bankrupt – it was an awful time for us. You know, I sometimes wonder why I stay with him, and when things get really bad, I've even thought of leaving him.

V: Perhaps it's because you still love him.

M: I suppose I do. You know it's not easy to leave someone you've been with a long time – even if they are ruining your life. I'm so confused, Vanessa. What do you think I should do?

Lesson 10.4 Track 3.11

Vanessa, Michelle

V: Well, it's obviously very difficult for you, Michelle. No wonder you're confused and upset.

M: Mmm, I don't know which way to turn, to be honest, that's why I've phoned you. I need some good advice.

V: OK, first of all, I think you need to talk to someone about the debts you have. A real professional.

M: Yes, but I don't know any professional person who could help us.

V: But I do, Michelle. At the end of the programme, I can give you the name of someone who can advise you how to deal with your debts.

M: Great, thanks very much.

V: And you could also contact your local Citizens Advice Centre – their services are free. If possible, you should both go there. OK?

M: Mmm, OK.

V: Another thing. Could I ask you, do you have a joint account with your husband?

M: Yes, actually I do. Our account's in both our names.

V: Well, you know, it might be a good idea to have a separate bank account. Just for the time being. Until your husband gets his finances in order. And tell me, do you have access to the Internet?

M: Yes, I use it at work. And also at home, when my husband isn't using the computer.

V: Great! Well, if I were you, I'd check the Internet to see if there are some websites offering help – for free, of course. And there's another thing you can do. I'd advise you to contact a finance company. They might be able to help you. Why don't you look into it? Your bank might be able to advise you and recommend a reputable company.

M: All right, I'll think about that. But what about my husband's spending problem? What can I do about it?

V: Mmm, it's a serious problem, it's vital that you do something about it. Or should I say, it's vital he does something about it. Why don't you have a serious talk with him? Tell him his spending is threatening your marriage, because it is. Advise him to seek professional help. There's an association he can join, they have experts who'll help him to control his addiction. I'll give you details later.

M: Thanks, Vanessa. You've given me some good ideas. I must say, I feel a lot better talking to you.

V: Good. I'm pleased to hear it. One final bit of advice. You might consider getting some counselling yourself. You've had a tough time recently, life's been difficult. You know, you need to think about your relationship with your husband. If he goes on destroying your life, you may have to consider divorce. I know you don't want to do that, and I hope it doesn't come to that, but it's essential that your husband changes his behaviour or it'll make you very unhappy, and possibly destroy your marriage. Think about it.

M: Mmm. Well, thanks very much, Vanessa. Please give me the addresses you mentioned.

V: Of course I will. My staff will contact you at the end of the programme, and you'll get everything you need. Goodbye Michelle, and good luck!

Lesson 11.1 Track 3.12

1 Ayla, from Turkey

When I'm outside Turkey, travelling for my job, I miss the smell of strong Turkish coffee, and the smell of the food. I really miss our typical Turkish breakfast of white cheese, bread, eggs, honey and olives. I think also of the rain in my home town, and holidays where my family and relatives come together. I miss the prayers we hear five times a day from the mosques. I also think Turkish hospitality is wonderful. I miss visiting friends, relatives and neighbours and the way that Turkish people really try hard to make their guests feel comfortable. Another thing I miss about Turkish culture is the respect for older people.

2 Carola, from Germany

When I lived abroad, I missed cycling to places. I didn't see many people on bikes, everyone used cars all the time, even for short distances. Children were taken to school by their parents, and my host father drove to a nearby petrol station to get his newspaper. I thought about getting a bike, but there were no cycle paths in my area, and I felt I'd be a kind of 'outsider' if I cycled to work in the morning.

I also missed small local supermarkets where you can walk to do your shopping. In Germany, we have many small supermarkets in all parts of cities or towns, and you can get everything you need there. They are not huge and anonymous, like the big supermarkets in some other countries.

Talking of food, I missed German bread and German rolls. Bread tastes a lot better in my country, I can tell you.

3 Anna, from Russia

When I worked abroad what I missed most was certain emotional aspects of our culture, not material ones. I certainly missed the Russian style of friendship. In my country, people will discuss all kinds of very personal problems, even intimate problems with you. And they expect friends to forget their own problems and do everything to help you out. But outside Russia, I noticed people are more individualistic, and even with good friends, the conversations are more superficial, they take less time, and people tend to be more focused on their own problems.

Also, I missed Russian jokes and loud laughter. Russians often organise parties at someone's home, old friends come together and spend hours eating and drinking around a big table, discussing things, singing, dancing. One final thing. I missed our traditional Russian winter, going down snow-covered hills on a toboggan with my young son, skiing and skating, playing snowballs and making snowmaidens with our fluffy snow.

4 Danielle, from Cameroon

What did I miss when I was abroad? Definitely the food. In Cameroon, everything we eat is fresh, no processing, artificial stuff or colouring. I remember we had to literally chase the chicken, kill it, and then cook it. It took almost the whole afternoon. And then I missed the spices. We took the tomatoes, basil and peanuts straight out of the field, it was wonderful! When we wanted a treat, all we had to do was go to the mango or guava or avocado tree and pick it. And if we wanted a snack, we would go to the cornfield to get some corn. I tell you, I had no problem keeping slim.

The weather, I missed that too. Cameroon is a tropical country, so we have some very good weather. Believe it or not, what I missed most was the sun of course, but also the tropical rain. I tell you, when it beats down on top of a tin roof, it produces a sound that's like a lullaby, it makes you feel sleepy.

5 Alessandra, from Italy

I feel comfortable living in foreign countries, especially in Europe. I like the variety of cultures you meet just travelling a few hundred kilometres. But I miss something that just isn't there. It's the sound of my typically Italian language where I grew up. It took me a long time to realise its effect on me. When I hear people speaking my Italian dialect, then I let myself dive into a very private comfort zone. It's a blend of feelings consisting of love, trust, comfort and being 'home'. For me, I've lived and worked in various places around the world, but I've never experienced that anywhere else, except in my home country.

I'm studying in England now and I definitely miss not being able to express my ideas as soon as they come into my mind. I just can't communicate easily and precisely what I think in English, and that frustrates me.

Of course, I miss knowing where to go to find what I need. Being Italian, it means I miss good food, the sun and friendly people. I miss so much, but I'm really enjoying being in England.

6 Nancy, from Argentina

I've travelled all over the world. What do I miss? Well, the first thing that comes to mind is the more relaxed atmosphere we have in the streets, you know, socialising and meeting friends for coffee or dinner. It's a very spontaneous culture. You don't need to make arrangements a long time in advance. You just phone a friend, and then meet them at home or outside only a few minutes after your phone call.

I should mention our drink, I miss it a lot when I'm overseas. It's called *mate*, it's a traditional drink in a special container. You pour a kind of green tea herb (called *yerba mate*) into the container, you add boiling hot water and then sip the tea. It's a kind of ritual. You pass the container around with a group when you get together at someone's home – it's a bit like the Indian tribes used to pass round the 'pipes of peace'. You chat, have fun and talk philosophically about life, the state of the world and so on. Friendship and bonding are very important in Argentina. I missed all that socialising when I was in England and the United States.

Lesson 11.2 Track 3.13

I emigrated to Chicago just over ten years ago. I think I suffered from culture shock the whole time I was there. The countryside outside the city was stunning and the people were wonderful, but I just couldn't get used to the weather conditions. The winters were bitterly cold and they seemed to last for a lifetime. Before I went to work, I usually looked out of the window to see what the weather was like. Sometimes the sky was blue and cloudless, and there was plenty of sunshine. 'Ah,' I would think, 'a nice, mild winter day.' But when I went outside, the cold would hit my face within minutes. My face went numb and really hurt, and if the wind was strong, I was soon shivering with the cold. I used to hate that walk to the subway, it was so painful.

But the summer wasn't much better. It was quite hot, and often humid – it made me feel really uncomfortable. And then when you went into a café to cool down, the air conditioning was always on and most places were freezing cold. I just couldn't put up with the heat outside and the icy conditions in the buildings – it drove me crazy. One day I woke up and said to myself 'I don't enjoy living here.'

I've been back in England for a few months now. That's been a bit of a culture shock as well. I'm still trying to adjust to my home country. People talk about TV programmes they loved, and I can't join in the conversation because I've haven't seen them. And a lot of the TV presenters and personalities look strange to me. So much older, I remember them as young men and women, now they're middle-aged. And take sport, for example, I followed ice hockey in Chicago, but everyone here talks about football. I haven't heard of most of the players, so I can't pretend to be interested.

I'm just not fitting in at the moment, I feel like a fish out of water, to be honest. I've no idea how long it'll last. But if I don't adjust soon to conditions here, I'll start to wish I was back in Chicago!

Lesson 11.3 Track 3.14

1

When my wife and I were on holiday in Istanbul, Turkey, we decided to visit a market. My wife persuaded me to travel there by *dolmus* – one of the small minibuses which hold about 20 passengers. We sat in the middle of the bus, and after about ten minutes, an old woman came from the back seats, tapped me on the shoulder and put two coins in my hand, muttering something in Turkish. I didn't understand, but thanked her and put the coins in my pocket. A few minutes later, the bus driver stopped and spoke to the old woman. She pointed at me, and didn't look very pleased. The bus driver started waving his arms about and shouting at me in broken English, 'You bad person. You get off my bus, you don't give me money.' I suddenly realised that the woman had given me the coins to pass on to the driver to pay for the journey. I was so embarrassed.

I admitted taking the money and apologised for not giving it to him. He just wouldn't listen. He warned me not to get on his bus again. I regretted travelling by *dolmus* and we never did it again. During the rest of our holiday, we travelled by taxi and ferry-boat!

2

I made a terrible social gaffe in Spain the first time I went there for work purposes. I'd refused to do the orientation programme because I'd been to Malaga for a week a few years before – it was great: sunny beaches and loads of other expatriates – really enjoyed myself. But when I went there for a week to work it was totally different. I'd arrived in the afternoon and there was a car to take me to the hotel from the airport. I'd missed lunch so I had a snack at about 3 o'clock. Then, knowing that my hosts had insisted on picking me up at 9 o'clock and that I'd agreed to meet them in the hotel lobby, I thought I would have my supper before going out for the evening. Big mistake! I hadn't realised that the Spanish eat very late. So there I was in a very nice restaurant having to choose a meal at 11 o'clock when I felt stuffed full from my supper earlier. They encouraged me to order lots of different dishes. I tried to eat but couldn't manage more than two or three mouthfuls. My hosts thought I must be unhappy or ill. I could see that they were very concerned so I decided to tell them the truth. They nearly fell off their chairs laughing and told me to forget about eating any more food. In a funny way, my social gaffe worked out OK in the end because everybody was laughing so much that we were able to talk business in a friendly atmosphere. But I never went anywhere new ever again without a full briefing.

Lesson 11.4 Track 3.15

Part 1

Hello, everyone. My name's James and I'm from Canada. This morning I'm going to talk to you about my fascinating home town of Toronto. I've divided my presentation into three parts. First of all, I'll start with some background information, then I'll move on to the main sights. Finally, I'll outline some other experiences a visitor should try when they come to Toronto. If you don't mind, we'll leave questions to the end.

OK, I'll start with some basic information. Toronto is the capital city of the province of Ontario, and it's situated on Lake Ontario. Until 1934, it was called York. It's got a population of approximately 2.4 million, so it's a fairly large city. It's an important industrial, commercial and cultural centre.

Toronto's getting better and better these days, as more and more people come from all over the world to settle here. They enrich our city greatly with their skills and talents and they help to create the lively, friendly, cosmopolitan atmosphere the city is famous for.

Track 3.16

Part 2

So, what are the main sights of the city? Well, there are many things to see, but let me focus on three: the CN tower, City Hall and Casa Loma.

OK, why is the CN Tower worth seeing? Well, it's a tall building, a very tall building. Actually, it's the tallest structure in the world; it's 1,815 feet high. Built in 1976 by Canadian National Railways, it overlooks the city and you can see it wherever you are in the city. It's truly gigantic, incredible, and awe-inspiring. Go up the tower and you get a fantastic view of the city. And if you're very brave, why don't you stand on the glass floor, 342 metres off the ground, then look down? And if you can do that, why not take the elevator and go on up to the Sky Pod? That's another 34 storeys higher!

Another great sight is the City Hall. There was a worldwide competition in the 60s to design it, and a Finnish architect, Viljo Revell, won the competition. Unfortunately, he died before it was opened in 1965. It's beautifully designed, and far ahead of its time. Now it's a very popular tourist attraction, in fact it's probably the most popular attraction. In front of it is Nathan Phillips Square. The Square is an entertainment venue, it offers free concerts, ice-skating and on New Year's Eve, a huge celebration takes place there.

Finally, Casa Loma. What can I say about this extraordinary castle? It was called a 'rich man's folly'. People thought Sir Henry Pellatt, the owner, was crazy to spend so much money on building the castle in 1914. It cost 3.5 million dollars, a huge sum in those days. And he went bankrupt trying to maintain and develop it. Ten years later, its value was just 27,000 dollars. It has so many interesting architectural features: 60 large rooms, an immense Great Hall, where 2,000 people can be entertained, a beautiful library, secret underground passages and magnificent gardens. It's a MUST place to visit.

Track 3.17

Part 3

Finally, I'll talk about some things a visitor should definitely do when they come to Toronto.

Well, how about trying some waffles for breakfast? They're sort of pancakes – with maple syrup – delicious, and typically Canadian food.

Secondly, if you like sports, you should go to see an ice hockey match featuring the local Maple Leaf team. They've won many championships and are one of the top ice hockey teams in North America. Ice hockey is physical, fast and exciting. It's a rough game, a contact sport, but thrilling and skilful.

I'd also like to suggest that visitors should try and experience the Caribana festival, which takes place every year from mid-July to early August. It is one of America's largest street festivals and is based on the Trinidad carnival. The first one took place in 1967, when the city's Caribbean community celebrated the 100th anniversary of Canada. It just got bigger and bigger so that today it attracts more than a million visitors.

To sum up, I'd just like to say that Toronto is a modern, exciting, and welcoming city just waiting to be explored. I do hope you will be able to add it to your list of destinations and we look forward to showing you the very best which Toronto has to offer.

That's all from me. Any questions?

Lesson 11.5 Track 3.19

Presenter, Guest

P: ... and welcome to today's edition of *Daybreak*, where my guest is Professor Mary Robinson, the author of a new book on improving reading skills.

G: Hello, Pam, and good morning everyone.

P: Yes, hello, Mary, and thanks for joining us. Perhaps we could start with you telling us a bit about why you wrote the book?

G: Yes, sure. Well, I've noticed that among the sort of students I meet at the university, there seems to be a decline in the amount of reading they do, both for their studies and for pleasure. This is a real shame because there is a clear link between the amount you read and your ability to express yourself. Also, it seems that reading is the best way of acquiring knowledge. For example, research into how people acquire knowledge has shown that people who watched more TV were more likely to get general knowledge questions wrong, and this is independent of intellectual ability.

P: Really, how interesting.

G: Yes, it seems the more reading you do, the better, whatever it is. Reading increases vocabulary, improves your general knowledge and keeps your memory and reasoning abilities working well.

P: That's got to be a good thing! So what tips can you give for improving reading?

G: Obviously, it depends on the sort of reading you're doing. However, I think students are often not selective enough about what they choose to read and then they focus too much on details. It's very important to get an overall idea about what you're reading and to make full use of any headings and subheadings to help guide your reading, and stop you wasting time reading unnecessary information. Also, I think it's crucial to engage with what you read. People often think of reading as a one-way process, but in fact it should be a two-way process ...

P: Can you explain what you mean there?

G: Of course. To be an effective reader, you should always be thinking about what the writer may say next, and also questioning what you read. Think about if you agree or disagree with what you are reading, with the opinion of the writer, with their logic, conclusions and arguments ... that sort of thing.

P: Right. Anything else?

G: Well, one particular problem that I've noticed is foreign students who focus too much on unknown vocabulary. This can make reading very time-consuming as they constantly stop to look up words in their dictionaries.

P: Yes, I see. In fact, I think people often do that in their own language too.

G: When they're studying, indeed. However, often, you can work out the meaning of the word by reading on and looking at the context it's used in, or at least make an educated guess. For people who want to improve their reading speed, a good tip is to use your finger, but not to follow the words on the line. No, the secret here is to move your finger down the page as you read, as this will train your eyes to move more quickly down the text and keep you moving forward.

P: That's a good tip. Well, thank you very much, Professor, and good luck with the book.

G: Thank you, Pam.

Lesson 12.1 Track 3.20

1

I absolutely detest mobile phones ... cellphones, whatever you want to call the horrible things. OK, yes, they're practical in emergencies, like when your car has broken down. But most of the time they're a pest, an absolute nuisance, and a pain in the neck. I loathe them. I was sitting on the train this morning and at least five people were shouting into their phones – why does everyone have to speak so loudly? And why do some of them give you their life story? It's so incredibly rude. I just want to sit in peace on the train and read my newspaper. I had to put my headphones on to listen to my state-of-the-art MP3 player just to drown out their noise. And restaurants, don't get me started on that. People shouting on phones in restaurants – so incredibly inconsiderate – why don't they just go outside to take their stupid calls?

2

What's my favourite piece of technology? That's easy, my portable DVD player. I've used it so much since I bought it, the chrome surface is really worn and the machine looks old. I don't care, I won't change it. It's really easy to use and it's certainly durable. It never breaks down, not even if I drop it, and that often happens. I love films, it's my main interest. As soon as I buy a new DVD, I want to watch it right away. The DVD player is so handy for that. It takes me just a few seconds and I'm watching the film. I even take it on the train with me. I have an hour's journey to work, so I'm never bored with my portable player. My fellow travellers seem to like it too. I've often caught them sneaking a look at the film I'm watching. So … three cheers for portable DVD players. What a great invention!

3

I suppose the last piece of technology I bought was a shredder, you know, for shredding documents and things like that. Everyone kept telling me to buy one because they, ... because of identity fraud – other people finding out information about you and using it to, I don't know, to steal from your bank account or get a passport in your name, that kind of thing. So I've just bought a shredder, and it's all right. It was cheap enough and it's pretty user-friendly, but I don't like it ... the idea, I mean. I don't like the idea of having to destroy important documents so other people can't use them. It's just that it shows what kind of world we live in now, I suppose, and I don't want to believe it. The other thing about the shredder that I don't like is the fact that it isn't very environmentally friendly – it uses quite a lot of electricity which isn't very green to start with, and apparently, you can't put shredded paper in the recycling bin. I think it's different from council to council, but where I live, they won't take shredded paper because the pieces are too small and can't be sorted mechanically for recycling.

Lesson 12.4 Track 3.21

1

I come to work by car. Parking's a terrible problem. There's not enough room in the company car park for all the cars, but they still let you drive in, and then you spend ages looking for a space, and there just isn't one. It's so annoying, such a waste of time. If the computer's so good, why can't it stop people going in if there's no space?

2

I like the general office, it's open plan and very friendly. But goodness, the air conditioning's awful. The office gets boiling hot during the winter and it's icy cold some days during the summer. Would you believe it, I had to put on a thick jumper while I was working in the middle of August? The system just doesn't work properly. You can keep your new computer – it's no good at all for controlling the temperature. I'm fed up with it. I preferred my old office – it was fine, and I always felt comfortable in it.

3

We'd all like to use the little kitchen for a quick coffee or to heat up a pizza. It was a good idea to have the kitchen next to our office. But we can't use it, because when you heat something up, the fire alarm goes off and you get a cold shower from the sprinkler system. Last week, I was soaked to the skin before I could get out! I tell you, the new computer system is no good, and never will be.

4

It's the lighting system that bothers me – it's too sophisticated. When I leave the office, it turns off the light, that's great. But the trouble is, it often turns off the lights when I'm in the office, working – that's really annoying. I never had a problem with the lights until the new computer was introduced. It's so sensitive. If you don't move around, it often switches off the light – it really drives me crazy at times.

Lesson 12.4 Track 3.22

Director, Rosa

D: Hello, Rosa, can I join you?
R: Oh, … yes, certainly.
D: I'd like to have a chat with you, is that OK?
R: Yes, of course, how can I help?
D: Well, it's about work really. You see, I know a lot of staff aren't happy at the moment. Could I ask you, how do you feel about everything?
R: Well … er …
D: You can be frank with me, Rosa, I promise you, it won't go any further.
R: OK, well actually, I'm really worried. I read that article, someone showed it to me, and, I don't know, I'm worried about my job. I've got three children and my husband's unemployed. I can't afford to be out of work.
D: Look, I understand how you feel. But I can assure you, we're going to put things right. Please don't lose faith in us, even if you are a bit down at the moment.
R: It's not just me, I think we're all unhappy at the moment. We feel, I don't know, let down. Everything's changed so much.
D: How do you mean, changed? Is it because you're not happy with the move to this building?
R: No, it's not that, it's the new computer system. I just can't work with it. I think I'm doing the right thing, you know, operating it correctly, then something goes wrong, and I get all the blame, when really it's the fault of the computer.
D: Mmm, it's true, there's certainly been a lot of teething problems with the new systems – no doubt about that.
R: Yeah, but please don't blame it on us when things go wrong.
D: So, … what's gone wrong recently then?
R: Lots of things. Like, last week the computer crashed – it took almost a day and a half before we could use it. Subscriptions started piling up, I had to do overtime to cope with all the extra work, and did I get any thanks? No, I entered the wrong details a couple of times, and my team leader had a go at me. Said I was no good at the job.
D: Mmm, that doesn't sound very fair to me, I must say. Anyway, don't worry, Rosa, we know you're one of the best workers in the company. Everyone knows that. And I guarantee we'll sort out the problems. You won't be out of a job, you have my word for that.
R: I hope you're right. You know, with the old computer system, I was always on top of my work. People used to say what a great worker I was.
D: I can see how you feel and we're going to do something about it, I promise. Tell me, are you free next Wednesday? There's going to be a meeting after work. An informal one, a chance for people to say how they feel and make suggestions. I've asked the Head of Human Resources to lead the discussion. Would you be willing to represent the admin staff? You're very popular with your colleagues. I know you'd be a good choice.
R: Well, I suppose so – if they all agree.
D: Great. I'll talk to them, but I know they'll be happy for you to represent them. And stop worrying about your job. Things'll get better, I guarantee that. We've contacted the supplier of the computer systems. They're confident they can sort out the problems and get things working again soon. Please tell your colleagues that.
R: OK, I'll do that.
D: Right. I hope you have a good meeting on Wednesday. I'll get my assistant to send you details.

Lesson 12.5 Track 3.23

Part 1

So, what is plagiarism? Well, basically, it's using the work of other people without saying where you got your information from, in other words, without acknowledging the author. If you use the same words that someone else has used in an article or lecture, for example, you are guilty of plagiarism. Of course, you're free to use the same words provided that you give a reference to the author and the source of the quote, I mean the article or book or whatever. If you just rewrite sentences from another text in your own words, completely different from the original, you're probably not plagiarising. You're doing a loose paraphrase, and that's OK, it's acceptable. You're plagiarising too if you use other people's ideas without saying whose ideas they are; obviously some ideas are just general and known by everyone, but ideas described by one person must be acknowledged.

Now, something that often surprises my students – you're also not allowed to copy work from another student, even if they give you permission, and submit it as your own. So, for example, if you discuss an essay with a friend of yours and then compare what you've written, you really must not take sections from your friend's essay and then use them in yours. It's not collaboration – it's plagiarism. I think it goes without saying that you can't take a chunk of text from the Internet and put it in an assignment without acknowledgment. It's totally unacceptable. So, to sum up, you mustn't quote, copy or paraphrase closely what you've read or heard, without giving the source.

You know, I've heard of cases where students not only don't write the material they submit, but they don't even read it before giving it in! Incredible! The main problem is, some students often plagiarise without realising they're doing it. That, of course, is why I'm doing this lecture.

Lesson 12.5 Track 3.24

Part 2

I'm often asked if you should use quotations from your source material. The answer is 'yes' but not too many, if possible. A lecturer wants your own thoughts and ideas about a subject, not just the ideas of other writers. They also want you to evaluate critically the material you've used. They're interested in your response to the topic. If you quote, however, you must write the words accurately, and use quotation marks around the words you're quoting, and of course, you should put a reference to the source with each one, in brackets.

Why do people plagiarise? I think, often, it's because they don't have confidence in their own ability or ideas. They feel safer using the ideas of other writers or speakers. Or it could be that the student's studying in a very competitive environment. So, they feel they have to copy the work of well-known writers to get a good mark or high grade. Another reason is, some students are just too lazy to think about the material they're reading; it's too much effort for them to write notes in their own words. OK, those are some of the reasons why people plagiarise. What's wrong with plagiarising? Well, it's a kind of stealing, isn't it? It's intellectual theft, and that's not acceptable.

These days, students use the Internet a lot for research. That's understandable, but it makes plagiarism very easy. It's also very risky now for students to plagiarise material from Internet sources and from any other sources, such as books or other students. There's software available now, such as Turnitin, to spot plagiarism. Staff can check quickly and effectively if they feel a student has copied material. So, the answer is, don't plagiarise, as you'll probably get caught!

Review 10–12 Track 3.25

Tara, Henry

T: Can I have a word with you, Henry?
H: Sure.
T: I'm very behind with my coursework.
H: Are you finding the course too difficult?
T: Not really. That's not the problem.
H: Well, is there something wrong at home?
T: Erm …
H: You can be frank with me, Tara. I promise you, it won't go any further.
T: Things have been quite difficult recently with … with my flatmates.
H: Why don't you tell me all about it?
T: It's hard to explain. It seems so stupid …
H: Look, I understand how you feel. Just tell me in your own words.
T: OK. It's the evenings really. You see they love listening to music and they have really powerful stereo systems. In fact they play music almost every night. But that's the time when I need to work on my assignments.
H: But why is that a problem for you?
T: Well, the music is so loud I can't really concentrate on my work.
H: Mmm, that doesn't sound very fair to me, I must say. It might be a good idea to tell them how you feel.
T: I'm not sure. I mean … I don't want to stop them enjoying themselves.
H: If I were you I'd just ask them to turn down the volume.
T: Well, I did ask them once and they turned it down. But they just started playing the music loudly again the next night.
H: You might consider talking to your landlord about this. He probably doesn't know about this noise problem.
T: Maybe. I suppose I could try talking to him.
H: And stop worrying about it. Things'll get better, I'm sure about that.

AUTHORS

Far left: Simon Kent
Centre left: David Falvey
Centre: Gareth Rees
Centre right: Ian Lebeau
Far right: David Cotton

Intermediate and Upper Intermediate levels

David Falvey studied Politics, Philosophy and Economics at the University of Oxford and did his MA in TEFL at the University of Birmingham. He has lived in Africa and the Middle East and has teaching, training and managerial experience in the UK and Asia, including working as a teacher trainer at the British Council in Tokyo. He is now Head of the English Language Centre at London Metropolitan University. David is co-author of the successful business English course *Market Leader*.

Simon Kent studied History at the University of Sheffield. He has 20 years' teaching experience including three years in Berlin at the time of German reunification. Simon is co-author of the successful business English course *Market Leader*. He is currently Senior Lecturer in English as a Foreign Language at London Metropolitan University.

David Cotton studied Economics at the University of Reading and French Language and Literature at the University of Toronto. He has over 30 years' teaching and training experience, and is co-author of the successful *Market Leader* and *Business Class* courses. He has taught in Canada, France and England, and been visiting lecturer in many universities overseas. He is currently visiting lecturer at London Metropolitan University.

Elementary and Pre-intermediate levels

Ian Lebeau studied Modern Languages at the University of Cambridge and Applied Linguistics at the University of Reading. He has nearly 30 years' experience in ELT – mainly in higher education – and has taught in Spain, Italy and Japan. He is currently Senior Lecturer in English as a Foreign Language at London Metropolitan University.

Gareth Rees studied Natural Sciences at the University of Cambridge. Having taught in Spain and China, he currently teaches at London Metropolitan University and University of the Arts. He also develops English language materials for the BBC World Service Learning English section and he makes films which appear in festivals and on British television.